# Practical Robotics
# in
# C++

*Build and Program Real Autonomous
Robots Using Raspberry Pi*

**Lloyd Brombach**

www.bpbonline.com

**FIRST EDITION 2021**

**Copyright © BPB Publications, India**

**ISBN: 978-93-89423-46-4**

## Distributors:

**BPB PUBLICATIONS**
20, Ansari Road, Darya Ganj
New Delhi-110002
Ph: 23254990/23254991

**DECCAN AGENCIES**
4-3-329, Bank Street,
Hyderabad-500195
Ph: 24756967/24756400

**MICRO MEDIA**
Shop No. 5, Mahendra Chambers,
150 DN Rd. Next to Capital Cinema,
V.T. (C.S.T.) Station, MUMBAI-400 001
Ph: 22078296/22078297

**BPB BOOK CENTRE**
376 Old Lajpat Rai Market,
Delhi-110006
Ph: 23861747

To View Complete
BPB Publications Catalogue
Scan the QR Code:

Published by Manish Jain for BPB Publications, 20 Ansari Road, Darya Ganj, New Delhi-110002 and Printed by him at Repro India Ltd, Mumbai

www.bpbonline.com

# Dedicated to

*The book is dedicated to past, present and future roboticists.*

# About the Author

**Lloyd Brombach** lives in Rochester Hills, MI, USA. He is a co-captain of the Wayne Robotics Club competition team. He has competed in robotics challenges as far back as NASA's 2007 (Autonomous) Lunar Regolith Excavation Challenge, and as recently as the 2019 Intelligent Ground Vehicle Challenge leading the teams' path-planning and obstacle-avoidance software development.

A controls engineer with 15 years of experience, he combines two years of schooling in electronics, control theory, sensors, microcontrollers with a four-year engineer apprenticeship program to design and implement custom electro-mechanical solutions for his employer and mentor new members of the robotics club. A firm believer in maintaining a diverse and modern skillset, he has returned to the university classroom to update his resume once again – this time with a computer science degree.

# Acknowledgments

I've received so much support, understanding, and encouragement while writing this book that it's difficult to know where to start.

I need to thank my mom for convincing me as a child that I can do anything. My dad for showing me where to start. My coworkers for picking up my slack when I've been distracted - especially Mo. My friends and family for making do without me for most of the last years' worth of get-togethers because I had to research, write, and make graphics (let's face it – I'm the most fun out of the group). Dr. Pandya for his mentorship and the members of the Wayne State University Robotics Club and Intelligent Ground Vehicle competition team for both the learning and teaching experiences. The BPB Publications team – from convincing me to tackle the project to staying right here with me until the end.

There isn't enough credit to give my wife, Jen, for her incredible patience, understanding, and support. From putting up with and even feeding the Wayne Robotics team for late-nighters. For tolerating my trips away and 14 hour days for conferences, builds team meetings, and even just working in the office or basement. For never complaining when I brought robots camping, and rarely when you tripped over them around the house – you are the real MVP in this book and my life.

To my readers, for embracing the exciting and complex world of robotics. For their enthusiasm as well as understanding that no matter how hard an author tries, every work is likely to have shortcomings. I appreciate forgiveness, corrections, and feedback, so readers of future versions, as well as the Practical Robotics online community, can be saved all possible frustration.

To these and so many others who have supported and influenced me in ways that steered my path and made this book possible:

Thank you.

# Preface

Finding clear guidance for building an autonomous robot is a challenge, partly because there are so many subjects involved, and partly because existing resources tend to be focused on their one specialty. Books on electronics don't talk about mapping or path planning, and books on robotics algorithms don't include the control theory necessary to be able to interface software with motors and feedback sensors. And too many books and tutorials for all subjects seem to require the reader to have already a degree — or at least some advanced mathematics — to be able to follow along.

Are you ready for the good news? This book will save you years of studying the parts of these subjects that aren't necessary for you to be able to build and program your first autonomous robot. This book will instead give you a clear roadmap and provide a complete foundation of knowledge to get you well into the game. I will also give you guidance on what to study next in each subject, so you can focus on and explore the parts you find most exciting.

What I won't do is give copy-and-paste tutorials without making sure you understand what you are doing. Although all of the code is here in print and available to download at github.com/lbrombach, my goal is not to have you build and program the example robot precisely. Instead, I encourage and empower you to design, build, and program robots your way, using my examples as guides. I will give you a serious kick-start, but how far you go from there is limited only by your imagination and determination.

I wrote this book after working with university students with a wide range of experience and abilities. From newcomers with no experience at all to graduate students who already have degrees in computer science, electrical, and mechanical engineering, none of them came in knowing how to build and program a robot. Our best programmers didn't know how motors or sensors worked, and our electrical engineers didn't know how to turn sensor data into useful numbers in code. Semester after semester, we co-captains found ourselves teaching the same basics of every subject over and over, and we wished for one manual that could give all of our team members a well-rounded foundation. Specifically, we needed lessons that were simple enough for the newer students to understand, yet in-depth enough that the graduates could still learn from them. This is that manual, and it requires nothing more to get started than basic C++ knowledge and a hunger for learning.

This book will appeal to both beginners as well as the most experienced programmers. I wrote code I felt would be easy for an inexperienced programmer to follow, knowing that more experienced programmers should have no problem implementing their own best coding practices. To my beginner programmers: This book uses C++ syntax to show how the algorithms work, but don't think of it as "a programming book." As your coding skills improve, you'll see more and more where I avoided C++ features I thought a beginner might not understand yet and took shortcuts like using global variables to make the examples easier on the eyes. All the programs are working examples but may not be examples of "best coding practices." I wanted very much to avoid an entire book of suddenly overwhelming code, and I try to give some warning and a little guidance as the C++ gets unavoidably a little more advanced along the way.

Delivery robots, warehouse robots, household robots, hobby robots, farm robots — each has its unique purpose and operating environment. Yet, they are all built upon fundamentals you will learn in this book. I advise against rushing to the tutorials; instead, get comfortable and read the book through, then come back for the hands-on experience.

Are you excited? I hope so because it's time to get started.

We have developed five sections where you can find the following topics:

**Section 1:** An introduction to computers for robotics. The section is divided into two chapters, the first focusing on selecting and setting up laptops and Raspberry Pi computers and the second chapter learning more about the Raspberry Pi general purpose input/output (GPIO) hardware interface pins, including basic electronics and using code to interact with hardware.

**Section 2:** The second section, called "Robot Project Starters," focuses on the knowledge needed to build the robot platform that can then be programmed with autonomous behaviors in later sections. Five chapters discuss the types of robot platforms available and acquiring or building one type of motors and motor control, communication between the different devices on a robot, miscellaneous helpful hardware, and wiring the computer and the rest of the robot.

**Section 3:** This section teaches robot logic matters in six chapters. One chapter focuses on controllers for both individual processes like a single motor as well as controllers of a complex system of systems and another chapter on coordinating the dozens of processes and a vast amount of data traffic an autonomous robot requires. The remaining four chapters in this section cover the primary autonomous robot matters of getting the robot to move by itself, mapping for navigation, how the robot can track itself, and autonomously finding a path that avoids obstacles.

**Section 4:** This section is called "Making Sense of Sensor Data" and explores, in-depth, into sensors useful for the above sections and more. Seven chapters total, five cover using sensors used for robot tracking (odometry), detecting obstacles with ultrasonic sensors, laser range finding (LIDAR), GPS, and other beacon-based location systems. Additionally, a chapter is dedicated to fusing the data from multiple sensors for a more reliable system and another dedicated to using cameras for computer vision.

**Section 5:** The final section is a single chapter that guides the reader through everything learned in the previous chapters to build and program an autonomous robot.

# Foreword

Excitement is growing in the field where robotics, microprocessors, computing, and advanced autonomous algorithms come together. This book is being introduced at a technological, robotics-centered turning point: Robots already play a dominant role in the areas of mobility, manufacturing, agriculture, health care and supply-chain management, yet some estimate the industrial robotics market will expand nearly 12% annually to over $33 billion in the next decade. Meanwhile, the medical robotics market is expected to reach $100 billion by 2024. I predict a robotic revolution coming that will help us solve many of the critical issues we face, now and in the future.

Robotics has and will continue to integrate with many aspects of our economy and daily life. Order something on Amazon? A Kiva robot finds your items on the shelf and brings it to the packing area. Need to clean your house? A robotic vacuum will do the trick. As our world population grows, humans will face tremendous challenges, and robots will be increasingly used to help us farm more efficiently, fight fires from land and air, and even pick up our kids from soccer practice.

But with this rapid industry growth comes a critical need for skilled engineers and researchers — a workforce that understands how the hardware, intelligent algorithms, software design, and sensors come together to solve difficult and critical robotics-related problems. Practical Robotics in C++ will play a key role in inspiring that workforce with a very practical, hands-on approach to learning robotics. By taking a big-picture view, the book engages readers and helps them better understand robotics basics. It covers a broad subject by focusing on its key aspects, including the Robot Operating System (ROS), microcontroller integration (e.g. the Raspberry Pi), key current sensors (e.g. Lidar, GPS, encoders, inertial measurement unit, etc.) and software design.

The thing that makes Practical Robotics in C++ stand out is that it shows you how to integrate different existing technologies to make a functioning robot while, at the same time, explaining key algorithms (like path planning, autonomous navigation, etc.) in enough detail that the reader can adapt what he or she learns to virtually any robotics project. This book is written in such a way that readers will come away with a solid foundation for a working robot. More importantly, it will entice the reader to continue research and experimentation into more advanced areas of robotics.

I met Lloyd Brombach when we started a robotics club at Wayne State University in Detroit; I am the faculty mentor, and Lloyd, a student in computer science, is a co-captain. We entered the Intelligent Ground Vehicle Competition, and Lloyd oversaw the main Robot Operating System (ROS)-based software for path planning and obstacle avoidance. What I noticed was that he is a very persistent yet patient person who has a keen intellect and extreme tenacity. As we got to talking, I found out that he had completed the 140.6-mile Ironman contest in 2012 — an athletic event that requires not just incredible physical endurance, but also tremendous mental fortitude. He has brought that same relentless determination to this book, and in my mind, he is not only an Ironman but also a Silicon man.

One could say he has really found his element.

Abhilash Pandya, Ph.D
Associate Professor, Department of Electrical and Computer Engineering
Director, Computer Assisted Robot Enhanced Systems (CARES) Laboratory
Wayne State University, Detroit

# Downloading the code bundle and coloured images:

Please follow the link to download the
*Code Bundle* and the *Coloured Images* of the book:

# https://rebrand.ly/2af84

# Errata

We take immense pride in our work at BPB Publications and follow best practices to ensure the accuracy of our content to provide with an indulging reading experience to our subscribers. Our readers are our mirrors, and we use their inputs to reflect and improve upon human errors if any, occurred during the publishing processes involved. To let us maintain the quality and help us reach out to any readers who might be having difficulties due to any unforeseen errors, please write to us at:

**errata@bpbonline.com**

Your support, suggestions and feedbacks are highly appreciated by the BPB Publications' Family.

## BPB is searching for authors like you

If you're interested in becoming an author for BPB, please visit **www.bpbonline.com** and apply today. We have worked with thousands of developers and tech professionals, just like you, to help them share their insight with the global tech community. You can make a general application, apply for a specific hot topic that we are recruiting an author for, or submit your own idea.

The code bundle for the book is also hosted on GitHub at **https://github.com/bpbpublications/Practical-Robotics-in-C-**. In case there's an update to the code, it will be updated on the existing GitHub repository.

We also have other code bundles from our rich catalog of books and videos available at **https://github.com/bpbpublications**. Check them out!

## PIRACY

If you come across any illegal copies of our works in any form on the internet, we would be grateful if you would provide us with the location address or website name. Please contact us at **business@bpbonline.com** with a link to the material.

## If you are interested in becoming an author

If there is a topic that you have expertise in, and you are interested in either writing or contributing to a book, please visit **www.bpbonline.com**.

## REVIEWS

Please leave a review. Once you have read and used this book, why not leave a review on the site that you purchased it from? Potential readers can then see and use your unbiased opinion to make purchase decisions, we at BPB can understand what you think about our products, and our authors can see your feedback on their book. Thank you!

For more information about BPB, please visit **www.bpbonline.com**.

# Table of Contents

**1. Choose and Set Up a Robot Computer**............................................................ 1

What is a Raspberry Pi?........................................................................................ 1

*What's the difference then?* .......................................................................2

*So the Raspberry Pi is the only choice for a robot controller?* ...................2

*Isn't the Raspberry Pi for schools, hobbyists, and toys?*
*I wanted to learn about real robotics.* ........................................................3

Raspberry Pi models and why not all are suitable for our purposes.............. 3

*Raspberry Pi Zero and Raspberry Pi ZeroW*..............................................5

*The Raspberry Pi 2B* ..................................................................................5

*The Raspberry Pi 3B - Best choice!!*..........................................................6

*The Raspberry Pi 3B+* ...............................................................................6

*The new Raspberry Pi 4* .............................................................................7

Operating system choices.................................................................................... 7

*Raspbian* .....................................................................................................8

*Ubuntu* ........................................................................................................8

Operating system installation and setup........................................................... 9

*Full Ubuntu desktop on laptop or desktop PC* .........................................10

*Lubuntu on your Raspberry Pi* .................................................................11

Programming environment (IDE) installation and setup .............................. 14

*Visual studio code for the laptop or desktop PC* ......................................14

*Code blocks for the Raspberry Pi*.............................................................15

Conclusion ......................................................................................................... 16

Questions............................................................................................................ 16

**2. GPIO Hardware Interface Pins Overview and Use** ..................................17

Introduction ...................................................................................................... 17

What are GPIO pins........................................................................................... 18

*So what exactly does the GPIO do?* ..........................................................19

*Electronics for programmers 101*..............................................................19

Types of output data.......................................................................................... 24

Types of input data ..................................................................................... 26

*Some common electronics hardware* ........................................... *27*

*Breadboards* ................................................................................... *27*

*GPIO pins as outputs* ................................................................... *31*

*Two pin numbering systems* ......................................................... *32*

GPIO pins as inputs ..................................................................................... 33

Accessing the Raspberry Pi GPIO with C++ programs ............................. 35

Installing PIGPIO .......................................................................................... 35

*Installing and setting up the PIGPIO library* ............................. *36*

*Making sure Code::Blocks can link to PIGPIO* .......................... *37*

*Running PIGPIO programs* ......................................................... *38*

*Our first GPIO project – hello_blink* .......................................... *38*

*Digital input to control a digital output – hello_button* ............ *42*

*GPIO event callback functions* ................................................... *43*

Conclusion .................................................................................................... 46

**3. The Robot Platform** ....................................................................................**49**

Introduction ................................................................................................. 49

Objective ....................................................................................................... 50

Considering the size and operating environment ...................................... 50

Differential drive versus Ackerman (car-like) steering .............................. 52

*Differential drive* ......................................................................... *52*

*Ackerman steering* ........................................................................ *53*

Ready-made robot platforms ....................................................................... 53

*Large pre-built robots* .................................................................. *53*

*Small pre-built robots* .................................................................. *54*

Tips for building your own robot ................................................................ 56

*Building materials* ........................................................................ *56*

*Batteries* ......................................................................................... *57*

*Drive trains* .................................................................................... *57*

*Robot parts sources* ...................................................................... *58*

Re-purposing robot vacuums or remote-controlled cars ......................... 59

*Robot vacuums with the interface* .............................................. *59*

*Interfacing with a Roomba* ..................................................................... 61

*Un-freezing your Roomba* ..................................................................... 65

*Robot vacuums without an Interface* ........................................................ 66

Hacking remote-controlled cars and trucks ............................................. 67

Conclusion ........................................................................................ 69

Questions ......................................................................................... 69

**4. Types of Robot Motors and Motor Control** .................................... **71**

Introduction ..................................................................................... 71

Objectives ........................................................................................ 72

Motor types ...................................................................................... 72

*Alternating current (AC) versus direct current (DC) motors* ................. 73

*Brush-type DC motors* ......................................................................... 73

*Servos* ............................................................................................ 74

*Stepper motors* ................................................................................. 75

*Brushless DC motors (also known as BLDC)* ...................................... 76

Introduction to the transistor and motor drivers .................................. 77

*The most basic control: On/Off* ......................................................... 77

*Transistors* ..................................................................................... 78

Pulse width modulation (PWM) .......................................................... 81

*PWM to create analog voltages* .......................................................... 81

*PWM as a control signal* ................................................................... 83

Motor drivers and motor controllers .................................................. 84

*Motor drivers* ................................................................................... 84

*Controlling motors with an L298N dual H-Bridge motor driver* ........... 86

*Motor controllers* ............................................................................. 90

Conclusion ........................................................................................ 91

Questions ......................................................................................... 91

Bonus challenge ................................................................................ 91

**5. Communication with Sensors and other Devices** .......................... **93**

Introduction ..................................................................................... 93

Objective ......................................................................................... 93

Binary (logical) signals ...................................................................... 94

*Debouncing switches* ............................................................ *95*

*Wheel encoders* ..................................................................... *96*

*Binary signals from analog sensors* ...................................... *96*

*Binary communication summary* ........................................... *97*

*Serial communication primer* ................................................ *97*

*UART serial* .......................................................................... *98*

Set up a Raspberry Pi and test UART serial communication ......... 99

*Fixing error opening serial port* .......................................... *103*

I2C communication primer ............................................................ 104

*To set up and use an I2C device with the Raspberry Pi:* ....... *105*

*Example and test program: hello_i2c_lsm303* ..................... *106*

Conclusion ..................................................................................... 110

Questions ....................................................................................... 111

**6. Additional Helpful Hardware** .............................................. **113**

Introduction .................................................................................. 113

Objective: ...................................................................................... 114

Power supplies .............................................................................. 114

*5 volt supplies* ..................................................................... *114*

Adjustable power supplies ............................................................ 115

Relay modules .............................................................................. 115

Logic level converters ................................................................. 116

FTDIs ............................................................................................ 117

Arduinos ....................................................................................... 118

Digisparks ..................................................................................... 119

Conclusion .................................................................................... 119

Questions ...................................................................................... 120

**7. Adding the Computer to Control your Robot** ..................... **121**

Introduction .................................................................................. 121

Structure ....................................................................................... 122

Objective ....................................................................................... 122

The steps ....................................................................................... 122

Step 1 - Mount and run power to the computer: ......................... 123

Interface (wire) the computer to the rest of the Robot:...................................124

Conclusion ...........................................................................................126

Questions..............................................................................................126

**8. Robot Control Strategy** ...............................................................**127**

Introduction.........................................................................................127

Structure..............................................................................................127

Objectives ............................................................................................128

Robot control: The big picture versus the small picture .................................128

The fundamental control loop.................................................................130

*Observe and compare* ............................................................*130*

*React* ...............................................................................*130*

*Affect*...............................................................................*131*

Open-loop and closed-loop controllers: ....................................................133

Designing a big picture (also known as the master) controllers:...................135

Designing a small picture (also known as a process) controllers: .................137

*Bang bang controllers (also known as On/Off controllers)* .....................*137*

*Proportional controllers* ........................................................*138*

*Designing controllers to accept some error*.................................*142*

*Setting a minimum output* ....................................................*143*

*Beyond proportional controllers* .............................................*143*

Conclusion ..........................................................................................144

Questions..............................................................................................144

**9. Coordinating the Parts** ...............................................................**145**

Introduction:........................................................................................145

Structure:.............................................................................................146

Objective..............................................................................................146

What is the robot operating system? ........................................................146

ROS versus writing your robot control software...........................................147

ROS and the commercial robotics industry ...............................................147

ROS setup ...........................................................................................148

*ROS melodic installation on your laptop or desktop* .............................*149*

*ROS kinetic installation on your Raspberry Pi 3B*...............................*149*

ROS overview and crash-course ....................................................... 152

    *Packages, nodes, publishers, subscribers, topics, and messages*.............. 153

A handful of helpful tips ................................................................ 160

Creating and writing ROS packages and nodes ........................... 160

    *The ROS file system*.................................................................... 161

    *Creating ROS packages* ............................................................. 161

    *Writing ROS programs (Nodes)*.................................................. 163

    *Downloading, reviewing, and running the chapter download programs* ............................................................. 171

Making life easier with roslaunch and .launch files...................... 172

Conclusion ................................................................................... 173

Questions...................................................................................... 174

**10. Maps for Robot Navigation**.............................................**177**

Introduction................................................................................. 177

Objectives..................................................................................... 178

Angle, heading, and distance conventions.................................... 178

Receiving sensor data .................................................................. 180

Occupancy grid maps................................................................... 182

Building occupancy grid maps (OGMs) with sensor data ........... 184

    *Marking the occupied cells*........................................................ 187

    *Marking the free cells* ............................................................... 190

    *Completing the map*.................................................................. 190

    *Publishing the map as a ROS Message*....................................... 191

Transforms in ROS....................................................................... 193

    *Understanding transforms*......................................................... 193

    *How transforms are used in ROS* .............................................. 194

    *Publishing transforms with the static transform publisher* .................. 196

    *Publishing transforms from nodes with a transform broadcaster* ......... 197

    *Getting transform data in your nodes* ....................................... 199

    *Viewing transform data from the command line* ......................... 201

Mapping made easy with Gmapping............................................201

    *Gmapping 101* .........................................................................201

*Getting Gmapping* ............................................................ *202*

*Running Gmapping and parameters in launch files* ................ *202*

*Steps to create a map* ....................................................... *205*

Visualizing a live map ........................................................... *205*

Saving a Map and using it later ............................................. *206*

*Saving maps* ..................................................................... *207*

Load previously saved map .................................................... *207*

Conclusion ........................................................................... *208*

Questions ............................................................................. *208*

**11. Robot Tracking and Localization** .......................................... **211**

Introduction ......................................................................... *211*

Objectives ............................................................................ *212*

The robot pose ..................................................................... *212*

*Converting Euler angles to quaternions* .............................. *214*

*Converting quaternions to Euler angles* ............................. *215*

Odometry and dead reckoning ............................................... *216*

*Wheel odometry* ............................................................... *216*

*Calculate the distance traveled for each wheel* .................... *220*

*Calculate the total distance the robot has traveled* ............... *221*

*Calculate the change in heading angle theta* ........................ *222*

*Add the change in heading to old heading theta* ................... *222*

*Calculate the distance moved in the x direction and the y directions (also known as translation)* ................................ *223*

*Add the distances calculated to the previous pose estimate* ... *223*

*Dead reckoning* ................................................................ *224*

Publishing odometry data in ROS .......................................... *226*

*Odometry transform publisher* .......................................... *229*

Further tracking and localization ........................................... *231*

*Manual pose updater* ........................................................ *232*

Fiducials ............................................................................... *232*

Laser scanner based localization ............................................. *233*

GPS and GNSS ...................................................................... *234*

Beacon-based localization systems .................................................235

Conclusion ....................................................................................235

Questions.......................................................................................236

**12. Autonomous Motion**.................................................................**237**

Introduction.................................................................................237

Objective........................................................................................237

ROS robot motion overview .......................................................238

The motor controller - simple_diff_drive.cpp .........................238

The simple_diff_drive motor controller code steps................239

The differential drive motor controller code outline .............240

The differential drive motor controller code ........................241

The drive controller: simple_drive_controller.cpp ................250

Drive controller steps...........................................................250

Conclusion ...................................................................................259

Questions.......................................................................................259

**13. Autonomous Path Planning**......................................................**261**

Introduction.................................................................................261

Objectives ......................................................................................261

Path planning methods and challenges......................................262

Challenges..............................................................................262

Path planning methods .........................................................262

Obstacle inflation ........................................................................263

Costmaps ...............................................................................264

A* path planning..........................................................................267

How it works ..........................................................................268

The A* algorithm by the steps...............................................271

Walking through an A* routine.............................................272

Writing the A* program as a ROS node.....................................279

The standard stuff, helper functions, and main() ................279

The heart of your A* Node: find_path()................................294

Conclusion ....................................................................................301

Questions.......................................................................................302

**14. Wheel Encoders for Odometry** ................................................................**303**

Introduction ...............................................................................................303

Objective ....................................................................................................304

Wheel encoders 101 ...................................................................................304

Optical encoders .........................................................................................304

Hall effect encoders ....................................................................................305

Wiring encoders ..........................................................................................305

The Encoder tick publisher - tick_publisher.cpp .....................................307

*Encoder tick publisher code* .................................................................*309*

Conclusion ..................................................................................................314

Questions ....................................................................................................314

**15. Ultrasonic Range Detectors** .........................................................................**315**

Introduction ...............................................................................................315

Objective ....................................................................................................316

HC-SR04 ultrasonic range sensor basics ...................................................316

*Reading HC-SR04 by the steps* ............................................................*316*

Wiring the HC-SR04 ..................................................................................316

Ultrasonic range data publisher: ultrasonic_publisher.cpp .......................317

*Ultrasonic range publisher by the steps* ...............................................*317*

*Ultrasonic range publisher code* ..........................................................*319*

Ultrasonic range data for object detection .................................................323

Conclusion ..................................................................................................324

Questions ....................................................................................................324

**16. IMUs - Accelerometers, Gyroscopes and Magnetometers** ..........................**325**

Introduction ...............................................................................................325

Objectives ...................................................................................................326

Accelerometers ...........................................................................................326

*Accelerometer shortcomings* .................................................................*327*

*Publishing IMU Data in ROS* .............................................................*328*

*The ROS sensor_msgs::Imu data type* .................................................*328*

*The IMU message publisher code* .........................................................*330*

Gyroscopes ..................................................................................................335

*Gyroscope shortcomings*.................................................*336*

*Adding gyroscope data to the IMU node* ...........................*336*

Magnetometers...................................................................*338*

*Magnetometer shortcomings*.............................................*338*

*Adding magnetometer data* ..............................................*339*

Mounting the IMU...........................................................*341*

Conclusion ......................................................................*342*

Questions........................................................................*342*

**17. GPS and External Beacon Systems** .................................**343**

Introduction....................................................................*343*

Objectives.......................................................................*344*

How beacon systems work.................................................*344*

GPS and GNSS basics......................................................*345*

*GPS/GNSS accuracy* ......................................................*346*

GPS/GNSS-RTK for 2cm accuracy....................................*347*

GPS/GNSS limitations.....................................................*347*

GPS/GNSS data ..............................................................*348*

*NMEA data strings* ........................................................*348*

*Some key lat/long data representations*.............................*350*

Publishing GPS/GNSS data in ROS...................................*351*

*The ROS package: nmea_navsat_driver* ..........................*351*

*Installing the nmea_navsat_driver package* ....................*352*

*Reading ROS package documentation* .............................*353*

*Running the nmea_serial_driver node with parameters*.......*354*

Conclusion .....................................................................*355*

Questions........................................................................*356*

**18. LIDAR Devices and Data** ...............................................**357**

Introduction....................................................................*357*

Objective.........................................................................*358*

LIDAR basics .................................................................*358*

LIDAR limitations...........................................................*359*

LIDAR types ...................................................................*359*

*Unidirectional (single point) LIDAR*........................................................360

*2D LIDAR* ..................................................................................................360

*3D LIDAR* ..................................................................................................361

*Salvaged robot vacuum LIDAR*................................................................362

LIDAR selection considerations..................................................................363

LIDAR data: The sensor_msgs::LaserScan message ...............................364

LIDAR mounting considerations.................................................................366

Setting up, running, and testing a common LIDAR unit ......................367

*Setting up an RPLIDAR by following these steps:*.................................368

Visualizing the LaserScan message ...........................................................370

Conclusion .....................................................................................................372

Questions.........................................................................................................373

**19. Real Vision with Cameras**..........................................................................**375**

Introduction...................................................................................................375

Objectives.......................................................................................................376

What is an image? .........................................................................................376

*Image attributes* ..........................................................................................377

*Pixel coordinates* ........................................................................................377

*Checking or installing the required software*...........................................379

*ROS Kinetic* ................................................................................................379

*ROS Melodic*................................................................................................379

*Testing OpenCV in ROS* ...........................................................................380

Image processing software (OpenCV) and ROS: .....................................381

*Step 1: Publishing images in ROS*............................................................382

*Installing the usb_cam_node* ...................................................................383

*Running the usb_cam_node* ......................................................................383

*Test the camera output*...............................................................................384

*Step 2: Subscribe to image in a different node* .......................................385

*Create your ROS vision package*...............................................................386

*Coding the image message subscriber* .....................................................387

*Step 3: Use cv-bridge to convert the RGB image ROS uses to
a BGR image OpenCV can work with* ........................................................388

*Step 4: Perform desired operations on the image*..................................389

*Step 5: Publish any non-image data as their own ROS message*...........389

*Step 6: Convert modified image back to RGB*........................................390

*Step 7: Publish result image under its own topic* ................................390

*More image processing basics* ...............................................................391

*Kernels, apertures and blocks* ..............................................................391

The importance of working on copies instead of original images ................392

*A word about lighting* ...........................................................................393

*Step 4 revisited - more possible OpenCV operations* ...........................393

*Converting color format: cvtColor()*.....................................................393

*Blurring images: blur(), medianBlur(), GaussianBlur()* ....................394

*Edge detection: Canny()*.........................................................................395

Edges on image to numerical lines: HoughLinesP() ....................................396

*Image masking: bitwise_and()* .............................................................401

Filtering by Color: cvtColor() and inRange() ...............................................403

Miscellaneous helpful ROS tool .....................................................................408

Advanced OpenCV and beyond ......................................................................408

Cloud-based image recognition .....................................................................409

Conclusion .......................................................................................................409

Questions..........................................................................................................410

**20. Sensor Fusion** ...........................................................................................**411**

Introduction ....................................................................................................411

Objective...........................................................................................................412

Sensor fusion made easy .................................................................................412

The Bosch BN0055 absolute orientation sensor...........................................412

*Provided data* ........................................................................................413

Improved odometry.........................................................................................414

Integrating the BN0055 – The hardware and ROS publisher.......................415

Integrating the BN0055 – The odometry node .............................................416

*Step 1: Subscribe to the IMU message*...................................................416

*Step 2: Verify orientation is not marked Do Not Use* ...........................417

*Step 3: Convert quaternions to Euler angles*.........................................418

*Step 4: Save Offset information IF this is first IMU message* ................. 418

*Step 5.1: If NOT the first IMU message – Save the IMU heading*.......... 419

*Step 5.2: Apply the new heading in the odometry calculation function* ...... 420

Sensor fusion 2 – A more comprehensive approach ..................................... 421

*The Kalman filter* ................................................................................... 421

The covariance matrix .................................................................................. 423

Covariance matrices in ROS messages ......................................................... 425

The robot_pose_ekf node .............................................................................. 426

*Installing robot_pose_ekf* ........................................................................ 426

*Running the robot_pose_ekf* .................................................................... 427

A final note on transforms and roslaunch .................................................... 428

Conclusion .................................................................................................... 429

Questions ...................................................................................................... 429

**21. Building and Programming an Autonomous Robot ....................431**

Introduction ................................................................................................. 431

Objective ...................................................................................................... 433

Part 1 - Building the physical robot platform ............................................... 433

*The robot platform – General overview and parts list* ................................ 433

*Wheel/motor modules* ............................................................................. 435

*Motor driver(s)* ....................................................................................... 436

*Caster wheel* .......................................................................................... 436

*Battery and charger* ................................................................................ 437

*Chassis/base* .......................................................................................... 438

*Computers* ............................................................................................. 438

*LIDAR or another ranging sensor* ........................................................... 439

*Wheel encoders* ...................................................................................... 439

*IMU* ....................................................................................................... 439

*Voltage converter for computer* ............................................................... 440

*GPIO header breakout board* .................................................................. 440

*Camera* ................................................................................................... 441

*Voltmeter* ............................................................................................... 441

*Miscellaneous materials* ......................................................................... 442

*Assembling the robot platform*..................................................*443*

*Mount the wheel modules and caster*.......................................*445*

*Mount the motor driver, terminal strips, and computer power supply* ......*446*

*Prepare the GPIO breakout board*...........................................*447*

*Mount the computer, GPIO breakout board, and IMU* .......................*447*

*Complete wiring and mount battery*.........................................*447*

*Mount LIDAR and camera*..................................................*448*

Part 1 - Conclusion .........................................................*449*

Part 2 - Programming your robot........................................*451*

*Programming – General overview*...........................................*451*

*Programming your robot – Detailed steps* ..................................*452*

*Run your autonomous robot!* ...............................................*464*

*Some troubleshooting tips*...................................................*465*

What next? ................................................................*466*

*Dynamic obstacle avoidance* ................................................*466*

*PID controllers* ............................................................*466*

*A master controller that manages various routines or tasks*.................*466*

*Implementing the map to odom transform (full localization)* ...............*467*

*Keep an eye on facebook.com/practicalrobotics and youtube.com/practicalrobotics*...................................................*467*

Conclusion ................................................................*467*

**Index**.........................................................................**469**

# Introduction

Finding clear guidance for building an autonomous robot is a challenge, partly because there are so many subjects involved, and partly because existing resources tend to be focused on their one specialty. Books on electronics don't talk about mapping or path planning, and books on robotics algorithms don't include the control theory necessary to be able to interface software with motors and feedback sensors. And too many books and tutorials for all subjects seem to require the reader to already have a degree — or at least some advanced mathematics — to be able to follow along.

What has finally allowed me to understand enough about robotics to design and build my own was taking the relevant bits and pieces from a combination of:

- A two-year course in electronics and automation technology;

- Two years of computer science, programming, and mathematics;

- A year of studying sensors, microcontrollers, and digital communications;

- A year of studying robotics software and algorithms;

- Years of experience designing and repairing industrial and commercial equipment automation controls;

- A lifetime of building and hacking electronic and electro-mechanical devices (apologies to my wife for the robot vacuum incident);

- Dozens of books and online courses; and

- Dozens of independent and cooperative robotics projects, including NASA's 2007 (Autonomous) Lunar Regolith Excavation Challenge and the 2019 Intelligent Ground Vehicle Challenge.

Are you ready for the good news? I'm going to save you four or more years of studying the parts of these subjects that aren't necessary for you to be able to build and program your first autonomous robot. This book will instead give you a clear roadmap and provide a complete foundation of knowledge to get you well into the game. I will also give you guidance on what to study next in each subject, so you can focus and explore the parts you find most exciting.

What I won't do is give copy-and-paste tutorials without making sure you understand what you are doing. Although all of the code is here in print and available to download at github.com/lbrombach, my goal is not to have you build and program the example robot precisely. Instead, I encourage and empower you to design, build, and program robots your own way, using my examples as guides. I will give you a serious kick-start, but how far you go from there is limited only by your own imagination and determination.

I wrote this book after working with university students with a wide range of experience and abilities. From freshmen with no experience at all, to graduate students who already have degrees in computer science, electrical, and mechanical engineering, none of them came in knowing how to build and program a robot. Our best programmers didn't know how motors or sensors worked, and our electrical engineers didn't know how to turn sensor data into useful numbers in code. Semester after semester, we co-captains found ourselves teaching the same basics of every subject over and over, and we wished for one manual that could give all of our team members a well-rounded foundation. Specifically, we needed lessons that were simple enough for the newer students to understand, yet in-depth enough that the graduates could still learn from them. This is that manual, and it requires nothing more to get started than basic C++ knowledge and a hunger for learning.

This book will appeal to both beginners as well as the most experienced programmers. I wrote code I felt would be easy for an inexperienced programmer to follow, knowing that more experienced programmers should have no problem implementing their own best coding practices. To my beginner programmers: This book uses C++ syntax to show how the algorithms work, but don't think of it as "a programming book." As your coding skills improve, you'll see more and more where I avoided C++ features I thought a beginner might not understand yet and took shortcuts like using global variables to make the examples easier on the eyes. All the programs are working examples but may not be examples of "best coding practices." I wanted very much to avoid an entire book of suddenly overwhelming code, and I try to give some warning and a little guidance as the C++ gets unavoidably a little more advanced along the way.

Delivery robots, warehouse robots, household robots, hobby robots, farm robots — each has its unique purpose and operating environment, yet they are all built upon fundamentals you will learn in this book. I advise against rushing to the tutorials; instead, get comfortable and read the book through, then come back for the hands-on experience.

Are you excited? I hope so, because it's time to get started.

Lloyd

# CHAPTER 1
# Choose and Set Up a Robot Computer

In this chapter, we will be covering the following topics:

- What is a Raspberry Pi?
- Raspberry Pi models and why not all are suitable for our purposes
- Operating system choices
- Operating system installation and setup
- Programming environment (IDE) installation and setup

## What is a Raspberry Pi?

The Raspberry Pi is a small, `single-board computer` (SBC). All that means that unlike your home desktop PC that might have a motherboard with slots or connectors for a processor, memory, video processor, and other components that you can swap and customize at will, an SBC is manufactured with these all permanently fixed to a single board. There is no changing or upgrading them without replacing the whole board. They don't have or run from a hard drive - the operating system runs from a micro SD card. There are several SBCs available today, but the Raspberry Pi is hands-down the most popular because of both it's very low-cost and massive community support - if you have a problem, there are many thousands of Raspberry Pi enthusiasts eager to help you on social media groups or the official Raspberry Pi foundation-user forums at *www.raspberrypi.org*.

Despite their minimal size (the biggest is about the size of a deck of cards), Raspberry Pis are fully functioning computers running a complete operating system (usually Linux) and capable of doing much of what your desktop PC can do such as web browsing, playing videos, connecting to printers and cameras, emailing, etc., as well as several things your desktop PC can't do without adding extra hardware like directly reading buttons, sensors or signalling the most common motor-controllers directly thanks to the **General Purpose Input/Output** (**GPIO**) header that we'll spend all of *Chapter 2, GPIO Hardware Interface Pins Overview and Use* getting used to. Also, thanks to its GPIO header, small size, and simple projects Raspberry Pis get used for, they sometimes get confused for a type microcontroller such as an Arduino. Still, the fact is these are in two entirely different classes.

# What's the difference then?

Among the big differences is the ability to write, compile, and execute programs directly on a Raspberry Pi. At the same time, a microcontroller requires you to write your programs and compile them on a computer, then download them to the microcontroller - which requires at least a USB cable and sometimes even a whole programming circuit. Once this is done, that program (which is limited to a much smaller amount of available memory, by the way) is the only thing your microcontroller can do until you repeat the whole process. A Raspberry Pi can run multiple programs at once - one of which can even be your microcontroller programming software. Since it is typical to be running multiple programs at once for all but the simplest of robots, we are going to exclude Arduinos and other microcontrollers from the list of suitable robot brains for our purposes.

# So the Raspberry Pi is the only choice for a robot controller?

Not at all. Although it is a fantastic choice, most of the robot code we will be writing throughout this book will work just fine on any other computer without any modifications. The exceptions being anything to do with the GPIO. On other computers, we have to use external hardware to do their job, and that requires different code. It's often not cost-effective to dedicate a regular laptop and the extra hardware, cost, and space requirements for a relatively simple robotics project, but sometimes it's worth the trade-offs. As we'll see later, computer vision takes a lot of computational power. This can go a lot faster if the computer has something called a **Graphics Processing Unit** (**GPU**). These specialized processors are designed to handle operations on image data in large chunks at a time, making them magnitudes faster than a regular CPU. *Nvidia*, one of the most prominent manufacturers of

GPUs, released its low-cost single-board computer in 2019 called the `Jetson Nano`. At a price point of `$100 US` and including a legitimate, 128 core GPU and 40 pin GPIO header compatible with the Raspberry Pis, it's bound to become a common name in the robotics world. Between the even lower price (making it available to more people) and huge community support network that the Jetson just doesn't have yet (although it's rapidly growing!), I still have to give the title of *Ideal learning computer for robotics* to the Raspberry Pi. That's why we've chosen to do our example projects with a Raspberry Pi for a controller.

## Isn't the Raspberry Pi for schools, hobbyists, and toys? I wanted to learn about real robotics.

You can indeed find a Raspberry Pi in the hands of all manner of toys and hobbyists, but that just speaks for its high power at a remarkably affordable price. Universities love for them how much teaching can be done on them for so little money, and I recently traveled to an international robotics summit and was surprised at the number of commercial robot companies that deploy their autonomous robot products with a Raspberry Pi as a controller. Following *figure 1.1* shows just one example.

*Figure 1.1: Ubiquity Robotic's Magni is just one of a number of commercially available robots powered by a Raspberry Pi. source: Ubiquity Robotics*

Magni and other commercial, Raspberry Pi-based robots can do things like security patrol, work in warehouses, office or baggage delivery, serve as cocktail waiters, and plenty more. I think you'll find a Raspberry Pi far more capable than *just a toy* and highly recommend starting your robotics-learning career with one.

## Raspberry Pi models and why not all are suitable for our purposes

Take a look at the comparison chart on the following *figure 1.2*. These are the most popular and readily available models of Raspberry Pi. I have omitted the less-common (and older) A and B models and place them in the *not suitable for our purposes* category. This is because of factors such as slow speeds, lack of memory, and a lot of software packages we might benefit from just won't run on them. They certainly could be made to work, but even in the cases where I might use one, I would generally use a *Zero* or *ZeroW* models instead. It's just a better deal for the money.

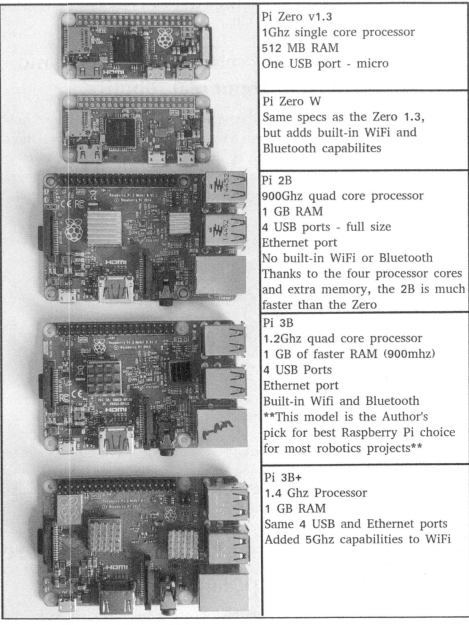

| | |
|---|---|
| | Pi Zero v1.3<br>1Ghz single core processor<br>512 MB RAM<br>One USB port - micro |
| | Pi Zero W<br>Same specs as the Zero 1.3,<br>but adds built-in WiFi and<br>Bluetooth capabilites |
| | Pi 2B<br>900Ghz quad core processor<br>1 GB RAM<br>4 USB ports - full size<br>Ethernet port<br>No built-in WiFi or Bluetooth<br>Thanks to the four processor cores<br>and extra memory, the 2B is much<br>faster than the Zero |
| | Pi 3B<br>1.2Ghz quad core processor<br>1 GB of faster RAM (900mhz)<br>4 USB Ports<br>Ethernet port<br>Built-in Wifi and Bluetooth<br>**This model is the Author's<br>pick for best Raspberry Pi choice<br>for most robotics projects** |
| | Pi 3B+<br>1.4 Ghz Processor<br>1 GB RAM<br>Same 4 USB and Ethernet ports<br>Added 5Ghz capabilities to WiFi |

*Figure 1.2:* A comparison of the most popular Raspberry Pi models.

Before you run off and buy the most powerful Raspberry Pi listed (or the new Raspberry Pi 4 – not pictured), please read the rest of this chapter as there are reasons the 3B+ or 4 may not be the best choice.

## Raspberry Pi Zero and Raspberry Pi ZeroW

The Raspberry Pi *Zero* and *Zero W* models are great little machines for a meagre price, but I'm afraid they just haven't got what it takes to be real robot controllers, except perhaps the most basic of obstacle avoidance bots. (The *Zero W* is a regular *Zero* with built-in Wi-Fi and Bluetooth adapters). I tend to use them where a microcontroller would probably do the job. Still, I might want to remotely reprogram it or perform functions that it makes easier than a microcontroller such as display or web access functions, or where I want the batteries to last a long time - the Zeros have no close competition among the other Pis as far as being low-power goes.

The problem arises from both its lack of memory and its single-core processor. This is less of a problem if you are an old Linux pro and are happy without a GUI, but if you like to use an **Integrated Development Environment** (**IDE**), the little Zeros are going to struggle. Try running your IDE over **Virtual Network Computing** (**VNC**) for remote access, and you might as well forget it. For these reasons, I tend to limit my use of Zeros to things with smaller programs that I don't mind editing from a plain text editor and compiling from the command line.

Also, be aware that the *Zero* models require an adapter to output to a standard HDMI monitor, and another to plug in a standard USB device like a keyboard. In the case of the less-expensive *Zero 1.3*, you will need a separate Wi-Fi adapter as well, which means you need a USB hub to have both Wi-Fi and keyboard, plus you have to buy and solder in your header pins for the GPIO. All this makes it less affordable than it seems at first glance.

**Verdict:** *Not for a fully autonomous machine.*

 We love the Raspberry Pi Zeros and it can be tempting to buy one for your project to save money. Still, plenty of folks new to the little computers have been disappointed when they discover that they have to buy extra adapters or how painfully slow they are – especially when using the graphical user environment.

## The Raspberry Pi 2B

The *Pi 2B* is the first model I find genuinely suitable for a real, autonomous robotics project. The full gigabyte of memory and quad-core processor makes it start to feel like a real computer and less like I'm trying to surf the Internet with a slow dialup connection back in 1995. You will have to buy a USB adapter for Wi-Fi if you don't have one lying about, but that's about it. Unlike the Zeros, it comes with header pins already soldered on so you can start plugging devices straight away.

*Notice: I said* **start** *to feel like a real computer - The Pi 2B is still on the sluggish side at some things like web browsing or when running remotely over VNC.*

This is a way of remotely controlling one computer from another, and it can be done from across the room or the planet. There are other ways to accomplish remote control of a computer, but VNC allows the sharing of the graphical environment so you can do everything with a remote machine as if you were plugged right into it. This can be very useful when developing robots.

**Verdict:** Acceptable choice, but unless you already have a USB Wi-Fi adapter lying around, you can get the even faster 3B model for about the same cost. Even if your robot doesn't need faster, You will greatly appreciate the faster machine, whether you are developing and testing your code or operating your finished project (as if these projects are ever truly finished). I get impatient when I click and have to wait and wait, then my attention wanders, and before long, I'm outside chasing squirrels with my dog and nothing has gotten done.

## The Raspberry Pi 3B - Best choice!!

The Raspberry Pi 3B is the best choice, in my opinion, because it strikes the best balance between power consumption, speed, and built-in features. In exciting news, it was the first model to come with on-board Wi-Fi and Bluetooth, saving you from having to buy USB adapters. The new, faster CPU feels almost zippy compared to the 2B. While the 2B can usually get by with just a heat sink, the 3B benefits from a heat sink and a small fan for cooling - especially in an enclosure. If the chips get too hot, they automatically throttle back to slower speeds so technically nothing is required, but heat sinks and fans cost can be had for just a couple dollars. This is worth every penny in the name of productivity.

**Verdict:** We have a winner! Of all Raspberry Pi models, I'll choose this one for all of my mobile robot projects.

## The Raspberry Pi 3B+

The Raspberry Pi 3B+ is not the best choice for a robot controller despite its faster processor – especially for mobile robots. It is a fine machine, but I've read more than one unofficial test that indicated only a modest speed improvement (about 10-15 percent faster) but at the cost of 50 percent greater power consumption. This is an essential factor for a mobile robot running on batteries, and while I haven't measured battery drain-time with a clock, the difference is noticeable. The extra power also means you've got to step up the cooling, but the 3B+ does add the 2nd Wi-Fi band, which is nice but not necessary.

**Verdict:** Everything we are going to do should work just fine on the 3B+ as well as the 3B (or 2B, for that matter), so the choice is yours. I keep my 3B+ model on my desk, where it can stay tethered to the wall outlet and use regular 3B Pis on my robots.

## The new Raspberry Pi 4

Shortly after I began writing this book, the Raspberry Pi Foundation released the brand new model 4B. A yet again faster processor, options up to 4 GB of memory, and other significant hardware changes make for a faster machine, indeed, but this required a significant overhaul of software packages as well to make them compatible. At this time (February 2020 – some 7 or so months later), the operating system and other software developers are still struggling to make compatible packages and operating systems that we use in robotics. It can be made to work, but forget simple installation methods – for even a simple robot, I had to do a lot of standard packages installing and compiling from source.

Even if the software catches up to the hardware and use becomes as easy as the Pi3B, I don't see a lot of benefit for the extra power consumption – which by all accounts is A LOT (even compared to the 3B+).

While the Pi4B has excellent potential, it's just not ready for those of us more interested in our projects than fighting with software installations. I wholeheartedly have to discourage the Pi4B for those newer to Linux for the time being. If you need a more powerful machine, I recommend you have a look at the `Nvidia Jetson Nano` – it's far more powerful and much better supported for not a lot more money. The only thing I can think of I'd want a Pi4 on a robot for is faster computer-vision work and machine learning, and the `Jetson Nano` is designed very much for that.

# Operating system choices

Just like any other computer, there are several operating systems to choose from for your Raspberry Pi. No, I'm afraid Windows isn't one of them, and we wouldn't want to slow the little machine down with that much baggage anyway. There is a version of Android out there that some folks are experimenting with on the Raspberry Pi, but I understand that it's pretty buggy and crash-prone. Let's just talk about a couple of versions of Linux.

# Raspbian

If you're at all experienced with the Raspberry Pi, you're almost certainly familiar with the official OS – Raspbian. Easily the most popular Raspberry Pi operating system and has the biggest pool of community support. Raspian is a great place to start for getting used to Linux and the Raspberry Pi for a lot of projects, and I encourage you to take some time following some small project tutorials you find interesting to get used to Raspbian, Linux in general, and the Raspberry Pi itself. It is not the operating system I am going to suggest for robotics or use in our projects in this book, however. The reasons for this will become apparent soon enough.

 **Raspbian is just what the Raspberry Pi Foundation calls its line of custom Linux distribution (usually called *distro* for short). There have been a lot of versions or releases, so when asking the internet for troubleshooting helps, you need to specify which release. The releases have names like *Jessie* or most recently (as of February 2020) *Buster*. Raspbian distros are based on Debian versions of Linux.**

Raspbian definitely could be used for big robotic projects like we are about to undertake. Still, it's going to require either a lot more coding or the ability to tweak and fiddle software installs. I just want to get my robots going, so I'll pass for robotics, but go for it if you get satisfaction out of making these things work!

Minimalists can also choose the *Lite* version of the different Raspbian versions. This is a bare-bones operating system without all the automatically installed extra software packages or even a graphical interface – everything is done from terminal windows.

 **A neat benefit of the Raspberry Pi operating from a micro SD card is how easy it is to swap them. I often travel with a Raspberry Pi, and a quick swap of the SD card is like having an entirely different machine for a different purpose.**

# Ubuntu

Those new to Linux are often surprised at how many versions there are. Debian, Ubuntu, Mint, Red Hat, Fedora, CentOS barely scratch the surface. Likewise, you'll usually find many versions of each of those. We call those *flavors*.

The flavors available for Ubuntu are many, but I just want to talk about two:

*The full desktop version of Ubuntu* and a more minimal version called *Lubuntu*.

The full version of Ubuntu is too heavy for the humble Raspberry Pi, and, from some experimenting with several flavors, I have found it most comfortable to get everything we need up and running on a version called Lubuntu. This still provides a graphical environment but skips a lot of the extras. Some of the extras are nice, but I have a nickname for extras that I don't use - *bloatware*.

If you're planning to use a full-size desktop computer or laptop for robotics, I suggest installing the full desktop version. This is, in fact, my daily OS and what I'm using to type this book with. You can even install it without giving up your Windows operating system by installing it as a *dual boot*. This allows you to choose whether you want to run Ubuntu or Windows at each boot. I highly recommend this option, even though I find myself rarely using my windows boot anymore. Ubuntu can replace almost everything, but once in a while, I need a program made for Windows. Yes, there is a Windows emulator called **Wine** that allows you to run Windows program from Linux distros like Ubuntu, but I don't see the point in fiddling with a known-to-be-buggy software in the software when I can reboot in seconds thanks to solid-state hard drives.

Another invaluable feature of having Ubuntu on your main computer and Lubuntu on your Raspberry Pi is how easy it is to control one machine from the other with SSH remotely. Yes, there are ways to do this with a Windows machine on one end, but none are easier than opening a terminal window on your laptop by pressing *Ctrl + Alt + T*, then typing ssh -X lloyd@lloyds_raspi.local at the command prompt. A little more on SSH later. For now, know that you're going to find it incredibly useful so you don't have to try to follow your robot around the room, forest, or ocean while carrying a keyboard and display.

Another benefit to running Ubuntu on all machines involved in a robotics project goes beyond remote control of one machine or another, but cooperating on the robot processes. I'll be introducing you to a very powerful (*and free!*) software later on that gives robots the ability to cooperate, among other things. This runs efficiently on Ubuntu and Lubuntu but can be complicated on other distros.

# Operating system installation and setup

Next, let's get you set up with a computer running an appropriate version of Linux. If you're terrified to install Linux on your regular computer, you can try it out by booting from the USB stick loaded with it and run right from there. It will be slower, but Ubuntu supports this. If you are ready to set up a Raspberry Pi 2B, 3B, or 3B+, I recommend you skip what I have posted below and *Chapter 9, Coordinating the Parts* – there is a shortcut by way of a ready-to-use image of a Raspberry Pi operating system, along with a lot of other software we're going to have to set up later anyway. It is maintained by a private company, so I include the do-it-yourself instructions in case they decide to pull it for whatever reason. Unless you like to do it all yourself, follow the instructions in *Chapter 9: Coordinating the Parts* then come back for the *Code Blocks setup* instructions.

 When talking about computer operating systems, and image is a file that contains an already set up operating system instead of an installation package. Rather than following a bunch of setups prompts, you can load an image and start running right away. You can also make an image to back up your system once you have it just the way you like it or before you tinker with it. Then making an *oops* is not as big of a deal.

# Full Ubuntu desktop on laptop or desktop PC

I'm not going to spend a lot of time talking about installing the full desktop Ubuntu on your laptop or desktop computer. Just don't forget that this isn't the version we want for our Raspberry Pi. If you are going to put a full laptop on your robot, then you could use this version. Whether you install Ubuntu as the only operating system or install alongside Windows as dual boot is up to you. Dual boot even on your robot won't hurt, except it does take a few extra seconds to boot up because you have to click which OS to boot into or wait for the timer to run out, and it will automatically boot into a default choice.

Whichever you decide, make a backup of your hard drive first – even if you have a brand new machine with nothing you need on it. As easy as it is to install, there is always room for something to go wrong, and it's sad not even to be able to revert to an operable machine to download or research things you need to get all fixed up.

To get started, just head over to *https://ubuntu.com/download/desktop* where they have instructions for installing Ubuntu onto machines running other Linux distros, Windows, or even macOS. Essentially, you're going to download what's called an image, copy it to a USB stick, reboot into that USB stick and follow the on-screen directions from there. I recommended installing the latest version that is tagged with **Long Term Support (LTS)**. Even if newer versions are available, there is no guarantee they are sticking around, and developers for other software tend to develop for LTS versions. As of July 2019, the LTS version of choice is *Ubuntu 18.04.2 LTS*.

# Lubuntu on your Raspberry Pi

This process is going to start with another machine. However, you could also do it from your Raspberry Pi if it's already running Raspbian or something else as long as you have another micro SD card handy that the Raspberry Pi is not running on. You might get by with an 8 GB, but that's cutting it close, and I recommend at least a 16 or 32 GB. Be warned that going higher than a 32 is probably overkill and requires jumping through some extra hoops because of format differences, so we aren't going to use one of those for anything in this book. There is a shortcut to all this. I'm going to show you in *Chapter 9, Coordinating the Parts*, but that comes with some minor compromises and relies on a private company keeping their website and OS image current, so I am going to show you how to do everything yourself. I would be lying if I said I didn't enjoy how quick and easy it is to set up with the shortcut method, but doing it yourself will help you understand what is happening on your Raspberry Pi – useful for troubleshooting if strange things start happening down the road.

From your shiny, new Ubuntu computer you hopefully set up as described above, the following steps install Lubuntu on a micro SD card:

1.  In a web browser, select the Lubuntu version from *https://ubuntu-pi-flavour-maker. org/download*.
2.  Go to your **Downloads** folder.
3.  Right-click on the file that starts with lubuntu and ends with .img.xz.torrent.
4.  Select **Open with Transmission**.
5.  In **Transmission**, highlight the file, set the destination (which can be the same as the **Downloads** folder) and press the green play button to start downloading. See the following *figure 1.3*.

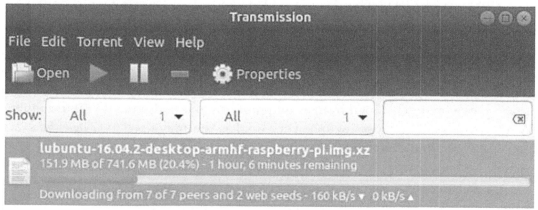

***Figure 1.3:*** *The Transmission control screen*

1. When it signals complete, you can stop the torrent and close transmission.
2. Use the file browser to navigate to the **Downloads** folder.
3. Right-click the file that starts with lubuntu and ends with .img.xz.
4. Select open with disk image writer then the restore disk image window will pop up.

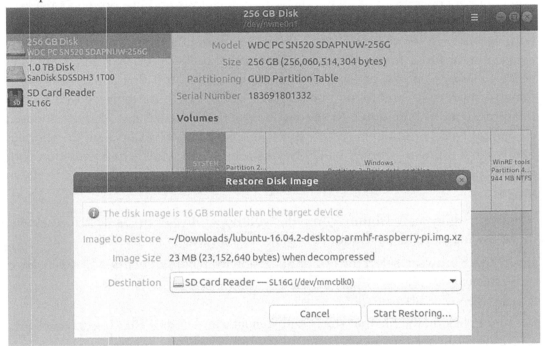

*Figure 1.4: The Disk Image Writer*

5. Pop your micro SD card into an adapter then into your computer and select it.
6. Double-check that you have your selected your SD card and not your computer's hard drive!
7. Click **Start Restoring…** and wait a while.
8. When it's done, eject the SD card, stick it into the slot on your Raspberry Pi, and power the Pi up with a power supply and cable rated for 2.4 amps.

That's how you'd get started from a computer running on Linux. If you're running Windows or macOS, it's going to be very similar. You may need to *Google* the exact procedure, but in the end, you are doing the same things:

1. Downloading the Lubuntu for Raspberry Pi image.
2. Burning the image to a micro SD card.
3. Putting micro SD card in Raspberry Pi and powering up.

I know it's tempting to buy the cheapest micro SD cards, but there are many reasons to skip those. Besides that the storage size is often much smaller than advertised; the read/write speed is often far slower as well. This makes a tremendous difference for us because the whole operating system runs from the micro SD, and its speed can cause a faster Raspberry Pi to run as slowly as a cheaper model. Buy a quality, name-brand 16 or 32 GB one from a reputable source.

Make sure you've plugged your Pi into an HDMI monitor before you plug it into power, or it may turn the HMDI output off. Then you'll spend a while scratching your head, wondering why it doesn't work. If it hangs up on the initial *rainbow screen*, the first things to try are a new power supply and cable – just because it works for your phone doesn't mean it can carry enough current for a Raspberry Pi. These are a bit hungry – especially the 3 and 3B+. Don't try to power them from your computer's USB port either, or you risk damaging it. Get a proper 2.4 amp or greater power supply. I suggest a 3 amp or greater.

Your first boot will be pretty typical of any new computer. You'll follow on-screen prompts to set things up like language and time zone. Make sure you choose to connect to the Wi-Fi the first time they give you a chance, as it will save you some extra updating later. You can, of course, use Ethernet instead but your robot isn't going to want to be tied down, so you'll want Wi-Fi anyway if available.

The first thing in Linux you need to get familiar with is *Ctrl + Alt + Tab*. This launches a terminal window with a command line. If ever you can't figure something out or everything seems frozen, try to summon a terminal window and shutdown or reboot from there before just pulling the plug. The sd cards are corruptible if the power is cut while the card is being written to. There usually is no recovery from there, and you have to start all over by reflashing the card with a new image. Once you have a terminal window, you can use `sudo reboot` or `sudo shutdown now` to do whichever you want to do safely.

 The sd cards are corruptible if the power is cut while the card is being written to, so it is essential to avoid cutting power to the Raspberry Pi without properly shutting down.

The second thing you should do is use `sudo raspi-config` to launch a unique Raspberry Pi configuration tool. With this, you can change your user name and password from the default. Then go to the **interfacing options** tab and enable at least the options for camera, SSH, I2C, and Serial. You'll be wanting all of those for our projects. You should also go to advanced options and choose to **Expand Filesystem** because of the way the Imagewriter leaves you with main partitions that waste most of the sd card's capacity.

Finally, you want to update your repositories and packages. Don't worry if you don't know what this means yet, use *Ctrl + Alt + T* to open a terminal, then run:

```
sudo apt update
```

```
sudo apt upgrade
```

Press *Y* to continue when asked and go for a walk - this may take a while the first time you run it.

# Programming environment (IDE) installation and setup

To use or not to use an IDE is, of course, up to you. I like to use one for all but my smallest programs for helpful features like organizing include files and autocomplete. For the sake of getting those who like their IDEs but are new to Linux or the Raspberry Pi, I'm going to cover just enough to get an IDE up and running.

## Visual studio code for the laptop or desktop PC

I have grown very fond of VS Code. While technically a text editor and not an IDE, it has so many plug-ins and functions that it blurs the line. One reason I started using VS Code over regular Visual Studio was project-compatibility when working with others – true IDEs like Visual Studio tend to add a bunch of extra little files and folders to your project package and working with someone using a different IDE, or even a different version of the same IDE makes for no end of hassle and headache. For this reason alone, I have adopted the VS Code as my programming environment on my laptop and desktop PCs but, unfortunately, it does not yet run on Raspberry Pis. To install on your Ubuntu computer, open a terminal window with *Ctrl + Alt + T* and run the following commands:

```
sudo apt install snapd
```

```
snap remove vscode
```

```
snap install code --classic
```

The first command installs Snap – which is your doorway to a place developers make their software available and easily installable. You could compare to maybe the App Store on your cell phone. The second command makes sure we don't have any problems because of anyhold installations of VS Code. The third command uses a snap to install VS Code as prepared for Linux. If prompted for a `sudo` or administrative password for permission, just give the computer what it asks for. To run VS Code in Ubuntu, click on the *apps* icon in the corner and type `VS` or `code` to find it. Then right-click on it when you see it, and either run or select **add to favorites**. The latter option permanently mounts an icon to the launch bar on the side of the screen. See the following *figure 1.5*:

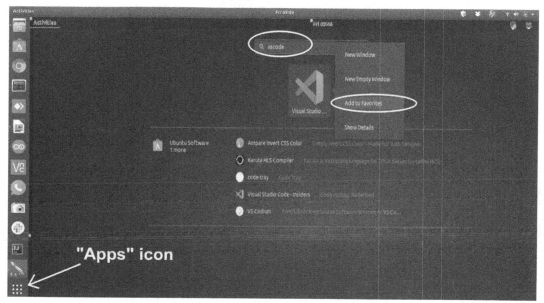

**Figure 1.5:** *Adding VS Code to the favorites bar*

I am, however, sad to say I have not found a way to run VS Code on a Raspberry Pi. I tried a couple of methods I found on the internet, but none have worked. This brings us to an option that could work well for either your laptop or your *Raspberry Pi: Code Blocks*. I keep VS Code on my laptop and Code Blocks on my Raspberry Pis.

# Code blocks for the Raspberry Pi

If you don't have a personal favorite IDE already for the Raspberry Pi, give Code Blocks a try. There are lighter-weight IDE's, but I found others I've tried to be more hassle getting set up than they were possibly worth. Code Blocks is pretty simple, so I'm sticking with it. To install:

```
sudo apt install codeblocks
```

Run by simply typing `codeblocks` at the terminal command prompt. To start a project, click **Start Project** -> **console application** -> **c++**. Then enter your project name and where you want it and click on **Next**.

On this screen, your default compiler should be in the compiler field. You should have GNU GCC Compiler already installed, and Code Blocks should detect it for you. When prompted, it's fine to make it your default compiler unless you have a personal preference for another. If you do, you are probably experienced enough that you don't need my help installing and setting it up. Go ahead and make sure both `create release` and `create debug` are selected and click on **Finish**. On the left, you'll see your project, and under it, a folder called **Sources**. Double click on **Sources,** and you'll see all the files in the project. Double click on main.cpp, and you'll see a Hello World! the program is already written. Click **Build**->**Build and run** and a little terminal should pop up with your greeting. Now you're all set to go!

 One last thing – if Code Blocks is unstable and randomly crashes on you, you can likely fix it by disabling the symbols browser. This is done by clicking the editor option in the **Settings** tab. Then in the left pane, select **code completion**. One the code completion window opens, click the symbols browser tab and check the box for `disable symbols browser`. This has worked on every one of my Rasberry Pis so far.

# Conclusion

In this first chapter, we've taken a big first step and have chosen the computer we will control our first robot with, and install some version of Linux installed on it. If we are new to Linux, we've even issued out first Linux commands to set up some basics and install a coding environment we'll use to develop software throughout the rest of the Practical Robotics in C++ experience.

Since the Raspberry Pi is such a popular, affordable, and especially-well suited choice for a robot's computer, we are going to spend *Chapter 2, GPIO Hardware Interface Pins Overview and Use* learning how to use the primary feature that sets it apart from most small computers that came before it – the GPIO pins. We will use these heavily in robotics to bridge the gap between software and the physical world our robot lives in, so let's spend some time getting to know them.

# Questions

1. What is the minimum usable Raspberry Pi model?
2. What is the operating system of choice for robotics?
3. How do you open a terminal with a command prompt in Linux?

CHAPTER 2

# GPIO Hardware Interface Pins Overview and Use

## Introduction

The GPIO pins are what have made the Raspberry Pi computer such a blockbuster hit, and it's time to learn precisely why. This chapter is going to be a crash course in the general basic electronics knowledge you need to use similar input/output pins on any similar computer or microcontroller, as well as how to use the Raspberry Pi GPIO pins with your programs for both controlling devices and reading information from sensors, switches, etc. Bookmark this chapter if you're not an old pro at the Raspberry Pi GPIO or basic electronics, as you'll be using this info a lot in your robotics career.

In this chapter, we will be covering the following:

- What are GPIO pins
- Electronics for programmers 101
- Types of output data
- Types of input data
- GPIO as outputs - explaining the relevant electronics basics
- GPIO as inputs - explaining the relevant electronics basics
- How to access Raspberry Pi GPIO with C++ programs
- Hello_blink – your first digital output program

- Controlling digital output with a digital input
- Callback functions: Calling function with a digital input

# What are GPIO pins

As computer programmers, we can write software that can do some cool stuff with numbers, images and data. Still, when it comes to making something happen in the physical world, we need a way to interface the ones and zeroes in our programs with hardware items like switches and motors. This is what GPIO pins are all about – *bridging software and hardware*. Until motors and switches learn to read the monitors and follow our wishes, one of the most powerful tools we have as developers of robots is the GPIO pins on our controller – whether that's a microcontroller or a **Single Board Computer** (**SBC**) like the Raspberry Pi.

Until fairly recently, we would have to write programs on a computer, then use some extra hardware to program a microcontroller that would then use it's GPIO pins to handle the hardware stuff. Alternatively, we could wire another interface device to a serial or USB port, and that device would handle the hardware in response to a program on a computer. These are still common and valid tools but come with extra hassle and expense that isn't always desirable. Thankfully, the Raspberry Pi Foundation came along in the year *2012* and developed a little single board computer that came with 26 GPIO pins on the same little board as the CPU and memory. This was the *Raspberry Pi 1 Model B*, and the educational and hobby worlds fell in love. *Figure 2.1* shows the layout of the original 26-pin GPIO header, as well as the newer 40-pin GPIO header.

```
    3.3v  ■ ■  5v              3.3v  ■ ■  5v
  GPIO2   ■ ■  5v            GPIO2   ■ ■  5v
  GPIO3   ■ ■  ground        GPIO3   ■ ■  ground
  GPIO4   ■ ■  GPIO14        GPIO4   ■ ■  GPIO14
  ground  ■ ■  GPIO15        ground  ■ ■  GPIO15
  GPIO17  ■ ■  GPIO18        GPIO17  ■ ■  GPIO18
  GPIO21  ■ ■  ground        GPIO21  ■ ■  ground
  GPIO22  ■ ■  GPIO23        GPIO22  ■ ■  GPIO23
    3.3v  ■ ■  GPIO24          3.3v  ■ ■  GPIO24
  GPIO10  ■ ■  ground        GPIO10  ■ ■  ground
   GPIO9  ■ ■  GPIO25         GPIO9  ■ ■  GPIO25
  GPIO11  ■ ■  GPIO8         GPIO11  ■ ■  GPIO8
  ground  ■ ■  GPIO7         ground  ■ ■  GPIO7
                             XXXXX   ■ ■  XXXXX
                             GPIO5   ■ ■  ground
                             GPIO6   ■ ■  GPIO12
                             GPIO13  ■ ■  ground
                             GPIO19  ■ ■  GPIO16
                             GPIO26  ■ ■  GPIO20
                             ground  ■ ■  GPIO21

  26 Pin Raspberry Pi        40 pin Raspberry Pi
  GPIO pin layout            GPIO pin layout
```

*Figure 2.1:* *The original 26 pin and current 40 pin Raspberry Pi GPIO headers.*

In the following years, the Raspberry Pi GPIO header evolved to 40 pins instead of 26 but kept the same layout so devices and hats from the early models could still work on the newer Pis. Today, the 40 pin Raspberry Pi GPIO header is something of a standard, and numerous competing SBC manufacturers have copied the layout and are 100 percent compatible with any circuit made for the Raspberry Pi. This makes sense if they hope to compete because of how many accessory devices are now made for the Raspberry Pi by third parties.

 **Mess around with Raspberry Pis for a while, and you're going to come across things called hats. Hats are just accessory hardware devices designed to fit right on top of the GPIO pins. They can be time-savers, but I've never been a big fan because they require specific GPIO pins that might already be taken and tend to block access to a bunch of pins even though they only need a few for themselves. I prefer to save pins and hassle down the road by running my wires to a standalone device.**

## So what exactly does the GPIO do?

The short answer is that they either output some voltage to turn something *On* or *Off*, or read an input voltage. To get a better understanding than that, let's go over some electronics basics.

## Electronics for programmers 101

I'm going to spare you a whole lot of technical detail, but electricity is all about electrons and electrons moving. If you have more in one place than you do in an adjacent place and connect the two with a conductor, the electrons will try to move from the place with more to the place with less – and can do work along the way. This is how a battery works - *there is a negative side with a whole lot of electrons and a positive side with a relative lack of electrons*. If you connect the two sides with a conductive wire, the extra electrons will rush from the negative side to the positive side, creating heat and an electromagnetic field.

I'm sure you've heard the terms *volts*, *amps*, *power*, and perhaps *ohms*. These are all terms used to describe certain things about electricity, and we need a basic understanding of each of them to be able to design our circuits or safely modify example circuits to suit our specific requirements. The short definitions of the essential terms are:

- **Volts:** Unit of measure of electrical pressure or intensity
- **Amps:** Unit of measure of electrical current (flow)
- **Ohms:** Unit of electrical resistance

- **Watts:** Unit of electrical power. *Volts * Amps = Watts*
- **Series:** Electrical components arranged end-to-end, with only one lead from each attached to a common point
- **Parallel:** Electrical components arranged side-by-side, having a common point of attachment for the leads from both ends

I think one of the easiest ways first to understand basic electricity is to think of it as a fluid – *like water*. (The calculations for water systems and electrical systems are quite similar). Our conductors (wires) will be like pipes, and the rest – well, read on.

 **Caution: In a Direct Current (DC) circuit such as something battery-powered, the electrons always flow in the same direction. Electronics projects having a computer rely heavily on this trait. In an Alternating Current (AC) circuit, the electron flow changes direction many times per second. This is handy for changing voltages and transmitting power over long distances, but bad for most of the components in our robots and bad for you if you go messing with the higher voltages that frequently accompany AC without proper training. Let's stick with batteries and DC power supplies, OK?**

`Volts` are the unit used to measure voltage, which can be thought of as electrical intensity or pressure. When you have water pressure in a pipe, that's potential energy waiting for a chance to do some work. Voltage is much the same – it's just a bunch of electrons all excited to do some work. And just like opening a valve on your pressurized garden hose opens a path for the water to spray all over, the moment there is a path from a place of greater potential (voltage) to a place with less potential, electrons are going to start flowing. We call that flow *current*. *Figure 2.2* illustrates how we represent both incomplete and completed paths for electrical flow in wiring diagrams called schematics.

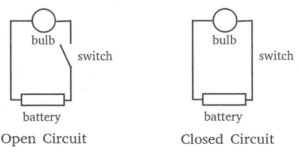

Open Circuit          Closed Circuit

*Figure 2.2: Schematic drawings of an incomplete (left) and completed (right) path for electrical flow*

We call completing the path for electricity to flow "closing the circuit" or "completing the circuit." When you turn on a lamp with a switch, you have closed the circuit. Before that moment, there was no path for electricity to get to the light bulb.

Ampere (`Amps`) is the unit used to measure current, which is a count of how many electrons are flowing per second. Back to our water analogy, if you have greater pressure in the hose you will have more gallons flowing per minute. Therefore, if we have greater voltage present when we close a circuit, we will have greater current. If you wanted to reduce water flow, you might do something to resist the flow like close the valve some. If you need to change the amps flowing through a wire or device, you can also increase or decrease the resistance.

`Ohms` are the unit we used to measure resistance to electrical flow. Without resistance, the flow of electrons can approach infinity. (Well, it'll get high enough to melt the wire or fry the devices, anyway.) We never want to power a device directly from our GPIO pins – we need to add some resistance. Thanks to the wonders of modern, cheap manufacturing of entire assemblies of components, many devices are available that have resistors built-in.

Volts, amps, and ohms have a rigid relationship that we can understand with a very simple math formula: $V = I*R$. $V$ stands for voltage in volts, $R$ stands for resistance in Ohms, and I don't know what genius decided that we have to use $I$ for current, but $I$ stands for current in amperes. As any mathematical expression, we can move things around to solve for any of these values if we have the other two. For example, if we know a power supply has *5 volts*, and we measure a device with our multimeter set to ohms and it reads *10 ohms*, *5 volts* divided by *10 ohms* is *.5 amps*, also known as *500 milliamps*. This relationship is known as `Ohm's Law,` and I highly recommend you spend some time studying up on it far more than we can in this book, but I have provided a very basic chart in *figure 2.3*. You're going to want to be very comfortable with these formulas.

| Volts = Amps*Ohms | Watts = Amps*Volts | |
|---|---|---|
| V = I*R | P = I*V | P = Watts |
| I = V/R | I = P/V | V = Volts |
| R = V/I | V = P/I | I = Ohms |
| | | E = Sometimes used for Volts |

*Figure 2.3: Ohm's and Watt's laws*

**Watts** are a unit for power and, according to *Watt's Law*, are the product of volts and amps. This is important to know because many devices will come rated in watts. Motors, for example, will come rated in either watts or horsepower (*One HP = 746 watts*). If you have a *12 volt, 120 watt* motor, you can calculate amp draw by dividing watts by the voltage. *120 watts/12 volts = 10 amps.* Now you know your motor controller had better be rated to handle *10 amps* at the very least, preferably more. Sometimes a watt-rating is more of a warning. As in, *this resistor can only dissipate 1 watt.* This means divide *1 watt* by your voltage to determine how many amps you can allow flowing through the resistor. Divide amps by *1000* to convert to milliamps. If you apply *5 volts* to a *1 watt* device, how many milliamps must it handle?

*(Hint: 1 watt / 5 volts = _____ amps. And _____ amps * 1000 = milliamps)*

**Series** and **Parallel** describe how components are arranged. Serial circuits are arranged with the end of one component wired to the beginning of another, and the end that component goes into the next and so on. A parallel circuit is arranged so the beginning of each component is wired together, and the end of each component is wired together. In practical electronics, we frequently use a combination of series and parallel circuits together where two or more parallel circuits are placed in series or several series circuits are placed in parallel. We cleverly call these *series-parallel* circuits.

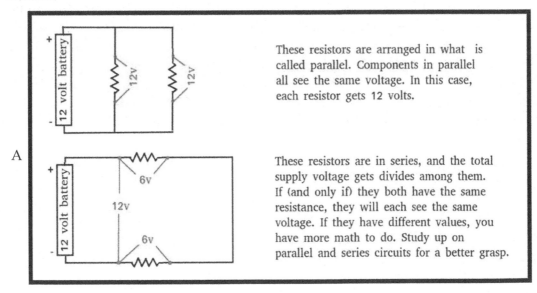

These resistors are arranged in what is called parallel. Components in parallel all see the same voltage. In this case, each resistor gets 12 volts.

These resistors are in series, and the total supply voltage gets divides among them. If (and only if) they both have the same resistance, they will each see the same voltage. If they have different values, you have more math to do. Study up on parallel and series circuits for a better grasp.

A `multimeter` for directly measuring voltage, resistance, and current is an inexpensive but indispensable tool that you'll need to get familiar with. They are all different, so you'll need to read your user manual to make sure you're in the correct mode and range for whatever you want to measure. When choosing a multimeter, take care to check how many amps it can handle in current mode. Some of the smaller, less expensive ones are very convenient to toss in your computer bag but can only handle a couple hundred milliamps. If you are only going to own one, buy one that can handle *10-20 amps*.

To measure voltage, place the test leads in parallel with the part of the circuit you wish to measure. To measure a GPIO pin, you'd place one lead on a ground pin and the other **VERY CAREFULLY** on the pin you want to check. The chances of slipping and touch the lead to two or more pins at the same time are high, so it is not recommended to measure directly at the pins. Instead, place a jumper wire on the pin and measure at the other end of that.

 **Caution: When two things get connected electrically where they aren't designed to (say you were poking around the GPIO pins with a test lead from your multimeter), it is called a short circuit or simply a short. This usually has undesirable consequences, and if the potential between the two points is great enough, too much current will flow, and something will fry. Many projects have gone up in smoke when a GPIO pin was accidentally shorted to a ground pin while probing with test leads.**

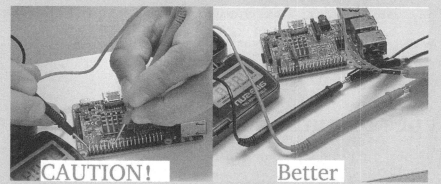

*Figure 2.5: Risky and safer ways of measuring voltage on a crowded header*

To measure DC current flowing through a circuit, we wire our meter in series with the circuit. A meter configured for reading current has a resistance of almost zero, and placing it in parallel with a circuit is creating a direct short and damage or at least blow a fuse on a lot of inexpensive multimeters. *Figure 2.6* illustrates measure voltage getting to an LED and measuring the current flowing through an LED.

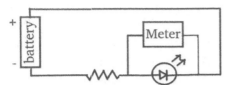 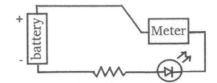

Measuring the voltage reaching the LED. Voltage will vary from component to component in a series circuit so be sure to measure in the right place.

Measuring current flowing through the LED. Fun fact: In a series circuit such as this one, the current flow is the same no matter where you measure

*Figure 2.6: Measuring voltage versus measuring current*

To measure ohms, place the leads in parallel with the part of the circuit you wish to measure. Measuring resistance in the circuit can be useful, but you must keep in mind that the reading can be influenced by parallel paths that you can't easily see. Removing even one lead of the component you want to test will guarantee you measure only the resistance of the parts you connected your leads to.

 **Caution: Your skin and body can conduct electricity and will read some resistance of its own. If you're ever wondering why your resistance reading is off or is jumping all over the place, ask yourself if you've become part of the circuit. To correct the situation, make sure you're not touching both ends of the meter. Little jumper wires with alligator clips are nice for making connections while keeping you out of the circuit.**

Now that you have an idea of what voltage is, let's look at how the GPIO pins either manipulate or measure voltage to do their job. We'll start by look at the different ways a GPIO pin could send a signal out to the world.

# Types of output data

GPIO pins are technically only capable of two conditions: *Either zero voltage* or *full-voltage*. *ON* or *OFF*. *True* or *False*. That's it. Yet humans have devised numerous, creative ways to manipulate these two conditions to represent many different types of output data. Here are a few you will almost certainly be using in your robotics careers.

- Digital output
- Analog output
- Asynchronous serial
- Synchronous serial

**Digital Output** data means the GPIO pin is being driven to a logical value of *0* or *1*, also known as binary or Boolean values. A pin in digital output mode goes *Low* to represent *false*. This typically means it will read *0 volts*. A digital output pin will be driven *high* to represent *true*. The voltage reading will be whatever your particular board uses for *high*. A Raspberry Pi's digital output will be *3.3 volts*. This voltage or lack of voltage is meant to be read by another device, not to do any real work. *Hi/Low, one/zero, True/False, ON/OFF* are all ways of describing the digital output values.

**Analog Output** data is more akin to floating-point values because instead of simply being on or off, we can represent almost any value in between *0* and our voltage that represents *high*. Calling it analog is somewhat misleading because GPIO pins cannot truly make any voltage except it's logical *high* or *Low*. To **fake** an analog value in between, the pin is switched *ON* and *OFF* many times per second, giving us a pulsating voltage that can be smoothed to its average value. This is called **Pulse Width Modulation** (**PWM**). We'll learn more and implement PWM in *Chapter 4, Types of Robot Motors and Motor Control*.

Other output types from GPIO pins are some implementation of one of these and are usually some form of communication with other devices. Serial communication, where we send bytes of data one bit at a time, is one classic example. We'll learn much more about communication in *Chapter 5, Communication with Sensors and Other Devices*.

**Asynchronous Serial Communication** is when a sending machine rapidly changes the voltage level on a wire from *Low* to *high* and back in a pattern the receiving machine can decode. You might think of it as a Morse code for machines, and usually, it's done over a pair of wires so each machine can both talk and listen. The Raspberry Pi has two specific pins for this (*Tx* for transmitting and *Rx* for receiving), although modern CPU speeds and software allow us to simulate a hardware UART with most any of our GPIO pins. Asynchronous Serial communication is excellent but is very prone to getting *hung up* where both sides are waiting for data, but neither is sending. I prefer to use it for one-way communication with sensors that just start streaming data when power is applied.

**I2C** is another communication protocol with special pins. With a serial protocol like the asynchronous serial method above, you can't have multiple devices on the same pins or wire because they'll interfere with each other's *1's* and *0's*. With I2C, each device gets an address and only speaks when addressed. You can have up to 127 devices on a single I2C bus that takes up only two of your GPIO pins plus power and ground. This is incredibly handy for adding and changing sensors without having to rewire the whole robot. I2C is technically *I squared C* is frequently pronounced *I two C*.

# Types of input data

Just like we have various types of output data to send signals or information out from the computer, we have a variety of ways to read signals or information into the computer from other devices. Generally, we have:

- Digital input
- Analog input
- Asynchronous serial
- Synchronous serial

**Digital input** is going to sound familiar because it's just reading the digital output of another device. What do I mean? Let's say you have a pin of your Raspberry Pi set as input and wired to the output pin of a microcontroller that operates at the same voltage. The microcontroller is in charge of the voltage on the wire, and if it sets it to *0*, the Raspberry Pi will read this voltage and return a *bool* value of *0* or *false* to the software that called it. If the microcontroller sets its pin high, the Raspberry Pi will interpret and return a *bool* value of *1* or *true*. Besides microcontrollers, you can read any device that can drive the digital input pin *high* and *low*. Wheel encoders (which we'll use later), motion detectors, and light sensors are all examples of devices that work by setting a digital pin *high* or *low*. Your program running on a Raspberry Pi or microcontroller can use an input pin to read this signal, then take further action as needed.

**Analog input** is when we measure more than a binary *On/Off* value. It literally measures the voltage on a pin. Analog inputs might be used to monitor the battery charge level or to read a sensor that has an analog output. Sensors that do not stream digital data will often vary voltage as its output signal instead. Care must be taken not to exceed a GPIO pins voltage rating, so we'll often add some hardware like a couple of resistors arranged into a voltage divider to bring it down to a safe range.

Also note that the Raspberry Pi does not have any ability to read analog values at all directly, so we need extra hardware in the form of **Analog to Digital Converter (ADC)**.

**Serial and I2C inputs** are special cases because they are part of two-way communication methods. We'll cover these when we get to *Chapter 5, Communication with Sensors and Other Devices*.

Note that when we measure voltage, what we are actually doing is comparing voltages. The meter registers the difference in voltage between its two test leads. By putting one lead on ground and the other lead on a *5 volt* pin, the meter shows us *5 volts – 0 volts = 5 volts*. If we instead put the negative (black) lead on a *3.3 volt* pin and the positive (red) lead on the same *5 volts* pin, the meter will indicate *1.7 volts* because *5 volts – 3.3 volts = 1.7 volts*. Typically in electronics, we are referencing some voltage compared to ground, but be aware that you might get different readings if your reference probe isn't on the ground.

Caution: Because different boards and microcontrollers use different input and output voltages, it is very important to make sure you either select ones that operate at the same voltage or are prepared to add extra hardware to match the voltages. Connecting the pin from a *5 volt* device to Raspberry Pi GPIO pins will damage the Rpi. Level shifters and voltage dividers are two ways of matching voltages.

## Some common electronics hardware

Before we start connecting wires and devices in the next section, I want to bring up some electronics hardware basics that are going to make your life easier to understand now. If you've been around electronics much, you can probably skip the next page or two except for the graphic of which pins on the Raspberry Pi header are useful for what.

## Breadboards

No, they're not for cutting bread. These are small, plastic boards with a bunch of little holes in it, and the holes in each row are internally connected. This allows you to place some components and wires to build complete circuits for testing without having to spend time screwing terminals or soldering connections that may just have to be changed. They come in many sizes, but a common one is pictured below.

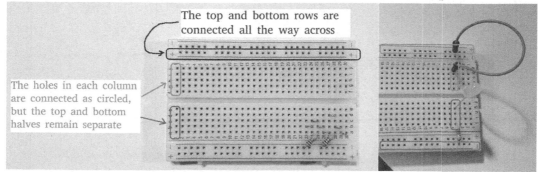

*Figure 2.7: A common breadboard*

Breakout boards are another great accessory for a robot project. There are many types of breakout boards, which are meant to make connecting to the GPIO pins easier. They frequently have screw terminals and a little room to add your components, as well as labels that correspond with the GPIO pin they are connected to. This helps reduce mistakes made trying to count across a long row of unmarked pins. Trust me when I say that connecting directly to the GPIO pins can get messy without a breakout board for all but the smallest projects. Having one or more of the breakouts boards pictured below is worth every penny.

***Figure 2.8:*** *A variety of breakout boards that make it easier to connect a lot of things to your GPIO header*

Some breakout boards, like the two on the left, are made to be plugged directly onto the GPIO header. The two in the picture on the right are each connected to Raspberry Pis with a `40` pin ribbon cable. If you only buy one to start, I recommend the type that plugs into a breadboard and connects them to the GPIO header with a ribbon cable. This is as handy as it gets for learning to use and testing circuits on the GPIO.

`Switches` are devices for opening and closing circuits and go in series with the device you want to control. When you flip a switch to *On*, it does the same thing as if you touched two wires together to complete a path for electricity to flow. In fact, sometimes instead of bothering to wire a switch for little test circuits, I simply plug a jumper wire in to close the circuit and unplug it to open the circuit. Be careful if you use this method – it's easy to get careless and let the dangling end of the wire make a short circuit, then POOF. Safest to immediately plug it into an unused section of a breadboard or, better yet, use a switch.

You can get all sorts of switches like those in *Figure 2.9* below– toggle switches, button switches, lever switches, float switches, and the list goes on forever. Of these switches, some stay on when you actuate them while others are **momentary** and turn off the moment you let go. Momentary switches (and relays, below) come with *normally open* or *normally closed* contacts. Normally open is the kind of switch people tend to automatically think of, as pressing the button closes the circuit. Normally closed has the circuit already completed, and pressing the button opens the circuit.

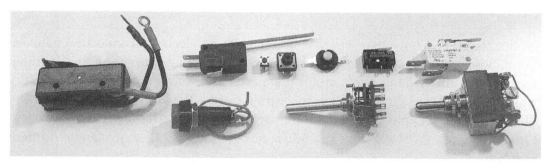

***Figure 2.9:*** *An assortment of switches in all shapes and sizes*

A relay is a special kind of switch that is activated with an electrical signal instead of by hand. This is of particular interest to us because our GPIO pins are not powerful enough to power anything, but we need to be able to turn things on and off with our programs that control them. There are solid state relays with no moving parts, but we are going to focus on the electromechanical type.

A relay has two essential parts: a switch and an electromagnet. You may recall from elementary school that an electromagnet is made by wrapping a tiny wire into a coil and passing electricity through it. We usually refer to the electromagnet simply as **the coil**. Each has its own pair of leads to connect to. The pair for the switch and the pair for the coil are not connected. *Figure 2.10* shows how a relay works and how it compares to a regular switch.

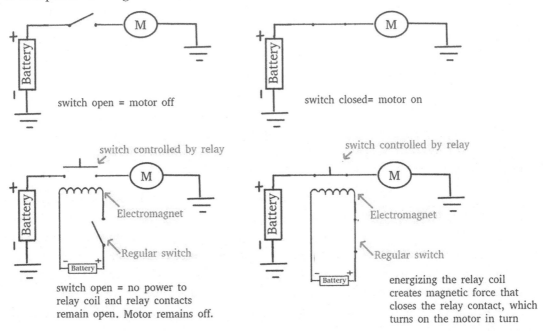

switch open = motor off

switch closed= motor on

switch open = no power to
relay coil and relay contacts
remain open. Motor remains off.

energizing the relay coil
creates magnetic force that
closes the relay contact, which
turns on the motor in turn

*Figure 2.10: A relay vs a regular switch*

Notice that relays have two separate circuits with no electrical connection between them. Sometimes you will hook both circuits to the same power source, but often we need to turn on a big, beefy motor that needs 24 or more volts with a 3.3 *volts* signal from a Raspberry Pi or microcontroller. **NOTE** that powering the relay coil directly from GPIO pins will draw too many amps. We learn how to do it safely in *Chapter 4, Types of Robot Motors and Motor Control. Figure 2.11* shows an assortment of relays.

*Figure 2.11: An assortment of relays*

Like switches, relays come in all shapes and sizes. They come with normally open and normally closed contacts (often both on the same relay!). You can find relays with coils that require just a few volts or coils that require a couple of hundred volts. The large relay on the right has a visible electromagnet coil and is used for turning whole-house air conditioners on and off. The relays on the board with the extra components are called relay modules. These are my favorite because the extra circuitry required between the GPIO pin and the relay is built-in, and I can simply run a jumper wire directly to the pin on the relay module board.

# GPIO pins as outputs

Now that you know some electronics basics, we can talk about how to wire your GPIO pins as digital outputs. Since we are using a Raspberry Pi, that means the pins we set as digital outputs will always either be either `0 volts` or `3.3 volts`. If you can turn on a tiny LED light, you can turn on a `10 KW` motor. It all starts with the Rpi outputting `3.3 volts` – hardware does the rest.

`Two important words of warning:`

1.  Raspberry Pi GPIO pins can only provide `3.3 volts` at `16 milliamps` – which is very, very little. This is enough to light an LED, but not activate a relay without an amplifying transistor.
2.  LEDs have almost no resistance of their own, so we must add our own to limit current and avoid damaging the GPIO pin. `2.2k ohms` should do for typical, small-sized hobby LEDs.

 **Caution: DO NOT try to power devices from GPIO pins. Trying to run the smallest fan or motor will instantly fry your pin and maybe your Rpi. Even powering a relay will require amplifying circuitry like a transistor.**

Wiring your GPIO as output is as simple as making sure the other device can handle your GPIO's voltage and adding a resistor somewhere in the circuit to limit current. In the LED circuit below, it doesn't matter if the resistor goes before or after the LED as long as it is in series and has a value that will keep current low enough to keep both devices safe. This means if your GPIO pins can handle `16 milliamps`, and your LED is only rated for `10`, you should use Ohm's law to calculate the value needed to keep current below `10 milliamps`. In practice, I have to admit that I frequently just grab a resistor that I know is technically `too` `big` because usually incredibly little current is required to light an LED or be read by GPIO pin on another device. I'd always instead draw less current if possible, then reduce the resistor value if necessary. *Figure 2.12* shows how to include a current-limiting resistor in an LED circuit.

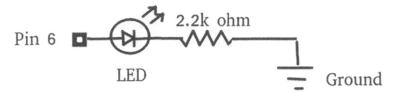

*Figure 2.12: Using a resistor in series with an LED to limit current drawn from the GPIO pin*

The above example presumes you are following along with a Raspberry Pi, and pin 6 is available. LEDs won't work if they are backward, so test it by plugging the wire into *3.3 volts* on your breadboard instead of pin 6. If the LED does not light, reverse it.

**Caution: The Raspberry Pi has two different numbering systems for the same *40* GPIO pins – the physical pin numbers and the GPIO (also known as Broadcom) numbers. For the rest of this book, we'll use the GPIO numbers. Take care not to confuse the two and accidentally fry your Pi.**

## Two pin numbering systems

The Raspberry Pi has two different numbering systems for the same 40 pins because matching the pins on the Broadcom microprocessor to the physical pin numbers was not practical. This is an unfortunate source of confusion for newcomers to the Rpi, but it doesn't take long to get the hang of it. The first number system is the physical number system. Finding a physical pin is as easy as counting starting at the bottom left of the header oriented horizontally. Finding the GPIO pin number requires a chart like the one in *figure 2.13*. I keep a printed one on my bench and found an Android app called **RPiREF**, so I always have one on my phone as well.

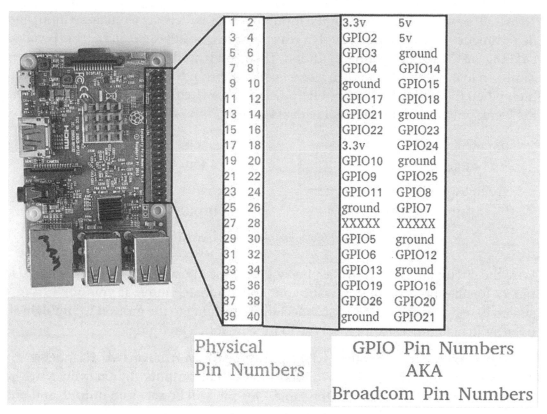

| Physical Pin Numbers | | GPIO Pin Numbers AKA Broadcom Pin Numbers | |
|---|---|---|---|
| 1 | 2 | 3.3v | 5v |
| 3 | 4 | GPIO2 | 5v |
| 5 | 6 | GPIO3 | ground |
| 7 | 8 | GPIO4 | GPIO14 |
| 9 | 10 | ground | GPIO15 |
| 11 | 12 | GPIO17 | GPIO18 |
| 13 | 14 | GPIO21 | ground |
| 15 | 16 | GPIO22 | GPIO23 |
| 17 | 18 | 3.3v | GPIO24 |
| 19 | 20 | GPIO10 | ground |
| 21 | 22 | GPIO9 | GPIO25 |
| 23 | 24 | GPIO11 | GPIO8 |
| 25 | 26 | ground | GPIO7 |
| 27 | 28 | XXXXX | XXXXX |
| 29 | 30 | GPIO5 | ground |
| 31 | 32 | GPIO6 | GPIO12 |
| 33 | 34 | GPIO13 | ground |
| 35 | 36 | GPIO19 | GPIO16 |
| 37 | 38 | GPIO26 | GPIO20 |
| 39 | 40 | ground | GPIO21 |

*Figure 2.13:* *The 40 pin Raspberry Pi GPIO header - physical pin numbers vs GPIO Pin numbers*

We will use the GPIO or Broadcom numbers for the remainder of this book, so `pin 6` for our purposes is different than physical `pin 6`. This is how PIGPIO and other libraries reference the pins, and it how most breakout boards are labeled as well.

# GPIO pins as inputs

Using GPIO pins as inputs is slightly more involved than using them as outputs because we must do something to keep the voltage on the pin stable when whatever device we are reading is not actively outputting a signal. This is called `pulling up` or `pulling down`.

**Caution: It's essential never to leave a digital input pin** *floating*. **Floating is when the pin is neither pulled up to** *high* **nor pulled down to** *low* **nor held at a certain analog level by some device. If we omit the pull up resistor in the circuit below, the input pin would be floating whenever the switch is open. Floating pins are to hardware what uninitialized variables are to software: Unpredictable and should be avoided.**

To use a Raspberry Pi pin as a digital input to read a switch, set a pin as an input and tie it directly to *3.3 volts* through a resistor of maybe *10k-30k ohms*. This is called **pulling up** to avoid a floating condition. Then you would run another wire from the same pin to *0 volts* (also known as *ground*), but through a switch. The pin will read high when the switch is open, but if you close the switch, the ground can overcome the weak pull up and the pin will read *Low*. See *figure 2.14* below.

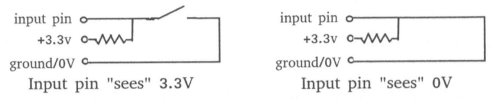

Input pin "sees" 3.3V        Input pin "sees" 0V

**Figure 2.14:** *Reading switch position with a digital input*

Wire the circuit above to your Raspberry Pi so we can use it in a few moments. Use pin *27* for the input pin if you want your code to match mine. If you don't have a switch to use, you can simply disconnect the wire going to the ground to simulate an open switch, taking care not to let the loose wire touch anything.

To read a signal from another GPIO pin (perhaps you have two Raspberry Pis working together) or any other digital device that outputs digital values at the correct voltage, it's more or less the same. One pin will be set as an output, and one will be set as input. We know that each requires a suitable current-limiting resistor, but the good news is that both pins can share the resistor. See *figure 2.15* below.

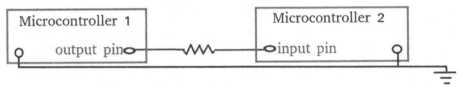

**Figure 2.15:** *Reading the GPIO output from one device with the GPIO input on another device*

Unlike reading a switch that can leave an input pin floating, when reading a GPIO pin with a GPIO pin, the output pin should always be driven high or driven low by the program controlling it. This means we don't necessarily need a *pullup*/*pulldown* resistor to prevent a floating input.

 **Two devices must share a ground for the electrical signal to pass from one to the other.**

Recall that the Raspberry Pi does not have any means of reading analog signals without extra hardware. Most devices we are going to use will communicate with the Raspberry Pi with serial or I2C, and I'll show you how to do that when we talk about sensors in *Chapter 5, Communication with Sensors and Other Devices.*

 **Note that if you are handy with a soldering iron, you can solder resistors (very carefully!) directly to the LED leads to saving clutter on your boards (and because it's faster to prototype). The two LED circuits pictured are both equivalents to the diagram above, but the yellow LED circuit takes more space and time to set up.**

*Figure 2.16*

# Accessing the Raspberry Pi GPIO with C++ programs

The ability to control GPIO pins from the same, tiny computer we can write our programs on and mount on a small, battery powered robot is why we love the Raspberry Pi so much. With other computers, we have the extra hassle of running cables to extra hardware and needing more power and space. With the Raspberry Pi, bridging the gap between software in a computer and the physical world is as easy as four easy steps:

1. Install a GPIO software library
2. Set up your IDE to link to PIGPIO
3. Include the correct header file in your program
4. Make function calls to the library

# Installing PIGPIO

Of the several software libraries available to manage control of the GPIO pins with C++ code, PIGPIO has emerged as my favorite. Far more than just managing the back end of turning the pins on and off or reading them, PIGPIO has some great utility functions to handle the nitty-gritty details of several communication protocols, pin monitoring with callback functions, creating PWM waves, and more. It is well-documented at *http://abyz.me.uk/rpi/pigpio/* and the developer is very active on the raspberrypi.org forums and provides wonderful support. I have to give many thanks to the developer, Joan, for such an excellent library.

# Installing and setting up the PIGPIO library

This is our final step before we can start doing projects. Some Linux distros meant for the Raspberry Pi will come with PIGPIO installed (like the Ubiquity Image from *Chapter 9, Coordinating the Parts*). You may be able to skip this installation (but come back if something isn't working – it's possible your distro came with an older version). Otherwise, I've repeatedly tested the following steps from the PIGPIO web site to install it on several Raspberry Pis, but check *abyz.me.uk/rpi/pigpio/download. html* for the latest instructions if you have any issues:

1. Stop any PIGPIO service already running
2. Download the latest version
3. Unzip the download
4. Change directory to the newly created `pigpio` folder
5. Run `make`
6. Run `make install`

You'll do these steps from the command line, so open up a terminal and use the following commands. (lines starting with '#' are comments, and you don't need to enter those).

```
#step 1

sudo killall pigpiod


#step 2

wget https://github.com/joan2937/pigpio/archive/v74.zip


#step 3

unzip v74.zip


#step 4
```

```
cd pigpio-74
```

```
#step 5
```

```
make
```

```
#step 6
```

```
sudo make install
```

**Installed?** Great! You can find some test programs on the PIGPIO download page I linked above if you want to be sure. When you're satisfied, we need to make sure Code::Blocks knows how to find the correct libraries when it's time to compile.

# Making sure Code::Blocks can link to PIGPIO

Now launch Code::Blocks by clicking the **Start** menu, then looking for it in **Programming**. Once it starts, open your hello_world program we created in *Chapter 1, Choose and Set Up a Robot Computer*. Then click on **Settings** in the top menu bar and select **Compiler**. This will open the **Global Compiler Settings** window.

Once it opens, click on the tab that says **Linker**, then the **Add** button under the **Link Libraries** field. Click on the three dots to browse and navigate to where the file libpigpiod_if2.so is installed. Usually, that will be the /usr/lib directory. I have circled the critical things in *Figure 2.17*.

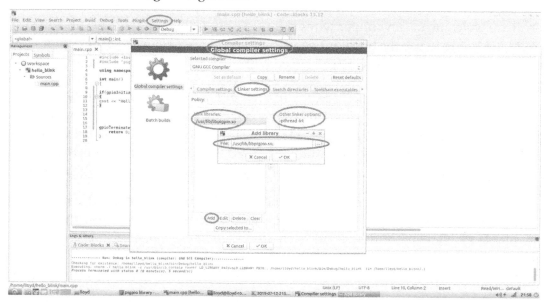

***Figure 2.17:*** *Adding the PIGPIO library and necessary linker options to Code Blocks*

Click on the `libpigpiod_if2.so` filename, then **OK** to add it to the link libraries. Then click on the **Other linker options** field on the right and add -pthread and -lrt by typing them in. Make sure to click **OK** at the bottom to save, and we're ready to start some real projects!

# Running PIGPIO programs

We are going to use the PIGPIOD (PIGPIO daemon) method, where we always have the PIGPIO daemon (background process) running that interacts with the GPIO pins. Any programs we launch will use this daemon as kind of a messenger to the pins. To start the daemon, just open a terminal and start it from the command line. I do this pretty much automatically when I boot up.

```
sudo pigpiod
```

It is slightly easier to run PIGPIO programs standalone than going through the daemon, but if you want to run a second GPIO program, it has to run through the first program (using it as a daemon) anyway. Since using the daemon and going standalone use different function calls, we are going to skip the standalone method completely to save you some hassle of learning two different sets of functions and writing different versions of the same programs. As you'll see going forward, our robots run many individual small programs rather than one large one.

# Our first GPIO project – hello_blink

`hello_blink` will be our first project and will use one pin and an LED (and resistor). You are welcome to run jumper wires right from the GPIO pins to your breadboard, but I am going to use the breakout board I showed you in *figure 2.16*. Set up pin *6* as an output with an LED as shown in *figure 2.12*.

 Most of the pins that are not *5v, 3.3v,* or GND can be used for GPIO, but there are good reasons to reserve specific pins for other purposes. For example, I like to save GPIO pins *2,3,4, 14,* and *15* because if I use them as GPIO, they aren't available for serial and I2C communications. You can learn more than we can cover here at the raspberrypi.org website.

Now, let's start coding! I am breaking the code down into bite-sized chunks, but if anything is confusing or you just prefer to see the entire programs, they are all available for viewing or download from *https://github.com/lbrombach*. I have several repositories for code from this book, and you'll find code from this chapter in `practical_chapters`. In case you're not familiar with `git` or GitHub, you can clone (copy) the repository from the terminal. Make a directory you want to copy the repository to, change to that directory, the use git clone. For example:

```
mkdir ~/practical
```

```
cd ~/practical
```

```
git clone https://github.com/lbrombach/practical_chapters.git
```

Back to writing code - Open Code::Blocks or your editor of choice on the Raspberry Pi. Create a new C++ console application called `hello_blink`. For a PIGPIOD program to compile and execute successfully, it must do the following (assumes PIGPIO daemon is already running):

1. Include the header file `pigpiod_if2.h`.
2. Assign aliases for pin numbers (optional).
3. Handshake with the daemon and get a `handle`.
4. Set pin modes and desired initial state.
5. Verify the handshake went *OK* before continuing (optional, but prudent).
6. Perform normal program functions.
7. Disconnect from daemon.

Steps *1* and *2*, I handle in the global space as you might expect:

```
//step 1
```

```
#include <pigpiod_if2.h>
```

```
#include <iostream>
```

```
//step 2
```

```
const int LED = 6;
```

```
using namespace std;
```

Nothing unusual here. Next, I write a function called `PigpioSetup()`. This is called from `main()` to handle steps 3 and 4.

```
int PigpioSetup()
```

```
{
```

```
//step 3
```

```cpp
    char *addrStr = NULL;

    char *portStr = NULL;

    //handshake with daemon and get pi handle

    int pi = pigpio_start(addrStr, portStr);


    //step 4 - set the pin mode and initialize to low

    set_mode(pi, LED, PI_OUTPUT);

    gpio_write(pi, LED, 0);


    return pi;

}
```

pigpio_start() returns an integer handle that will be used to identify this program to the daemon every time it makes a function call. That's why you see pi as the first argument in the setmode() and write() function calls that follow. Next, we write our main() function that calls PigpioSetup() and handles steps 5, 6, and 7.

```cpp
int main()

{

    //initialize pipiod interface (starts step 3)

    int pi = PigpioSetup();

    // step 5 - check that handshake went ok

    if(pi>=0)

    {

        cout<<"daemon interface started ok at "<<pi<<endl;

    }

    else

    {

        cout<<"Failed to connect to PIGPIO Daemon

            - Try running sudo pigpiod and try again."<<endl;
```

```
        return -1;

    }


    ///step 6 - normal program run and function calls

    //set pin 6 high to turn Led on

    gpio_write(pi, LED, 1);

    //sleep for 3.2 seconds

    time_sleep(3.2);

    //turn led off

    gpio_write(pi, LED, 0);


    //step 7 - disconnect from pigpio daemon

    pigpio_stop(pi);

    return 0;

}
```

And that's it. In Code::Blocks, compile and run with the *F9* key. You will likely get an *unable to initialize GPIO* error. If so, you can save your work and restart Code::Blocks with sudo permission by typing `sudo codeblocks` at the terminal command prompt. Be advised that any new projects or files you make while Code::Blocks is run with `sudo` permission won't be able to be edited later without `sudo` permission. You may prefer to run your program from the command line. Unless you changed the output directory when you set up the new project, you'd find the executable in `...hello_blink/bin/Debug`. Navigate to the folder and run with `sudo ./hello_blink` or run it from anywhere with the absolute path. In any case, be prepared to enter your admin password. For me, it runs if I type `sudo /home/lloyd/CPP/hello_blink/bin/Debug/hello_blink`

If everything went according to plan, our LED should have come on for *3.2* seconds, then turned off. Now let's expand on our last project and read a GPIO input pin – flashing our LED in response to a button press.

## Digital input to control a digital output – hello_button

Controlling a GPIO pin as an output is a good start, but we also need to be able to read a GPIO pin as an input. In our second program, `hello_button`, we'll tie the two together so the LED comes on in response to a button (or other) switch connected to a GPIO input pin. Start with the circuit from `hello_blink`, then wire a switch of some sort to pin *27* as an input, as shown in *figure 2.14*.

To write `hello_button`, start a new project (console application) in Code::Blocks called `hello_button`, then do the following:

1. Copy all of the `hello_blink` code into it.
2. Alias pin 27 as `BUTTON`.
3. Set pin 27 mode.
4. In `main()`, add a `while(1)` loop with an `if(condition)` block inside the loop.
5. Put the code that blinks the LED inside the `if()` statement.

Steps 1 and 2: Copy the `hello_blink` code into the new program and add the alias for pin 27, so you now have two `const` declarations in the global space.

```
const int LED = 6;
```

```
const int BUTTON = 27;
```

Step 3: Then, in the `PigpioSetup()` function, set the mode for pin 27 to input.

```
set_mode(pi, LED, PI_OUTPUT);
```

```
gpio_write(pi, LED, 0);
```

```
//set pin 27 mode as input
```

```
set_mode(pi, BUTTON, PI_INPUT);
```

Steps 4 and 5: Put the code that blinks the LED into an `if` the condition that checks the state (voltage level) present on pin 27, which we called `BUTTON`. IF the condition is met, the blink code will run. Otherwise, the `while()` loop continues forever, checking pin 27.

```
    while(1)

        {
```

```
if(gpio_read(pi, BUTTON) == false)

{

//set pin 6 high to turn Led on

gpio_write(pi, LED, 1);

//sleep for 1.5 seconds

time_sleep(1.5);

//turn led off

gpio_write(pi, LED, 0);

   }

}
```

The function to check a pin is gpio_read(). You may notice that I wrote the condition to execute if the button == false. The false indicates the logic level at the pin is *Low*. I wrote it this way because the diagram in *figure 2.14* shows the pin pulled *high* with a resistor and closing the switch pulls the pin logic level *Low*. It is very common to use this arrangement instead of pulling the pin low and the switch driving it high when closed, but it works either way. I encourage you to spend a little while experimenting with both.

 **Note – I wrote the** if(gpio_read(pi, BUTTON)==false) **the long way, but like every other logical condition, it is common to see the** ! NOT **operator used in place of writing out** == false. **It's a little more subtle, so keep your eyes open when reading code – even later in this book. This would look like:** if(!gpio_read(pi, BUTTON)).

Compile and run hello_button with **F9** (or from the command line). The LED should be *OFF* until the if() condition catches the switch closed, then the LED should illuminate for however long you have in the time_sleep() function call. The while(1) loop is infinite, so the program will never end until you use *Ctrl + C*.

# GPIO event callback functions

You may be familiar with event-based callback functions from other coding experience – these are functions you don't call in your code like a normal function call, but rather are called automatically upon some event happening such as a mouse click or *Esc* key pressed. For our purposes, it is very useful that PIGPIO provides us an easy way to set up callback functions that are called in response to a GPIO pin changing state. This can be specified for low-to-high (RISING_EDGE), high-to-low (FALLING_EDGE), or either (EITHER_EDGE).

I consolidated the code a little bit to make the program easier on the eyes, but it still follows the template of hello_blink and hello_button as far as setting up PIGPIO and pins. hello_callback runs for *60* seconds, and every time it detects that pin 27 goes from *low* to *high* (you've pressed the button), it increments a counter and displays the running total. Go ahead and start another new console application in Code::Blocks or a blank .cpp file in whatever editor you choose if you're comfortable compiling from the command line. The code must include the following:

1. Include the header file pigpiod_if2.h.
2. Assign alias for pin number 27 (optional).
3. Define the callback function.
4. Handshake with the daemon and get a *handle.*
5. Set pin modes.
6. Verify the handshake went OK before continuing (optional, but prudent).
7. Initialize a callback.
8. Perform normal program functions.
9. Cancel the callback.
10. Disconnect from daemon.

Steps 1 and 2 are the same as before:

```
#include <iostream>

#include <pigpiod_if2.h>


using namespace std;


const int BUTTON = 27;
```

Step 3 – Defining the callback function. The callback function must be defined as type void. You can name it what you want, but you must have the correct number and types of arguments. This just increments the variable i and prints the value to the screen every time it is called.

```
void button_event(int pi, unsigned int gpio, unsigned int edge, unsigned int foo)
```

```
{

    static int i = 0;

    cout<<"Button pressed. Press count = "<<i++<<endl;

}
```

Steps 4, 5, and 6 are just like the other `hello_programs` so far, except I included them in `main()` to keep this short.

```
int main()

{

    char *addrStr = NULL;

    char *portStr = NULL;

    int pi = pigpio_start(addrStr, portStr);

    if(pi>=0)

    {

        cout<<"daemon interface started ok at "<<pi<<endl;

    }

    else

    {

        cout<<"Failed to connect to PIGPIO Daemon - Try running sudo pigpiod
        and try again."<<endl;

        return -1;

    }

    //set pin 27 mode as input

    set_mode(pi, BUTTON, PI_INPUT);

//steps 7, 8 , 9, and 10 here
```

```
    return 0;

}
```

Same old stuff, right? Step 7 is new – Initializing the callback:

```
int callbackID=callback(pi, BUTTON, RISING_EDGE, button_event);
```

Calling the pigpio function callback() returns an int ID; you need to keep the same way you keep the handle we've been storing in the variable pi. This is so you can disconnect it from the daemon when you're done with it. I save it in callbackID. The arguments for callback are your pi handle, the pin number, RISING_EDGE, FALLING_ EDGE, or EITHER EDGE, and the name of your callback function.

Steps 8, 9, and 10 are shown here. For step 8, all I do is sleep for 60 seconds, but you could do anything.

```
//step 8 - let the program run for 60 seconds

time_sleep(60);

cout<<"60 seconds has elapsed. Program ending."<<endl;


//step 9 - cancel the callback and end the pigpio daemon interface

callback_cancel(callbackID);

//step 10 – close connection with PIGPIO daemon

pigpio_stop(pi);
```

Canceling the callback is essential to prevent it from becoming a zombie process in the daemon if this program closes without letting the daemon know.

Now you can compile and run the program. You'll likely notice that every time you press to close the switch, the counter increments a lot more than once. No, your code isn't broken. Switch contacts don't snap closed as cleanly as you'd think, but instead, bounce open and repeatedly closed before settling. You'd never notice looking at a light, but our processors are so fast they catch it and count many events instead of one. This is called **switch bounce**, and I cover debouncing in *Chapter 5, Communication with Sensors and Other Devices*.

# Conclusion

Whew, we've covered a LOT in very little time. We covered the electronics basics necessary to design and adapt simple circuits we'll need to interface sensors and motors with our computer, and we learned how to use the PIGPIO library to read and write values to GPIO pins to bridge the space between computer programs and devices in the physical world.

As with all new things, there are all sorts of nuances and tricks you'll pick up to make life more comfortable or cleverly implement some circuit that doesn't fit textbook instructions. Don't worry if you still have questions; we'll be drawing plenty more diagrams and writing more and more code along the way. You can always refer back to this chapter, but it's also not the last time we'll see this stuff in action. We've also only touched the very tip of what we can do with PIGPIO, and you'd be doing yourself a favor to look over the rest of the available PIGPIO function calls at *abyz. me.uk/rpi/pigpio/pdif2.html*.

With that, it's time to look toward something more exciting than blinking lights on a breadboard. *Chapter 3, The Robot Platform* about the robot platform – the base and body of the machine we hope to make intelligent enough to navigate and accomplish tasks all by itself. We are going to discuss design considerations, where to buy one, how to build one, and what can be re-purposed and used as the robot base that we can continue to build on for years of learning, experimenting, and further developing robotics techniques.

# CHAPTER 3
# The Robot Platform

## Introduction

A robot platform is the base machine that entirely becomes a robot when you add the sensors and programming we will learn throughout this book. This chapter is all about choosing and acquiring the right type of robot platform for the mission you have chosen for it. Whether you are considering designing and building your own, building one with guidance from plans or a kit, purchasing one already-built, or hacking a device you may already own, we will explore the pros, cons, and provide some things to think about for each.

We are going to focus on mobile robot platforms, but even among these, many factors must be considered. It is important to spend a little time in this chapter to help you make an informed decisions and save a lot of time and money when building your first autonomous robot.

In this chapter, we will be covering the following:

- Considering the size and operating environment of your robot
- Differential drive versus Ackerman (car-like) steering
- Ready-made robot platforms
- Building your robot from scratch

- Re-purposing (also known as *hacking*) robot vacuums or remote-controlled cars for a robot platform

# Objective

Gain enough insight into the different robot platform options to be able to make a decision that will provide the best learning opportunity and satisfaction.

# Considering the size and operating environment

I understand that big, beefy robots are fun to build. But before you decide your first robot project is going to be big and strong enough to walk the dogs and haul several bales of hay around the farm, let me suggest that you'll get there sooner by starting with a smaller robot.

I learned the hard way years ago that big robots not only take a lot more money and time to build, but also aren't nearly as convenient as small robots. That lack of convenience results in a lot of lost learning opportunities because it will be raining, or you don't have the time to try a quick thing because you have to drag your robot outside or you are across town. If it is a smaller robot, you can take it with you or at least leave it on in your workshop -logging in during your lunch hour from work or your beachfront vacation spot. I'd be very hesitant to leave a robot that can do real damage alive in the garage – trust me when I say that crashes are going to happen. Look over *figure 3.1* as follow:

*Figure 3.1: Large robots are usually less useful for learning at first*

Rule of thumb? Never make a robot bigger than it has to be for its mission. The big robot on the left in *figure 3.1* can barely turn around in the small shop, while the smaller robot on the right can easily sneak between tables and chairs. Even though the big robot can fit through the door, it fits just barely and the level of precision required of its sensors and control programs are painfully frustrating to achieve. If it needs to be a large robot to handle certain tasks or terrain, the designer should consider that extra room allowed between the robot and tight spaces it needs to fit can save hours of frustrating programming and fiddling. This could be accomplished by making the base smaller or even just mounting the wheels under or closer to the robot's body.

If this is your first robot, I suggest that you decide that *Learning* is the primary mission. Having a little patience and learning faster with a smaller robot will pay off when you finally build your big bot and can get it going in days or weeks rather than years - All of the skills and most of the software are entirely transferable.

With that lecturing out of the way, you still get to decide what suits your purposes. I still have to suggest keeping things as compact as possible because having a little extra room to maneuver allows for less precise sensors and much, much simpler code. The shape of a robot can affect its maneuverability as well.

 **Do you know why many robotic vacuum cleaners are round? Because square robots have a greater tendency to get stuck against a wall or in corners, but a round shape has no corners to catch. It's not an insurmountable problem, but solving a problem with hardware design can be weeks or months faster than solving it with software. Not to mention far less frustrating.**

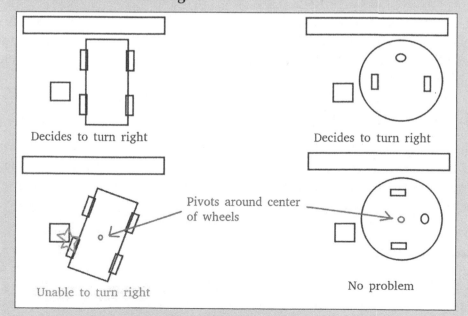

Decides to turn right          Decides to turn right

Pivots around center of wheels

Unable to turn right          No problem

*Figure 3.2: The maneuverability advantage of round robots over rectangular robots*

Small robots are simply more nimble, but will still need adequate ground clearance and wheel diameter for the terrain it's going to operate on. That may limit just how small you can go.

If it's a robot meant to operate outdoors, *will it operate on grass or pavement?* Wheel slippage is quite the annoyance to your robot's navigation and motor control software (and thus, you – the programmer), so keep in mind that grass can be slippery – especially if damp. The big robot in *figure 3.1* is designed to handle grassy terrain and has all-terrain vehicle tires that are far less likely to slip and give false speed and distance data than smaller or smooth wheels. Getting the undercarriage or axle of your robot stuck on a rock or branch is a bummer, too. So more significant, knobby tires are better for non-pavement terrains. A robot operating on pavement might get away with small skateboard wheels, although I don't advise it.

An indoor robot can get away with much smaller, smoother wheels but still consider whether it will have to handle carpet. For the same reasons a grass-going robot needs bigger wheels outdoors, a carpet-going robot needs bigger and more textured wheels inside. Even robot vacuum cleaners designed for carpet can slip and get stuck once you've added a few pounds of extra hardware. Don't ask why I'm so confident of that...

# Differential drive versus Ackerman (car-like) steering

The differential drive is steering by making the wheels (or tracks) on each side of the machine turn at different speeds. Ackerman steering, for our purposes, is pivoting the front wheels to turn the vehicle – like a car. Let's consider a few things about each.

## Differential drive

To understand differential drive, you might picture how a tank or bulldozer steers. If the left side is set to full speed and right side set to half speed, the machine will move in an arc to the right. If we stop the right side entirely, the machine moves in a tighter arc. Finally, we can even reverse one side and pivot the machine in place.

This is the easiest method of steering and allows the most precise control for maneuvering in tight spaces. This is what I recommend for low-speed robots and definitely for learning robotics with when possible, but be aware that with more giant robots with four or more wheels can be damaging to grass because of the wheels skid in a sideways arc as the machine pivots. This can be minimized or eliminated by using two drive wheels and one or two wheels that freely swivel (like the robot on the left in *figure 3.1*).

## Ackerman steering

`Ackerman steering` is a common wish-list item I would caution against for a first robot. For our purposes, we are going to define Ackerman steering only as *pivoting the front wheels together to turn the vehicle in an arc,* although there is technically a good bit more to it than that.

My reason for recommending against Ackerman steering is simply that it adds a great deal of complexity in path planning – especially in tight places or when getting the robot unstuck. Imagine your robot finding itself coming to a dead-end at the end of a narrow passage. With differential drive, it's merely a matter of pivoting in place to retreat. With an Ackerman vehicle of the same size, it becomes a multi-step algorithm of going forward in turn, turning the tires and reversing, turning wheels again, and going forward, and it could go on for a while or may not be possible at all. Not only that, but the robot has to analyze several steering algorithms against the current problem and be able to choose which to apply. Robotics is hard enough without adding a lot of extra decision-making and geometry math with no real benefit until you need to steer at higher speeds.

# Ready-made robot platforms

Ready-made platforms can be fantastic time-savers if they meet your mission requirements and budget. Some are bare-chassis that are little more than four wheels and two motors attached to a base like a remote-controlled car without the remote control stuff or a body. I'm going save talking about how to use them for the remote-control car section.

For this section, I want to talk about the ready-made platforms that come with everything installed and ready to go. They range from the size of a cereal bowl to the size of a 4 wheel drive all-terrain vehicle. Maybe bigger.

## Large pre-built robots

Larger, stronger, (and often outdoors-worthy) ready-made robots can be found in your mission requires and budget allows – see *figure 3.3* below). These are usually built with commercial applications in mind, but still make for fantastic learning machines - or you can just have a blast running the pre-installed software routines. **Ubiquity Robotics - Magni**, on the left, actually comes with a Raspberry Pi installed and several abilities like telepresence and *follow* modes. **Waypoint Robotics Vector™**

robot has a capacity of up to *272Kg* (*600Lbs*), but I caught it acting as a cocktail server at a party (right).

*Figure 3.3:* *Ubiquity Robotic's Magni (left - photo credit Ubiquity Robotics) and Waypoint Robotic's Vector™ (right)*

And finally for the large, pre-built class: I'd be cheating you if I didn't bring up a company called *Clearpath Robotics*. They not only have an incredible line of proven autonomous robot platforms for both land and sea (*figure 3.4* below), but they have stellar tutorial pages and open-source simulation packages. You can get the hang of operating their *Jackal* and *Husky* Robots without even owning one. Find them at *http://www.clearpathrobotics.com*

*Figure 3.4:* *Clearpath Robotics Jackal(left) and Husky(right) autonomous ground vehicles. photo credit: Clearpath Robotics*

## Small pre-built robots

The great thing about small robots is that everything about controlling them is the same as it is for giant robots. Aside from tweaking a few values to account for the different motors and handling characteristics, you could pretty much use the same controller and software. Longer range sensors and some extra safety features are highly advisable for larger machines, of course.

For smaller robot platforms, the name *TurtleBot* is almost synonymous with commercially available robot learning platforms. Early models were the size of (and based on a special version of) a popular robot vacuum, and larger than the version *3* you can find today. The *TurtleBot3* is modular and customizable but starts with a mobile base, Raspberry Pi, LIDAR, and the software you need to get going. You can add things like cameras and even manipulator arms, and, despite the base version being small enough to use on a table, it is great for learning everything to program autonomous wheeled vehicles. There's a lot of tutorials and community support out there as well. Possibly the best bang for your buck in the *ready-to-go robots* category.

There are plenty more to choose from in varying sizes, configurations, and of course, price. Look for robotic specific stores online for this class of robots. A few online shops that come to mind first for complete robots, kits, and robot parts and sensors in general are: *www.pololu.com*, *www.robotshop.com*, and *www.robotis.us*. Perfectly capable robots can that fit in the palm of your hand can be found - Following *figure 3.5* shows several found in the **Computer-Assisted Robot-Enhanced Systems** (**CARES**) laboratory at *Wayne State University in Detroit, MI.*

***Figure 3.5:*** *A few palm-sized, off-the-shelf robots found in a research laboratory at Wayne State University's College of Engineering*

Pre-Built robot pros:

- The fastest way to get started
- Reliability as the design has likely been tested and tested
- Support available

Pre-Built robot cons:

- Expensive
- Less customizable

# Tips for building your own robot

Completely do-it-yourself robots are very satisfying and allow for the most customization, but be aware that it takes much longer than you probably expect because you are now responsible for every little detail. And there are a lot of details – drilling a hole for every single screw, running every wire, finding a way to secure every wire, getting the motors and axles perfectly aligned – it all adds up. I'm not trying to discourage you from giving it a go, but I want you to be informed before making the decision. If you're still game and see it through, you're going to have some serious bragging rights and I'd love to see your handiwork – please send me pics to the *Practical Robotics Facebook* page (*facebook.com/practicalrobotics*)!

 **I did decide that this book would feature a robot project you can build yourself with minimal tools, expense, and experience - so the highest number of people can participate. The lessons in this book are intended so you come away with the knowledge to program any robot platform, so you are free to use a purchased one or build something different and still follow along.**

There are so many possible variations that I can't give a lot of specific direction except for the project build we will build in *Chapter 21, Building and Programming An Autonomous Robot* but here are a few general tips about the power to keep in mind:

## Building materials

`Aluminum` is light and relatively strong and makes a great frame if you have some tools and patience (although it is faster to build with than steel, below). If you have the ability and unique welder to weld it, that's even better – the rest of us have to drill holes and bolt the pieces together. Beware of the little metal shavings that get everywhere and can short circuit your electronics if you're not careful to vacuum thoroughly.

`Steel` is much more substantial than aluminum (and messes with certain sensors we'll talk about later) but can be welded with an ordinary welder. It's challenging to cut and drill, so prepare to spend a lot of time compared to aluminum.

Both steel and aluminum leave sharp edges when cut or drilled, so extra care must be taken to avoid vibrations from cutting through insulation and shorting wires.

`Plastic` is an ok material for smaller robots, but I think most useful for making various clamps, hinges, and mounts if you have access to a 3D printer. I have seen some very minimal (but still elegant) robots that were completely 3D printed, but so far, these have all been too small to carry the sensors and computer we need for our purposes.

Wood as a robot building material is something I would have turned my nose up at in the past, but I have come to embrace it for the ease of working and speed of building. Plywood makes a smooth base for mounting components - and because screw zip right in, rearranging or swapping components until you have it just right is a snap. Hardwoods make good frame members, although this type is not so weather-resistance as an aluminum machine.

## Batteries

You want a battery that can handle deep-cycling (draining the battery much beyond 50%). I am a big fan of power-tool batteries for small-medium robots up to maybe the size of a vacuum-type and sealed lead-acid batteries from electric scooters for bigger robots. Don't use a regular car-battery because they are intended to produce short bursts of a lot of amps, and running them down as we do for robots will quickly damage them. Disposable batteries are not practical at all and will quickly cost more than buying something rechargeable.

As far as battery voltage, I like to find something that suits the highest voltage device on the robot (usually the main motors) then reduce that with DC-DC converters for any other voltages I need – like 5v to power my Raspberry Pi.

## Drive trains

Drive trains consist of the motors, the wheels, and everything in between that connects them. What connects them usually starts with a gearbox because motors spin too fast but lack torque by themselves. Sometimes a sprocket and chain or belts as well for further gear reduction or just mounting reasons. If your robot is small enough, you can get a wheel and motor module that comes pre-assembled with a gearbox, and you only have to mount one thing. If you're not that lucky, you'll have to mount motors, separate axles in bearings for the wheels, sprockets, and tensioners.

Scratch-built robot pros

- Most customizable
- Might be less expensive
- Most bragging rights
- The most learning

Scratch-built robot cons

- Very time-consuming
- No manufacturer support
- Can end up wasting materials making revisions – increasing cost

**Big bots mean big motors, and big motors may surprise you with how very many amps they can draw. This *4x4* AutoNav robot in *figure 3.6* was a blast to build and operate, but the team learned the hard way not to underestimate how many amps big, beefy motors can draw when the emergency-stop button went up in smoke during a test. All wiring had to be rerouted through a *200 amp* relay.**

*Figure 3.6: Joy, the Wayne State University Robotics club entry to the 2019 Intelligent Ground Vehicle Challenge*

# Robot parts sources

*Amazon* and *eBay* can be excellent sources of parts, but the sheer number of search results can make it challenging to find precisely what you need if you don't know the exact name of it. On the other hand, sometimes you can find things you didn't know existed that will help your project. Other online retailers that cater to robotics and electronics projects may not have as big of a selection, but usually have categories set up for easy browsing. Some online retailers useful for robot parts are:

- *banebots.com* – Mostly drivetrain parts.
- *robotmarketplace.com* – Mostly drivetrain parts, some electronics
- *digikey.com* – electronics
- *mouser.com* – electronics
- *pololu.com* – a little of everything. Great for sensors with tutorials and sample code.
- *adafruit.com* – electronics geared towards making it easy for hobbyists. Tutorials.
- *robotshop.com* – a little of everything.

Shopping locally for components is not as easy as it used to be. In the *U.S.* the only place I know of with a good DIY section is Microcenter if you're lucky enough to live near one. They carry Raspberry Pis, microcontrollers, a decent selection of electronic parts and some types of (small) motors in addition to being a complete computer center. They also have some small robot kits. I am fortunate that I can stop on my way home from work for a lot of the things I used to get from *Radio Shack* before their demise.

# Re-purposing robot vacuums or remote-controlled cars

Re-purposing robot vacuums are probably my favorite way to build indoor robots - the reasons are many:

- It can be found much cheaper than ready-made platforms – especially if you find a used one or even salvage a broken one.

- Pre-installed motors and maybe motor controllers mean your drivetrain is already done for you.

- Pre-installed sensors! Wheel drop-sensors, bumpers, cliff-detectors, beacon sensors, wheel encoders, it's fantastic not to have to mount and wire all that!

- Some come with a charging dock, which is a must if you hope to leave your robot unattended for any length of time. A robot that comes with one will save you a ton of engineering time.

- You learn more about how the parts work together than with ready-made platforms that are delivered up and running, but they save you a lot of the tedium of building your own from scratch.

I classify robot vacuums into one of two categories:

- With interface
- Without interface

## Robot vacuums with the interface

This first category is for robots with a connector and software interface of some sort. These might be the best for those with limited electronics skills because wiring requirements are minimal – sometimes just a USB cable.

A great candidate for this type is any robot in the *Neato Botvac* series like the one in *figure 3.7*. A connection is as secure as a USB cable and running a terminal software like Screen. Its onboard LIDAR (laser ranging unit) allows for making very accurate maps for autonomous navigation. I haven't personally done much with the *Neato Botvac* besides a simple test connection - mostly because my wife still hasn't forgiven me for taking out the vacuum parts of our last robot vacuum to make room for an auxiliary battery. You can find how-to instructions for connecting to the *Neato* online and, once connected, can just type `help` for a list of available commands.

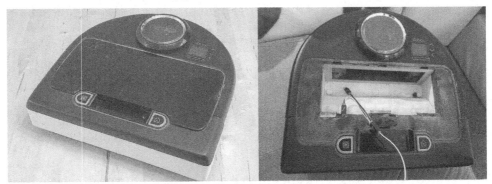

*Figure 3.7: Neato Botvac with LIDAR and simple interface*

Another popular robot vacuum model, the *Roomba* by *iRobot*, also has a well-documented interface. *iRobot* themselves provided a fantastic document with detailed instructions called the *Open Interface Spec (OI)* for reading the sensors and writing commands. What they lack in LIDAR they make up for with the open interface, a myriad of extra sensors, navigation beacons, and not only a dock, but the ability to simply send a command and the robot will seek the dock and handle docking all by itself. I added a *Neato Botvac* LIDAR myself since they can be found cheap on *eBay* (see *figure 3.8*). It's a fair trade for self-docking if you ask me.

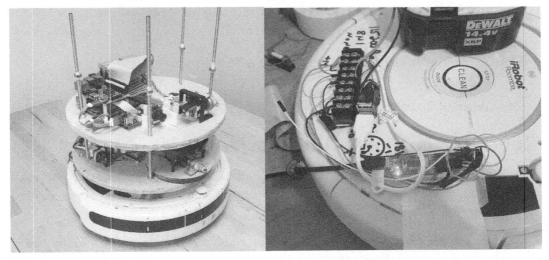

*Figure 3.8: An iRobot Roomba turned Frankenbot to my wife's dismay. It is a little more involved to connect than just plugging in a USB cable. The din connector location is circled.*

# Interfacing with a Roomba

Models in the *500, 600, 700,* and *800* series are preferred. The earliest models (*400* and earlier) either had a different interface or none at all, and it seems the newest (*900*) series does not support this function either.

 **If the following about serial communications seems foreign to you, we spend more time in chapter learning about different communication via serial and other means.**

Connecting to your Roomba open interface is just a standard serial connection at *115200* baud, *8* data bit, no parity, one stop bit, no flow control (*115200, 8N1*). Still, the OI spec sheet has directions for changing it if necessary. You'll find the *7* pin mini din connector under a cover on top of the robot. Everyone else will tell you that you need to order the correct din connector, but I'm going tell you that sticking regular breadboard wires into the individual holes works just fine to experiment.

Communications could be done with the serial UART on the Raspberry Pi GPIO pins *14* and *15*, but the Roomba UART speaks at *5 volts,* and the Rpi has *3.3 volt* pins (*we talked about matching voltages in the last chapter, right?*). Since going from UART to UART will require voltage-shifting circuitry anyway, it's much easier to do so with a USB device called an **FTDI**. *Figure 3.9* **below shows wiring an FTDI to the Roomba's connector**.

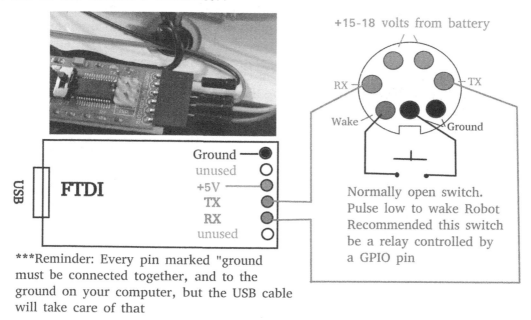

+15-18 volts from battery

RX — TX

Wake — Ground

Normally open switch. Pulse low to wake Robot Recommended this switch be a relay controlled by a GPIO pin

USB | FTDI

Ground
unused
+5V
TX
RX
unused

***Reminder: Every pin marked "ground must be connected together, and to the ground on your computer, but the USB cable will take care of that

*Figure 3.9: Connecting to the Roomba din connector through an FTDI. That's not a mistake — TX of one device goes to RX of the other and vice versa.*

These are the basic steps for getting communication with your Roomba via USB port.

- Wire your *FTDI* and wake button as pictured above (*figure 3.9*)
- Plug in your *FTDI* and power *ON* your Raspberry Pi
- Initialize *PIGPIO*
- Open a serial port
- Close the switch manually or via a relay controlled by your Raspberry Pi for *50-150* milliseconds. If successful, Roomba will respond with an audible beep.
- Send command *128* to start the open interface and put the robot in *passive* mode. It will not move in *passive* mode
- Send *131* to start *safe* mode. A robot can now move if commanded
- Command away. Request data packets or send motor commands or even commands for pre-programmed routines like clean or dock
- Send *133* to put Roomba to *sleep*
- Close, serial port
- Terminate *GPIO* library

*iRobot* has released a couple of versions of the open interface over the years, and earlier versions have some differences in commands and capabilities. If something isn't working, double-check that the interface specification document you are reading matches your model. Below is an example program to get you started.

hello_roomba.cpp is a simple program with a few sample functions for communicating with your Roomba using the PIGPIO library. Note that you'll have to study the PIGPIO documentation and the Roomba OI documentation for this to make sense, these are here to make it easier for you to understand how the OI and PIGPIO work together. Find the PIGPIO documents at *http://abyz.me.uk/rpi/pigpio/ pdif2.html*. For the Roomba OI docs, you'll need to *google roomba oi* and find the one that works for your model.

```
//hello_roomba.cpp

#include "pigpiod_if2.h"


using namespace std;


int pi = -1;
```

```
int serHandle = -1;

//used to make sure roomba awake and listening
void wake(){
    int R1 = 23; //This is assuming the wake relay is on pin 23
    set_mode(pi, R1, PI_OUTPUT);

    gpio_write(pi, R1, 0);                      //pulse wake relay
    time_sleep(.1);
    gpio_write(pi, R1, 1);

    serial_write_byte(pi,serHandle,128);        //send start command
    time_sleep(.15);
    serial_write_byte(pi,serHandle,131);        //set to safe mode
    time_sleep(.15);
}

//drive in reverse at 80mm/sec
void rev()
{
    char driveString[] = {137, 255, 136, 0, 0};
    serial_write(pi, serHandle, driveString, 5);
}

//drive forward at 120mm/sec
void fwd()
{
    char driveString[] = {137, 0, 120, 127, 255};
```

```
        serial_write(pi, serHandle, driveString, 5);
}


//stops wheel motors
void stop()
{
    char driveString[] = {137, 0, 0, 0, 0};
    serial_write(pi, serHandle, driveString, 5);
}


//puts Roomba to sleep and frees program resources
void shutdown()
{
    serial_write_byte(pi,serHandle,133);
    time_sleep(.1);
    serial_close(pi, serHandle);
    pigpio_stop(pi);
}


//main() wakes Roomba, drives it forward for 5 seconds. Pauses
//for one second, reverses for 5 seconds, the shuts everything
//down
int main()
{
    char *addrStr = NULL;
    char *portStr = NULL;
    //handshake with daemon and get pi handle
    pi = pigpio_start(addrStr, portStr);
```

```
//open serial port
serHandle = serial_open(pi, "/dev/ttyUSB0",115200,0);

wake();
fwd();
time_sleep(5);
stop();
time_sleep(1);
rev();
time_sleep(5);
stop();
shutdown();
}
```

## Un-freezing your Roomba

During your experimenting with the interface to your Roomba, there are bound to be times that it seems to freeze up. This is most likely because you set it to expect a certain amount of data and it's still waiting for some of it - And it will wait forever and ever. You can remove the battery to reboot, but I've learned to keep a small program handy that blasts the Roomba with a whole bunch of sleep commands. This satisfies the number of bytes Roomba was expecting to receive and puts it in sleep mode so you get listen for the audible confirmation when you try to re-initialize by pulsing the wake pin low. I don't know why but sometimes I have to run the force_sleep program a couple times. Here is the program roomba_sleep.cpp that sends the sleep command 100 times.

```
//roomba_sleep.cpp

#include "pigpiod_if2.h"


using namespace std;
```

```
//puts Roomba to sleep
{
    int pi = -1;
    int serHandle = -1;
    char *addrStr = NULL;
    char *portStr = NULL;
    //handshake with daemon and get pi handle
    pi = pigpio_start(addrStr, portStr);

    //open serial port
    //serHandle = serial_open(pi, "/dev/ttyUSB0",115200,0);
    serHandle = serial_open(pi, "/dev/ttyAMA0",115200,0);

    for(int i = 0; i < 100; i++)
    {
        serial_write_byte(pi, serHandle, 133);
        time_sleep(.01);
    }

    time_sleep(.1);
    serial_close(pi, serHandle);
    pigpio_stop(pi);
}
```

# Robot vacuums without an Interface

The second category of robot vacuums is the ones without an easily exploitable interface. It's always worth checking around online to see if anyone has posted interfacing instructions for the specific model of robot vacuum you have. Still, I generally expect that you'll need to connect to the motors and sensors yourself and write all of your code instead of using the original controller. It still saves you a ton of work and is a fantastic platform for our purposes. See *figure 3.10* below.

**Figure 3.10:** *Early Roomba models like this early 400 (left) or this unknown robot vacuum chassis (right) don't have the same software interface, but still save us a lot of hardware mounting*

 **If you are skilled with electronics, you can sometimes find the motor controllers on the existing control board and use that instead of installing your own. Often, the board is so cluttered or takes up so much space that it's not worth it. If you do look for it, it's probably an H-bridge type made of 4 transistors mounted carefully together.**

# Hacking remote-controlled cars and trucks

Hacking remote control cars have some of the advantages of hacking vacuums but lack the sensors. But they are cheap and come in many shapes and sizes so you could find one that would work indoors and outdoors. Some thoughts on converting remote control cars to robots:

- They come with a battery pack for their electronics, but you don't want to run your Raspberry Pi from this. Add a dedicated power supply like a power bank big enough to charge a laptop.

- Most remote-controlled cars have Ackerman steering, but the differential drive is still preferred for our purposes. If possible, select a tank or bulldozer model.

A particularly amusing entry into the 2019 Intelligent Ground Vehicle Challenge by *Ohio University Professional Autonomous Vehicle Engineers* (*OU-PAVE*) falls somewhere between built-from-scratch and hacking a remote control car. The crowd favorite, it started its life as a toddler ride-in vehicle. (refer *figure 3.11*)

***Figure 3.11:*** *Pathfinder by Ohio University Professional Autonomous Vehicle Engineers (OU-PAVE). Photo credit: Russ College of Engineering and Technology, Ohio University*

The *OU-PAVE* team has done remarkable work on *Pathfinder*. Not only on refining its autonomous abilities to follow a path and avoid obstacles, but *Pathfinder* was used as a platform to develop and test guidance and control algorithms that were then loaded into a full-sized car (*Kia Soul EV*).

As a testament to how a small, less expensive, and more convenient robot for learning and developing is entirely transferable to any size robot and can ultimately save you time – The *OU-PAVE* team was able to get the software working on the *Kia Soul* in just a few hours of testing and tuning. You can see some great videos of *Pathfinder* in action on *OU-PAVE's Facebook* page at *facebook.com/PAVEOhioU*.

Re-purposing vacuums and remote control cars pros:

- Can be a big time-saver
- Sometimes built-in sensors
- You learn more than buying a completed robot platform
- Very high fun-level
- Can be very inexpensive

Re-purposing vacuums and remote control cars cons

- Sometimes limited room for customizing
- Can be challenging to add encoders to an existing drivetrain if it doesn't come with them
- Your spouse or child isn't always happy with you when they find you've taken their vacuum or toy apart

# Conclusion

In this chapter, we talked about your choices for a robot platform. You learned some benefits and drawbacks of various features and the importance of choosing a robot appropriately-sized for its purpose. We talked about buying, building, and hacking robots – and even learned how to talk to the computer that controls a Roomba robot vacuum, and issue drive commands to it. All of these are essential considerations to help you make the best choice for you since you're going to be spending a lot of time learning how to turn this platform into an autonomous machine.

Before we get too far into autonomous behaviors and programming robots, we have some more basics to work through. One of the most fundamental things we do as roboticists are to write software to control motors - to move robots or even just a part or tool on a robot. That's why *Chapter 4, Types of Robot Motors and Motor Control* is so important – we'll learn about the different types of motors and how to control them.

# Questions

1. What are some disadvantages of large robots?
2. What are some challenges of Ackerman steering compared to differential drive?
3. Why is it inadvisable to use a car battery to power your robot?

# Chapter 4

# Types of Robot Motors and Motor Control

## Introduction

Motors are a central part of every robot. Whether they are spinning wheels or propellers, actuating legs, positioning control surfaces or even sensors, a great deal of our time as roboticists is spent directly controlling or figuring out what to do next with motors. This chapter is about learning the different motor types available and how to control them.

In this chapter we'll learn the basics of how motors work, the different types of motors, and the hardware and software we need to control them. Even the most sophisticated robot project come down to getting the right signal to the right type of motor, so a solid grasp on motor control in critical for robotic success. Code in this chapter is available for download at *https://github.com/lbrombach/practical_chapters*.

In this chapter, we will cover the following:

- Motor types
- Motor control – speed and direction
- Introduction to the transistor and motor controllers
- Pulse width modulation (PWM)

- Generating a PWM signal with a Raspberry Pi
- Control a motor with a Raspberry Pi – Tutorial

# Objectives

Gain an understanding of motor types and their uses. Write a simple motor control program and control a motor with it.

# Motor types

Motors are devices that turn electrical energy into mechanical energy in the form of a rotating shaft. This shaft can be attached to propellers, wheel, or joints of robot arms either directly or indirectly (through gears, sprockets, or pulleys) to create motion we need to accomplish some task. Our most obvious need is turning wheels to move our robot, and this is the use-case we'll focus on.

All electric motors work by using magnetic fields arranged to repel or attract other magnetic fields. You may remember from science class that magnets have magnetic fields that flow through the North and South poles. These magnetic fields are directional (also known as *Polarized*), and magnets will attract or repel each other based on how their fields are oriented towards each other (two North or two South poles will repel each other, while a North and a South will be attracted to each other). A permanent magnet has to be physically turned around to reverse its magnetic field, while the field of an electromagnet can be reversed by reversing the flow of electricity through it. See *figure 4.1* below for an illustration.

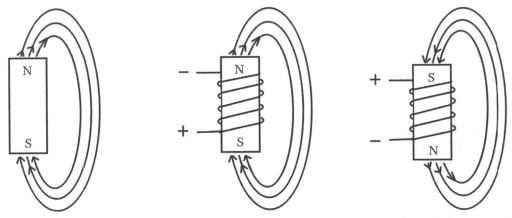

Permanent magnets always have the same polarity

Reverse the polarity of the power to an electromagnet to reverse the polarity of the magnet

*Figure 4.1: Permanent magnet vs electromagnet magnetic field polarity*

I don't intend to get much deeper into motor theory, but this much is important - Motors have a stationary part and a rotating part, each with their own arrangement of magnets pushing and pulling on each other. We have to have a way to reverse the polarity of specific magnets at specific parts of the rotation In order to keep the motor spinning instead of locking in place. There are different ways to accomplish this, which is why we have different motor types.

# Alternating current (AC) versus direct current (DC) motors

When looking for motors, the first big decision is whether you want to use an AC or DC motor. You may even have motors from power tools or an appliance like a washing machine and you're wondering if you can use it for your robot. Let's look over a few key characteristics of AC and DC motors before deciding which we want to use in a robot.

| DC Motors: | AC Motors: |
|---|---|
| Run directly from battery | Extra electronics to run from battery |
| Lower, safer operating voltage | Higher, dangerous voltages |
| Easy speed control | Complex speed controller |

Without question you want to use DC motors for your project. DC motors are simple to use, requiring only that we apply a (usually) safe voltage to them. AC motors require the polarity of a (usually) dangerously high voltage to reverse many times per second, and this require electronics well outside the scope of this book.

For the purpose of mobile robotics, AC motors honestly have nothing to offer us over DC motors until you get into human-transporting self-driving vehicle territory. Disregard my above warning if you are *Elon Musk*, but for the rest of this book any time I mention a motor it will be a DC motor.

# Brush-type DC motors

Until recently, brush-type (also known as **brushed**) DC motors have been the most common type of motor you'd find in anything powered by battery. It probably still is, but the brushless DC motors we'll talk about below have become more and more common. Brushed DC motors can be found in all manner of department store toys, power tools, car window motors and many more. I couldn't possibly name all the places you'll find them.

They get their name because they use electrically-conductive brushes that slide across something called a **commutator** to accomplish the switching the poles of electromagnets. This is how they are kept alternately pushing and pulling against permanent magnets mounted in the motor body. They spin fast, so will almost always need a gearbox to be useful to us.

You can identify a motor as brush-type because it came out of something that was battery powered and it only has two wires going to it. Don't be fooled by extra wires going towards a motor – The salvaged wheel module from a robot vacuum in *figure 4.2* below appears to have more than two wires, but closer inspection shows several wires going to a sensor and only two wires going to the motor itself.

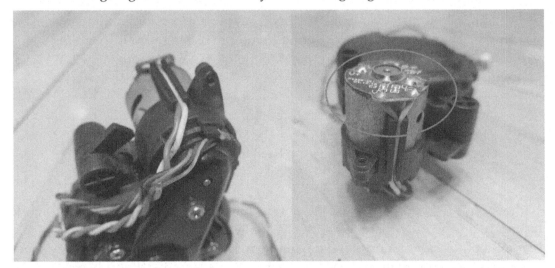

*Figure 4.2:* *Salvaged brushless DC motor from robot vacuum, still attached to it's gearbox and wheel*

Brush-type motors are the least expensive motor, very reliable, and simplest to control – all you have to do is vary the voltage to speed them up or slow them down. To me, that makes up for them being a bit noisier than brushless motors. I definitely recommend those newer to electronics use this type for robot drive motors.

## Servos

You might also hear these called **servo motors**. Servos are actually a combination of some type of motor, a gearbox, and electronics module that allow for fairly precise positioning of the output shaft. They come in different sizes and voltages from hobby to industrial, but I'm only going to talk about the hobby types like the one in *figure 4.3* below.

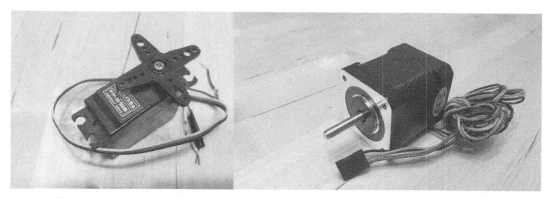

*Figure 4.3:* *A common hobby-grade servo (left) and a Common stpper motor (right)*

The servos you are likely to encounter and use have a brush-type DC motor in them, but instead of varying the voltage to control them directly, we supply a constant voltage (usually *5-12* volts DC) plus a special control signal and let the on-board electronics do the rest. The control signal we send is typically a `Pulse width modulation` (`PWM`) signal that we'll talk about later in this chapter, but it may sent via one of the communication protocols we learn in *Chapter 5, Communication with Sensors and Other Devices.*

For the most part, servos are intended to rotate a limited range (less than a full-circle – maybe up to *270* degrees) and hold a certain position, but they have been hacked to allow continuous rotation. This was such a popular hack that some manufacturers have started selling them this way as well and even started selling little wheels that bolt right on where you would normally attach a lever arm. They can be used to drive the smallest of robots, but I generally think of servos as positioning devices.

# Stepper motors

Stepper motors (right image in *figure 4.3*) are another type of DC motor used for positioning – often with great precision. Unlike a brush-type motor that has a commutator to control the reversing of the polarity of a single electromagnetic coil (also known as `winding`), steppers have two or more DC coils that are energized one at a time - sometimes one is energized and the other reversed. The controlling of which coil is energized when is done with electronics outside of the motor. *Figure 4.4* below illustrates a permanent magnet in a stepper motor being pushed and pulled by energizing different coils with different polarities.

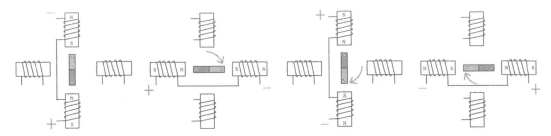

*Figure 4.4: Stepper motor windings and magnetic field rotation*

When the controller switches which coil is energized and the shaft turns to line up with the magnetic field, it is said to have stepped. By varying the voltages and direction of current flow through the various coils, stepper controllers can move the shaft in full steps, half-steps, or even smaller fractional steps. You keep track of position by counting the number and direction of steps commanded.

Stepper motors are not used for robot drives, but rather for positioning things like joints of robot arms or grippers. Four wires going to a motor itself (and not sensors attached to the motor) are a pretty good indicator that you have a stepper.

## Brushless DC motors (also known as BLDC)

Brushless DC motors belong in a category next to brush-type DC motors because, unlike servos and stepper motors, they are both the type I would consider using for robot drive motors. The BLDC is a cousin to the stepper motor, however, and I thought having the stepper motor lesson first would help you understand the BLDC.

Both the BLDC and the stepper motors use multiple electromagnetic coils and an external controller. The BLDC typically has more coils and adds sensors for detecting shaft position, along with a more sophisticated controller that requires those position sensors to decide which coils to energize next. This controller is called an electronic speed controller and allows for much higher speeds than you could achieve with a stepper motor.

BLDC motors are very responsive, have decent power, and are much quieter than brush-type motors thanks to not having brushes scraping around. They are pretty universal on drones and hoverboards, and more and more electric bicycles.

# Introduction to the transistor and motor drivers

We are generally going to use a driver for every type of motor, although servos have them built in and we only have to send the right signal to it. All motor drivers serve the purpose of amplifying a small signal from our GPIO output pins to something big enough to power the electromagnets inside our motors. In the case of electronics speed controllers for BLDCs, they also have to have some smarts. Before we get ahead of ourselves, let's learn the basics.

## The most basic control: On/Off

On/Off control generally does not provide enough control for autonomous robot drive wheels, but is sometimes perfect for things that have to be spun continuously or moved from end-to-end without precision in between. A linear actuator that raises an instrument might be able to simply *turn on* until it hits an end switch, for example.

We saw how a simple On/Off switch or relay would be wired back in *Chapter 2, GPIO Hardware Interface Pins Overview and Use, figure 2.10*. Instead of using a second battery and a manual switch to turn our relay coil on, we can use a GPIO pin. Just don't forget that you can't drive a relay coil directly from a GPIO pin – you need an interface that we'll get to shortly. Check out following *figure 4.5*:

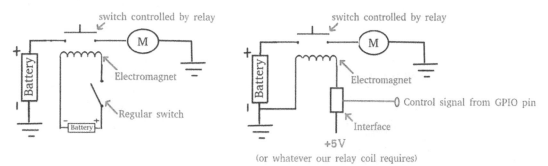

***Figure 4.5:*** *Activating a relay with a GPIO pin*

That covers just the off and on control of a brush-type DC motor. If we want to reverse the direction of a brush-type DC motor, we have to reverse the polarity of the voltage going to it. We can do that with a double-pole, double-throw switch. These are available as manual switches or electromagnetic relays, so full On/Off and direction control of a motor could be done with two relays and two GPIO pins - as in following *figure 4.6*:

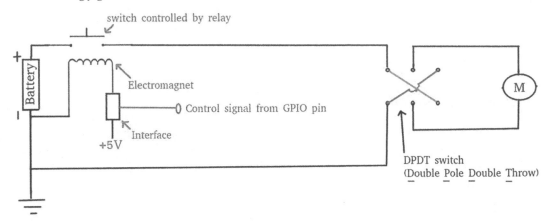

*Figure 4.6: Reversing a motor by reversing voltage polarity with a Double Pole Double Throw switch or relay*

A **double pole, double throw** (**DPDT**) switch is like two single pole double throw switches that throw at the same time. Handy if you want to arrange like this to reverse the voltage going to the motor. Each center pin connected to the motor is connected to either the pin to its left, or the pin to its right – the upper and lower halves switch at the same time but are not connected to each other.

Earlier, we talked about controlling brush-type motor speed by varying voltage. While you certain could switch a *12 volt* battery for a *6 volt* battery and watch the motor speed drop by half that obviously won't do for our autonomous vehicle. Fortunately, we can control the voltage to our motors by our software and some electronics instead of re-wiring by hand every time we need to change speed.

## Transistors

When On/Off control of a motor isn't good enough, we turn to transistors. In the name of finishing this book this year, I'm going to limit our discussion to a generic transistor concept: Amplifying a small, fragile signal to supply a much bigger signal, voltage, or current to a bigger device. A few transistors are pictured in *figure 4.7*.

***Figure 4.7:*** *Transistors. The middle one mounted to a heat sink.*

*We did this with a relay, right?* In *figure 4.5*, we applied a paltry `5 volts` from some microcontroller and were able to energize a motor that could have well been operating at `300 volts`. A few advantages transistors have over relays are:

- The ability to control how much voltage or current gets through by varying the control signal.
- Faster switching speeds
- No mechanical parts to wear out

Mechanical relays could never switch fast enough to be used to control a brushless DC motor, and would quickly wear out even if they did. Unlike a relay, the control signal side and the power side do have an electrical connection.

The basic transistor has 3 leads called either `collector`, `base`, and `emitter`, or `drain`, `gate`, and `source` depending on the type. The differences are beyond our scope, but very interesting and useful as you dive deeper into electronics. For our purpose, we can consider them doing the same things and I'm going to refer only to drain, source, and gate from now on.

There is resistance between the source and drain that determines how much voltage can get through. How much resistance depends on how much control signal (voltage, in this case) is applied to the gate. Look over *figure 4.8* below – in this case we are driving a motor, but we could just as easily be controlling voltage to a light or a heating element.

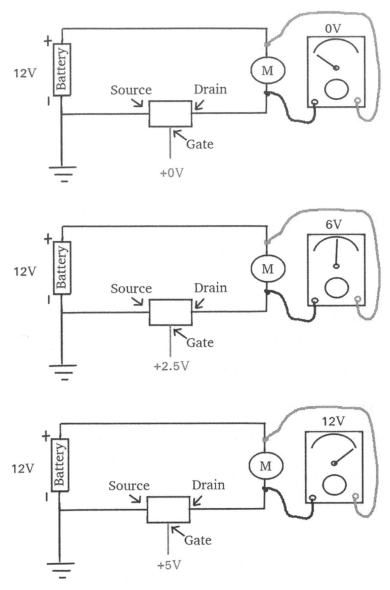

**Figure 4.8:** *Controlling output voltage and by varying the input voltage to a transistor*

Imagine that the motor in *figure 4.8* is rated for *12 volts*. If the transistor is not supplied with any voltage to its gate, the gate remains closed and the motor will not spin. If the transistor is of the type that is *fully on* at *5 volts*, supplying *5 volts* to the gate will allow the motor to spin at full speed because the *12 volts* from the battery will get through. Intermediate voltages can be supplied to the motor by supplying voltages between *0* and *5 volts* to the gate.

Unlike the power-hungry relay coil, the gate of a transistor can often be driven directly by a GPIO pin with just a resistor to limit current. In fact, we could put a relay coil in the circuit in *figure 4.8* instead of a motor (although I don't bother building my own circuits to drive relay coils anymore, thanks to cheap pre-assembled relay modules we'll talk about in *Chapter 6, Additional Helpful Hardware*).

 **It's not unusual to drive a transistor with a transistor. Transistors that are *fully on* at 3.3 or 5 *volts* are called logic level transistors, and often don't have the final output capacity required by themselves.**

Pretty neat, huh? But I can hear you asking now - If a GPIO pin can only be On or Off, *how do we vary voltage to the gate of a transistor?* Allow me to introduce to your new friend: PWM.

# Pulse width modulation (PWM)

PWM is a very common way of manipulating the normal *On/Off* signal from a GPIO pin to make it more versatile. While we are still limited to turning the GPIO output either on or off, we can switch the output fast enough to carry more information. We'll talk about how this is used for complex communication of numbers and text information in *Chapter 5, Communication with Sensors and Other Devices* but for now let's look at two common ways this rapid switching is used as part of a motor control:

1. To Create an analog voltage with a digital output.
2. To provide a control signal that includes information about desired output.

Technically these can both be a control signal, but in the case of number one it may also be a direct hardware driver. Hang tight and hopefully the rest of this chapter clears this up – just be aware that I am going to refer to number one as an analog voltage and number two as a control signal. Let's take a look at both types of PWM.

## PWM to create analog voltages

This first use of PWM is how we would directly control the voltage we send into a transistor gate. You can output an average voltage of any value from *0 volts* to the normal *high* level of the GPIO pin, and it's roughly as simple as varying the *duty cycle*. Duty cycle is just how we describe what percentage of the time our pin is in the *On* condition. Following *figure 4.9* shows a graph of two PWM output signals.

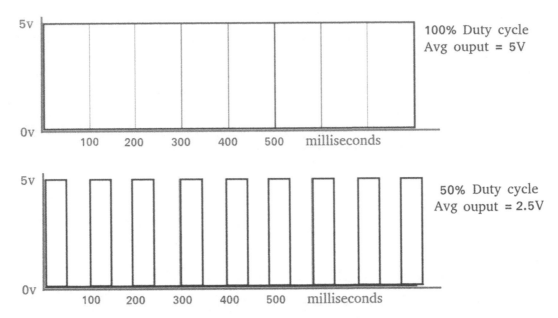

*Figure 4.9: PWM signals at 100% (top) and 50% (bottom) duty cycles*

The top PWM signal in the image above has the same effect as being always on. In the bottom PWM signal the output is energized only half of the time, so the average voltage is half of the pins *high* voltage level. These signals are said to have a period of `100ms` (which is a pretty long period, but I used it to make the example easy to interpret).

 **The** *analog* **signals created by PWM are very choppy and may need to be smoothed for good results in some applications. We won't need to for our purposes, but you can research** *low pass filter* **for more information if the need arises.**

Our software doesn't usually speak in percentages. Instead, it breaks up a constant period of time (which can often be set by the programmer) into a certain number of slices. PIGPIO and other popular microcontroller libraries divide a period into *255* slices by default, so setting a duty cycle of *255* means *255* out of *255* slices of every period are *On*. That is the same as simply setting the pin high. To output a voltage *50%* of our pin's normal *high* voltage, we'd set the duty cycle to *127* (*50% of 255 = 127.5*).

We still aren't capable of much current, but we can feed this analog voltage into the input (*gate*) of a transistor. The PIGPIOD library makes it easy to produce a PWM signal on a Raspberry Pi GPIO pin. To output a PWM signal on any Raspberry Pi output pin, use the `set_PWM_dutycycle()` function as in the code below:

```
//start a PWM signal on pin 26 on this Rpi,

//with a duty cycle of 50% would be:

set_PWM_dutycycle(1, 26, 127);
```

For the full function definition, as well as other PWM functions available in the PIGPIOD library, visit the PIGPIO page at *http://abyz.me.uk/rpi/pigpio/pdif2.html*.

# PWM as a control signal

The second way PWM is used is to communicate something to another device and is very commonly used to control the desired position of servos. It is generated the same as above, but instead of trying to achieve an average voltage with our *pulses*, we really are focusing on the width of each pulse. In fact, when we are creating an analog voltage above, we usually to refer to the duty cycle as we did above. When hardware expects a PWM control signal, it is the width of each pulse that is specified (and sometimes frequency).

To create a standard signal of this type, the period should be *20* milliseconds, and the *On* pulse will *.5 - 2.5* milliseconds long. A servo interprets this pulse to *know* what position it is being commanded to hold, with *1.5ms* being center. Since *1.5ms* is center, *.5ms* means turn fully counter-clockwise, and *2.5ms* means turn fully clockwise.

We could generate this signal by setting the period and doing some quick math to come up the duty cycle that matches our demand, but the PIGPIOD library makes it easier with a dedicated servo function. The example code below shows how to output a PWM control signal.

```
// generates a pwm signal with a period of 20 milliseconds

// and a pulse width of 2 milliseconds on pin 26

set_servo_pulsewidth(pi, 26, 2000);
```

The set_servo_pulsewidth takes three arguments:

- The Raspberry Pi handle we got during handshake with the PIGPIO Daemon
- The GPIO pin number
- The desired pulse width in microseconds

If you're looking at the PIGPIOD documentation, you'll see *frequency* used where we've talked about *period*. Frequency is just the number of cycles per second, so you can easily convert back and forth if necessary. Also note that you must multiply your desired pulse width in milliseconds by *1000* because our function expects the argument in units of microseconds.

# Motor drivers and motor controllers

The principles we've learned so far in this chapter are at the heart of more comprehensive devices called motor drivers and motor controllers that offer more functionality than the simple motor driver circuits I've shown you. They accomplish these extra functions by arranging a number of circuits together to handle multiple speeds, both directions, and sometimes multiple motors. They may also have their own microcontrollers running software algorithms to allow different means of communication or allow better control without burdening your main computer (or the programmer) with motor control details.

Let me say that you are likely going to hear *motor driver* and *motor controller* used interchangeably at some point, although they are technically different things. I can see where sometimes the line can get blurry because most devices sold as motor controllers are actually a board with both a motor controller and a motor driver. What is important is that you understand the functions of each and that both jobs get done. Let's look at each.

## Motor drivers

Motor drivers are the circuitry that handles supplying power to the motors based on their input signal. The circuit in *figure 4.8* is a simple motor driver, but can only move the motor in one direction. The most common type of motor driver for brush-type DC motors is an arrangement of *4* transistors called an **H-Bridge**. H-bridges allow you to control both speed and direction of brush-type motors without the reversing relay we talked about earlier.

An H-bridge is cheap and doesn't require any complicated controlling as all it does is vary voltage and polarity. It's good for a single motor winding (coil), but can be used in pairs to drive stepper motors. Stepper motor control is more involved that DC motor control because of that pesky requirement of coordinating the two windings.

A very common motor driver is the *L298N Dual H-bridge*. As its name suggests, it has two H-bridges and can control either one stepper motor or two brush-type DC motors that draw up to two amps. It requires a PWM signal to control motor speed and driving one of two pins low to set direction per H-bridge. Following *figure 4.10* is a common motor driver module based on the L298N.

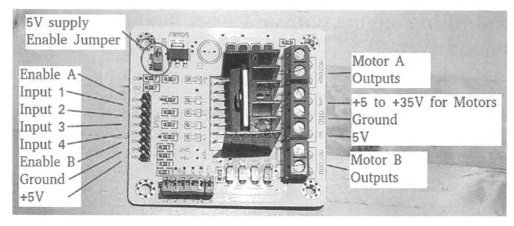

**Figure 4.10:** *An L298N-based dual motor driver by Velleman*

The *VMA409* by *Velleman* in *figure 4.10* is a L298N dual H-bridge driver on a handy little board with everything you need to interface with GPIO from a Raspberry Pi or a microcontroller and drive either two brush-type DC motors or one stepper motor. (The L298N is the large device in the middle, everything else as added by the module-manufacturer). Don't let all those connections intimidate you, it's pretty easy to use. Take a look at the wiring diagram in *figure 4.11*.

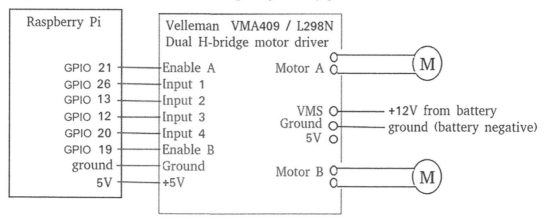

**Figure 4.11:** *Wiring diagram from Raspberry Pi to L298N module to motors*

*That's not so bad, right?* It looks like a lot of labels in *figure 4.10*, but in *figure 4.11* we can see that it's just 6 GPIO pins, a power sources, and a couple of motors. Bookmark this image – it is the same wiring diagram and pin assignments used for both the code we'll use shortly and robot project in *Chapter 21, Building and Programming an Autonomous Robot.*

# Controlling motors with an L298N dual H-Bridge motor driver

For this section, we are going use what we've learned so far in this chapter to write a simple program and control a brush-type DC motor with an H-bridge motor driver. I am using a *Velleman VMA409*, a pair of wheel modules scavenged from a robot vacuum, and a cordless drill battery. The Raspberry Pi is power separately, and it supplies *5 volts* to the driver board. Following *figure 4.12* shows my setup.

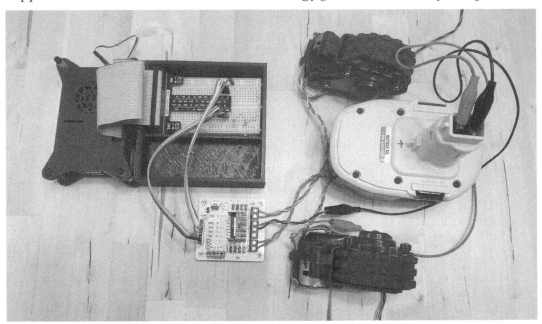

**Figure 4.12:** *A L298N based motor driver module all set up with a Raspberry Pi and a pair of robot vacuum motors*

Be careful when making temporary connections like this that wires don't short. Believe me when I say that sparks, fires, and battery explosions are not fun and can cause injury. Your wife can also cause injury if she finds scorch marks on her new dining room table. Be careful. Once you have safety assured, the steps for using an L298N-based motor driver like the *VMA409* for brush-type DC motors are:

Remove the *5V* supply enable jumper on the driver module to avoid *5V* getting back to your *3.3 volts* GPIO pins and to allow modulating speed.

1.  The wire your motors to the outputs – polarity doesn't matter because you can always switch the wires or change motor direction in software. Wire a power supply suitable for your motors – polarity does matter here. Make sure ground goes to ground.

2. Connect ground and *5V* to power the board. You can power the board with the *5V* supply on the Raspberry Pi, but it is important to never try to power a motor from those. Get a battery pack or my personal favorite – a power tool battery at the right voltage for your motors.

3. **Enable A**, **Input 1**, and **Input 2** are all for **Motor A**. The enable pin takes PWM signal to control motor speed. Drive input pin 1 low (or short to ground) to spin the motor in one direction, or **Input 2** low to reverse – maintaining your PWM signal the whole time. Never drive both input pins low at the same time. The **Enable B**, **Input 3**, and **Input 4** exactly the same but for **Motor B**.

See *figure 4.11* for the complete wiring diagram. Regarding *Step 4*, the code below is a sample program (`hello_motor.cpp` in your downloads) that uses the PIGPIO Daemon Library to run motor A at half-speed and full-speed, both forward and reverse for a few seconds each.

```cpp
#include <iostream>
#include <pigpiod_if2.h>


//define our GPIO pin assignments
const int PWM_A = 21;
const int MOTOR_A_FWD = 26;
const int MOTOR_A_REV = 13;


using namespace std;


//handshakes with Pigpio Daemon and sets up our pins.
int pigpio_setup()
{
    char *addrStr = NULL;
    char *portStr = NULL;
    //handshake with pigpio daemon and get pi handle
    const int pi = pigpio_start(addrStr, portStr);

    //set pin modes.
```

```
    set_mode(pi,PWM_A, PI_OUTPUT);

    set_mode(pi,MOTOR_A_FWD, PI_OUTPUT);

    set_mode(pi,MOTOR_A_REV, PI_OUTPUT);


    //initializes motor off Remember that high is "off"

    //and we must drive in1 or in2 low to start the motor

    gpio_write(pi, MOTOR_A_FWD, 1);

    gpio_write(pi, MOTOR_A_REV, 1);


    //return our pi handle

    return pi;

}
```

The first block above is all normal set up stuff like our necessary include files, constants and other global, and a function to setup our PIGPIO Daemon interface as well as our pin modes and initial pin states. The next block has the motor control function calls.

```
int main()

{

    int pi = pigpio_setup();

    if(pi < 0)

    {

        cout<<"Failed to connect to Pigpio Daemon. Is it running?"<<endl;

        return -1;

    }


    //when you're ready to start the motor

    gpio_write(pi, MOTOR_A_FWD, 0);
```

```
    // starts a PWM signal to motor A enable at half speed

    set_PWM_dutycycle(pi, PWM_A, 127);

    time_sleep(3); //3 second delay

    //starts motor at full speed

    set_PWM_dutycycle(pi, PWM_A, 255);

    time_sleep(3);


    //stops the motor

    gpio_write(pi, MOTOR_A_FWD, 1);

    time_sleep(1);

    //repeats in reverse

    gpio_write(pi, MOTOR_A_REV, 0);

    set_PWM_dutycycle(pi, PWM_A, 127);

    time_sleep(3);

    set_PWM_dutycycle(pi, PWM_A, 255);

    time_sleep(3);

    gpio_write(pi, MOTOR_A_REV, 1);


    pigpio_stop(pi);

    return 0;

}
```

Hopefully you're getting used to the PIGPIO daemon interface library and you're comfortable looking through the documentation online to clear up any questions, but I think you've got this well under control. Now is even a great time to stop and experiment with motor control. *Can you add a second motor to* `hello_motor`*?*

Motor drivers by themselves are very handy to keep around, but sometimes you can't spare four to six GPIO pins to control two motors or perhaps you want to write fewer lines of code. Let me introduce you to our good friend, the motor controller.

# Motor controllers

Motor controllers are the software and circuitry that take an input signal about what the motor needs to be doing, and generates and output signal that goes to the motor drivers. The `hello_motor` program we just wrote is a simple, open-loop motor controller. Don't worry if you don't know what *open-loop* means yet – we will spend a lot of time in *Chapter 8, Robot Control Strategy* learning different controller types.

While `hello_motor` exists on our computer, some motor controllers exist on other hardware. This is most commonly in the form of a module that has it's own microcontroller and motor drivers that can handle a lot of important details for us – like making sure the robot is actually going straight or calculating a current position from wheel rotation data.

Following *figure 4.13* shows one such motor control module.

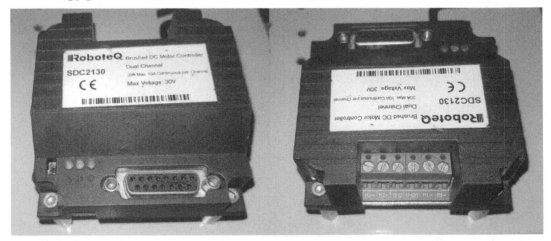

***Figure 4.13:*** *A complete motor control and driver module by Roboteq. Photo credit Dan Pollock*

Motor control modules like those in *figure 4.13* can be time-savers. As you'll find out, getting a robot to drive straight can be a challenge. We can do things with software and feedback from sensors to fix the problem, or we can turn to a self-contained control and driver solution that allows us to simply command a speed and forget about the details. The major downside of motor controller modules is that they are expensive.

 **Motor controllers for brushless DC motors are a special type called electronic speed controllers. These take inputs from position sensors in order to properly sequence the energizing of the coils.**

While the type of output signal is always the same for a given type of motor, the input signal could be PWM, serial, I2C, USB, Bluetooth, and while I haven't personally seen a motor controller that listens for various piano keys to be pressed, it could be done. My point is that there many different types of motor controllers and it's important to read the documentation to make sure it's going work for your project.

# Conclusion

We spent this chapter learning different motor types and how they work. We also learned how to control motor speed and direction with transistors and relays, as well as how to use modules that handle that low-level circuit work for us. Finally, we wired a motor to a common motor driver module and wrote our first program to control a motor's speed and direction with a Raspberry Pi.

These fundamentals are critical to our success as roboticists, and spending the time to understand them all is going to save you a lot of headache down the road.

Equally critical to our ability to make an intelligent robot is the ability to communicate between devices. We will spend the next chapter learning how to send and receive information via a number of standard protocols you are likely to need in order to communicate between your computer and motor controllers, sensors, and sometimes other computers.

# Questions

1. What type of motor is most suitable for a first robot-build?
    a. How do you reverse this motor?
    b. How do you control the speed of this motor?
2. A device that receives a PWM signal usually responds to one of two features of the PWM signal. This is usually the duty cycle or the.
3. What is the most common type of motor driver?

# Bonus challenge

Review what we learned in *Chapter 2, GPIO Hardware Interface Pins Overview and Use* about reading switches with GPIO pins. Add two buttons (or simulate if you don't have them) to your Raspberry Pi, and modify hello_motor to respond to button presses – one of the buttons should cause the PWM signal to the motors to increase by ten for each button press, the other button should cause the PWM signal to decrease by ten. For an extra challenge, make the motor reverse direction when the button pressing sends the PWM value below 0.

# CHAPTER 5
# Communication with Sensors and other Devices

## Introduction

What sets a robot apart from a remote-controlled machine is the ability to accumulate data from any number of sensors and make decisions based on that data. To get that data from the sensor to the robot's main computer, we have to be able to use whichever communication protocol the sensor is designed for – and there are several. This chapter is dedicated to learning common communication protocols that you will use over and over again in robotics.

In this chapter, we will cover the following:

- Binary (Logical) signals
- Serial communication primer
- I2C communication primer

## Objective

Gain working knowledge of binary, I2C, and serial communication protocols.

# Binary (logical) signals

Binary signals are logic-level signals used to convey a single bit of information. While all communication protocols we will discuss utilize binary signals, this section is dedicated to the most straightforward type – where a single bit of information is the entire message.

The most straightforward sensors convey only a single bit of information and are read like a digital input pin from *Chapter 2, GPIO Hardware Interface Pins Overview and Use*. This might be the state of a switch embedded in a bumper so the robot knows when it hit something, a switch embedded in a wheel so the robot knows when a wheel has gone over the edge of a stair, or a switch that a lever hits so the robot knows when an actuator has reached the end of its travel. These are usually called *bump sensors, wheel drop sensors,* and *end switches*.

The above sensors could be mechanical switches like we used in *Chapter 2, Gpio Hardware Interface Pins Overview and Use* for experimenting with inputs. Still, they could take several different forms – as long as they can drive a GPIO input across its threshold voltage. You can find switches that respond to temperature, magnetic reed switches that respond to the magnet, individual resistors and diodes that respond to the presence or absence of light, or even modules of complete circuits that can *switch* in response to the motion, moisture, or radio signals. In the end, we are merely reading the digital input for whether its voltage level is high or low. *Figure 5.1* below shows a number of switches and a sensor module we read the same way we read a switch:

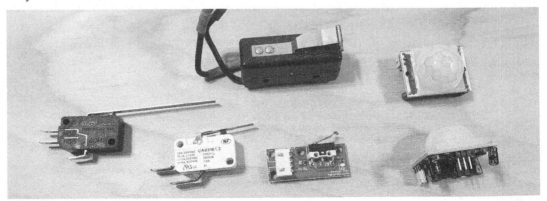

***Figure 5.1:*** *An assortment of lever switches and a couple passive infrared motion sensors*

Lever switches come in all sizes and are great for bump sensors and end switches. Also pictured are passive infrared sensor modules that have all the circuitry on board to drive a pin high or low in response to detected motion – it's not technically a switch, but the signal pin is read the same way as a switch.

# Debouncing switches

It won't matter for some applications, but if you need to be sure that every switching cycle is counted once (maybe you are counting the number of button presses to scroll menu choices), you need to debounce the switch to avoid every button press resulting in multiple increments.

**Beware of bouncing switches!**

**Mechanical switches don't close their contacts neatly, but rather vibrate or** *bounce* **open and closed several times. It happens so fast that you would never notice just turning on a light or something, but your processor is so fast that a single switching action might register as a several** *On/Off* **cycles.**

The easiest way to debounce is with software that reads the GPIO pin with the switch several times with a few milliseconds of delay in between. The code below is one way to do it.

```
bool checkPin(int pin){

    int i=0;

    while(1)

    {

        if(gpio_read(pi, pin)==0)

        {

        i++;

        }

        else

        {

        i--;

        }


        if(i>5) return 1;

        if (i<-5) return 0;
```

```
    time_sleep(.05);

    }

}
```

The above simple function plays a kind of tug-of-war by counting up every read the switch is closed and counting down every read the switch is open. Once it reaches a *consensus number,* it will return either true or false. The delay and *consensus number* can be played with because every switch will be different, but this works pretty well for every switch I've tried.

# Wheel encoders

Encoders are devices that help you keep track of how many times a shaft has turned. These will be read on a GPIO input pin as simple binary signals like a switch, but instead of just checking it for *On* or *Off* we monitor the pin to count momentary *pulses* as if someone were just tapping the switch. By counting pulses, we can determine how many times the shaft has rotated. Calculating how far a robot has traveled and turned with encoder pulse counts is known as **wheel odometry**. We will dedicate *Chapter 11, Robot Tracking and Localization* to learning all we need to know about it. *Chapter 14, Wheel Encoders for Odometry*, is dedicated to all the details needed to select, wire, and write code for wheel encoders to get that data in the first place.

# Binary signals from analog sensors

A variation of a digital sensor is technically an analog sensor with a defined threshold that software treats as a switching point. An example of this is an infrared emitter / receiver pair of diodes arranged to measure distance. The closer the object, the more infrared light gets back to the receiver, and the higher voltage is read by the analog to digital converter (dark objects can absorb much of the IR light and mimic further distance).

While technically what we are doing is reading a varying voltage level, I would say this arrangement is most commonly used in robotics as a switch that doesn't require physical contact. Take a look at the following *figure 5.2*:

Will the closer object or the further object result in the larger measured signal?

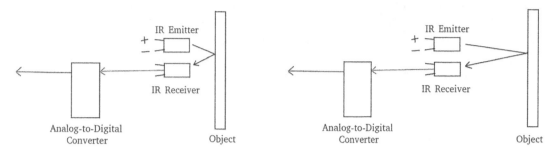

**Figure 5.2:** *An infrared transmitter/receiver pair*

The emitter is an LED that beams out infrared light, easy enough. Think of the receiver as a phototransistor that responds to light instead of the voltage applied to the gate. A receiver circuit measures the intensity of the infrared light coming back to infer a distance from whatever reflected the light. The receiving circuit is measuring voltage, and you pick a value to `switch` at. This method is how cliff sensors on many robot vacuums work – they are an infrared diode pair aimed straight down and usually read a very close distance. If they ever read more than an inch or so, the software calls it a `cliff` condition.

# Binary communication summary

When communicating a single bit of information, it is merely a matter of reading whether the logic level of an input pin is high or low – the pin doesn't know or care if it is hooked up to a switch or some other device that can change the voltage level above and below its logical threshold. This is a simple and very versatile tool but is inadequate on its own for sending large amounts of data. One time-tested method for sending large amounts of data still uses binary signals by sending them rapidly one after another. This is the very popular communication method simply known as `serial`.

# Serial communication primer

A lot of sensors provide much more data than we could get from reading the simple *On/Off* input that we have so far. We might need to read an analog value with an **Analog to Digital converter** (**ADC**) or receive an array of numbers from a sensor that provides multiple data points. Serial communication is the act of serializing data bits (to send one after the other), enabling us to send endless chunks of data from device to device.

Several communication protocols use serialization, but only one is conventionally called *serial*, while the others are known by more specific names. This is the early and still a very popular method using a Universal Asynchronous Serial Bus (UART) that transmits on one wire and receives on another. In this book (and almost everywhere else), this is what you should assume if I simply use the word *serial*. I will use other names for different serialized communication protocols.

## UART serial

To transmit data, the transmitting device toggles a digital output (TX) pin to send numbers in binary one bit at a time (`8 bits per byte`). The receiving device has to be set to monitor its input (RX) pin and receives the numbers, which can then be interpreted as needed and placed into a variable. The receiving program has to know which type of data to expect, or it cannot interpret it correctly. You can find a couple of serial communication tutorials that look deeper into these details on the Practical Robotics YouTube channel at youtube.com/practicalrobotics.

Only two devices can be on a standard serial line because if two ever transmitted at the same time, the receiving device would have no way of separating the `1`'s and `0`'s. The result would be garbage data.

The standard serial communication protocol is asynchronous, basically meaning that the transmitter and receiver don't share a clock signal or coordinate their efforts by the protocol – that's up to the programmer to do, if necessary. If it's not done carefully, the two devices can quickly end up in a state where they are both waiting for data and not doing anything else - and they will happily sit and wait forever while you wonder what went wrong.

Both devices have to be configured to run at the same baud rate and with a few other parameters set the same. Baud rate (also known as **Bits Per Second** (**BPS**)) is how fast the bits are streamed. Some ordinary baud rates are *9600*, *56000*, and *115200*. Always check the device documentation because it could be as low as *300* or even higher than *115200* – although reliability tends to degrade as speed increases.

The other parameters are:

- Number of data bits
- Parity (*yes*/*no*)
- Number of stop bits

When you read the serial communication section of a device, you will usually see it listed like this:

`9600 8N1`

This means *9600* is the baud rate, there are *8* data bits, *N* - No parity, and *1* stop bit.

Common libraries save us from needing to know the details of how each of these affects the actual stream of data; you just have to make sure they all match on both devices. Serial communication can take place via USB, Bluetooth, Ethernet, or GPIO pins.

**More than a byteful:**

**When sending data serially – whether via the UART serial, USB, I2C, and so on – you can only send one byte (value** *0 to 255***) at a time. Values in some of our example programs (and the rest of your robotics career) will often far exceed** *255.*

*What's a programmer to do?*

**You can send values that require 2 or more bytes by breaking the value down to its binary form, then sending those** *16* **or more bits in** *8* **byte chunks as if each were a value by itself. On the receiving end, we break those bytes back into bits, shift them around to line them up, then read the final value. Unfortunately, it's not always as easy as putting all the bytes side-by-side, as sometimes only** *4* **or** *6* **of the bits of one of the bytes are used, and the remaining mean something else entirely.**

**This is one of those topics a little outside of what I want to subject you to in this book but is a necessary evil. I am going to gloss over the topic here, but visit** *youtube.com/practicalrobotics* **for a full tutorial on combining bytes.**

# Set up a Raspberry Pi and test UART serial communication

The first step is the wiring. If the voltages on UART pins of both devices match, it's as simple as connecting ground and the two **TX**/**RX** pins. You have to criss-cross, so **TX** of each device is going to **RX** of the other, or else both will be transmitting on the same wire and listening on the same wire. One device has to transmit (**TX**) to the receive (**RX**) of the other. *Got it?*

**Good!** The easiest way to test your device's configuration is loopback, where you simply wire a jumper from the **TX** to the **RX** on the same device. See *figure 5.3* below for a serial wiring drawing, but note that it is not always necessary to have both **TX**/**RX** wires connected. Sometimes you only need to communicate one-way, and it's fine to leave the other wire Off.

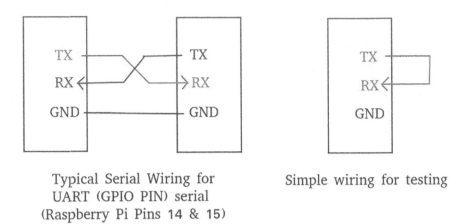

Typical Serial Wiring for
UART (GPIO PIN) serial
(Raspberry Pi Pins 14 & 15)

Simple wiring for testing

*Figure 5.3: Wiring for serial communication and for testing*

Next, configure your Raspberry Pi for serial communication with the GPIO pins. At the command line, type:

`sudo raspi-config`

Select `Interface Options`, then `Serial`. Answer `NO`, you do not want a login shell to be available over serial, and `YES,` you want the serial hardware to be enabled. Save and exit.

Now we want to make a change unique to the Raspberry Pi. It only has one hardware UART, and by default, it is assigned to Bluetooth. This leaves only a software UART (mini-UART, they call it) available for our GPIO UART pins. Don't worry about the details for now, but the hardware UART is preferable for us. Let's take it away from Bluetooth and assign it to our GPIO serial. Open the file `/boot/config.txt` with a text editor.

`sudo nano /boot/config.txt`

At the bottom, add the line

`dtoverlay=pi3-disable-bt`

And make sure the line `enable_uart=1` is somewhere in the file and not commented out with the # symbol. Then use *Ctrl + X* to exit and *Y* to save. See *figure 5.4* for an example of the finished `/boot/config.txt` file.

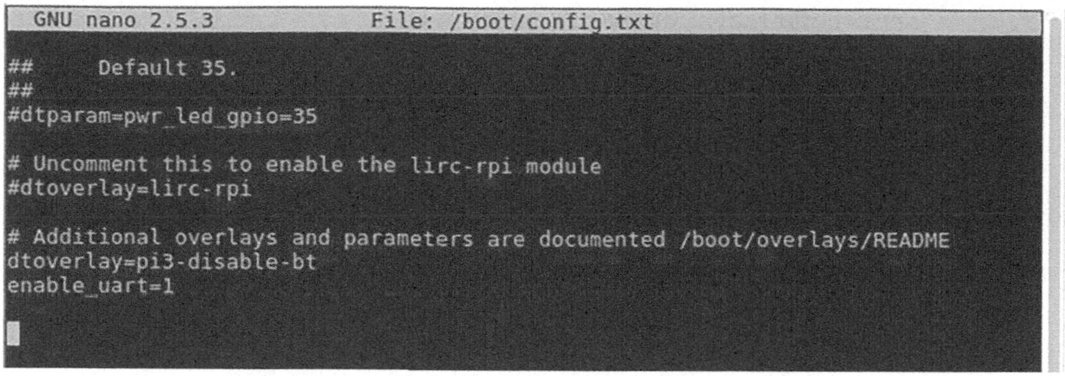

```
GNU nano 2.5.3                  File: /boot/config.txt

##        Default 35.
##
#dtparam=pwr_led_gpio=35

# Uncomment this to enable the lirc-rpi module
#dtoverlay=lirc-rpi

# Additional overlays and parameters are documented /boot/overlays/README
dtoverlay=pi3-disable-bt
enable_uart=1
```

*Figure 5.4: Editing the Raspberry Pi /boot/config.txt*

The hello_serial.cpp program below is a simple serial test program that opens a Raspberry Pi serial connection, checks for available data, writes three bytes, then reads three bytes. The TX pin must be wired directly to the RX pin in the loopback configuration shown in *figure 5.3*. The program is also in the chapter downloads at *https://github.com/lbrombach/practical_chapters*.

Serial test program: hello_serial.cpp

```cpp
#include <iostream>

#include <pigpiod_if2.h>


using namespace std;


int main()
{

    char *addrStr = NULL;

    char *portStr = NULL;

    int pi=pigpio_start(addrStr, portStr);


    int UARTHandle = serial_open(pi, "/dev/ttyAMA0",115200,0);

    cout<<"UARTHandle = " << UARTHandle<< endl;

    time_sleep(.1);

    cout << "Data available start: "
```

```
        << serial_data_available(pi, UARTHandle)

        << " bytes" << endl;

    serial_write_byte(pi,UARTHandle,6);

    serial_write_byte(pi,UARTHandle,'f');

    serial_write_byte(pi,UARTHandle,'F');

    time_sleep(.1);


    cout << "Data available after writing: "

        << serial_data_available(pi, UARTHandle)

        << " bytes" << endl;

    cout <<"Byte read = "

        << serial_read_byte(pi, UARTHandle)<< endl;


    cout << "Data available after reading a byte: "

        << serial_data_available(pi, UARTHandle)

        << " bytes" << endl;

    char inA = serial_read_byte(pi, UARTHandle);

    cout <<"Byte read = " << inA << endl;

    char inB = serial_read_byte(pi, UARTHandle);

    cout <<"Byte read = " << inB<< endl;


    serial_close(pi, UARTHandle);

    pigpio_stop(pi);

    return 0;

}
```

The first byte is written, read, and displayed as an integer. Then second and third bytes are written as a char, but the actual transmission is as an integer based on the ASCII code for those characters. The serial_read_byte function returns integers, so we have to convert it back to a char if that's how we want the data displayed. It is critical to know what type of data is being received so you can convert or interpret it appropriately. *Figure 5.5* below shows the output from the program if all goes well:

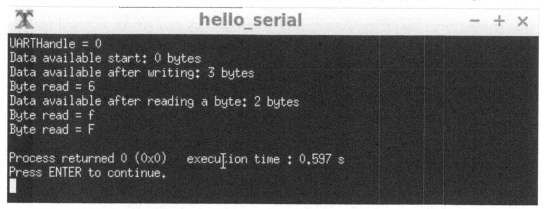

*Figure 5.5: hello_serial test program output*

The standard serial protocol works through several conduits. We have shown using serial from UART to UART (each device's TX/RX pins), but the protocol works with the same code with USB, Bluetooth, and others by just changing which serial device is opened. In the next chapter, I will show you to connect the TX/RX from a serial UART to your computer's USB port and make the minor software changes needed to use a USB port instead of a UART.

# Fixing error opening serial port

To use the communication ports in Linux, we need to have permission for the dial out group the port belongs to. The ports show as sub-folders in the /dev folder – most commonly you'll use:

- /dev/ttyAMA0
- /dev/ttyUSB0
- /dev/ttyACM0

You can see the entire list with:

```
ls /dev/tty*
```

Note that the 0 at the end is the first one that shows up and increments with the next device. If you plug in a second USB serial device, it may show up as dev/ttyUSB1.

If you know the port, you can permit that one for a quick test with:

```
sudo chmod 666 /dev/portpath
```

```
#example:

sudo chmod 666 /dev/ttyAMA0
```

That should clear up *permission denied* or *unable to open port* errors, but will have to be done every time you open a new terminal. The persistent solution is to add your user to the `dialout` group with:

```
sudo usermod -a -G dialout user
```

Then log out and log back in (or just reboot), and you should be good to go from then on.

# I2C communication primer

I2C is one of the most popular communication protocols for devices within a small system (like a robot), and you'll find modules using I2C for accelerometers, compasses, GPS, relays, and motor controllers to name a few. I2C allows us to not only read and write information to a device but to use the same two GPIO pins to communicate with over 100 different devices. The ability to run single, 4-wire cable to many devices greatly simplifies the adding of new sensors and keeps the wiring manageable. I2C is still a method of serial communication, but it's not *The serial* that we talked about above.

Two big things set I2C apart and allow multiple devices to share wires:

1. Individual device addresses that allow a *master* to make a call on the wire that all devices *hear*, but only the addressed device responds to.
2. Message acknowledgment. Unlike the standard serial protocol, I2C has message acknowledgments built-in, so we can be reasonably sure of receipt.

Like the standard serial protocol, we have standard software libraries to save us the trouble of learning and coding all the details. *Whew!*

To use I2C devices, we read and write to the device's registers. Registers are memory locations, and the state of the bits tells the device what to do or holds data we can read from the device.

The general usage of I2C goes something like this:

1. Open an I2C bus.
2. Write a value to a specific register to enable and set the device mode.
3. Read the register that holds that data byte we need. Frequently we will need to read and combine two registers (one byte each) to get a value.
4. Leave the device streaming or power it down, depending on program requirements.

**Caution: There are** *3.3 volts* **and** *5 volts* **I2C Devices. Make sure yours matches your master's logic level or be prepared to add a level shifter as we'll discuss in** *Chapter 6, Additional Helpful Hardware.* **(Raspberry logic level is are** *3.3V,* **and Arduino logic level is** *5V***).**

Wiring I2C devices are the same whether you have one or one hundred slaves. Each device needs power, a common ground, SDA (data line), and SCL (clock signal). Just keep adding them in parallel, as shown in following *figure 5.6*:

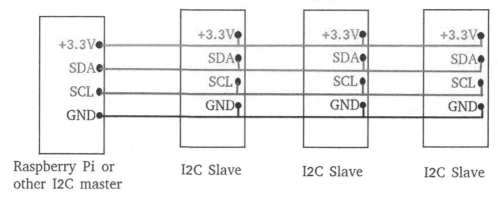

**Figure 5.6:** *Wiring I2C devices in parallel*

# To set up and use an I2C device with the Raspberry Pi:

First, make sure I2C is enabled by typing this at the command line:

```
ls /dev/*i2c*
```

It should return an I2C bus designation like /dev/i2c-1, with 1 being your bus number. If it instead it returns something about *no such file or directory*, run the Raspberry Pi configuration tool with:

```
sudo raspi-config
```

Then select Interface Options, Then I2C, then choose Yes, I'd like the ARM I2C interface enabled.

Now try the ls /dev/*i2c* command again to confirm you're good to go. Once you have confirmed your bus number (1), let's check the list of available devices on the bus with i2c-tools. If it's not already installed with your distro, install it with:

```
sudo apt-get install -y i2c-tools
```

Once that's done or if it's already installed, check for available devices with the i2c-detect tool. Don't forget the -y tag to avoid potential problems.

```
i2cdetect -y 1
```

This scans bus number 1 and returns a graph with the devices it found. You can see that I have three I2C devices available. `0x19`, `0x1e`, and `0x6b`. The `0x` is a convention that tells you that these are hexadecimal addresses. *Figure 5.7* below is a screenshot of my detected I2C devices.

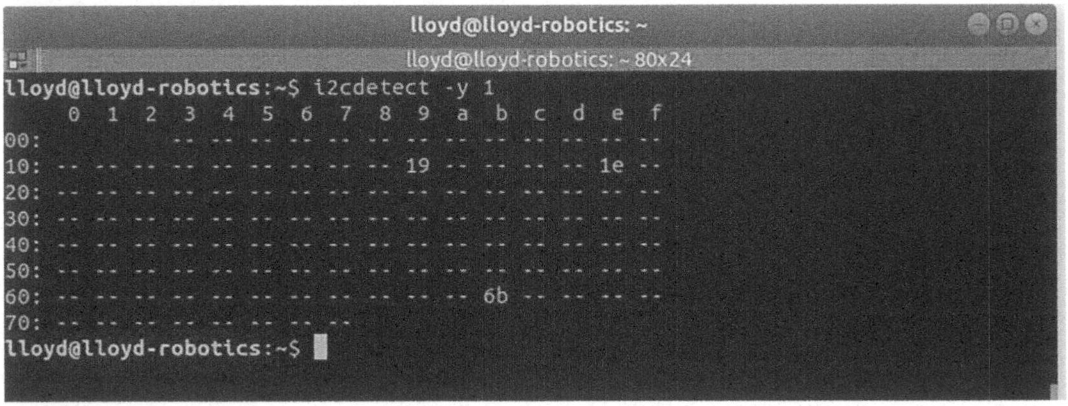

*Figure 5.7: The output of i2c-detect showing the three device addresses available on my I2C bus*

Your device documentation should tell you what the default address is. Still, sometimes manufacturers of modules get chips from different chip manufacturers and end up selling the same device with more than one possible default address. This is a big headache that the I2C `detect` tool helps with. Just run I2C `detect`, wire in the new device, and rerun I2C detect again and make a note of the new address. The newly listed address is your new device.

# Example and test program: hello_i2c_lsm303

We can't test our I2C program with a loopback as we did with `hello_serial`, so what follows is a program to read a few bytes from an LSM303 accelerometer at address `0x19`. Accelerometers are widely used for tracking a robot's position and orientation – we will spend *Chapter 16, IMUs: Accelerometers, Gyroscopes, and Magnetometers* learning more about them. For now, let's just get acquainted with I2C communications.

The LSM303 (and many other devices) gives a two-byte value for each piece of data. Registers only hold one byte, so we have to read them separately and combine them into an integer. If you have questions about the I2C functions, refer to the PIGPIOD C interface documentation. As usual, the `complete hello_i2c_lsm303.cpp` program is available to download from *https://github.com/lbrombach/practical_chapters*. This first block of code shows our setup and the outline of the structure in the `main()` function.

```
#include <iostream>

#include <pigpiod_if2.h>


using namespace std;


const int LSM303_accel=0x19; //accelerometer address

const int I2Cbus=1; //RPi typical I2C bus. Find yours with "ls /dev/*i2c*
"


int main(){

    //step 1.1 - initialize pigpiod connection

    //step 1.2 - open I2C connection and save I2C handle

    // step 2 - configure the device into the mode required and any
    parameters

    // step 3 - read bytes from registers

    // step 4 - combine bytes as necessary, convert is desired as well

    //step 5 - put device to sleep if done with it

    //step 6 - close I2C connection

    //step 7 - disconnect from pigpio daemon

    return 0;

}
```

The above sequence has us reading values just once exiting the program. Typically for sensors, we would keep looping, but we'll get to that later. Start the program as below, which starts typical of any PIGPIO program and adds a line to open I2C connection and get an I2C handle for each I2C device we want to use. In this case, it's just one device.

```
//step 1.1

char *addrStr = NULL;

char *portStr = NULL;

int pi=pigpio_start(addrStr, portStr);
```

```
/step 1.2

const int ACCEL_HANDLE=i2c_open(pi,I2Cbus, LSM303_accel,0);
```

Step 2 below has us first set the frequency register –by writing a value of `0x47` to register `0x20`, then another configuration byte at register location `0x23`. Many registers break up a byte into individual bits, so writing hexadecimal `0x09`, in this case, can set several config options because the device can interpret each `1` and `0` separately (`0x09` converts to binary `00001001`). If you need more info on reading and writing to device registers, the video tutorial on *youtube.com/practicalrobotics* titled *Reading and Understanding Sensor Datasheets* discusses the topic extensively.

```
// step 2 - set frequency, pause, then set a few more parameters

i2c_write_byte_data(pi, ACCEL_HANDLE, 0x20, 0x47); //set frequency

time_sleep(.02);

i2c_write_byte_data(pi, ACCEL_HANDLE, 0x23, 0x09);

time_sleep(.02);
```

The accelerometer provides readings for three axes – x, y, and z. Each reading requires us to combine two bytes into a single value.

Steps 3 and 4 in the block below has us reading both bytes for the x reading, then applying step 4 to combine the two bytes into a single value. It is essential to know the format of each byte being sent. In this case, only 12 out of 16 total bytes are part of my value, so I shift the **Most Significant Byte** (**MSB**) eight places to the left, perform a bitwise `OR` to combine them, then shift all 16 bits four places to the right to end up with a properly positioned final value.

Sometimes the value will use 10 bytes or even all 16 – you'll have to get this from the datasheet. It also may be unsigned or signed so it can represent negative numbers (as in this case). Bitwise operations and twos-complement are a bit outside of our scope here. I have video tutorials available for both topics at the *Practical Robotics YouTube* channel mentioned above.

```
    //step 3 - read the bytes

        int xLSB = (int)i2c_read_byte_data(pi, ACCEL_HANDLE, 0x28);

        int xMSB = (int)i2c_read_byte_data(pi, ACCEL_HANDLE, 0x29);

        //step 4 - combine the bytes
```

```
float accelX=(float)((int16_t)(xLSB | xMSB<<8)>>4);


//repeat steps 3 and 4 for y and z data

int yLSB = (int)i2c_read_byte_data(pi, ACCEL_HANDLE, 0x2A);

int yMSB = (int)i2c_read_byte_data(pi, ACCEL_HANDLE, 0x2B);

float accelY=(float)((int16_t)(yLSB | yMSB<<8)>>4);


int zLSB = (int)i2c_read_byte_data(pi, ACCEL_HANDLE, 0x2C);

int zMSB = (int)i2c_read_byte_data(pi, ACCEL_HANDLE, 0x2D);

float accelZ=(float)((int16_t)(zLSB | zMSB<<8)>>4);


//print the raw values

cout<<endl<<accelX<<” “<<accelY<<” “<<accelZ<<endl;
```

The datasheet will specify both the unit of measure and sometimes a multiplier to achieve that unit. In this case, the raw data is in milliG's, so a level and stationary device will read (close to) 0 on x and y axis and roughly 1000 milliG on the z axis. It's not listed in the steps, but below is a short bit of code to indicate if the device is roughly level.

```
if(accelX < 50 && accelX > -50 && accelY < 50 && accelY > -50)

    cout<<”The device is fairly level”<<endl;

else

    cout<<”The device is not level”<<endl;
```

And finally, steps 5, 6, and 7 in the following code block are just closing up operations:

```
//step 5 - put device into sleep mode

i2c_write_byte_data(pi, ACCEL_HANDLE, 0x20, 0x00);

//step 6 - close I2C port

i2c_close(pi, ACCEL_HANDLE);

//step 7 - disconnect Pigpio daemon

pigpio_stop(pi);
```

If everything is right, you should see an output similar to that shown in *figure 5.8* below. Don't forget that the PIGPIO daemon must be running.

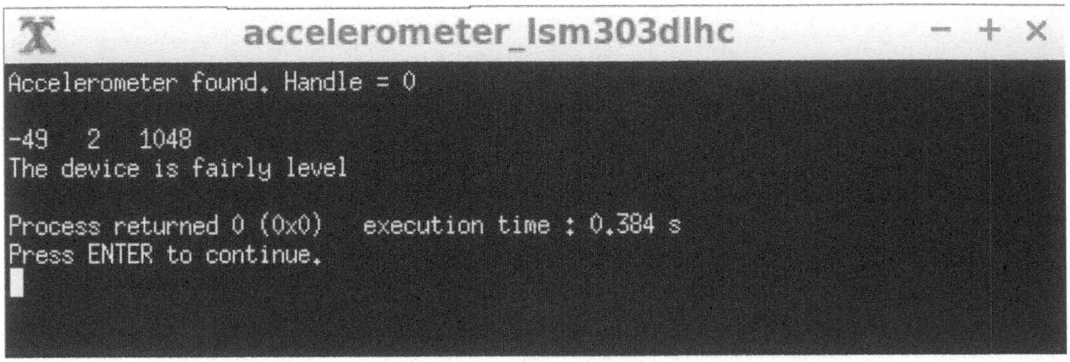

**Figure 5.8:** *Output from hello_lsm303 I2C test program*

hello_i2c_lsm303.cpp is, of course, specific for the lsm303 accelerometer. Still, the process is typical, and if you have a different I2C device, you can modify this program by using your device address and register addresses. There may be errors in the final values unless the code to combine bytes is also changed to match your device's format. Again, check out the *Practical Robotics YouTube* channel for further tutorials on both of these if you need them.

# Conclusion

In this chapter we've learned three of the most common ways communication is done between devices. We learned to read switches that might be embedded as sensors, sensor modules that output a signal just like a switch would, and how to send and receive more than one bit of data at a time with two serialized communication protocols – one known merely as serial and one called I2C that allows us to talk to many devices over the same pair of wires. There are many optional subjects in the robotics field, but these skills will be needed in every case.

Robots have a lot of little parts working together, and sometimes these parts need other parts to support or interface with them. We will spend the next chapter looking at various hardware that doesn't fit neatly into other chapters, but that you will likely need for your robot projects.

# Questions

1. What is it called when a computer reads a switch making contact many times instead of once? What is the solution?

2. Technically it is a distance measuring method, but infrared emitter/receiver pairs are most commonly used as what in robotics?

3. What parameters must match on both ends for standard serial communication to work?

4. If we have several I2C devices all wired to the same communication lines, how does each one know that it is the device being queried?

# CHAPTER 6
# Additional Helpful Hardware

## Introduction

Robots have a lot of parts, and sometimes these parts need other parts to support them or interface them with the rest of the machine. In this chapter, we are going to cover some hardware that isn't specifically Raspberry Pi or Robotics related, but you'll find very helpful or even necessary when building robots. Some of the things I'm including do a required task, and you need something to do the job on every robot build. Other things may not always be required, but are included so you know they exist and what they can do for you.

In this chapter, we will cover the following

- Power supplies, 5V and adjustable
- Relay modules
- Logic level converters
- Voltage dividers
- FTDIs
- Arduinos
- Digispark

# Objective:

To learn how some commonly supporting hardware is used and how to choose the one for your project.

# Power supplies

In addition to a battery pack suitable for powering your motors, your robot is going to need at least one regulated power supply for the computer and other electronics. For our purposes, we want to use DC-to-DC voltage converters that can handle an input voltage at least as high as our main battery supplies and have current (*amps*) capacity for enough for everything you'll power with it. To determine how many amps you need, just add up the current required by each device.

## 5 volt supplies

You'll generally need a *5 volt* power supply with plenty of amp capacity for all the devices it will power – including sensors, servos, relays, and a computer if you're using a Raspberry Pi. A *3 amp* module is the least I ever use, but I will almost always go with at least a *5 amp* converter for my *5 volt* supply if I can. Cutting it too close can lead to sagging voltage and erratic behavior of your electronics.

Many *5V* devices will come with USB connectors; many will come with screw terminals or just holes in a circuit board you have to solder to. As a starting point, I usually get *5 volt* supplies with USB outlets, then plan to solder my wires to the supply circuit board and make a rail or terminal strip that I can easily tap from as needed. See *figure 6.1* below.

***Figure 6.1:*** *Adjustable and Fixed DC to DC converters and a USB to screw-terminal adapter*

The top left device is an adjustable DC to DC converter with solder pads, and the bottom left device is a fixed 5 volt converter with a USB plug for the output. The device on the right is an adapter that allows you to tap the 5 volt connections from a USB port without soldering, just be careful to draw only minimal current from your computer USB port. I usually use them with fixed 5V power supplies that sometimes have multiple USB plugs.

# Adjustable power supplies

Probably the second-most-common voltage you'll need for sensors is 3.3 volts, but because these devices don't have any sort of standard connector I don't bother buying dedicated, fixed 3.3 volts supplies. The current needed for 3.3 volt devices is also usually small enough that I don't mind taking it from a Raspberry Pi if I have one on board. If I do need more, I'll use an adjustable-voltage DC to DC converter that I always keep on hand because they are useful for so many things.

 **Amp capacity ratings on electronics are the maximum they can supply or** *source*. **Don't worry if a supply is rated for more than your device says it needs because a device will only draw what it needs. For example, a Raspberry Pi3B will only draw the** 2 **or** 2.5 *amps* **that it needs even if the power supply is rated for** 100 *amps*.

# Relay modules

In the old days, using a relay with a microcontroller meant wiring half dozen components to drive the relay coil while protecting our output pin. It wasn't difficult, but it sure was tedious and time-consuming. Today, we have easy access to modules like the one in *figure 6.2* below that have all these already components mounted and wired - for less than I used to pay to make my own.

*Figure 6.2: A four-relay module by Sainsmart*

These relay modules by *SainSmart* (and generic copies) are among the most commonly available and are listed as *5v* relays. However, they have built-in *opto-isolators* that typically respond well to *3.3 volts* on the input side. What that means is you can apply *5 volts* to JD-VCC to power the relay coil, and it is electrically separate from the VCC you could power from the microcontroller or Raspberry Pi *3.3 volts* (to do this you have to remove the jumper between JD-VCC and VCC). Also, note that these are *active low* relays – you apply a *low* signal to energize the coil and a *high* signal to de-energize.

The basic modules take one digital signal from your microcontroller for each relay, but you can get modules that communicate via serial or I2C that allow you to control dozens of relays with just a couple data wires.

# Logic level converters

Sooner or later, you are likely to have two devices that communicate at different voltages. If it's a one-way communication where a higher voltage signal needs to be read by a lower-voltage device, you can get away with a simple voltage divider. For other situations, you'll want to use a proper logic level converter that can step voltages up or down to match the need.

**Voltage dividers** are made by placing two resistors in series, then using a connection between them for our input pin. This works because one end of the two resistors forms a circuit from our higher voltage device to the ground, and we are tapping a lesser voltage from the center of the circuit. The voltage at the center tap will depend on the higher voltage level and the ratio between the two resistors. *Figure 6.3* shows an example voltage divider circuit and the formula to calculate the output voltage.

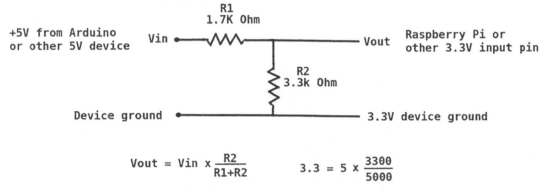

$$Vout = Vin \times \frac{R2}{R1+R2} \qquad 3.3 = 5 \times \frac{3300}{5000}$$

*Figure 6.3: Voltage divider wiring, formula, and formula example*

Voltage divider resistor values can be almost anything within reason as long as the ratio remains the same. Go too low, and you risk drawing too much current or go too high, and not enough current will flow to trigger the input device. Also, remember that *3.0 volts* are above the logical threshold for most *3.3 volt* devices, so if you don't have the exact resistor values *close enough* can be ok.

Logic level converters (also known as *logic shifters*) allow you to step a signal either up or down. Typically, they come on a board with multiple *channels*, making it a snap to interface multiple pins from one device to another. *Figure 6.4* shows a level shifter with four channels. Having four channels means the module has four level shifters that can be used for separate signals.

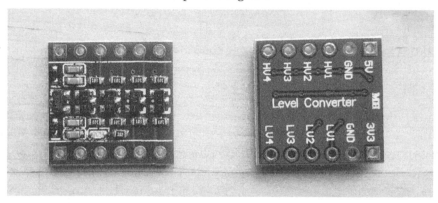

*Figure 6.4:* *A 4 channel bi-directional logic-level converter*

Early logic shifters only worked in one direction - that is, they could only shift up, or they could only shift down. Bidirectional logic shifters like the TE291 breakouts pictured in *figure 6.4* can shift in both directions, making them the most versatile and the only type that can be used to match levels for I2C communication circuits.

# FTDIs

FTDI is an acronym for a brand name (**Future Technology Devices International**). Still, it is synonymous with a specific chip used for interfacing USB with the UART-type serial (UART type) communication pins. This allows us to use UART-type serial devices and sensors with a Raspberry Pi if the serial GPIO pins are taken, or even with a regular computer. *Figure 6.5* shows two modules designed around the FTDI chip.

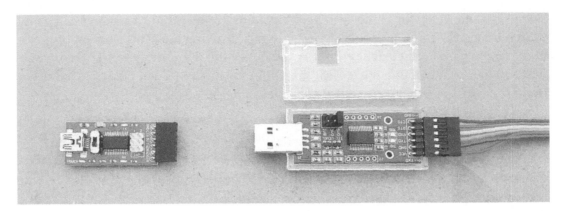

*Figure 6.5:* FTDI devices

The FTDI device on the left is switchable for *3.3* or *5 volt* operation, while the one on the right has a jumper for selecting *5, 3.3,* or *1.8 volts* and does not require a separate USB cable.

Using the USB port for serial communication is the same as using the GPIO UART serial pins except that you have to open a different port. Usually, this will be /dev/ ttyUSB0 unless you have another device plugged into USB, then it may be /dev/ ttyUSB1. To open the USB port and test an FTDI with hello_serial from *Chapter 5, Communication with Sensors and Other Devices* change line 12 from

```
int UARTHandle = serial_open(pi, "/dev/ttyAMA0",115200,0);
```

to

```
int UARTHandle = serial_open(pi, "/dev/ttyUSB0",115200,0);
```

With this one change made, you should be able to loop back the tx/rx pins on the FTDI and see the same output as you did when running hello_serial with your GPIO UART pins.

# Arduinos

If you've been into electronics in the past decade or so, you've no doubt at least heard of Arduinos. These are great little microcontrollers built onto a circuit board with various accessory hardware - like connectors, regulators, and LEDs already connected and soldered for you.

Arduinos are great interface devices between the robot and any computer – even those without their own Input and Output pins. Of particular use to us is that most versions have a built-in analog to digital converters, giving them one ability even the Raspberry Pi does not have. You program Arduinos with C++ in their special editing environment (Free download), and, once programmed, the Arduino automatically starts running it's routine upon applying power. See *www.arduino.cc* for more information about Arduinos.

# Digisparks

With so many microcontrollers available, these little guys have to be my favorite for small tasks. While they are not technically Arduinos, they are programmed with the same software and libraries and have many of the same characteristics – making them honorary Arduinos, in my book. A Digispark is pictured alongside an Arduino in *figure 6.6* below.

*Figure 6.6: An Arduino Uno R3 (left) and a Digispark (right)*

Digisparks are built around the `ATTtiny85` microcontroller with minimal memory for a program. Still, they are built onto a tiny circuit board (about the size of my thumb-tip) that plugs directly into a USB port for easy programming without cables. They come with *6* input/output pins and can PWM to control motors, read analog voltages and convert them to digital values, control relays, and more. Any time I need a straightforward task done, I reach for a Digispark.

# Conclusion

In this chapter, we've just touched the surface of some available hardware that you will likely need for your robot projects. We've learned how to choose a power supply, how to interface devices that have different configurations (USB to GPIO pin serial) or operate at different logic voltages, and how we can use microcontrollers to extend the capabilities of our primary computer.

We'll use at least some of these devices in the next chapter, where we add the central computer to our robot, wire it up, and test each component and interface. This is an important milestone, as having the completed robot platform allows us to focus on learning the part of robotics that gives them their smarts and autonomy – the software.

# Questions

1. You need to select a *5 volt* power supply for a robot with the devices listed below. What is the lowest rated (current) power supply you can use? Why is it a good idea to use a bigger one?

   *2.5 amps*          - Raspberry Pi 3

   *350 milliamps*   - LIDAR

   *125 milliamps*   - USB camera

   *60 milliamps*     - Motor driver control circuit (not motors)

   *35 milliamps*     - GPS/IMU/Misc Sensors

3. When can you use a voltage divider instead of a logic level shifter?

4. What is one thing an Arduino can do that a Raspberry Pi cannot?

# CHAPTER 7

# Adding the Computer to Control your Robot

## Introduction

It's time to install a computer that your robot will use to learn new tricks and make decisions on its own. This is the main controller that will take data from sensors, saved information about the environment, and your programming to become something much more capable than a remote-controlled toy.

The instructions in this chapter assume you've got a robot chassis with a battery, power supply suitable for your computer, wheel modules (with wheel encoders), and a motor driver. If you're not there yet, don't worry a bit – you can read through the chapter so you have a better idea of what to expect when you do start building. I highly recommend reading through the whole book before you start building or buying parts.

These instructions go with the robot build in *Chapter 21, Building and Programming, and Autonomous Robot* – the wiring diagrams, pin numbers, and sensors mentioned will match that final project. If you haven't read *Chapter 21* yet, you might want to look it over to get a good overview of the project. Similarly, you might benefit from reading the first few pages of *Chapter 14, Wheel Encoders for Odometry*, before you proceed with this chapter.

In this chapter, we're going to get your computer mounted and interfaced and tested with necessary sensors and motor drivers. This computer is going to be your primary interface to the rest of your robot's hardware, so it is essential to get it wired up and each component tested. After that, we can put down the tools for a while and focus on what I think is the most exciting part about robotics: `The programming`.

# Structure

In this chapter, we will be covering the following:

- Mount and run power to the computer
- Interface to wheel motors and test
- Interface to wheel encoders and test
- Optionally mount and test LIDAR and IMU

# Objective

Complete and test the basic robot platform.

# The steps

The following chapter is written very much for this book's example robot. If you are a bit more advanced and using this book and a more of a guide than a step by step, you may have chosen different hardware. It is fantastic if that is the case, but I obviously cannot document every possible hardware combination. The general steps are the same, but you'll have to do more homework on your own for wiring and coding instructions:

1. Mount and power the computer.
2. Wire computer to motor drivers and test that they respond to software.
3. Wire wheel encoders to computer and test that we can read them with software.

*Steps 1-3* are the basic requirements to start applying what we learn in the following chapters. With these steps complete, we can start learning to drive the robot and use feedback from the wheel encoders to keep track of its position. I've also included an `inertial measurement unit` (`IMU`) in the wiring diagram – it is optional but included in the final project. This is an I2C device, so any I2C devices you decide to add will connect to these same pins.

# Step 1 - Mount and run power to the computer:

Find a place on your robot to secure the computer – Ideally, layout every part you will need and decide now where they will go so you don't have to move things later. Some considerations when choosing a mounting location:

- Leave room to access all power, USB, video, camera, and other connectors – don't forget a little extra room for plugging in and unplugging!
- Speaking of connectors, don't forget they'll stick out a bit. If you mount a Raspberry Pi close to the edge of your robot, cables can overhang the robot and catch on things.
- Leave room for airflow for cooling. Packing the computer into a small space may look cool, but will likely lead to overheating sooner rather than later. You could add a cooling fan if this is what you want to do.

If it's a Raspberry Pi you're mounting, the mounting holes provided fit M2.5 screws and standoffs, but a careful person can drill the holes bigger to accommodate M3 screws if that's what you have. For easy building and prototyping, I've found that M3 standoffs hold well when screwed directly into a hole drilled into the wood. *Figure 7.1* below shows a Raspberry Pi and GPIO breakout headers secured this way.

***Figure 7.1:*** *Nylon standoffs for mounting and stacking components*

Once you've secured the computer, find the right place to secure your 5 volt power supply if you haven't and run power to the Pi. Use a shorter cable rather than a longer one and wire tie excess into a neat bundle. Don't plug it in just yet – complete the rest of the wiring first to avoid heart-breaking oopsies in the form of accidental shorts.

# Interface (wire) the computer to the rest of the Robot:

Now we need to wire the GPIO pins to the rest of the robot's hardware. Rather than trying to plug wires directly onto the computer's GPIO pins, I suggest using a breakout board with numbered screw-terminals. I'm using the one pictured in *figure 7.2* below. Optionally, prepare the empty circuit-board area with an I2C bus as described in *Chapter 21, Building and Programming an Autonomous Robot* before adding a bunch of other wires.

*Figure 7.2:* *A nicely labelled screw-terminal GPIO pin breakout board*

Whichever interfacing board you choose, mount it and connect it to your computer. The breakout board pictured below fits right onto the Raspberry Pi **40** pin GPIO header. Others use a **40** conductor IDE cable – this is the same cable that was once the standard cable for connecting hard disk drives.

With your breakout board mounted, you can wire your robot's hardware to it. Refer to *Chapter 4, Types of Robot Motors and Motor Control*, or *Chapter 14, Wheel Encoders for Odometry*, if you have questions. Also, remember that things might vary if you have chosen different components. You should have at least the following devices to wire if you want to follow our example build with a Raspberry Pi closely:

1. Wire the left wheel motor driver - recommended pin **21** for *PWM*, pin **26** for enabling *Forward*, pin **13** for enabling *Reverse*. Refer back to *Chapter 4, Types of Robot Motors and Motor Control* for motor wiring diagrams. Once it's wired, test

it for operation with `hello_motor` also from *Chapter 4* – taking care to make sure the pin numbers in the code match your wiring.

2.  Wire the right wheel motor driver - recommended pin **12** for *PWM*, pin **20** for enabling *Forward*, pin **19** for enabling *Reverse*. Then repeat the testing you did for the left wheel.

3.  Wire the right wheel encoder signal wire to pin **23**. You can test with the `hello_callback.cpp` from *Chapter 2, GPIO Hardware Interface Pins Overview and Use* or wait until we get through *Chapters 9, Coordinating the Parts,* and *Chapter 14, Wheel Encoders for Odometry. Chapter 14* has the final program we will use to read the encoders, but requires some foundational knowledge in *Chapter 9.* Either have the motor powered or turn the wheel by hand during the test, and make sure the pin numbers in the program match your wiring. Refer to *chapter 5* for wiring diagrams.

4.  Wire the left wheel encoder signal wire to pin **22** and repeat the tests you did for the right wheel encoder.

*Figure 7.3* below shows the complete diagram for the robot project built-in. This robot uses an *L298-based* motor driver, a pair of Roomba robot vacuum wheel modules with built-in hall-effect encoders, and an **LSM303** (*DLHC version*) IMU.

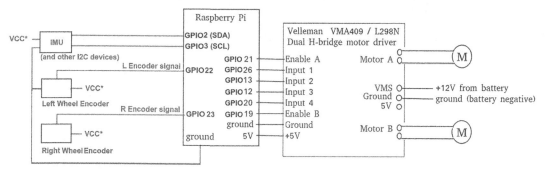

*VCC is the appropriate positive voltage for your devices
The Hall Effect encoders in the wheel modules I use are 5V
and the LSM303 IMU I use is 3.3V.
As always, check your device's documentation.*

***Figure 7.3:*** *The complete wiring diagram for this book's robot project*

A final step that can be done now or later is to add the IMU and any other I2C devices to the SDA and SCL (standard I2C pins – GPIO **2** and **3**). Test with an appropriate program, for example, the `hello_lsm303` IMU test program from *Chapter 5, Communication with Sensors and Other Devices.*

# Conclusion

This chapter should have been relatively straightforward and we should have mounted the robot's main computer and interfaced it to the motor drivers and wheel encoders. If everything went as planned, you should now have a basic robot platform that just needs a little code to get moving.

If any part doesn't work, I encourage you to review the past chapters and work and research until you've solved the problem before moving on to the next section. Don't be too discouraged – the best of us have learned far more by fixing mistakes than we ever could have by reading books alone.

When your robot platform is working and you're ready to move on, it might be a good time to pat yourself on the back and take a little break. When you come back, maybe bring a pencil and paper for just a little math as we learn some essential concepts in robot control. We'll learn how a couple of relatively simple control concepts work, and how one, in particular, is repeated over and over to make increasingly complex control decisions.

# Questions

1. Why should one resist the urge to pack the computer into a small space? What can be done to help the problem if you do?
2. If your Raspberry Pi GPIO breakout board doesn't attach directly to the pins, what kind of cable can you use to connect it?

# CHAPTER 8
# Robot Control Strategy

## Introduction

We spent the first seven chapters building a foundation of knowledge about robot hardware – learning everything from basic electronics to interfacing sensors with a computer that will be the brain of our autonomous machine. With that behind us, we can now look forward to the software that makes our robot more intelligent and able to perform tasks like navigating from place to place on its own.

In this chapter, we will learn some essential control fundamentals that can be applied to robotics as well as most other automated systems. We'll discuss the difference between controlling the overall machine and controlling specific parts of it (like a single motor) and learn how to do both. These are essential concepts that you'll need to write every level of robot control software or even get the best results out of software that already exists.

## Structure

In this chapter, we will cover the following:

- Robot control: The big picture versus the small picture
- The fundamental control loop

- Open-loop and closed-loop controllers
- Designing a big picture (also known as the master) controllers
- Designing a small picture (also known as a process) controllers

# Objectives

To learn the different types of robot controllers and gain an understanding of the first control loop. Use the first control loop in proportional controllers, and explore the nesting of simple control loops to handle complex processes.

# Robot control: The big picture versus the small picture

Imagine you are sitting in your cubicle at work, just starting an assignment your boss requested you complete by the end of the day. You have all the knowledge and tools and should have just enough time, so it's not a big deal. Now imagine that the cubicle next to yours is suddenly on fire. If you get up and leave, you won't likely be able to complete your task for the day - You have to make a decision, and fast!

After taking a moment to realize what is going on, you would likely weigh your options in order of importance: Your job is essential, but surviving takes a higher priority. Hence, you decide that some action besides sitting and continuing to work is required. Now you have to decide whether getting up and leaving is the best choice, or perhaps you could extinguish the fire and save the company a lot of damage.

*Is it worth the risk?*

*Would you be rewarded for your dedication or fired for violating company policy?*

This is an example of what I call your big picture controller (also known as **master controller**) at work. Your master controller can be thought of as the head honcho or big decision-maker of an organization like a business with hundreds of employees. While the manager might decide what overall task is to be completed next, he or she can't be bothered with every detail of what every employee is doing.

So your internal master controller decides you'd better leave the building and let the professionals fight the fire – great! It gives the order and sets it own resources back to paying attention for new information – because *what if there is a new danger that would necessitate another change of plans?* As far as your master controller is concerned, it gave the order, and these small picture things happen pretty much automatically.

But they don't happen automatically. It may feel automatic to us because we don't have to think about it actively. Still, they're in a motor control part of your brain dedicated to deciding which muscles to contract and in what order so you can stand up and move toward the exit. In case you're curious, physicians call the motor control part of your brain the *motor cortex*.

And the human body's motor controller is just one of many that worry about their own, specific little functions and nothing else. Your body has different controllers to regulate body temperature, blood pressure, and breathing rate – to name just a few. All of them take some inputs (some data about the state of the thing they are in charge of) and decide what to do next to achieve the desired condition. *Figure 8.1* below attempts to illustrate how several controllers in a robot work together to complete a task.

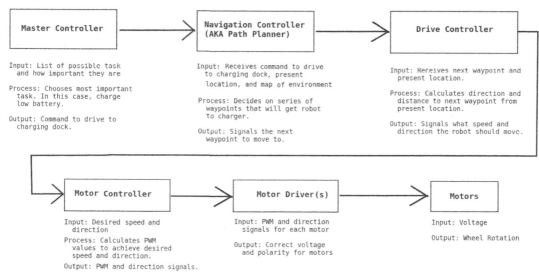

*Figure 8.1: Several layers of controllers are usually required to accomplish any task*

What I want you to take away right now is that when we talk about the `controller` in robotics, it is essential to know which one is being referred to. I'll try to be specific, but be aware in conversation people seem to assume often you know exactly which controller they are talking about and do not specify unless you ask. In essence, at least that's my experience in the controls industry. I could probably mail each of you this book for free if I had a dollar for every time I was asked to look at a problem with `the controller` without being told which one.

# The fundamental control loop

Controllers all use a general idea called a control loop that isn't too different from how we humans process information and make decisions. The general idea is that we follow specific steps over and over. Humans usually do it without thinking about it, but our robots are going to have to be programmed very explicitly to accomplish even simple control functions. Different texts use slightly different terminology for these necessary steps, but what they mean is the same:

1. Observe and compare
2. React
3. Affect

## Observe and compare

In this step, an assessment is made of the current state of the thing we want to control. This *thing* might be location, orientation, temperature, speed, angle of a joint, or countless other things. This *thing* is more formally known as the **process variable**, while the state is a measurement of its current condition. Look over *figure 8.2* below.

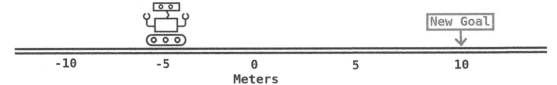

*Figure 8.2: Process variable, state, and error*

The controller compares the current state of the process variable (which is the location of the robot) with the desired state and calculates an error. The error is the difference between current and desired states. If our robot in *figure 8.2* only moves forward and backward and it is currently **-5** meters from home, if we give it a new destination of **10** meters, the error is *10 - (-5) = +15 meters*.

## React

Now that we have an error, we calculate and output an appropriate signal to the appropriate device to bring our error as close to *0* as we can get it. The device that affects change is usually known as the **actuator** and might be a heating element or motor driver, but depending on the level of our controller might be an entire system with its own controllers that handle the details on a small scale.

# Affect

Affect is the actual corrective action - such as the speed of the motor changing in response to our react step above.

Once this sequence is complete, we either assume the job is done, or we return to the first step and once again observe where we are, compare it to where we want to be, and so on. In programmer-speak, you might look at this sequence as a function called over and over in a loop until the function that called it decides that the task is complete or no longer necessary.

Consider this simple temperature controller function that could be part of your home thermostat's program:

```
void control_temp(int temperature, int desiredTemp){


    if (temperature < desiredTemp)

      {

         stop_air_conditioner();

         start_furnace();

      }

    else if (temperature > desiredTemp)

      {

         stop_furnace();

         start_air_conditioner();

      }

    else

      {

         stop_air_conditioner();

         stop_furnace();

      }


}
```

In this example, the process variable or *thing* we want to control is the temperature of our home. The state is the actual measured temperature and is passed to the controller function as the variable *temperature*.

Let's look at how it relates to our 3-step cycle:

**Observe and compare:** In this case, the observation step is handled by the argument temperature and desiredTemp being passed to the function. The variable temperature is the actual temperature in your home, and desiredTemp is the temperature we set the thermostat to. If they weren't passed as arguments, the control_temp() function would have to get this data by calling other functions itself.

However we get information to our function, the if/else statements compare the actual temperature and the desired temperature. The results of this comparison dictate what happens in the next step:

**React:** Once we've identified which comparison condition applies, we call the function needed to output the signal needed to turn on the furnace or air condition. If the actual and desired temperatures are the same, the error is 0, and we use the final else statement to make sure neither the furnace nor the air condition is running.

**Affect:** Happens in all the furnace and air_conditioner functions. These are controllers of sorts themselves that sequence and directly activate fans and gas valves, and so on.

 Notice that in the react step that when we send a signal out, we first make sure any conflicting equipment is shut Off. Here we don't want to heat and cooling on at the same time. In your robot, you may have to be careful not to send both forward and reverse enable signals to a motor driver.

In the actual writing of a controller function, our job stops to react. We have to know what our signals should do in the affect phase, but how that takes place is the job for either hardware or some other function. For the controller function we are writing at this moment, we are going to worry about only the three things every controller needs:

1. Input(s)
2. A function that makes the control decisions
3. An output

It sometimes helps to picture these in the flow diagram in *figure 8.3* below.

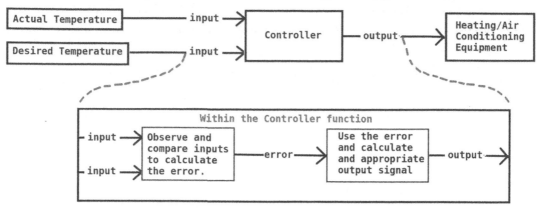

*Figure 8.3: The basic components of a controller: Inputs, a controller function, an Output*

*I know, I know.* You didn't buy this book to learn about controlling furnaces, but I wanted to drive home that these control fundamentals are universal – while the details change with the application, what I wanted you to see was the building blocks do not. See *figure 8.4* for a diagram that may feel more relevant.

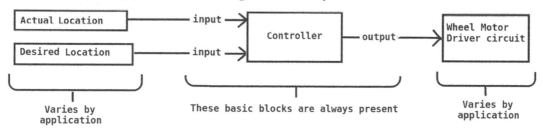

*Figure 8.4: Controllers all boil down to Inputs, a controller function, and an Output*

It's easy to see how these building blocks are the same. As we move on and start building more and more onto these blocks and even nesting them, I want you to hang on to some of the best advice my father ever gave me if you begin to feel lost or intimidated:

> *"Slow down and remember that these things are all the same - just different."*

# Open-loop and closed-loop controllers:

The simplest type of controller is called an open-loop controller. In this type, the controller takes its inputs, calculates an output, but does not monitor progress towards the goal. A closed-loop controller, on the other hand, takes repeated measurements of the progress we call feedback. Consider the robot control scenario from *figure 8.2* - the actual location was **-5M,** and the desired location was **10**.

An **open-loop controller** attempts to take advantage of known information, and presumes the outcome will be acceptable. It does not have feedback to *close the loop*, and I have wonder why it's called a loop at all when it looks more like a straight line – see *figure 8.5*.

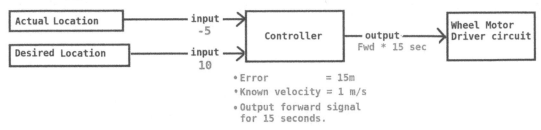

*Figure 8.5: An open loop control process handling the scenario in figure 8.4*

The controller calculates the difference between the actual and desired locations (the error) as **15M**, divides that by the anticipated velocity of **1** meter per second, then outputs the *go forward* signal for **15** seconds, and the system simply presumes that the robot ended up in the correct location.

In practice, though, it is not very likely that the robot ended up where we wanted it. Wheels can slip or get stuck. Batteries get low and mechanical parts like bearings to get old and dirty, causing velocity to be less than expected. What if your robot is a boat or aircraft? Now the wind and current will play a role in the final position. These or any number of factors routinely cause results that are different than what was calculated – and that makes open-loop control inappropriate for most robot control applications.

A **closed-loop controller**, on the other hand, can be well-equipped to handle the unexpected factors by monitoring progress towards the goal. Assuming our robot can't merely read the tape measure markings on the floor, we can use our sensors to measure how far we've traveled. This is constantly fed back as an input, so our drive controller can re-evaluate if it's still doing the right thing. The control diagram would look like *figure 8.6*.

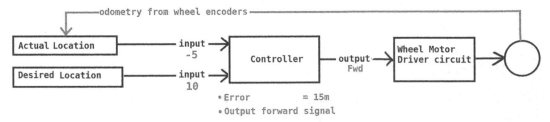

*Figure 8.6: A closed loop controller using feedback from wheel odometry to handle the scenario in figure 8.2*

In this simplest example of a closed-loop controller at work, the error is calculated, and the output is simply set to start the robot moving forward. Many times per second, odometry data is added to the input, and a new error calculated. The output continues driving the robot until the error reaches 0 without regard to how long it takes. Hopefully, we are in agreement that we should use closed-loop controllers for almost all of our autonomous robot controllers.

# Designing a big picture (also known as the master) controllers:

With so many different robot platform types, robot missions, and hardware variations, it won't be possible for me to give a comprehensive *how to* on master controllers. I do, however, want to give you some general ideas and a starting point that you can adapt as your project evolves.

I put master controllers in a separate subsection from other controllers because of a couple of notable differences that affect how we write our controller function:

1.  Instead of inputs being integer variables that we can directly compare to calculate an error, inputs are more like a list of possible actions. Our controller function has to decide which task is most important right now.
2.  Instead of outputting an integer value, the master controller will typically call a function that is going to act as a controller for a whole task. This controller will act as a sequencer that commands several things to happen in a particular order. This second controller is a master controller in its own right, but we usually try to give each of these a unique name to reduce confusion.

*What are we to do if we can't directly compare these inputs as integers?* We can assign integer values to them. Let's say we have a robot capable of the following routines:

- Dock and charge
- Update its map of the environment
- Follow user manually-entered drive commands
- Check the dog's water bowl
- Vacuum the floor

We can sort these into an array called the task list, in order of importance. *Figure 8.7* shows a simple array of strings (a robot's task list) sorted by importance.

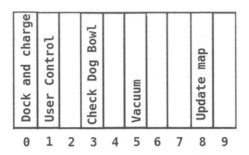

*Figure 8.7: Ordering tasks into an array by priority or importance*

*Notice the blank elements?* That is intentional because projects inevitably evolve, and tasks are added and removed. Leave yourself room. If memory is not an issue, there's no reason the size of this array can't be *100* or more. It would also work well to use a more advanced data structure if that is in your programming toolkit.

In addition to this array, let me introduce you to something called a **priority array**. This is a parallel array of the same size as the task array, but the data is of type bool. By lining these arrays up, the priority array element that corresponds to each task can be set as false if the task does not request, or true if the task is requested.

Our master controller function would iterate over the priority array and find the first (highest priority) task that is being requested, look up what that task is in the task list, and call the necessary function to handle that task. *Figure 8.8* should help illustrate the concept.

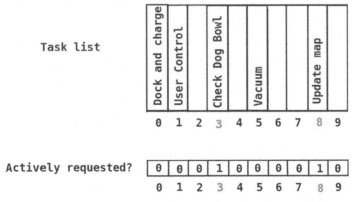

*Figure 8.8: Task list and priority array lined up*

There are two elements in the priority array set to true – check the dog bowl and update the map. Since taking care of a living creature is more important than checking to see if any new walls have been built, the programmer chose to place keeping the dogs watered in a higher priority position. When the master controller iterates over the priority array, it will see that element [3] is the most essential task being requested at the moment. It can then check our task array and see that element [3] means it is time to take care of the dogs and start that sequence. Updating the map will wait until other, more critical tasks are satisfied.

**The simple parallel array master controller model works well, but more advanced programmers might prefer one array of struct or class objects instead. The master function would just check a data member and then directly call a member function that starts the works in motion.**

You might be wondering: *What decides which elements in the priority array get set? Can you guess?* **Yep** – another controller that works independently of the master controller or other functions. Fortunately, these are usually simple functions with simple Boolean (true/false) outputs. The battery monitor would check the battery voltage, and if it's lower than some desired level, set element [0] to true for the master controller to catch on its next loop through. Another controller would flag element [1] if a user were sending commands, and the other tasks on this list are probably based on the time elapsed since last completed.

# Designing a small picture (also known as a process) controllers:

I find our small picture controllers more satisfying to design and code than big picture controllers, even if they involve a little more detail and math.

## Bang bang controllers (also known as On/Off controllers)

We've already talked about this simplest type of controller without naming it when we looked at the thermostat function control_temp() earlier in this chapter. The controllers response to any difference between the actual and desired state is to turn the responding element On or Off. There is no *gentle* response if the error is small and a little nudge would do.

Bang bang control cannot be used where precise control is required because, by the time our sensors indicate that it's time to turn off the output signal, we've often exceeded our desired state causing the controller output to *bang* in the other direction.

Not only does precision suffer, but the heat and abrupt forces of rapid reversal (or even just rapid start/stop) can also be hard on mechanical and electrical parts.

For these reasons we don't often see it in robot drives, but sometimes it's useful for accessory tasks – like the battery monitor function that controls the flag in *figure 8.8*.

# Proportional controllers

This is the type of controller I am going to focus on for this book. Imagine that you want to move your car from a spot in the driveway to inside the garage – the desired location is maybe *8* meters from the actual location. `Would you slam on the gas to pull your car in?` I am guessing you would barely give any throttle at all – just enough to nudge the car forward. What if the car was *50* meters away? You might give a bit more gas but still wouldn't try to achieve freeway speeds.

This is the idea behind a proportional controller – an output signal (your foot on the gas, in the above example) that is proportional to the magnitude of the error. Now we're talking about a practical controller suitable for robot drive motors.

Let's get right to designing a proportional drive controller to control our 1D robot's velocity, starting with the basic formula:

$$output = gain * error$$

*It's not too bad, right?* To design our controller we have to consider what our output range is – usually for a robot drive controller we want to output velocity in meters per second, so our minimum desired out would likely be *0* m/s, and our maximum would depend on our hardware and environment (not yet considering where we might have to reverse and output a negative velocity). I am going to assume a robot with a maximum desired velocity of *1* m/s.

To get our gain value, we have to ask ourselves: `At what amount of error do I want my robot to achieve full speed?` We certainly don't want it jumping to full speed to move a few centimeters – but we don't want it wasting time at low speeds if it has to cross a football field, either. What is realistic or desirable here will depend on the mass of your robot and some other factors, and you'll likely be adjusting this gain value during some testing. I am thinking that taking *2* meters to accelerate to and from *0* to *1* meter per second is reasonable, so I want to achieve my maximum output when the error has reached two meters.

So having identified as many variables as possible, we can start working our equation in *figure 8.9*.

```
output = 1 m/s          output = gain * error
gain   = ?                   1 = gain * 2
error  = 2 m
                         gain = 1/2 = .5
```

Plug gain in to get our function formula:  `output = .5 * error`

*Figure 8.9: Basic proportional drive controller gain calculation*

With our gain calculated, we can write our function that takes input x for error and calculates an output that steadily increases from *0* to *1* m/s as we approach an error of *2* meters. Look over the output graph in *figure 8.10*; there are a few specific things I hope you notice.

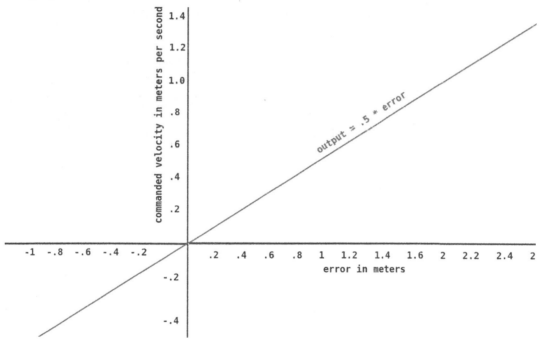

*Figure 8.10: Output graph of example proportional controller*

The first thing I want you to notice is that this is just a straight line (also known as **linear**) function in the slope-intercept form. If you recall from *Algebra* whenever it was you took that, the formula for a linear function is $y = m * x + b$ where m is the slope and b is an offset up or down the *y axis*. Our proportional controller formula is the same. Although I omitted writing the offset b for simplicity and because I presumed that our robot would be stationary with an output of *0*. That may not always be the case; however – a drone fighting gravity or a boat fighting a steady river current would always need that offset included or a different type of controller function entirely. *Figure 8.11* shows a comparison between the proportional control formula and the standard linear equation.

```
output = 1 m/s          output = gain * error + offset
gain   = ?                   1 = gain * 2 + 0
error  = 2 m
offset = 0               gain = 1/2 = .5
```

        Proportional Controller Formula

```
y = output = output      y = m * x + b
m = slope  = gain        1 = m * 2 + 0
x = input  = error
b = offset = offset      m = 1/2
```

          Standard Linear Equation

Resulting Formula:
output = .5 * error + 0

Resulting Formula:
y = .5 * x + 0

*Figure 8.11:* *The proportional controller formula and the standard linear equation*

The second observation is that our proportional controller happily handles negative error values and appropriately outputs a negative velocity command; we just have to catch that negative value to make sure our motor drivers reverse the motors. See the example cases in *figure 8.12* below and notice the output of the second case.

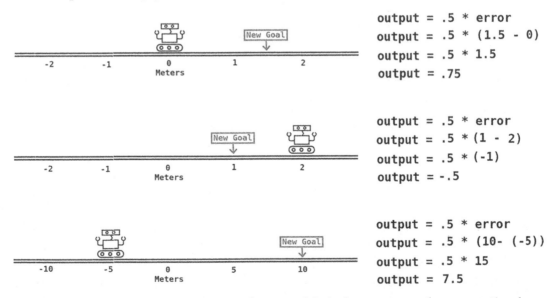

```
output = .5 * error
output = .5 * (1.5 - 0)
output = .5 * 1.5
output = .75
```

```
output = .5 * error
output = .5 * (1 - 2)
output = .5 * (-1)
output = -.5
```

```
output = .5 * error
output = .5 * (10- (-5))
output = .5 * 15
output = 7.5
```

*Figure 8.12:* *A positive, a negative, and an out-of-desired-range output from proportional controller*

*Whoah! What happened in the third case?* We had previously decided that our maximum velocity should be *1* meter per second, yet our controller is commanding *7.5* m/s. Unless our hardware is not capable of exceeding *1* m/s, it will be the programmer's job to catch out-of-bounds cases and handle them. A simple if statement right before we output the signal will do, like in the following sample code:

```
void Velocity_Controller()

{

const int k = .5; //Our gain. usually denoted with a 'k'

const int offset = 0;

const int MAX_VELOCITY = 1;

int cmdVel = 0; //our output. Stands for "command Velocity"

int desired = 0; //desired location

int current = 0; //current location


while(1)

    {

    desired = Get_Desired();

    current = Get_Current();

    int error = desired - current;

    cmdVel = k*error+offset;


    if(cmdVel > MAX_VELOCITY)

        {

        cmdvel = MAX_VELOCITY;

        }


    publish(cmdVel);

    time_sleep(.1); //delay to set 10 HZ publish frequency

    }

}
```

This controller could be implemented as is (for a robot that moves only forward and backward), but it honestly borders on pseudocode. Learn from it how a controller might be coded, but in practice, we are probably going to get our inputs a different way. As for the publish(cmdVel) function call, all that means is that it will publish the output value in a way that our motor controller can read it and, in turn, output the appropriate PWM and direction signals for the electronic motor driver circuit.

 **It might be tempting to skip a step and write a velocity controller that directly outputs a PWM signal. In my opinion, this would be a mistake for reasons that should become apparent in the very next chapter.**

## Designing controllers to accept some error

I hate to be the one to give bad news, but you're rarely going to achieve a state with 0 error, no matter how well you code your controller.

You might measure your robot's position with a tape measure and think it's where it belongs, but *is it really precisely on that 2 meter mark that you think you see?* Or *is it 2.000001 meters?* Because your robot would keep trying to correct for that extra micrometer but probably never get it just right. This is a problem because if the robot never reports that it has arrived at the assigned goal location, it will not continue to its next task.

To deal with this problem, we have to give some boundaries that we call close enough. If our robot has to go to the 20 meter mark on a track to retrieve a bin in a warehouse, instead of coding:

```
double desired = 20;

while(current != desired)

    {

    keep_trying();

    }
```

We need to code something along the lines of:

```
double cushion = .01;

while(current < desired - cushion || current > desired + cushion)

    {

    keep_trying()
```

}

Which of the above two functions will allow the robot to stop and report that it's ready for the next step?

## Setting a minimum output

One shortcoming of the proportional controller is that a robot will never actually reach its goal location with only the output from the proportional formula. As the robot gets close, the formula will output some very small signals that will be too small to move the robot at all.

This minimum level will vary by an individual robot but consider as an example that PWM signals to motor driver boards commonly have a range from *0* to *255*. If the robot is close enough, the proportional formula will output something as low as *10* or *20*, but many motors won't turn at all with a PWM signal that's less than *50* or *60* or *100* – it depends on the motor. For this reason, it is necessary to include a minimum PWM value – if the drive controller is asking for a value less than what will turn the motors, we have to output instead of the minimum that will turn the motor. It is also possible to monitor wheel speed and increase the PWM signal while wheels have a speed of 0. This can help get the robot moving – which takes more power (and a greater PWM sgnal) than to remain moving once started.

## Beyond proportional controllers

While the proportional controller we will use in this book is a great starting point and miles ahead of the bang bang controller, there may come a time that you find it's not performing as well as you need it to. For all it's pure greatness, the proportional controller (also known as `P controller`) still has its shortcomings.

Sure, crude offsets can be made if we do need some constant output other than *0* to maintain the desired state. Still, it's not very accurate – especially if we have to counter varying external forces like wind or as our speed increases, and we want to make corrections on the go. Smoothly covering that last little distance as a robot approaches, but has not yet reached its goal, is another situation in which proportional-only controllers struggle. For these situations, adding integral and derivative influences to our proportional controller can increase responsiveness and make for an overall more robust controller. This is known as the `proportional integral derivative` (`PID`) control.

PID controllers allow us a level of precision and responsiveness that the simple proportional controller cannot match but comes at the cost of a higher level of mathematics than I wanted to force upon everyone here. Those of you comfortable with some essential calculus should not have a hard time adding the $I$ and $D$ components to your $P$ controllers – there are several tutorials to be found on the Internet.

# Conclusion

Controllers are such an essential part of every automated machine you would do well to make sure you understand the material in this chapter – researching further if necessary (recommended regardless, as we have only scratched the surface). Start noticing the key control loop in everyday machines and find it embedded deep within any code you are trying to decipher. Make control loops as second nature as can be, because almost everything else you in robotics is going to rely heavily on them.

We learned about master controllers and process controllers, how they all take an input, make a decision, and output some signal. We also learned how several simple controllers could be chained together to accomplish more complex tasks, and we studied proportional process controllers in some detail. Finally, we learned the basics of a master controller that can make the big decisions for our robots.

Now that we understand controllers and are beginning to see how many there are, we've got to be wondering how we keep it all manageable. Fear not – for our next chapter is about keeping coordinating the parts and keeping them manageable. Take a break. Hydrate. Stretch your legs or take a nap. When you come back, we are going to learn how to use software that makes it relatively easy to organize and coordinate dozens of little programs. Widely used in academics and research (and increasingly in commercial robots), **Robot operating system** (**ROS**) provides many helpful tools for running and troubleshooting your robot.

# Questions

1. Your drone has a forward airspeed of *6* meters per second. You programmed it to fly *30* meters in still air, then stop and hover with an open-loop controller. How many seconds will the drone fly? How many meters did the drone end up flying if the tailwind unexpectedly picked up to *2* meters per second?

2. Calculate a proportional controller formula for a robot with a desired top speed of *4* meters per second when the error is *6* meters.

3. What is a situation that the proportional controller is not ideal for, and what is the solution?

# CHAPTER 9

# Coordinating the Parts

## Introduction:

There is no way around it; autonomous robots have a lot going on. We've covered eight chapters worth of foundational knowledge – like we were gathering the ingredients for a gourmet recipe. I'm not much of a cook, but I know the good ones have a system for keeping their kitchen well-organized with everything they might need readily available but nothing in the way. We need a similar approach to build our robot's software package, or things will quickly become an unmanageable mess – sometimes even a burned mess!

In this chapter, we'll add a powerful software to our toolbox that can help us coordinate the dozens of input, output, and controller functions that need to freely share information between each other (and sometimes between different computers). Keeping the many functions and bits of data across an entire robot is an essential piece of the robotics puzzle, and what you learn in this chapter can save you months or even years getting your robot deployed. Let's get cooking.

 **More than other chapters, we're going to need some necessary Linux command-line skills. If you're not at least comfortable navigating the file system, you really might want to take a break and find a quick Linux intro.**

# Structure:

In this chapter, we will cover the following:

- What is the Robot operating system (ROS)
- ROS versus writing your robot control software
- ROS and the commercial robotics industry
- ROS setup
- ROS overview and crash-course
- A Handful of helpful tips
- Creating and writing ROS packages and nodes
- Making life easier with launch files

# Objective

To gain a useful familiarity with the Robot Operating System (ROS) and write our first robot control function.

# What is the robot operating system?

Despite its name, **Robot Operating System** (almost always just called **ROS**) is not an operating system – it is a de facto software framework that handles the communication between software components called **nodes**. It's much more a middleware than it is an operating system and currently runs best on Ubuntu flavors of the Linux operating system.

ROS nodes can be started and stopped on the fly, allowing you to make changes or even try completely different ones while the rest of a robot is still running. This is great because you can bring new sensors online, add new routines, or try different algorithms (for path-planning, for example) without recompiling and restarting the entire system. Nodes can be run on more than one computer, allowing for the sharing of processing duties or even collaboration between robots.

ROS does this by acting as a kind of information hub – any node can broadcast or publish information, and ROS makes that information available to any other node that subscribes to it. It serves as a master clock, parameter server, and package manager. Additionally, ROS comes with simulation, troubleshooting, and visualization tools ready to go when you choose a full installation (recommended).

# ROS versus writing your robot control software

Nothing is stopping you from choosing to write your software suite entirely on your own, except for perhaps the time commitment. You could certainly write the folders and folders of include files and classes, then some framework of your own to tie them all together and control the flow of data and processes. If that's your idea of a good time, then by all means.

I have to warn you that it can get big and messy – especially if you're still learning robotics basics at the same time.

In any case, going the `I can do this all myself` route usually results in a frustrated, half-implemented, minimally functional project that is slow to evolve. The original goal of having a robotics platform to try different techniques and tweak and perfect routines is often lost or slowed to a snail's pace. This was my experience when I thought `I don't need ROS - what's the fun if someone else wrote all the code?`

Since you're here, I'm going to assume you would rather spend your time learning and implementing robotics algorithms than writing code forever - ROS can help you do that. Enough ROS code is available (in working bundles called **packages**) that you can often get away with writing incredibly little code, or you can write your custom packages as you wish. Often the case is we want a working platform right away; then, we can choose individual packages to tweak and experiment with.

Early on, I underestimated how much more I could learn about robotics by using ROS and focusing on individual packages rather than writing the entire codebase myself. I'm going to encourage you to avoid that mistake and use ROS to learn how robots tick. You can always write your codebase from the ground up once you have a good handle on building and programming robot projects in ROS – and you'll save yourself a ton of time and frustration overall.

# ROS and the commercial robotics industry

I'm including this short section for those interested in a robotics career in the commercial sector and are concerned about ROS being a waste of their time. It's a legitimate question since not long ago, the feeling in the industry was that ROS is for academic institutions, and robotics companies don't use ROS. I am happy to tell you with certainty that the tide has turned.

Earlier in the robot revolution, many companies preferred to keep their software and techniques proprietary. The idea was that when they made big breakthroughs, they could be *the* company with such and such capabilities and leave their competitors in the dust. It seemed like a good idea, until none of them made the progress they had hoped for on their own.

CEOs of many robotics companies have realized that the industry as a whole has been slow to advance due to the lack of information sharing, and every company has a lot more to gain if the advancements are made that allow robots to become part of daily life for the average consumer. Further, they realized the benefits of being able to hire developers already familiar with some standard software and practices compared to having to spend sometimes months training new hires before they can start working on a proprietary project. I heard these statements first hand at the `2019 Robotics Summit` and Expo by CEOs and developers from dozens of companies. Their message both in seminars and in one-on-one chats could be summarized as: We started using ROS because it significantly increased our talent pool and speed of development.

If that's not enough to convince you of the power and impending prevalence, perhaps it would help to know that a consortium of companies (including many you know) has sent dozens of experienced developers to collaborate full-time on the software, standards, and conventions for ROS2. I am now a believer that ROS will have an even more significant presence in commercial robotics in the years to come, and hope you are too.

This is not a book about ROS, and you'll want to learn a lot more than we are going to learn here, but the rest of my examples and our final project in *Chapter 21* will use ROS. As such (Pandering to my personal belief that `paint-by-numbers` tutorials are largely a waste of time), it only fits that we cover enough of the basics that you can use ROS with your code, not just mine or what you can download. Let's get ROS set up on your computer; then we can dive right into the `how-to` part.

# ROS setup

At the minimum, you're going to need to install ROS on the computer acting as your robot's brain. Since we have been using a Raspberry Pi 3B with the *Lubuntu 16.04* operating system for our example projects, I will walk you through two ways of installing ROS on that. Additionally, I think you'll find it highly useful to install ROS on your laptop or desktop computer. If that's the case, I hope you have it loaded with *Ubuntu 18.04*.

ROS versions are released with alphabetically-increasing code-names, much like Linux distros are. There are two currently supported releases of ROS called *Kinetic* and *Melodic*, and no shortage of disagreement over which is *better*. I use both, and they have played well together as far as networking and message-passing, and I have yet to have one of my packages work on one but not the other. There are some differences in some packages (ROS code-bundles available for download) being supported on only one or the other. Still, in most cases of needing a package on the unsupported platform, I have been able to add them by git cloning the repository and compiling manually. Don't worry; I'll cover that in a bit.

What I'm saying is don't sweat too much over which is *the best* version. If you are running *Ubuntu 18.04*, *ROS Melodic Morenia* is the supported version, and installing that will be most comfortable. This may be the case with your laptop or desktop, but any Raspberry Pis you are installing on should be running *Lubuntu 16.04*, and the supported ROS version is *Kinetic Kame*.

*My recommendation?* Download and install the ROS version that is supported for your Linux version.

# ROS melodic installation on your laptop or desktop

To install ROS Melodic on your laptop or desktop, head to *wiki.ros.org/ROS/ Installation*, click on the option for **Melodic**, and follow the instructions carefully. You'll notice some newer options for installing on Debian Linux and even Windows. Still, as of this time, problems have been reported and fixing the little bugs you are likely to encounter is not well-documented enough for those new to ROS, in my opinion. I encourage you to stick to installing on Ubuntu (or Lubuntu).

# ROS kinetic installation on your Raspberry Pi 3B

To install ROS Kinetic on your Raspberry Pi 3B, you have two choices I have vetted, and I have one confession to make: You didn't have to install and setup Lubuntu the hard way that we did in chapter one. The easy way is a complete image with Lubuntu and ROS already running upon the first bootup. Still, it is provided via a private company's website, and they theoretically could decide to stop sharing it any time they wish. (I don't see that happening, but they could).

**Option 1:** To install ROS on your Raspberry Pi 3B *the easy way* to follow these steps:

1. Download the latest Raspberry Pi image from *ubiquityrobotics.com/download.*

2. Use a tool like *balenaEtcher* (download from *balena.io/etcher*) to write the downloaded image file to a micro SD card.

3. Put the micro SD card into your Raspberry Pi and boot it up. You can follow the instructions on their **Downloads** page to get going without a monitor, but I find it much easier to use a monitor anyway.

4. Unless you have a *Magni* robot - we want to stop their startup scripts because this is the exact image that gets shipped in their *Magni* robot, and your hardware is not likely the same. Do this with the systemctl utility from the command line:

   4.1. Stop the magni-specific startup scripts with sudo systemctl disable magni-base.

   4.2. Disable roscore autostart with sudo systemctl disable roscore.service.

5. Set the PIGPIO daemon to autostart at bootup (optional).

   5.1. Enables PIGPIO daemon to start at bootup with sudo systemctl enable pigpiod.service.

   5.2. Start the daemon right now with sudo systemctl start pigpiod.service

6. Optionally delete the Ubiquity packages in the catkin workspace we'll be discussing shortly. They won't hurt anything by being there, but I like an uncluttered workspace.

**Option 2:** To install ROS on your raspberry Pi 3B *the official way* is going to be a bit more involved. Before anything else, we must open the Lubuntu software center and set it to allow downloading from *restricted*, *universe*, and *multiverse* repositories. A couple of these are disabled by default, so don't skip this step.

1. Find the software center by clicking the menu button, then system tools. Click and open the Lubuntu software center.

2. Use the arrow and open the **Preferences** tab.

3. Open **Software properties**.

4. Check the boxes to allow from main, restricted, universe, and multiverse.

5. Close the software center.

With permissions all set, we can install ROS following these steps from *http://wiki.ros.org/kinetic/Installation/Ubuntu*. I highly recommend navigating to the installation page itself, so you better understand what you are doing and to make sure you have the latest information. These are all commands to enter on the command line.

1. sudo sh -c 'echo "deb http://packages.ros.org/ros/ubuntu $(lsb_release -sc) main" > /etc/apt/sources.list.d/ros-latest.list'

2. sudo apt-key adv --keyserver 'hkp://keyserver.ubuntu.com:80' --recv-key C1CF6E31E6BADE8868B172B4F42ED6FBAB17C654

3. `sudo apt-get update`
4. `sudo apt-get install ros-kinetic-desktop-full`

That is the official install part, but we still need to initialize `rosdep` and set up some environmental variables to allow us to use ROS commands from any terminal without navigating to a specific directory or typing long absolute paths for every command. The last line is to install some ROS dependencies as well as `rosinstall` - a tool that will undoubtedly make your life easier down the road.

1. `sudo rosdep init`
2. `rosdep update`
3. `echo "source /opt/ros/kinetic/setup.bash" >> ~/.bashrc`
4. `source ~/.bashrc`
5. `sudo apt install python-rosinstall python-rosinstall-generator python-wstool build-essential`

And finally, the last thing we need to do before we get started is set you up a workspace called a **catkin workspace**. While ROS is installed elsewhere, your catkin workspace is where you will organize your project. Any packages you create will go here, as well as many you clone from the internet. The build system known as catkin will help you set up, manage, and build your project.

1. `mkdir -p ~/catkin_ws/src`
2. `cd ~/catkin_ws/`
3. `catkin_make`

*Still with me?* Good! I know that was a pain, but we are finally done with the boring setup stuff and ready to start using ROS after a quick test!

**ROS quick-test**

Before we move on, it's worthwhile to make sure our installation went Ok and start roscore – which is the ROS master node. If you have problems with this little test, review and re-try the whole installation from the top – and read up on the ROS *Wiki* pages. Error messages often tell you exactly what is missing, and sometimes Googling the error message will take you to someone else's question about the same and answers from the community.

 **roscore is at the center of your ROS projects and must be started before any other nodes. If roscore is stopped and restarted, other nodes already running will have lost their connection and will need to be restarted as well.**

At the command prompt, enter the command:

```
roscore
```

And give it a minute to fire up. Hopefully, you get an error-free output similar to *figure 9.1*, below.

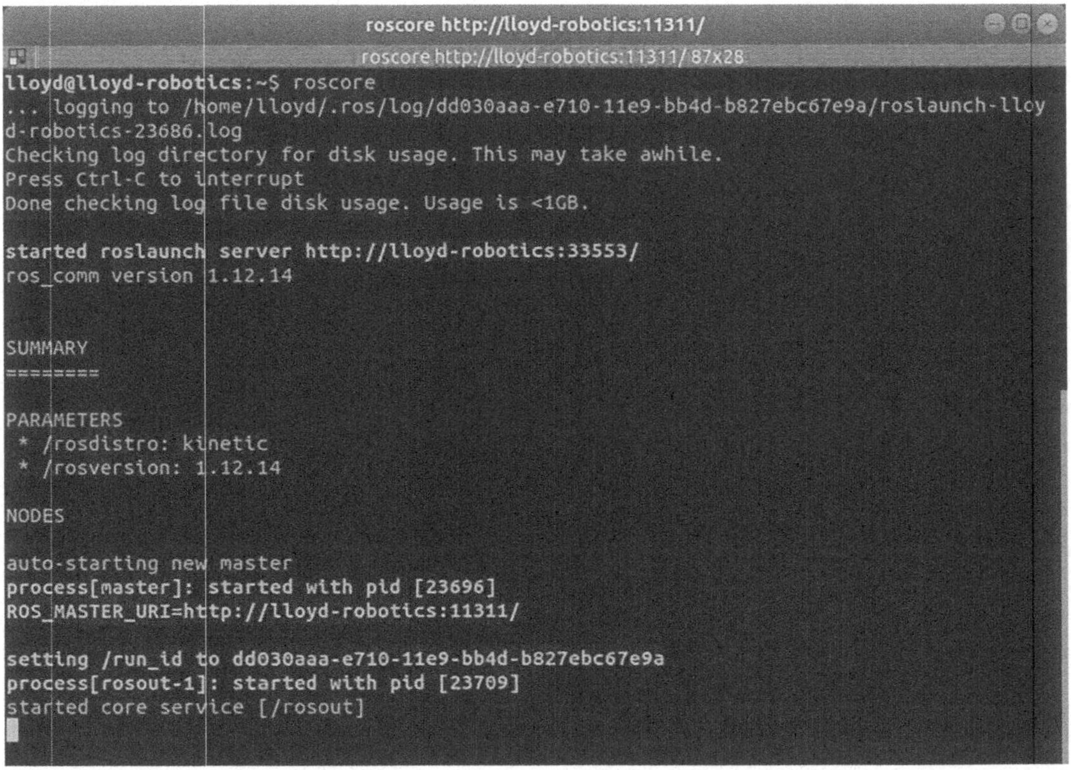

**Figure 9.1:** *A successful start of roscore*

*Good?* Congratulations – you have successfully started the ROS master node and can now start and stop other nodes at will. Now we can dive into learning how to use ROS!

# ROS overview and crash-course

ROS projects consist of nodes that each handle a specific task. You can almost think of them as functions in a program – they take some information, make some decisions, and send some information back out for a user, another function, or even a piece of external hardware.

Unlike a function that we might directly call and wait for a return value, ROS nodes act independently. Once set in motion, they will read and process information or broadcast messages whether any other node is listening or not if the information they need is available to them. This broadcasting information between nodes is called publishing a message to a topic while listening for published messages is called **subscribing**. For this reason, you will often here a node referred to as a publisher or subscriber.

Let's get our keyboards dirty with some publishers and subscribers. You can do these first tutorials with your laptop if you've installed ROS on it – you don't necessarily have to use your robot's brain yet.

# Packages, nodes, publishers, subscribers, topics, and messages

Nodes are bundled into related bunches called **packages**. With roscore already running, open a new terminal window and type the following command:

```
rosrun turtlesim turtlesim_node
```

- rosrun is the command to launch a node.

- turtlesim is the name of a package that has several cool nodes for learning how ROS works.

- turtlesim_node is the name of a node

When you hit *Enter*, you should see a blue field pop up with a turtle in the middle of it. For some basic things, you can consider it to be a simulated robot. turtlesim_ node is just one node in the package called turtlesim. You can see the other nodes available in the turtlesim package by opening another terminal window and typing the following:

```
rosrun turtlesim <tab><tab>
```

You should see the names of a few available nodes pop up, and the next line is the command prompt exactly where you left off, so you don't have to retype anything. Instead of starting another node just yet, hit *Ctrl + C* to quit and get back to an empty command line. The turtlesim_node window and list of available nodes in the turtlesim package are shown in *figure 9.2* below.

*Figure 9.2: The turtlesim_node (left) and available nodes in the turtlesim package (right)*

If you tried some arrow keys or mouse inputs to drive your turtle, you were undoubtedly disappointed by its lack of response. Don't worry, and it's not broken. Let's use the `rostopic` command to get our first clue as to what is going on. Type the following command:

```
rostopic <tab><tab>
```

And you'll see a list of available `rostopic` commands. *Do you see a pattern?* The `<tab>` key gives you a list of possible completions to any command you start typing. You can even type just the first few letters of a command, and it will autocomplete for you if there is only one choice. We are going to use the `list` command, so complete the command to see a list of currently active topics.

```
rostopic list
```

The first two topics listed, `rosout` and `rosout_agg` are present any time `roscore` is running. The topics directly relevant to our simulated robot-turtle happen to be bundled under the `turtle1` namespace. The output of your `rostopic list` command should look like *figure 9.3*.

```
lloyd@lloyd-robotics:~$ rostopic
bw     echo  find  hz    info  list  pub    type
lloyd@lloyd-robotics:~$ rostopic list
/rosout
/rosout_agg
/turtle1/cmd_vel
/turtle1/color_sensor
/turtle1/pose
lloyd@lloyd-robotics:~$ 
```

*Figure 9.3: The output of the rostopic list command*

To see what the `turtle1/cmd_vel` is all about, use `rostopic info`.

`rostopic info turtle1/cmd_vel`

And the output will list:

- The message type
- The nodes that publish the topic
- The nodes that subscribe to the topic

We'll come back to message types; for now, just know that `cmd_vel` is the commonly-used name for the ROS message used for issuing velocity commands. I want you to notice the publishers and subscribers. Our `turtlesim` is subscribing – just waiting to receive commands to move.

*Where do those commands come from?*

We can see that right now; nothing is publishing velocity commands. You've got a car in the driveway with the motor running, but no one sitting behind the wheel to step on the gas or turn the wheel! What you see on your screen should look similar to *figure 9.4* below.

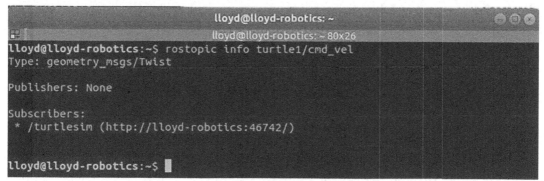

***Figure 9.4:*** *The output of the rostopic info command*

To publish velocity commands, we need to launch a suitable node. Open yet another terminal window and launch the node `turtle_teleop_key` from the `turtlesim` package.

`rosrun turtlesim turtle_teleop_key`

Now, as long as the window you just started `turtle_teleop_key` in is the selected window, pressing the arrow keys will make the turtle move.

*How does it do this?* In another terminal window, run `rostopic info` on the topic `turtle1/cmd_vel` again, and you'll see that the `turtle_teleop_key` node publishes velocity commands to the topic.

*Are you noticing another pattern?* The use of rosrun takes two arguments.

1. The first argument is the name of the package the desired node is part of.
2. The second argument is the name of the node itself. It's always.

```
rosrun <package name> <node name>
```

The final piece of the puzzle is the message type. Messages types are custom data types – class objects with one or more data members. Some messages contain just simple data members like integers, while some messages are a collection or several other messages. This just means when a node creates a message, and they are creating an object of a class. Sometimes that object contains several other objects as it's data members. Accessing the data members happens the same way as it does for accessing data members in non-ROS objects.

 Hopefully, you're comfortable enough with classes and objects in C++. I am trying to avoid them as much as possible for my code examples to keep them simple for beginners, but classes and objects are an integral part of ROS (and C++) as a whole. I can't recommend enough that you find some tutorials and get a solid understanding.

*Figure 9.4* showed us that the cmd_vel message publishes the message of type geometry_msgs/Twist. You can get a look at the data members in a geometry_msgs/Twist message with the rosmsg info command. Look over the output in *figure 9.5* or, better yet, try it yourself.

```
rosmsg info geometry_msgs/Twist
```

Notice that the geometry_msgs/Twist message contains two separate messages that both happen to be Vector3 messages (which are also part of the geometry_msgs package), and could be used in a node and published all by themselves if you wish. Using rosmsg info on the Vector3 message shows us that this is a collection of 3 floating-point values called x, y, and z. Don't just take my word for it.

```
rosmsg info geometry_msgs/Vector3
```

You can see the output of rosmsg info for both the Twist and Vector3 messages below in *figure 9.5.*

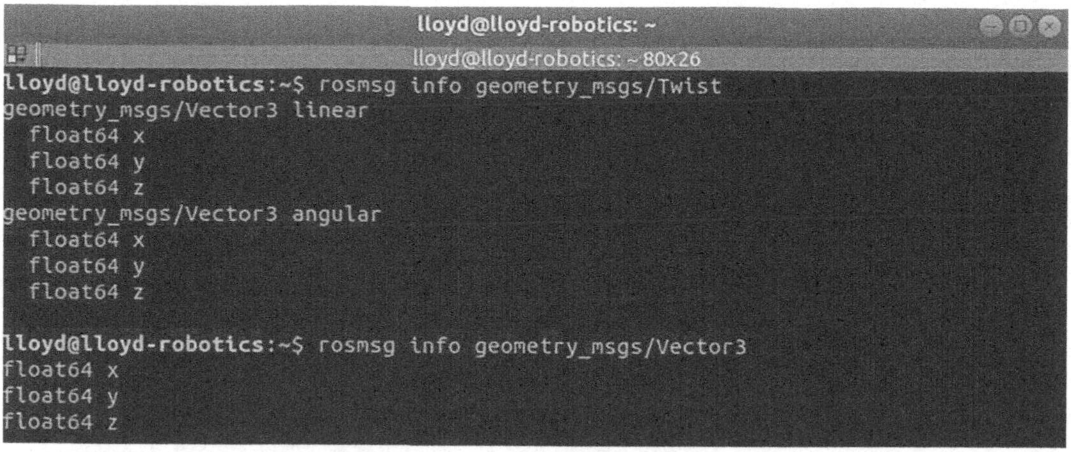

```
                         lloyd@lloyd-robotics: ~
                         lloyd@lloyd-robotics: ~ 80x26
lloyd@lloyd-robotics:~$ rosmsg info geometry_msgs/Twist
geometry_msgs/Vector3 linear
  float64 x
  float64 y
  float64 z
geometry_msgs/Vector3 angular
  float64 x
  float64 y
  float64 z

lloyd@lloyd-robotics:~$ rosmsg info geometry_msgs/Vector3
float64 x
float64 y
float64 z
```

*Figure 9.5: The output of the rosmg info command*

There are hundreds of ROS message types and, while `rosmsg info` is convenient, you should spend some time perusing *wiki.ros.org/common_msgs* to get an idea of the many, many messages already defined in ROS and spread out over several packages. You should also keep in mind that you can create your own custom message types if you can't find one that quite suits your needs. Reading over *wiki.ros.org/msg* can give you a much better understanding of messages.

As far as what these x, y, and z values are – these are the inputs to a drive controller. For a simple, non-flying robot we use the linear x value for forward velocity, and ignore the y value (unless our robot can move sideways without rotating) and the z value, as this would pertain to an aircraft or perhaps a climbing robot. The standard unit used for linear velocities in ROS is meters per second.

The angular values are for the rate of rotation – how fast we turn. For our wheeled robot, we usually can only rotate right and left – as viewed from the top down. This would be the angularz value, typically in radians per second. (I'll give a quick review of radians in *Chapter 10*)

You can use the `rostopic echo` command with any message listed when you run `rostopic list` to view the live-stream of the content of these messages. With `roscore`, a `turtlesim_node`, and the turtle_teleop_key all running, arrange your windows so you can see your turtle, your `teleop` window, and another terminal window with a command prompt and type the following:

```
rostopic echo turtle1/cmd_vel
```

Now click on your `teleop` window to make that the active window and drive your turtle around with the arrow keys. Observe the output of the echo window, and compare it to the motion of your turtle - A positive linear x value sends the turtle forward, a negative linear x sends it backward. ROS conventions tell us that a positive angular z value rotates the turtle clockwise, while a negative angular z rotates it counter-clockwise. See how I laid out my windows and the `rostopic echo cmd_vel` output in *figure 9.6* below.

***Figure 9.6:*** *Monitoring messages with rostopic echo*

Now that you know that a ROS message is just a collection of data being sent from one node to another node, I hope it's apparent that any node can publish or subscribe to any topic. For example, press *Ctrl + C* in your `teleop_key` window to close the node, then launch a node called `rqt_robot_steering` in the package also called `rqt_robot_steering`.

*Can you think of how to launch it? That's right!*

`rosrun rqt_robot_steering rqt_robot_steering`

A little GUI window pops up, allowing you to publish `cmd_vel` messages using sliders in the window. If you try to drive right away, you'll notice that it doesn't move your turtle just yet.

*Can you figure out why?* I left you a clue in *figure 9.7* below.

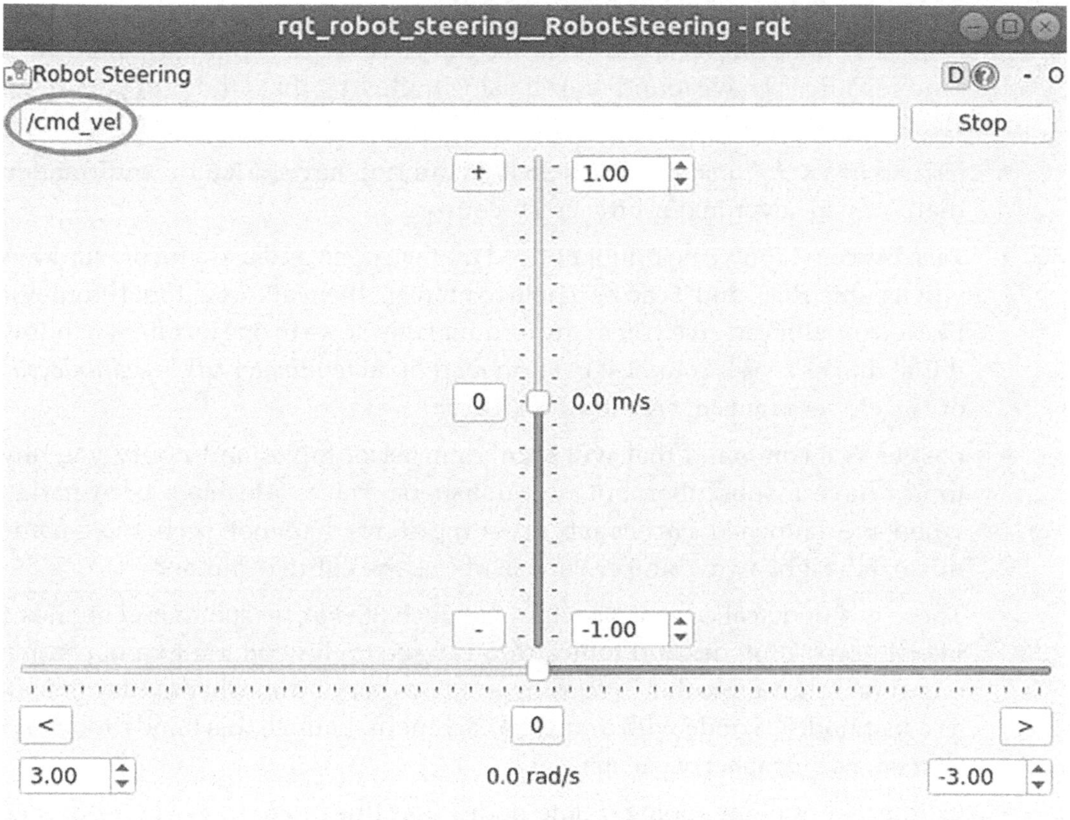

*Figure 9.7: rqt_robot_steering node*

Right! The `rqt_robot_steering` node publishes to the `/cmd_vel` topic by default, but our `turtlesim_node` subscribes to `/turtle1/cmd_vel`. Go ahead and change the topic in the field I circled in *figure 9.7* to match what our turtlesim is subscribing to, and voila! You'll find rqt_robot_steering a convenient node for testing and driving robots about.

Since any node can publish any topic and any node can subscribe to any topic, I hope it's not a stretch to imagine how they can be used to pass input and output messages from the controllers we learned in *Chapter 8*. Instead of a turtle on a screen, a motor controller can subscribe to the `cmd_vel` topic and set the PWM signal to the motor drive hardware based on the commanded values. Or, instead of using the `teleop_key` node to publish to `cmd_vel`, another node can automatically calculate the heading and distance to the next desired location and publish the `cmd_vel` messages to get our robot there.

# A handful of helpful tips

There are entire books on ROS, and what we can cover here is limited. There are a few tips and resources I have found myself using quite a bit that I thought you might appreciate.

- *wiki.ros.org/ROS/tutorials* – The ROS Wiki tutorials have FAR more information than we can cover in our little crash-course.

- `Terminator` – You've no doubt noticed that we open and use a lot of windows when using ROS, and it can be a pain to manage them all. A terminal emulator like terminator can give you many terminal windows in one terminal window if that makes sense. Your best bet is to read up at *terminator-gtk3.readthedocs.io* or *Google* `terminator terminal emulator`.

- `roswtf` is a command that will scan your list of topics and notify you any topics have a subscriber, but no publishers. This could have been handy when we launched `rqt_robot_steering` if we had not seen topic-name mismatch right away. Simply run `roswtf` as the entire command.

- There is a node called `rqt_graph` in the package `rqt_graph` that generates a visual graph of nodes and topics. You can see topics going into and coming out of nodes. A topic that is missing a subscriber or publisher is easy to spot as a leaf node – a node with a single attachment. Launch this handy tool with `rosrun rqt_graph rqt_graph`.

- Command line remapping. Some nodes don't have an easy way to change something like the topic name like `rqt_robot_steering` does. Instead of having to modify source code every time we need to match up topic or other names in ROS, we can remap at the command line. Read more about remapping at *wiki.ros.org/Remapping%20Arguments*.

- To manually clone a package from the Internet that doesn't work with `apt`, you can often just clone it with `git clone` from the workspace `src` folder (see *figure 9.8*) and recompile by navigating back to your `catkin_ws` directory and running `catkin_make` at the command line.

# Creating and writing ROS packages and nodes

To wrap up our ROS crash-course, we are going to create our package and add our first node to it. Once again, I cannot come close to sharing the wealth of knowledge in the ROS tutorial Wiki and suggest you follow them all or find a course dedicated to ROS to gain the best understanding. I'll cover writing a node that is specific to our example robot project, but the breadth of information will be smaller.

# The ROS file system

The packages that come installed live in /opt/ros/kinetic or /opt/ros/melodic, but packages you create will go in the catkin workspace you set up. The easiest way to get there is with the roscd command to get to your catkin_ws/devel folder, then cd .. to go up one level to catkin_ws. Use the ls command to list everything in the directory (If you're used to windows, you might be used to call directories folders). You should see the following three sub-directories:

- build
- devel
- src

# Creating ROS packages

You should refer to the ROS Wiki pages to learn more about what goes on in the build and devel directories; we are going to be using the src directory as a place to add our packages. The steps to create your own ROS package are:

*Step 1* Navigate your command prompt to the catkin_ws/src directory.

cd ~/catkin_ws/src

*Step 2* Create your very own package named practical:

catkin_create_pkg practical roscpp std_msgs

- The command catkin_create_pkg creates a new folder with the name of the package (practical) and two sub-folders for your include and source files. Additionally, the process creates the CMakeLists.txt and the package.xml files for the new package. Any time you want to create a new package use the format:

    catkin_create_pkg <new_pkg_name> <depend1> <depend2> <depend...>
- The arguments called depends are optional, but a good practice to include to avoid compilation errors. I know that the programs we write will need at least the packages called roscpp and std_msgs, so I included them when we created the package practical. You can also add them later in the package CMakeLists.txt file. *Figure 9.8* shows the general structure of the **Catkin Workspace** and how your packages and files fit in.

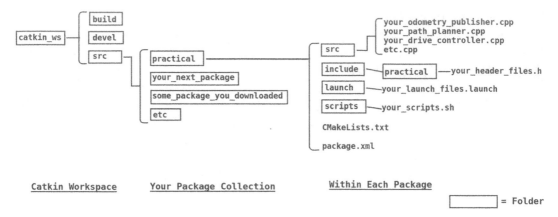

*Figure 9.8: The Catkin workspace file structure*

*Step 3* Edit the package CmakeLists.txt. Use your code editor to open the CmakeLists.txt in the new package you created, and remove the hashtag # to uncomment line 5 to enable C++11 support then save and exit. This isn't always required, but it will be if you use the PIGPIOD library with a Raspberry Pi. I don't think it ever hurts. *Figure 9.9* shows my edited CmakeLists.txt.

```
practical > M CMakeLists.txt
    1   cmake_minimum_required(VERSION 2.8.3)
    2   project(practical)
    3
    4   ## Compile as C++11, supported in ROS Kinetic and newer
    5   add_compile_options(-std=c++11)
    6
```

*Figure 9.9: Uncommenting line 5 in CmakeLists.txt to Enable C++11 compilation*

In the CmakeLists.txt, line with a # at the front are comments and ignored during compilation. Uncommenting a line means removing any # symbols in front of a line.

*Step 4* Create necessary resource folders

Create a folder we'll need later called launch. You should still be in the workspace's top-level src folder, so navigate to the practical and make directory launch

cd practical

mkdir launch

You can create folders for other resources like scripts, maps, config data for your nodes, etc. For now, the launch folder is enough.

# Writing ROS programs (Nodes)

*Great!* Now use your code editor and create your first ROS node. We'll make a proportional controller that subscribes to the turtle's location as an input and outputs a twist (velocity) message to command the turtle's velocity to get to a new location. In this first program, I keep it simple, and you simply set a desired goal x location as a `const` in the code (from `0-11`, knowing the turtle starts at `x = 5.54`). This program is available in the `downloads` as `go_to_x.cpp`.

The steps to create a ROS node are as follows:

1. Create a `.cpp` file in your `packages /src` folder.
2. Include `ros.h`, ROS message headers, and other files you need.
3. Define any constant values, global variables.
4. Write a setup function.
5. Write your callback functions.
6. Write any helper functions.
7. Write any controller functions.
8. Write your main function:
   8.1. Call your setup function
   8.2. Handshake with `roscore` and get a node handle
   8.3. Subscribe to any topics
   8.4. Advertise any publishers
   8.5. Loop as long as you need a program to run
       8.5.1. Set loop rate
       8.5.2. Call `spin()` to check callbacks
       8.5.3. Call your functions
       8.5.4. Publish message if not done in other functions
       8.5.5. Print node data to screen (optional)
   8.6. Shut down any hardware interfaces as necessary

## 1. Create a .cpp file

Create a blank file called `go_to_x.cpp` in your `practical/src` folder. How you do this will depend on your programming environment. In Codeblocks, you can click the new file button, then follow the prompts to include the full location path and file name. Still, I find this part of Codeblocks a bit clunky and often prefer to create and save a blank file from the command line with `nano` (or whatever your preferred text editor).

```
nano go_to_x.cpp
```

Then I usually save the blank file and open that in Codeblocks. It's just more efficient than Codeblock's new file utility – especially when you know you're creating several files at once.

**Step 2 and 3**:

Include ros.h, ROS message headers, and other files you need in your .cpp file, and declare global constants and variables:

```cpp
#include "ros/ros.h"

#include "geometry_msgs/Twist.h"

#include "geometry_msgs/Pose2D.h"

#include "turtlesim/Pose.h"

#include <cstdlib> //for abs()

#include <iostream>


using namespace std;


//declaring variables.

geometry_msgs::Twist cmdVel;

geometry_msgs::Pose2D current;

geometry_msgs::Pose2D desired;


//change GOAL to any value from 0 to 11

const double GOAL = 1.5;


//the coefficient (or gain) for our linear velocity calculation

const double Kl = 1;


//the distance we are willing to accept as "close enough"

const double distanceTolerance = .1;
```

This first section is nothing special. Just remember, we have to include the right header file for each message type we will use. Then you'll notice we create a few objects we need to access across several functions.

The object cmdVel is a Twist message. Twist messages are used to convey information about velocity, so well use it to issue velocity commands. cmdVel is just what I named the object for internal use, but we will publish it under the typical topic name cmd_vel.

The object current is updated whenever this node receives a new pose message in topic turtle1/pose. Then we use it again when we calculate the distance error in our x location.

 **In robotics, pose refers to the physical state of a robot (or even a component, like a robotic arm). For our turtle and simple wheeled robots, we utilize its** x **and** y **coordinates on a 2D plane, and its heading we call** theta. **More on that in** *Chapters 10 and 11.*

The object desired is where our goal pose will be stored. In this example program, we simply set the desired.x variable with a constant. In the future, we will set the desired.x, desired.y, and desired.theta with values we enter on the command line or from messages published automatically by our path planner!

## 4. Write a setup function

```
void misc_setup()

{

    desired.x = GOAL;

    cmdVel.linear.x = 0;

    cmdVel.linear.y = 0;

    cmdVel.linear.z = 0;

    cmdVel.angular.x = 0;

    cmdVel.angular.y = 0;

    cmdVel.linear.z = 0;

}
```

The misc_setup() function is useful for making sure we don't have uninitialized variables and any other setup housekeeping we want to keep separate from our main() function. I usually use one to set up the PIGPIO Dameon interface, serial or I2C interfaces, and definitely to initialize GPIO pins to a safe state, so the robot doesn't go berserk.

**5. Write your callback functions**

```
// callback function to update the current location
void update_pose(const turtlesim::PoseConstPtr &currentPose)
{
    current.x = currentPose->x;

    current.y = currentPose->y;

    current.theta = currentPose->theta;
}
```

The update_pose() function is our first callback function. We don't use the y or theta data members in this tutorial, but I included them so you can see how to access them in the future.

Callback functions don't get called with a normal function_call(), but instead happen automatically upon some event. In this case, update_pose() gets called when a message is published to the turtle1/pose topic. We will also frequently use callbacks for hardware events like counting our wheel encoder ticks.

**6. Write any helper functions**

```
double getDistanceError()
{
    return desired.x - current.x;
}
```

We just have one helper function, for now, that calculates the distance error on the x coordinates. In the future, these can become more involved and more numerous.

**7. Write any controller functions**

```
void set_velocity()
{
    if (abs(getDistanceError()) > distanceTolerance)
    {
```

```
        cmdVel.linear.x = K1 * getDistanceError();

    }

    else

    {

        cout << "I'm HERE!" << endl;

        cmdVel.linear.x = 0;

    }

}
```

The `if/else` statements in `set_velocity()` make up our proportional controller - like we talked about in *Chapter 8*. The further away our turtle reports that its current x location is from the desired x location, the greater the `cmd_vel` output. When we decide that the turtle is *close enough,* we set the output to 0.

**9. Write your `main()` function**

```
int main(int argc, char **argv)

{

    //9.1

        misc_setup();


    //9.2 register node "go_to_x" with roscore & get a nodehandle

    ros::init(argc, argv, "go_to_x");

    ros::NodeHandle node;


    //9.3 Subscribe to topic and set callback

    ros::Subscriber subCurrentPose =

    node.subscribe("turtle1/pose", 0, update_pose);


    //9.4 Register node as publisher

    ros::Publisher pubVelocity =

        node.advertise<geometry_msgs::Twist>("turtle1/cmd_vel", 0);
```

```cpp
    //9.5.1 set the frequency for the loop below
        ros::Rate loop_rate(10); //10 cycles per second

//9.5 execute this loop until connection is lost with ROS Master
    while (ros::ok)
    {
        //9.5.2 call the callbacks waiting to be called.
            ros::spinOnce();

        //9.5.3 call controller after the callbacks are done
            set_velocity();

        //9.5.4 publish messages
            pubVelocity.publish(cmdVel);

        //9.5.5 output for you entertainment
            cout << "goal x = " << desired.x << endl
                << "current x = " << current.x << endl
                << " disError = " << getDistanceError() << endl
                << "cmd_vel = " << cmdVel.linear.x<< endl;

        //We set the frequency for 10Hz, this sleeps as long
        //as it takes to keep that frequency
            loop_rate.sleep();
    }
    9.6 //we don't have any hardware to shut down

    return 0;
}
```

And finally, our `main()` function has to register our node with the master (also known as `roscore`), announce anything we want to publish and set callback functions to occur for any topic we subscribe to, and loop to keep everything happening. There is nothing fancy happening, but have a closer look at the act of declaring our publishers and subscribers in *figure 9.10* below.

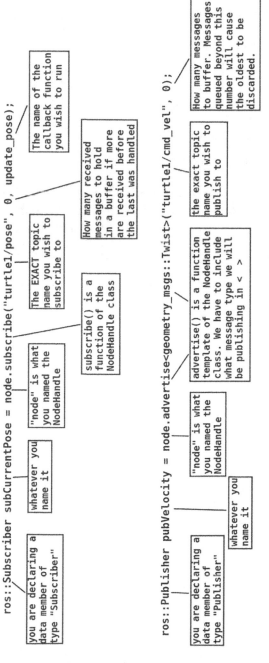

*Figure 9.10: Details of declaring ROS Subscribers and Publishers*

## Adding your program to CmakeLists.txt

Once you've saved your .cpp file we need to add it to your package's CmakeLists.txt so it compiles and becomes a node we can launch with rosrun. Open the file called CmakeLists.txt in the practical package and add these two lines near the bottom.

add_executable(go_to_x src/go_to_x.cpp)

target_link_libraries(go_to_x ${catkin_LIBRARIES})

You'll need to do this for every node you want to add to your package. For future use (when you are ready to use non ROS libraries like PIGPIOD), above your list of executable add these two lines as well:

INCLUDE_DIRECTORIES(/usr/local/lib)

LINK_DIRECTORIES(/usr/local/lib)

And when adding any node that uses PIGPIOD, you have to add libpigpiod_if2.so to your target_link_libraries. I've included a screenshot (*figure 9.11*) of the last lines in my CMakeLists.txt to give you an idea of how several .cpp files can be turned into nodes.

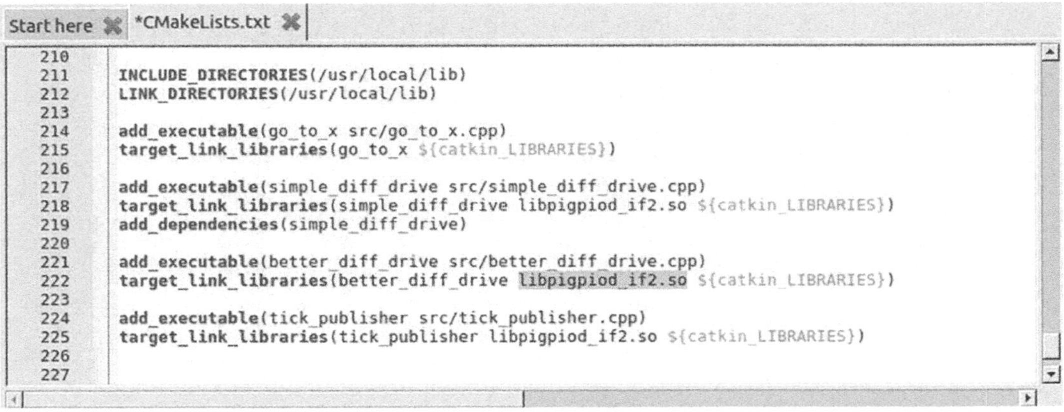

*Figure 9.11: Adding include directories and executable nodes to CMakeLists.txt*

Notice that you can optionally add node dependencies here. Once you're done editing and saving your CmakeLists.txt, all that's left is compile your package. You have to be in the catkin_ws directory (not a subdirectory), then from the command line use:

catkin_make

It might take a bit, depending on how much has changed since the last make. If you get a failed message, scroll back through the output, looking for the errors. Often the fatal stuff is red and gives a filename and line number – just like a regular C++ compile. If you're error-free, awesome! Let's try your node. Open three terminals and launch roscore in once, the turtlesim_node in another, and I the last try your new node:

```
rosrun practical go_to_x
```

You should see your turtle head right or left until it reaches the x location you set as GOAL in go_to_x.cpp. You can close that node, change the GOAL value between 0 and 11, recompile (catkin_make) again, then re-launch your node and watch the turtle head to its new location. You can also watch the working of the proportional controller in real-time. If anything goes wrong, try the troubleshooting tricks we learned earlier, like roswtf or rostopic echo turtle1/cmd_vel, to see what is broken. Finally, it your node – *experiment with it!*

# Downloading, reviewing, and running the chapter download programs

The following programs are available in the downloads folder for this chapter:

- go_to_x.cpp - Exactly the program we just wrote above
- simple_goal_pub.cpp – A program that accepts user input to publish goal x, y coordinates instead of having to change the code every time we want the turtle (or robot) to move.
- go_to_xy.cpp - In addition to moving to a position in the x direction, we subscribe to a message called waypoint that has both x and y coordinates. The turtle first turns toward the goal location, then moves toward it.

Both simple_goal_pub.cpp and go_to_xy.cpp are possible solutions to assignments in the *Questions* section at the end of the chapter. I recommend you first run them so you can see how they work, then try to write them yourself with the knowledge from *Chapter 8 and 9* before you peek at the code, but the code is there for you to learn from.

The code from this chapter is available as a standalone ROS package (called chapter9) as well as individual programs in the chapters downloads like the rest of the book. I did this so that you can learn how to download and run ROS packages and nodes that may not be available through the apt repositories. The robot project from *Chapter 21* is also available as a ROS package, but the code from the rest of the chapters are simply .cpp files in the chapters downloads.

To download the `chapter9` ROS package, navigate your command prompt to the `catkin_ws/src` folder and run:

```
cd ~/catkin_ws/src
```

```
git clone https://github.com/lbrombach/chapter9.git
```

```
cd ..
```

```
catkin_make
```

ROS will not let you have two programs with the same name in your `catkin_ws`, so rename your `go_to_x.cpp` file and any other files you have with duplicate names if it doesn't compile (don't forget to change your `CmakeLists.txt` to match). After you run the example nodes, you can move the `chapter9` folder out of the `catkin_ws` and put all of your program names back if you wish.

Since this package is called *Chapter 9*, you'll use that for a package name instead of `practical`. For example: With `roscore` and `turtlesim_node` already running, use two new terminals to run the following:

```
rosrun chapter9 go_to_xy
```

```
rosrun chapter9 simple_goal_pub
```

You should be able to type x and y coordinates in the `simple_goal_pub` window, and `go_to_xy` will issue `cmd_vel` messages to drive the turtle to wherever you tell it to go (within bounds). Take this time to run `roswtf` and `rqt_graph` to see how your ROS environment has changed from the simple examples earlier.

# Making life easier with roslaunch and .launch files

Opening from one to 30 terminal windows and individually launching that many nodes can take the fun (and productivity) out of a session. Fortunately, ROS has a tool available called `.launch` files that act sort of like scripts to automate the launching of nodes, remapping of message names, entering parameters, etc. You can have as many different launch files in a package as you wish to write.

Launch files are just `.xml` files you can make in your code or text editor. Place them in the folder you created earlier called `launch` and save them with the `.launch` extension. *Figure 9.12* is an example of a very simple – but still time-saving – `launch` file.

```
turtle_go_to.launch ×
launch > turtle_go_to.launch
   1    <launch>
   2
   3       <node pkg="turtlesim" type="turtlesim_node" name="turtlesim_node" />
   4       <node pkg="chapter9" type="go_to_xy" name="go_to_xy" />
   5       <node pkg="chapter9" type="simple_goal_pub" name="simple_goal_pub" output="screen" />
   6
   7    </launch>
```

*Figure 9.12: A simple launch file*

This launch file is named `turtle_go_to.launch` and automatically launches:

- `roscore`
- `turtlesim_node`
- `go_to_xy`
- `simple_goal_pub`

Yep – if `roslaunch` doesn't detect `roscore` running, it will launch it for you. This launch file is included in the *Chapter 9* download so you can try it yourself from the command line with:

`roslaunch chapter9 turtle_go_to.launch`

You can interact with `simple_goal_pub` in the terminal you launched from, but I caution against running nodes that take keyboard input from `roslaunch` because the output is cluttered by every node running. I included it so you know you can, but the output feature is best suited for displaying output from nodes – and sparingly at that.

Roslaunch has a lot more capabilities, and we'll touch on a few more along the way, and you can learn even more at *wiki.ros.org/roslaunch*. It's hard to live without once you get the hang of it.

# Conclusion

In this chapter, we've put a good scratch on the surface of one of the most popular and useful robotics software tools. The time we spend learning ROS basics will pay itself back fifty-fold and allow you to focus on the how and why of robot autonomy.

We've learned what ROS is, why it's useful, installed it, and learned how to launch its significant components and communication between nodes – which we can even create ourselves now.

These skills are going to come in handy in our next chapter, where we learn how our robots can make their maps that will become crucial if we hope for our robots to drive itself from place to place reliably autonomously. We'll learn the structure of robot maps, how they are made, and walkthrough using a ROS package that makes excellent maps for you.

# Questions

1. Write a publisher node for a topic called waypoint that publishes a message of type geometry_msgs::Pose2D. This node should ask the user to enter a goal x and y coordinates (float values) between 0 and 11, then publishes the most recently updated message.

2. Modify the go_to_x.cpp that we wrote earlier to subscribe to the waypoint topic and automatically update the desired.x value with data from the waypoint topic. This should result in the turtle moving to any x location the user inputs in the publisher node you wrote in question.

3. Bonus challenge: The node go_to_x ignores any y inputs. Copy your go_to_x. cpp file to a new node file called go_to_xy.cpp. Modify it to make its new goal include both x and y coordinates. Your controller should first aim the turtle to the correct heading. When the turtle's heading is *close enough*, have your controller calculate total distance and drive to the goal.

*Hints:* Here are some functions you can use to calculate the distance and angular errors. You'll need to include math.h, and you want to use atan2 instead of atan for reasons I don't want to tackle here. There are some great YouTube resources for trigonometry refreshers if you need them.

```
double getDistanceError()
{
    return sqrt(pow(desired.x - current.x, 2) + pow(desired.y -
        current.y, 2));
}


double getAngularError()
{
    double deltaX = desired.x - current.x;
    double deltaY = desired.y - current.y;
    //hypotenuse = a^2+b^2=c^2
    double distanceError = sqrt(pow(deltaX, 2) + pow(deltaY, 2));
```

```
    //absolute bearing to goal = arctan(slope)
    // and slope = (y1-y2)/(x1-x2)
    double thetaBearing = atan2(deltaY, deltaX);
    double angularError = thetaBearing - current.theta;
    return angularError;
}
```

# CHAPTER 10
# Maps for Robot Navigation

## Introduction

In one form or another, we use maps to get everywhere we go. Some of us remember unfolding paper maps to plan a trip; more recently, we mostly press a few buttons, and a digital version shows up on a screen. Even when we don't think we need a map, we often have one in our heads from previous experiences with where we are going. For me, this *map* is usually a top-down view (with varying accuracy and resolution) of the environment that I'm trying to navigate. However, this isn't to say that a map is required to get from point A to point B.

*Elon Musk* of *Telsa Motors* has stated that he doesn't believe his autonomous cars should be using detailed maps as we learn here, making the point that his robot cars should be able to navigate flawlessly even to places they've never been. I see his point, but I also think it's silly to force a system to forget the data it already has. Can you imagine having to find the bathroom or copier at work all over again every time you need to use it? `Sure, you could`, but aren't you more efficient if you make a mental note of where it is along with any obstacles in your way? You still may have to navigate around a co-worker along the way, but you generally know where the cubicles and doors are so your path is completed faster.

The autonomous car company *Cruise automation* mirrors my sentiment and operates a fleet of self-driving vehicles that manage incredibly effective decision-making on the busy streets of *San Francisco*. According to *Kyle Vogt* (President and CTO of *Cruise* in *June* of *2019*), these very human-like (and fast) decisions are possible thanks to precision maps that are regularly updated and shared by the fleet. When a car encounters something unusual like extra lines painted or traffic signs obstructed, it can often call upon prior data of the location and safely continue autonomous operation. Search on *YouTube* for *Cruise San Francisco Maneuvers* and try not to be impressed.

I hope I've convinced you of the benefits of building a map of a robot's operating environment because that is how the navigation algorithm we are going to learn works.

# Objectives

Understand the occupancy grid map, how to build one with robot sensor data, how to save it in a properly formatted file, and how to serve a saved map back to ROS for navigational purposes.

**In this chapter, we will be covering the following:**

- Angle, heading, and distance conventions
- Receiving sensor data
- The occupancy grid map (OGM)
- Building OGMs with sensor data
- Transforms in ROS
- Mapping made easy with Gmapping
- Visualizing maps with Rviz
- Saving maps
- Serving previously saved maps to your robot

# Angle, heading, and distance conventions

We are going to work with a lot of angles – whether we are plotting obstacles or describing the direction our robot is facing (also known as **heading** or **theta**). Many of us are accustomed to a coordinate system that measures angles in degrees, and straight-up (or *North*) is our reference of *0 degrees*, especially if it's been a long time since we've taken trigonometry. In robotics, however, we measure angles in radians, and our reference, or *zero*, point is to the right (due *East*, if you were looking at a standard map).

Perhaps you recall that there are *2\*PI* (or about *6.28318*) radians (or rad) in *360 degrees*. Instead of measuring our angles from *0* to *2\*PI*, we start at *0* and measure up to *PI* for a counter-clockwise angle, and *-PI* for clockwise angles. Should our calculations at any time give us a value above *PI*, simply subtract *2PI,* and the result will be an equivalent negative angle. Similarly, if our calculations lead us to an angle that is less than *-PI*, we can just add *2PI* for an equivalent positive angle.

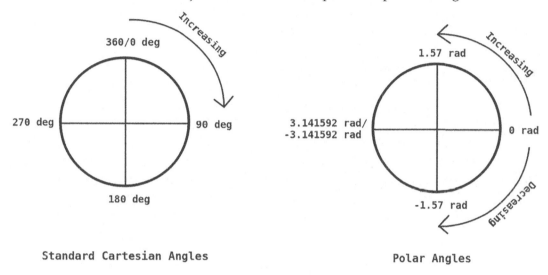

**Standard Cartesian Angles**                                    **Polar Angles**

*Figure 10.1: In robotics, a polar angle system is preferred over a Cartesian angles system*

A polar angle system helps solve the `Which is the shortest direction to turn` question and reduces some math conversions during the trigonometry in mapping and path planning. Because angles in degrees are so much more intuitive for most people, it is not uncommon to do conversions and use degrees in user interfaces.

In a three-dimensional world, three of these angles can be used to describe the complete orientation. This convention that uses angles of *-Pi* radians to *+Pi* radians for *roll*, *pitch*, and *yaw* (same as our heading or theta) is called the **Euler angles convention**. We will revisit Euler angles in the next chapter – for now, it is enough to know that the direction our robot is facing is one of three *Euler* angles.

Quaternions are another way to represent the orientation of an object in space that you'll need to be at least familiar with. Quaternions add a fourth variable to the orientation part of the pose data and are usually notated with a w. These are not as intuitive to visualize as *Euler* angles, and I would prefer not to include them at all in a fundamentals book such as *Practical Robotics in* C++ except that you'll need to know how to convert back and forth from Euler to quaternion for some very important software tools later. We will tackle conversions in the next chapter.

Another notable convention is that distances are measured in meters, so we use floating-point values for better resolution. If you are an American or otherwise raised using inches and feet like me, you may be tempted to try and use units you are more familiar with and *just convert when needed*. I'd like to caution against this, as each conversion inserts a chance for error or just plain forgetting – and there will be a LOT of them. Even *NASA* learned this lesson the hard way when a Mars orbiter crashed when they forgot to convert acceleration data from Imperial to metric. Save yourself from the bigger headache and just use the standard metric units.

# Receiving sensor data

You're going to need sensor data to build a map, and that data should come in the form of ROS messages your map-building node subscribes to. While it is possible to directly read raw sensor data and build a map in the same node, it is not advisable because you may need to swap out sensors for a different type at some point, and sometimes other nodes also need the sensor data. By writing a map-building node that can process any standard laser scan message, for example, it can automatically compensate for differences in scanner resolution, the field of view, and so on.

We're going to be working with the ever-popular laser scan message, but the idea would be the same if you were using other sensors with the different data types. Subscribing to a laser scan message is just like the subscriber we wrote in *Chapter 9, Coordinating the Parts* — we're just receiving a different data type. Let's look at an example map publisher node setup.

```cpp
#include <ros/ros.h>

#include <sensor_msgs/LaserScan.h>

#include <nav_msgs/OccupancyGrid.h>


ros::Publisher mapPub


//callback function runs when we receive a new scan message

void scan_to_map(sensor_msgs::LaserScan msg)

{

// use scan data to build and publish map here
```

```
}

int main(int argc, char **argv)

{

    ros::init(argc, argv, "map_builder");

    ros::NodeHandle n;

//subscribe to laser scan message

    ros::Subscriber scanHandler = n.subscribe<sensor_msgs::LaserScan>

("scan", 0, scan_to_map);


//advertise our publisher

    mapPub = n.advertise<nav_msgs::OccupancyGrid>("map", 10);


//loop through callback 10 times per second

    ros::Rate loop_rate(10);

    while (ros::ok)

    {

ros::spinOnce();

        loop_rate.sleep();

    }

}
```

With the basic subscriber/publisher set up, when a laserScan message with the topic name scan is received, the callback function receives it as an object locally called msg. Object data members are accessed with the standard. operator. For example, to print the minimum angle of the scan and the distance measured in element 100 to the screen, you could use something like

```
std::cout<<msg.angle_min<<endl;

std::cout<<msg.ranges[100]<<endl;
```

We will cover the `sensor_msgs::laserScan` message in greater detail in *Chapter 18, LIDAR Devices and Data*. For a complete picture of the laser scan data members and other sensor message types, you may need, visit *wiki.ros.org/sensor_msgs*.

# Occupancy grid maps

At the heart of this simple but effective map-type is the idea that we can represent a map of a physical world in a 2D array, or matrix, of cells. Imagine overlaying grid lines over the drawing of an apartment like I did in *Figure 10.2*. The dark lines are walls; there are some stairs, a sofa, table and chairs, and some various other furniture and appliances.

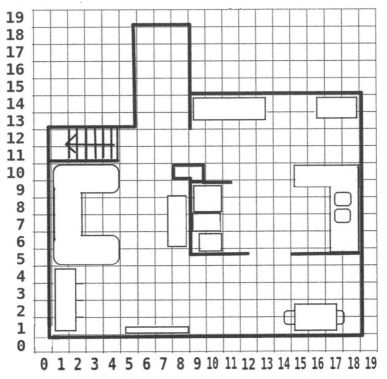

*Figure 10.2: Laying a grid over a scale-drawing*

With the grid overlay, we can quickly look up any cell by *(x, y)* coordinate and determine what is in it. If we are calculating a route, our path planner algorithm can see that point *(6, 6)* is an open space, while *(4, 6)* has a sofa in it, and *(8, 6)* has a TV stand.

That's a lot of details to indicate that our robot is free to travel through *(6, 6)* but not the others. Our path planner doesn't have to care if it's a wall that is in its way or a sofa or a dog – it either can go someplace or it cannot. Let's take the cluttering details out of each cell and simply mark them occupied or not. *Figure 10.3* is the same floor plan represented more simply.

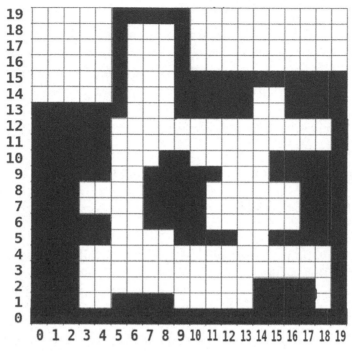

*Figure 10.3: A simplified representation of the same apartment in figure 10.2*

Now that our 2D array contains only simpler binary values, our path planning algorithm has very little interpreting to do. This becomes more important when we use less powerful machines like the Raspberry Pi, or as the array size grows due to either a larger space or higher resolution.

 **The examples in figures** *10.1* **and** *10.2* **use elements that appear to be about** .5 **meters each. Elements that large makes for less processing but also** *waste* **a lot of free space for reasons we'll talk about in a couple of moments. I'm a big fan of** .1 **meter elements, but** .05 **meters are also common.**

It is easy to be confused at first when working with maps because we always express the robot's position (pose) being x,y meters from the corner of the map (point 0,0) (and that is how we receive robot location data). Once we are doing calculations within the map, however, we have to convert that x,y in meters to x,y grid cell numbers by *dividing the x,y in meters by the map resolution*. For example, if our map has a resolution of .1 meters (10cm) per cell and the robot's location is reported as (1.5, 2.2), that means its real-world location is 1.5 meters to the right and 2.2

meters up from the lower-left corner (0,0) of the map. To do calculations for the map, however, we have to divide by .1 to find the location within the map cells. Within the map, our robot is located at a cell (15,22).

That's the general idea of how we structure maps for our robots. Pretty simple, right? As we get more advanced, the structure can be expanded to include a third dimension. You can imagine how a flying robot would need to know the height of each obstacle, as well. For ground vehicles, 3D data can be useful when you need to start navigating uneven terrain or other specialty routines. For basic navigation of reasonably level terrain, it offers no advantage.

# Building occupancy grid maps (OGMs) with sensor data

Building your maps with the following details is not necessary, and shortly I will introduce some mapping software that can handle all of these details for you. I do believe that this section provides important details on how mapping works, and skipping ahead to the *Mapping made easy* section can leave large gaps in your understanding. If anything, skip the code sections but read the algorithm comments.

When constructing a map, it's common to make the point (0,0) the left bottom corner of your robot's map instead of the center like we might have been used to from math class – this allows us to keep the robot in quadrant 1 of our grid, which contains only positive-numbered coordinates. Life is just much easier when you don't have to deal with negative numbers when it comes to addressing array indices and the math we are going to need.

In our example above, I talked about simplifying to binary values, but that's not quite the entire story. Beyond occupied or free, it's essential to know which spaces are unknown or unexplored. Additionally, sometimes our data is not concrete enough to declare one whether the space is free or occupied. The conventional solution is to mark every cell with a value from 0 to 100, where 0 is most certainly free space, and 100 is most certainly occupied. In-between values indicate how certain or not certain our system is that space is occupied. The individual software packages receiving and utilizing the map data can be set with threshold values to decide if a cell is occupied or not. A value of -1 is assigned to unknown or unexplored cells.

To start mapping, we need four things:

1. A blank or previous map to store our new data to.
2. To know the current x,y location of our robot within the map space, and its angular heading.

3.  To know where the sensor is located compared to the center of the robot.
4.  The distance and angular direction to an object we want to map.

To start with a blank map, we need to declare a 2D integer array large enough for our environment and initialize every element to -1. I know my test space is a bit under `10` meters by `10` meters, which is `1000` x `1000` centimeters. Since I want to use a `10cm` x `10cm` cell, I need a `100` x `100` element 2D array. In practice, the smallest map that will do the job will lend the best performance. It is similar with resolution — If I used `5cm` cells instead of `1cm` cells, my path planner could navigate more precisely and possibly squeeze my robot through tighter spaces but would have to evaluate up to 4 times as many cells. You have to decide what you need.

We will learn about robot tracking and localization in a later chapter; for now, we will manually supply the robot's position within the frame of the map we made. This should be much higher resolution than simply using the cell we occupy – we will want to be accurate to the centimeter (or even better, if possible) so we will use a float value in meters. I will call these pose variables `currentX`, `currentY`, and `currentTheta`.

And the last setup value we need is something called a **transform** in ROS. This provides information needed to compensate for the sensor not being located at the center of the robot. The robot views itself as a point in space that is at the center of where it rotates in a pure pivot. If a sensor is `.5` meters away, obstacles will be plotted inaccurately if we do not compensate for this difference. Again, for this section, we will manually add this offset and call them `transformX`, `transformY`, and `transformTheta`. In a proper ROS project, we usually lookup transform data that is broadcast by other nodes. We will do that and learn more about transforms later.

Now we need to talk about the fourth point – range data. For this tutorial, we are going to presume we are getting data from a scanning laser sensor – as is still the most common mapping sensor. You are by no means limited to a laser scanner – this can also be supplied by ultrasonic sensors, radar, special cameras, and even bump sensors that have a range of `0`. You can use any or all of these to add to your map, and each would have its own transform data.

Let's look at some variables and constants we would use for building an occupancy grid:

```
//PI is used a lot

const PI = 3.141592;


//declare new map array
```

```
int8_t newMap[100][100];

//initialize the location in the map grid as 49.5, 20. In practice
//we would have to divide the real-world robot location
//by the map resolution to find the map location given here.
double currentX = 49.5;
double currentY = 20.0;

//initialize the robot aimed straight ahead using polar heading
double currentTheta = PI/2;

//manually set our transform as if our laser is on the centerline
//but 10 cm forward of true center, and aiming straight ahead
double transformX = 0.1;   // .1 meters = 10cm
double transformY = 0.0;
double transformZ = 0.0;
double transformRoll = 0.0;
double transformPitch = 0.0;
double transformYaw = 0.0;

//normally supplied by laser_scan message
double ranges[360];
const double angle_increment = PI/180; // 2*PI/360 simplified;
const double angle_min = -PI;
const double angle_max = PI;
```

> **Given the information we set up above, we have a robot sitting in a blank world at a real-world pose of (4.95, 2.0) and aiming straight ahead at 0 radians. Since our map has a resolution of .1, we must divide the pose data by .1 to find that the robot's location among the map's grid is** x = 49.5 **and** y = 20.

For this tutorial, let's define a robot that is round and 30 cm in diameter – very close to the example project robot for this book. *Figure 10.4* may help you picture the robot's world as we start.

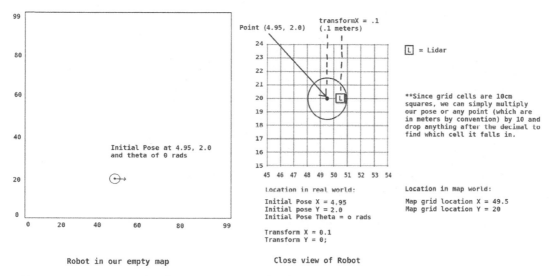

**Figure 10.4:** *An example of an initial map with robot pose and transform from laser to base_link*

Notice how and why transforming measurements from the lasers point of view to the base_link (robots' point of view) matters. If we did not compensate for the .1 meter offset, a scan now would plot obstacles in completely different grid cells than if we rotated 180 degrees and scanned again. This error only grows as the distance from the rotational center of the robot and the sensor grows – imagine how big the error might be if the sensor were mounted on the front of a car!

# Marking the occupied cells

Laser range data will be available in an array with as many elements as the device returns per complete sweep. We are going to call this array ranges[360] since our example project uses a laser scanner that provides 360 points at one-degree increments (but remember that angle increment data will be published in radians, not degrees). Also available will be the information you need to determine which array[] element contains the data for which angle, in the form of where the scan starts (angle_min), where the scan ends (angle_max), and the increment between individual data points (angle_increment). See the following *Figure 10.5*.

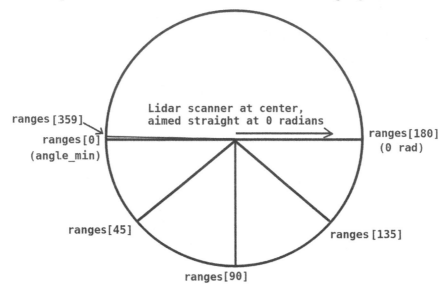

**Figure 10.5:** *Laser scan (Lidar) range data is published in ROS as an array with enough elements for however many measurements the scanner in a sweep*

Now that we know how the ranges[] array is oriented, we can iterate through the array and plot each measurement in our map. To do so, we apply trigonometry to the range and angle data to figure out the x, y coordinate of each obstacle detected. Don't forget that our robot won't always be pointed with a heading of 0 radians, so we must add the robot heading angle (theta) to the scanAngle. To calculate the x, y coordinate of an obstacle detected at a given range and angle:

1. Calculate the x and y distance between the laser scanner and the robots base_ link, because we must add these to the scanned range to plot them in the map accurately:

   xOffset = cos(pose.theta) * transformX

   yOffset = sin(pose.theta) * transformX

2. Calculate the relative scan angle in radians from the ranges[] element number using (relative to robot's heading):

   relativeScanAngle = angle_min+element*angle_increment

3. Calculate the actual scan angle - Add the robot's heading in radians to the relative scan angle in *Step 2*.

   scanAngle = pose.theta + relativeScanAngle

4. Calculate with x and y distances from the laser scanner to the object using the scanAngle from *Step 3*:

```
xDistance = cos(scanAngle)*range
yDistance = sin(scanAngle)*range
```

5.  The laser's x location is the robot's pose.x + xOffset, and its y location is pose.y + yOffset. Add the laser's x and y coordinates to x and y distances to the object to get its absolute x and y coordinates:

```
xCoordinate = xDistance + pose.x + xOffset
yCoordinate = yDistance + pose.y + yOffset
```

*Figure 10.6* walks through calculating the x, y coordinates of an obstacle detected in ranges[155] at a distance of .61 meters. This particular scanner covers 360 degrees in one-degree increments (like the XV11 Lidar or many others). The robot's heading is 45 degrees, or .785 rad (45 deg*PI/180 - .785 rad).

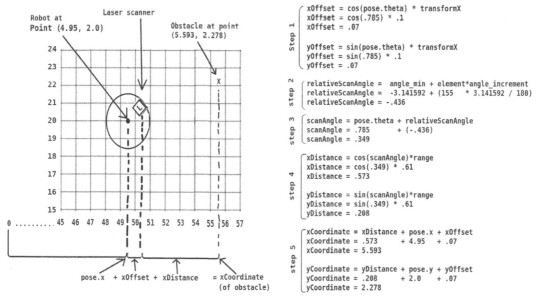

**Figure 10.6:** *Calculating the x, y location of an obstacle given range and direction(angle) data*

Because our map grid cells are .1 meters x .1 meters, we can easily find which element in our 2D map array (newMap[][]) the obstacle is in by multiplying the coordinates and dropping everything after the decimal. Note that no matter where in the cell the actual point falls, we will mark the entire cell occupied. Our object was detected in cell 55, 22, so we will assign the value of `newMap[55][22]` to `100` for occupied.

It is prudent to apply some filters and checks before marking cells as occupied – if the signal strength is too low, or the reported distance is either closer or further away than the sensor is rated for it is likely erroneous and should not be plotted. We can get fancy and begin to assign weighted values to individual scans, and vary the value in the element between `0` and `100` to reflect how likely the cell is occupied or not, but for our purposes, we will stick to assigning values of `0` for free, `100` for occupied, and `-1` for unknown.

## Marking the free cells

We're not done with the information we just spent all that time calculating because we can also use it to mark free space. Since laser scan or other robot-mounted sensor data can only show us the closest obstacle, we know with reasonable certainty that there is nothing between our sensor and the obstacle, and we can mark those all of those cells as free. One bit of caution, however – because many consecutive `scanAngles` will often pass through the same cells, it is important not to mark a cell as free if a previous computation marked it occupied.

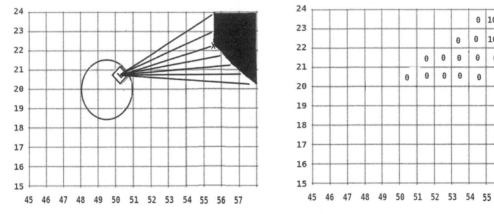

*Figure 10.7: A section of occupancy grid values after processing the pictured sequential elements from a* `ranges[]` *array having detected the pictured obstacle*

## Completing the map

A scan from a single point can leave a lot of unexplored space. You can manually drive the robot and keep updating the map as long as you have accurate pose data for every scan taken. This means having a working odometry node or pose estimator that can update accurately and continuously.

Processing scans while on the move must be done carefully, as you have to synchronize your scan message with your pose message to be sure they are each taken at the same time. Fortunately, the official ROS message type includes data members for you to use as a timestamp for your messages. You will also have to compensate for the scan *blur* that happens because a moving robot is in different places for each element of the scan. Fortunately, the software I am going to introduce shortly (Gmapping) takes care of these for us.

If manually driving around to map isn't what you had in mind, a simple technique to automate exploring is to write a node that locates the nearest unexplored area and publishes a nearby free cell as a desired location. Your path planner can drive you there, and you can scan and keep repeating until some desired percentage of the world is explored. If you want to try this, you may need to limit robot speed and acceleration to minimize pose estimate error and scan blur – even with Gmapping. Minimizing speed would be done at the drive controller, which we cover in *Chapter 12, Autonomous Motion.*

## Publishing the map as a ROS Message

Our map may be starting to shape up, but it's not going to be useful unless we can get it out to our path planner or visualization tools. We need to publish our map in the ROS message format many other packages are expecting.

The map we've built and work with is a 2D array we address with an [x][y] pair, but the standard nav_msgs::OccupancyGrid publishes the data as a 1D array (vector, actually). More experienced programmers might have worked with the 1D array to begin with, but the rest of us are going to have to copy the data one cell at a time. Fortunately, a simple nested *for loop* readily handles this business, which amounts to a process like that illustrated in *Figure 10.8.*

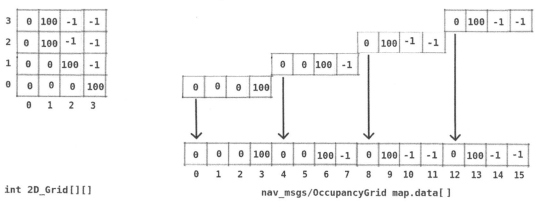

*Figure 10.8: Converting a 2D grid we've used as a map into a one dimensional Occupancy Grid array*

A pair of nested *for loops* make quick work of the job, iterating over the height and width that you set for the 2D array. The code to do this would look something like the code block below.

```cpp
#include <nav_msgs::OccupancyGrid.h>

void someFunction()
{
//creates a map object named "map"
nav_msgs::OccupancyGrid map;

//filling header and metadata
map.header.frame_id = "map";
map.info.resolution = .1; //meters per cell
map.info.width = 100; //covers 10 meters
map.info.height = 100; //covers 10 meters

//resize empty data field and initialize all to unknown
Map.data.resize(map.info.width * map.info.height);
For(int i = 0; i < map.data.size; i++)
{
Map.data[i] = -1;
}

//let's assume our 2d map array "newMap" already exists
//with the same width, height, and resolution

//iterate over and copy every element
for int(j = 0; j < map.info.height; j++)
{
```

```
for int(i = 0; i < map.info.width; i++)

{

map.data[map.info.width*2 + i] = newMap[i][j];

}

}


//publish the occupancy grid map with previously declared publisher "map"

mapPub.publish(map);


}
```

Map metadata is a data member of the `nav_msgs::OccupancyGrid` and is another message type on its own. At a minimum, we need to fill out the map `width`, `height`, and `resolution` (how many meters we want each pixel to represent). Visit *wiki.ros. org/nav_msgs* for a complete look at the *Occupancy Grid* and *Map Metadata messages*, as well as some other nav_msgs you will find useful.

# Transforms in ROS

Transforms are widely used to communicate location and orientation data. More specifically, transforms communicate the difference in location and orientation between two frames of reference. By linking the transform information between frame A and frame B, and also between frame B and frame C, we can compute the transform information from frame A to frame C. Let's take a close look at what this all means and how transforms are used in ROS.

## Understanding transforms

To understand transforms, you have to understand frames. Frames in ROS refer to different frames of reference for measuring and coordinates. If you ask your robot to find your dog and it only reported 2 meters to the right and 1 meter up, you will still have no idea what that means because you have no frame of reference - 2 meters right and 1 meter up from the sensor is different than 2 meters to the right and 1 meter up from the origin of the map. In this context, we are discussing two frames: The *sensor* frame and the *map* frame.

If you knew the exact distances between the sensor and the map origin, you could then convert a statement like 2 meters to the right and 1 meter up from the sensor to some measurement that makes sense in the map frame. Of course, this only works if the statement is made disclosing what the reference point is, so when we publish location data for anything in ROS, the message has a place to specify which frame the coordinates are about. For some clarity, look back at *figure 10.4*.

In *figure 10.4*, we have three frames of reference:

- The **laser** frame – The data the laser reports is about itself. Because the location of the laser is fixed about the `base_link`, the laser frame is considered the child of the `base_link` frame.

- The **base_link** frame – The base link is generally the point of the robot that the robot pivots around or otherwise the center of the robot. The `base_link` frame is where everything is measured about this point. `base_link` is the parent frame to the laser frame but is the child frame to the map frame.

- The **map** frame – This the highest frame in the hierarchy for this example. This is the parent frame for the `base_link` frame.

When we plotted obstacles detected by the laser scans earlier in this chapter, what we essentially did was to calculate the transform from the map frame to the laser frame, then plot the obstacles from that point. **Transforms** are what we call the measurement between two frames.

In practice, there is another frame in-between map and `base_link` called **odom**. Odom is short for odometry (which is how we track our robot's position), and the odom frame starts at the same place as the map frame (transforms of x, y, z == 0, 0, and 0) but wanders away as errors accumulate. More on that in *Chapter 11, Robot Tracking and Localization.*

## How transforms are used in ROS

We use transforms as a way of making sure every node has the measurements it needs to convert from frame to frame as needed. Some transform never changes and are considered static – like our `base_link` to laser transform. This data could be hard-coded into nodes that use laser data, but if we moved the laser, we would then have to change the code for each node. It is more efficient and less error-prone if publish transform data so it can be changed once and then be grabbed like any other published message.

Non-static transforms, like a map to `base_link`, are constantly changing and couldn't be hard-coded anyway. Sometimes transform data is redundant to other messages (The map to `base_link` data is the same as our pose data, for example), but both versions of the data have their uses. If you are the sender of such data, you need to be aware that some nodes will require the data as a message, and others will use the transform. You'll probably have to make sure both are available, and we'll do that in *Chapter 11, Robot Tracking and Localization,* as well.

If you are writing a node or otherwise in need of that data, knowing how to receive it both ways can be hugely beneficial. You can calculate the location of the laser in the map frame in three steps as we did above (from `map->odom`, from `odom->base_link`, then `base_link→laser`), or you can use a handy transform tool called `tf_lookup()` that calculates it all for you if you just ask for a `map  ->laser` to begin with. In fact, with `tf_lookup()`, you can request the transform between any two frames as long as they are linked. *Figure 10.9* below shows what is called a `tf` tree.

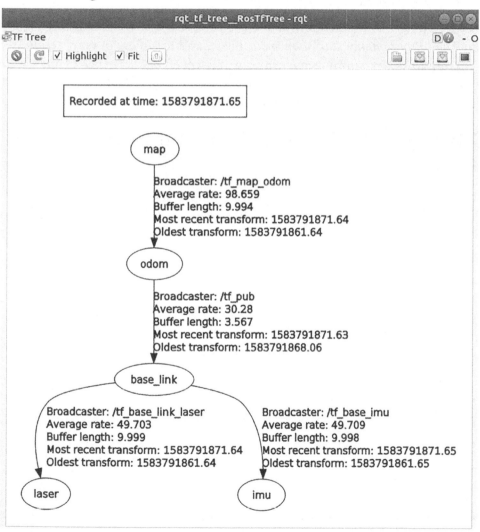

***Figure 10.9:*** *A tf tree generated by rqt_tf_tree*

It is important to not have any breaks in the tf tree. For example, if there is no odom to base_link **transform being broadcast,** tf_lookup **cannot calculate a request for map to** base_link **because the tree is broken.**

It's easy to see how tf_lookup is handy for even our relatively simple robot, but imagine having a gripper on the end of a robot arm with six joints of its own, and that arm is on a mobile robot. Subscribing to a message for each position transform and calculating the gripper's position and orientation in the map frame would be something between tedious and a nightmare! It would be far preferable to just call tf_lookup() for map→gripper.

The tf tree above is the actual tree for the project robot we'll build in *Chapter 21, Building and Programming an Autonomous Robot,* and this view of your active tree can be generated just by running rosrun  rqt_tf_tree  rqt_tf_tree. That's a handy way to remember which nodes are broadcasting, which transforms and to visually see if you've left anything missing that would break the tree.

# Publishing transforms with the static transform publisher

For transforms that never change, you can publish the data via a broadcaster in a node, but I think it's easier to manage them in your launch files. You're just starting an instance of the node static_transform_publisher from the package tf with arguments of:

1. Translation x
2. Translation y
3. Translation z
4. Orientation roll
5. Orientation pitch
6. Orientation yaw(theta)
7. The parent frame
8. The child frame,
9. The frequency to publish.

Going back to the example in *figure 10.4*, we use transformX of .1, transformY or 0, and transformTheta of 0. That entry in a launch file would look like:

```
<node  pkg="tf"  type="static_transform_publisher"  name="tf_base_link_
laser"

    args=".10 0 0 0 0 0 base_link laser 10" />
```

Alternatively, you can publish a static transform via command line with the same arguments:

```
rosrun tf static_transform_publisher .10 0 0 0 0 0 base_link laser 10
```

The command line option is handy for testing things or making quick changes, but is far too tedious to rely on. Embrace your launch files.

# Publishing transforms from nodes with a transform broadcaster

A transform broadcaster `tf::transformBroadcaster` isn't too different from a `ros::Publisher` object in that it registers itself in the ROS ecosystem and handles the passing of other message types – in this case `tf::Transform` messages. Add a transform broadcaster to a ROS node with the following steps:

1. Include the `tf/transform_broadcaster.h` file
2. Create the `broadcaster` object
3. Create the `tf::Transform` message object
4. Set the transform offset position
5. Set the transform offset orientation
6. Broadcast the `transform`

**See the code block below:**

```cpp
//step 1

#include <tf/transform_broadcaster.h>


//step 2 declare broadcaster object - can be in a function

static tf::TransformBroadcaster br;


//step 3 declare transform object - can be in a function

tf::Transform odom_base_tf;


void some_function()

{

//step 4 set tf origin data

base_laser_tf.setOrigin(tf::Vector3(x, y, z) );
```

```
//step 5 set tf rotation data

base_laser_tf.setRotation(tf::Quaternion(x, y, z, w) );


//step 6 broadcast transform

br.sendTransform(tf::stampedTransform(odom_base_tf,    ros::Time::now(),
"odom", "base_link") );

}
```

After declaring our broadcaster and transform objects (*steps 2* and *3*), we need to set the origin (*step 4*) with a tf::Vector3 argument with our x, y, and z location data. To set the orientation (*step 5*), we use the setRotation() function, but instead of the *Euler* angles we've been using, we have to use quaternions.

 **To build a node that includes tf or tf2 files, you'll need to add those two packages to your own package's CmakeLists.txt file. These go near the top in the section that looks like the following:**

```
find_package(catkin REQUIRED COMPONENTS

    roscpp

    std_msgs

    tf

    tf2

)
```

The above transform broadcaster could be put directly in a node that calculates the odometry data, but there may be times it is preferable to let another node broadcast it. For this reason, it is not uncommon to write a separate transform publisher node that listens for the odometry message and rebroadcasts that information as a transform - It is easier to exclude or include the transform broadcaster node as necessary in a launch file than it is to change code in the odometry node itself. A complete example of such a node is in the Downloads for *Chapter 11, Robot Tracking and Localization* as well as the complete robot package for *Chapter 21, Building and Programming an Autonomous Robot*.

# Getting transform data in your nodes

Getting transform data within a program is not difficult and can be more efficient than subscribing to a topic and processing every message whether you need it or not. With transforms, our program can look up a transform only when needed. The general steps to lookup transform in a ROS node are:

1. Include the `tf/transform_listener.h` file
2. Create a transform listener object
3. Create a transform object
4. Call `lookupTransform()` to load data into your transform object
5. Use `getter()` functions to access data
6. Convert quaternion data to Euler angles if necessary

**Have a look at the code block below.**

```
//step 1

#include <tf/transform_listener.h>


void some_function()

{

    //step 2

    static tf::TransformListener listener;


    //step 3

    tf::StampedTransform odom_base_tf;


    //optional

    if(listener.canTransform("odom","base_link",

        ros::Time(0), NULL))

    {

    //step 4

        listener.lookupTransform("odom", "base_link",

            ros::Time(0), odom_base_tf);
```

```
    //step 5

cout<<odom_base_tf.getOrigin().x()<<",    "    <<odom_base_tf.getOrig-
in().y()<<" "<<endl

    <<odom_base_tf.getRotation().x()<<", "

    <<odom_base_tf.getRotation().y()<<", "

    <<odom_base_tf.getRotation().z()<<", "

    <<odom_base_tf.getRotation().w()<<endl;


    //step 6 in chapter 11

    }

}
```

*Steps 1 – 3* are pretty normal and result in a listener object called **listener** and a transform object called odom_base_tf. One thing to note is that a listener object must be created statically because behind the scenes, it stores transform data for 10 seconds. If you create the object then immediately try to read from it, there will likely not be any information yet.

Not listed in the steps, but you could optionally use a listener function called canTransform() to check if a transform you want is available at all.

*Step 4* uses the lookupTransform() function to get the transform data placed into our transform object. Make sure enough time has elapsed since creating the listener object for there to be some data present. lookupTransform() takes the following four arguments:

- Frame 1
- Frame 2
- A time stamp you're looking for. Using ros::Time(0) indicates we want the most recent data
- The name of the object we want to store the transform data in

*Step 5* uses the getter functions getOrigin() and getRotation on our transform object. The rotation values are quaternion that we will convert to *Euler* angles in *Chapter 11, Robot Tracking and Localization.* There is also a complete ROS node file called tf_echo2.cpp in the Downloads for this chapter.

# Viewing transform data from the command line

Sometimes you need a quick look at a transform between a couple of frames. You can do this easily from the command line with the node `tf_echo` from the `tf` package. It's just like starting any other node, plus the `frame1` and `frame2` arguments. For example, to see the current transform for `odom` to `base_link`:

```
rosrun tf tf_echo odom base_link
```

The above command will start scrolling the transform data if the frames are available and connected. Fortunately, the orientation data is printed in both quaternion and regular (Euler) angle notation.

Additional command line `tf` utility nodes can be viewed by typing

```
rosrun tf <tab><tab>
```

But complete information for both the command line interface and C++ API can be found at *wiki.ros.org/tf*.

Not only can transform and the `tf` package streamline your code, many ROS packages you find online require certain transforms to be available to work. The mapping software I am about to introduce, for example, requires an `odom` frame to `base_link` frame transform as well as a `base_link` to laser transform.

# Mapping made easy with Gmapping

This is the part where I confess that my intent is not that you should write the map-making node yourself, and you don't need to study the previous section in great detail. It is, however, very important for you to understand laser scan and occupancy grid messages, and how occupancy grids are generated and what everything in them means. I couldn't think of a better way to teach that than to explain as if we are writing our own – and there's even a complete mapping node `.cpp` file in the `Downloads` for this chapter for you to get a better look at the whole picture. This node works but lacks some of the smarts and robustness of an industry-accepted mapping node: Gmapping.

## Gmapping 101

Gmapping is an open-source **simultaneous localization and mapping (SLAM)** software package widely used in robotics for over **10** years now. Gmapping uses odometry data (which we'll learn to publish in *Chapter 11, Robot Tracking and Localization*) and 2D laser scan messages to generate maps with a far more advanced algorithm than we read about above. Gmapping is capable of processing scans on the move and even computing the error between the odometry and the real-world. While it is an older package, Gmapping's convenient ROS wrapper node, extensive (and readily available) documentation, and effectiveness keep it widely in use.

The ROS *Wiki* page has a lot of information you'll need about running Gmapping and its many parameters. Find it at *wiki.ros.org/gmapping*. For more information about how Gmapping works, start at *https://openslam-org.github.io/gmapping.html*. There you'll find a description, a little about the authors, and links to the relevant academic papers with more details about the algorithm.

## Getting Gmapping

The easiest way to install Gmapping is with the `apt` package manager. Pick the command below that matches your ROS version and run it from the command line:

```
sudo apt-get install ros-kinetic-gmapping
```

or

```
sudo apt-get install ros-melodic-gmapping
```

This should install the Gmapping ROS wrapper we will use directly as well as the underlying code that is the `openslam_gmapping` package itself.

## Running Gmapping and parameters in launch files

This section is intended to be read so you know some of the things we'll have to learn and implement to achieve our first steps. Read over and bookmark this section, because you'll come back to it in *Chapter 21, Building and Programming an Autonomous Robot* as we put together an entire robot.

Gmapping requires a properly formatted laser scan message as well as transforms for the `base_link` to laser and from `odom` to `base_link`. You can run the `gmapping` node directly from the command line, and it will load default parameters, but you can't expect very good results unless you set the parameters to match your system. To run the basic node with default parameters:

```
rosrun gmapping slam_gmapping
```

While you could set a parameter or two via command line, there are far too many not to use a launch file. To set parameters in a launch file, we have to extend our previous entries by moving the terminating / to another <node> tag. For example, the code block below shows the single <node> tag entry we could use if we could live with default parameters.

```
<node pkg="gmapping" type="slam_gmapping" name="gmapping" />
```

The / at the end indicates this is the end of this node entry. In order to extend the entry to add parameter arguments or parameter remapping arguments, we will omit the / from the first <node> tag and add it to a second <node> tag. In between the two tags, we can add arguments using <param> or <remap> tags following the format below:

```
<node pkg="gmapping" type="slam_gmapping" name="gmapping" >

<param name="base_frame" value="base_link"/>

<param name="maxRange" value="8"/>

<remap from="scan" to="base_laser"/>

</node>
```

The above block is a single node-launch entry. It will start the slam_gmapping node but specifies that base_link is the name of the base frame, the maximum range of the laser is 8 meters, and that the node should listen for messages on the base_laser topic instead of the default scan topic.

Some key things to notice are:

- All arguments are passed as strings in quotes – even numbers
- Each tag must have a / to declare the end of that tag

Now that you know how parameters and to remap arguments are set in a launch file, let's look at a complete launch file for Gmapping.

```
<launch>

<!-- this is a comment in a launch file -->

<node pkg="gmapping" type="slam_gmapping"

name="slam_gmapping" output="screen">

    <param name="odom_frame" value="odom"/>

    <param name="base_frame" value="base_link"/>

    <param name="map_frame" value="map"/>
```

```
<!-- The maximum usable range of the laser for obstacle detection. Set
to less than maxRange -->

<param name="maxUrange" value="8"/>


<!-- The maximum range of the sensor - for marking of free space. Set
maxUrange < maximum range of the real sensor <= maxRange -->

<param name="maxRange" value="12"/>


<!--map->odom tf broadcast period in seconds.
0 to disable, but during mapping this is better than
a static transform fixing map and odom together-->

<param name="transform_publish_period" value=".05"/>


<!-- Initial map size and starting point (origin) -->

<param name="xmin" value="0"/>

<param name="ymin" value="0"/>

<param name="xmax" value="10.0"/>

<param name="ymax" value="10.0"/>


<!--delta = resolution of the map-->

<param name="delta" value="0.1"/>
```

```
</node>

</launch>
```

These are the basic parameters that we need to get right. When making a launch file for a single node, I tend to include every parameter even if I think the default value is fine because I want to make it easy to tweak and experiment. The above launch file (with some extra, less-critical parameters included) is available in the *Chapter 10* Downloads as well as the *Chapter 21* package. Read up on the rest of the parameters at the Gmapping *Wiki*.

# Steps to create a map

Creating a map is a multi-step process – mostly because you will nodes to command the robot, interpret those commands and turn them into output signals for the motors, publish laser scan data, and keep track of and publish the robot's location. We will learn each of these in the upcoming chapters. When you get to the mapping part in the *Chapter 21, Building and Programming an Autonomous Robot* project or are otherwise ready to try some mapping, come back here and follow these steps (covered with more detail in *Chapter 21*):

1. Run a launch file that will start sensors and everything you need to drive manually (we will create in *Chapter 21*).
2. Set your starting location and orientation.
3. Run your `gmapping` launch file (`roslaunch your_package_name gmapping_only. launch`).
4. Drive your robot around *slowly*.

If you have met all the requirements, Gmapping should start publishing a map on the topic `map` that can be viewed and saved for later use. As you drive and places become visible to the laser scanner, the map should fill in.

# Visualizing a live map

You may want to visualize the occupancy grid message as it's being updated and published. Rviz is a visualization tool that subscribes to ROS messages like occupancy grids and laser scans and outputs a visual representation of them. Once you have a map being published (which you can check with `rostopic echo -n1 map`), run the Rviz visualization tool if it's not already running with:

```
rosrun rviz rviz
```

When the window opens, follow these steps to display a map.

1. In the left pane, click on the **Add** button.
2. In the pop-up, click **map-building**.
3. In the left pane, a new heading for the map should appear. Make sure the topic listed matches the map topic being published.
4. Scroll up in the left pane to global options, under **Fixed Frame**, select or type `map`.

A map should appear in the main viewing window. See the following screenshot for a reference.

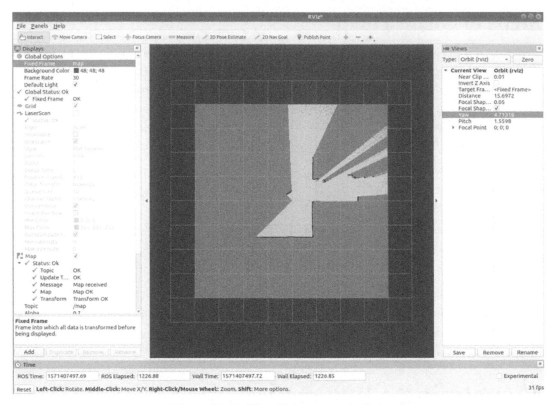

*Figure 10.10: Visualizing a map in Rviz*

If the map isn't visible, check for error messages in the left pane under the `map` section. Often the problem is that you're missing a necessary transform, or the topic is listed incorrectly – Rviz can't render when it doesn't have that information provided correctly. Double-check that the map is being published and that at least some of the data is not listed as `0` or `-1`.

Rviz is a great tool for visualizing much more than just maps. We can see our laser scans, robot position, planned paths, and more. There is a good bit more than we can fit here, but you can probably figure a lot out by experimenting. I also have a short tutorial for the Rviz basics at *youtube.com/practicalrobotics*.

# Saving a Map and using it later

While there's nothing to stop you from saving your occupancy grid data as a text file and writing your node that reads the text file and publishes the `OccupancyGrid` message, maps are traditionally saved as a `.PGM` image file that can be easily viewed and even edited in your favorite photo-editor. Editing is a handy tool to remove temporary things that got mapped (like my dog who wouldn't move) or fill in areas the laser missed (like my very reflective dishwasher).

## Saving maps

Saving maps is easy thanks to a package called `map_server`. You can try the command below first, but if your install didn't automatically include `map_server`, you could install it with:

```
sudo apt-get install ros-kinetic-map-server
```

-or-

```
sudo apt-get install ros-melodic-map-server
```

Choose according to your ROS version.

Save a map by launching the `map_saver` node (from the `map_server` package) with an argument for the filename:

```
rosrun map_server map_saver -f lvgRmMap
```

The `map_saver` node will now generate two files necessary for the traditional map – the `.PGM` image file and `.yaml` file with some map metadata. If your occupancy grid map is being published with a topic name other than the `map` you'll need to remap the topic name to match as we discussed in *Chapter 9, Coordinating the Parts. Figure 10.11* shows the two files in my file browser and the contents of the `.yaml` file after a quick, stationary scan of my living room.

lvgRmMap.pgm          lvgRmMap.yaml

*Figure 10.11: A saved occupancy grid map and its metadata file*

# Load previously saved map

Using a previously saved map is similarly easy with the `map_server` node in the same package. To start `map_server` publishing a map, just launch like any other node but add the .yaml filename as an argument – for example, to load my living room map:

```
rosrun map_server map_server lvgRmMap.yaml
```

Visit *wiki.ros.org/map_server* for more details and options about map_server and map_saver.

# Conclusion

Maps are a vital part of efficient robot navigation. All the skills you learned in this chapter – Using polar angles; subscribing to sensor data messages; what an occupancy grid is; and how to generate, save, and re-load occupancy grid maps — are foundational knowledge you will need with every autonomous robot project.

Of course, generating and navigating mapped spaces autonomously cannot be done without your robot being able to answer one of robotics most fundamental and challenging questions by itself:

*Where am I?*

In the next chapter, we will tackle the problem head-on and discuss some of the pros and cons of different methods used for a robot to track its position — and help you implement one method in great detail.

# Questions

1. Refer to *Figure 10.12* below. You're commanding your robot to turn and face the heading 50 degrees from polar zero. Of course, your robot only speaks in radians, so you'll have to convert. Pose theta data being published indicates the robot's current heading is at 2.0 radians. Calculate the error between the desired heading and current heading, in radians.

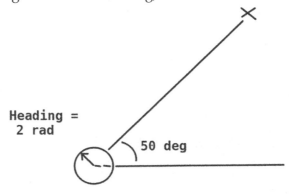

*Figure 10.12*

**2.** You have received a laser scan message from a Hokuyo laser with the listed characteristics. Which element of the `ranges[]` array would you access to determine the distance between the scanner and an object due north of the scanner (at `1.57` radians)?

Data read from scan message:

`angle_min: -2.35619449615`

`angle_max: 2.35619449615`

`angle_increment: 0.00436332309619`

# CHAPTER 11

# Robot Tracking and Localization

## Introduction

Robot tracking is continually comparing one set of sensor data to the previous and adding up the small changes to estimate the current position and orientation. Robot localization is the act of determining where the robot is located in its environment without tracking – more like if you are walked someplace blindfolded, then uncover your eyes and figure out where you are with all new clues. Without knowing where the robot is, we cannot intelligently give it directions to its next destination. Both tracking and localization are valid methods, and usually, the best results come from a combination of the two.

This chapter is all about answering, *Where is the robot?* in a form that can be used mathematically to plot sensor data to a map or to plot a path from the current location to another. Because we are focusing on autonomous robots, the robot will have to answer this question for itself.

# Objectives

Understand how to express robot position, calculate robot position from sensor data, and publish location data as a ROS message that other robot packages can use.

In this chapter, we will cover the following:

- The robot pose
- Odometry and dead reckoning
- Publishing odometry data in ROS
- Further localization
- Publishing pose data in ROS
- Fiducials
- Laser feature - Tracking and localization
- GPS/GNSS – It's value and limitations
- Beacon - Based localization systems

# The robot pose

To describe where a robot is, it won't nearly do to say *It's in the kitchen* or even more specifically *It's by the refrigerator*. Our path planning and mapping software requires numbers to do calculations, and even if the robot knows where the refrigerator is, *in front of* is not likely specific enough to calculate motor drive commands that don't result in hitting an obstacle. We need a much more specific and consistent way to describe to our robot's position and orientation – so we use a collection of numbers we call the **pose**.

There are several conventions for expressing a pose, but they all contain both position and orientation data (sometimes also called translation and rotation). Among the simplest pose conventions is a 2D pose we'll be using throughout this book – it contains x and y locations, as well as angular data (which direction the robot is facing) called **theta**. *Figure 11.1* below illustrates a 2D pose. This is what you've seen if you've already read the chapter on Mapping, which you should do now if you haven't. At the very least, read the section about *Angle, heading, and distance conventions*.

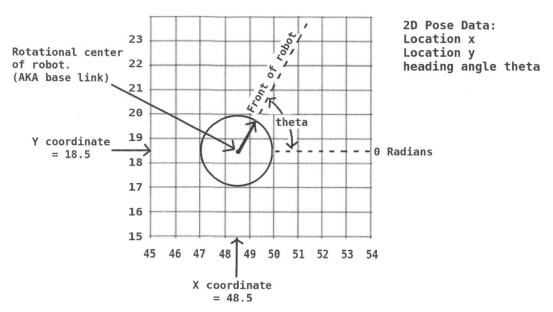

**Figure 11.1:** *The basic two-dimensional pose data*

There are, however, pose conventions for other purposes. A pose for a drone or even a ground-based robot that has to navigate a cave or several floors of a building would need a third dimension, z, expressing height above or below the reference plane. Rather than just angular data theta, which expresses yaw, these machines would also need data for roll and pitch. These refer to the angular rotation about the associated x, y, and z axis. This representation of *roll, pitch*, and *yaw* is called the **Euler angles** and is illustrated in *figure 11.2* below.

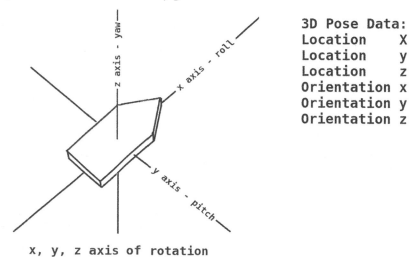

**Figure 11.2:** *A full 3d pose includes our 2D information, plus information for elevation, roll, and pitch*

Quaternions are another way to represent the orientation of an object in space that you'll need to be at least familiar with. Quaternions add a fourth variable to the orientation part of the pose data and is usually notated with a w. These are not as intuitive to visualize as *Euler* angles, and I would not include them at all in *Practical Robotics in C++* except that you'll need to know how to convert back and forth from Euler to quaternion for reasons we'll get to later.

*Figure 11.3* summarizes and gives an example of the 2D pose data we are going to use, how to represent it as a 3D pose with Euler angles, and a 3D pose with quaternions.

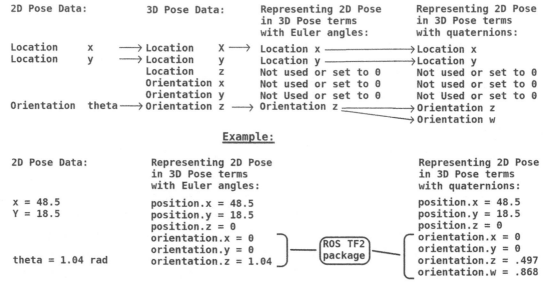

**Figure 11.3:** *2D pose vs 3D pose with Euler angles vs 3D pose with quaternions*

As the mathematics of the conversion is well outside the scope of this book, it is very fortunate that the ROS tf and tf2 packages you already have installed can do the conversions for you. To use these packages, you'll need list tf and tf2 in the find_package section of your package's CmakeLists.txt file.

# Converting Euler angles to quaternions

Converting Euler angles to quaternion for the nav_msgs::Odometry the message is a three-step process:

1. Create a tf2::Quaternion object.
2. Use the setRPY(roll, pitch, yaw) function to convert Euler angles to quaternion.
3. Convert the tf2::Quaternion to a geometry_msgs::Quaternion, which is the type used in odometry and pose messages.

```
#include <tf2/LinearMath/Quaternion.h

#include <tf2_geometry_msgs/tf2_geometry_msgs.h>


//step 1

tf2::Quaternion tempQuat;


//step 2

tempQuat.setRPY(0, 0, pose.theta);


//step 3

OdomMsg.pose.orientation = tf2::toMsg(tempQuat);
```

The `tf2::toMsg()` function accomplishes the same as copying the x, y, z, and w, data members from the `tf2::Quaternion` to the x, y, z, and w data members in the `geometry_msgs::Quaternion`. Note that you can access the tf2 data members as a function call – for example, to copy just the w member directly, you could use:

```
OdomMsg.pose.orientation.w = tempQuat.w();
```

# Converting quaternions to Euler angles

Converting in the other direction, I find the original `tf package` more straightforward than using the `tf2` package. Here are the steps:

1. Create and initialize a `tf::Quaternion` with the x, y, q, and, w values from the message you received.
2. Create a `tf::Matrix3x3` and initialize it with your quaternion.
3. Call `.getRPY()` with your orientation x, y, and z as arguments to hold the *roll, pitch, yaw* data.

The following example code assumes you have a `geometry_msgs::quaternion` called **orientation** as part of a pose message, and pose message called `myPose` where we want to store Euler angles (primarily for z, but we'll do all three):

```
#include <tf/transform_broadcaster.h>


//step 1

tf::Quaternion quat(orientation.x, orientation.y,
      orientation.z, orientation.x);

//step 2
```

```
tf::matrix3x3 mat(quat);
```

```
//step 3
```

```
m.getRPY(myPose.orientation.x, myPose.orientation.y,
```

```
    myPose.orientation.z);
```

The result is that `myPose.orientation.z` now holds our heading angle (theta).

One last note on quaternions. Any change to any of the three Euler angles will change all four of the quaternion values, so don't be surprised if you increase y to represent your robot being on an incline and it results in the x value being reduced. As I said, it's not very intuitive, and for now, the most basic familiarity and ability to convert is enough.

# Odometry and dead reckoning

Odometry is the act of using sensor data to estimate the position of our robot by measuring and adding up small changes – usually many times per second. Probably most associated with wheel odometry from our cars, odometry can be measured with wheel encoders or laser data, or even by tracking motion in data from cameras. Certainly not without its shortcomings, odometry is the oldest method of keeping track of a robot's location and still something of a standard today – albeit as just one component of a complete localization package.

## Wheel odometry

To track a robot's movement with wheel odometry, we turn to the encoders we discussed back in *Chapter 3, The Robot Platform*. We count the pulses from the encoders as the motor shaft turns and divide the number of pulses (called **ticks**) by the known number of ticks per meter. If the left and right wheels travel the same distance, our robot has gone straight. If the left and right wheels have traveled different distances, our robot has turned. The number of ticks per meter can be measured or calculated. We'll look at encoders and publishing tick data in detail in *Chapter 14, Wheel Encoders for Odometry*.

If you calculate, be aware that you'll likely have different real-world results depending on the surface the robot will be driving on, as soft surfaces like a carpet require a greater number of rotations to cover the same total distance compared to a hard floor. Outdoors, wheel textures, as well as hard pavement versus grass versus dirt, will also give different results for the same distance traveled. For these reasons, I prefer to directly measure the number of encoder ticks per meter on the surface I know I'll be on when possible. If the surface varies, I take several measurements and use the best average. To measure the encoder ticks per meter:

- Mark a starting point at the front of the robot. Be as precise as possible – I like to put a piece of tape where the caster wheel touches the ground if it has one. If the robot has 4 wheels and no caster, I put the tape across the robot's front wheels, then use a tape measure to precisely mark the center spot between the wheels.

- Start your tick counter (we'll code one in detail later) and drive the robot straight for some distance, preferably several meters. Don't worry about stopping at a precise location; what's important is that you drive more or less straight (some drift is ok) and that you accelerate and drive slowly to avoid the wheels slipping.

- Repeat the marking process, then measure as precisely as possible the distance in meters from start to finish. Move the robot, if necessary, to get an accurate measure.

- Add the left and the right number of ticks, then divide by two for the average. Divide the average number of ticks by the distance in meters for ticks per meter.

- Repeat several times to get the best average. You'll declare this in your odometry code as `const int TICKS_PER_M`.

- Measure your wheels from centerline-to-centerline and record it later as `const double WHEEL_BASE`.

Once you know the number of ticks per meter, you'll just need to know the distance between the two wheels and a steady stream of data from your `tick_publisher` node. *Figure 11.4* is an example of how I calculated these values for the project robot I built for this book.

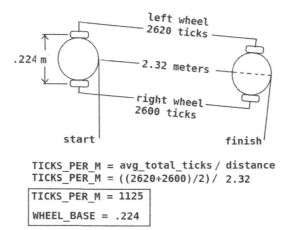

$$TICKS\_PER\_M = avg\_total\_ticks / distance$$
$$TICKS\_PER\_M = ((2620+2600)/2) / 2.32$$

$$TICKS\_PER\_M = 1125$$
$$WHEEL\_BASE = .224$$

**Figure 11.4:** *Measuring the ticks per meter and the wheel base - two constants we'll use for odometry*

From here, the math is straightforward with a little trigonometry. With each cycle, we'll receive the updated counts from the left and right wheel encoders. Ten times per second is a minimum target for frequency, but that'll be set in how fast the tick publisher publishes. With each cycle:

- Calculate the distance traveled for each wheel
- Calculate the total distance the robot has traveled
- Calculate the change in heading angle theta
- Add the change in heading to old heading theta
- Calculate the distance moved in the x and y directions
- Add the distances calculated to the previous pose estimate
- Publish the new odometry pose message for other nodes
- Save the new pose data to use in the next cycle

As a ROS node, the process would take place in three functions in addition to `main()`. One to update each left and right distances, one to do the rest of the calculations and publish, and of course `main()` to handle setup and looping, etc. Look over the general outline for this ROS node, then let's look at each step.

```
#include "ros/ros.h"

#include "std_msgs/Int16.h"

#include <nav_msgs/Odometry.h>

#include <geometry_msgs/PoseStamped.h>

#include <tf2/LinearMath/Quaternion.h>

#include <tf2_ros/transform_broadcaster.h>

#include <cmath>


//we will publish with and without quaternions

ros::Publisher odom_pub;

ros::Publisher pub_quat;


//odometry messages contain a pose message

nav_msgs::Odometry newOdom;
```

```
nav_msgs::Odometry oldOdom;

const double PI = 3.141592;

const double WHEEL_BASE = .224;

const double TICKS_PER_M = 2250;

double leftDistance = 0;

double rightDistance = 0;

using namespace std;

void setInitialPose(const geometry_msgs::PoseStamped &init_pose)

{

//set "last known pose" to init_pose message

}


void Calc_Left(const std_msgs::Int16& lCount)

{

//update leftDistance;

}


void Calc_Right(const std_msgs::Int16& rCount)

{

//update rightDistance

}


void update_odom()

{

//calculate and publish new odometry
```

```
}


int main(int argc, char **argv)

{

//subscribe to encoder messages

//establish and advertise publisher

//loop and call update_odom

}
```

**These code blocks will not compile if pasted together because I have declared odometry data types here, but below in the steps, I am using 2D pose data for readability. We will learn the odometry data type at the end of the chapter. An entire example node called `encoder_odom_publisher.cpp` is in the `Downloads` for this chapter and is included in the robot project `Download` in *Chapter 21, Building and Programming an Autonomous Robot*.

## Calculate the distance traveled for each wheel

To do this, we subtract the previous count from the new count. Care must be taken to handle integer rollover. Assuming you are receiving data as the typical 16 bit integer, when the count would exceed the maximum 16 bit value of `32768` the next count will wrap or roll-over to the minimum value of `-32768`. This wrapping works in both directions, and your code should be able to handle it.

A simple way to detect rollover is to look for large jumps in counts per cycle. If most cycles give `0` to `20` ticks, a jump of several thousand should mean that the counter has rolled over. This example callback function receives 16 bit integer called `lCount` and detects rollover as any tick count greater than `10,000` in one cycle. One other line of the note is that the function skips adding for a cycle if either the last count or the new count is `0` because if the nodes start up at different times for whatever reason, the function will automatically calculate huge distances traveled when there has been none. The 1/10 of a second glitch when rolling past `0` is a small price for avoiding a big error. The last count is still updated, so we pick up the next cycle. There should be an identical callback function for the right encoder counts message.

```
void Calc_Left(const std_msgs::Int16& lCount)

{

    static int lastCountL = 0;
```

```
//make sure we don't start up with false distance
if(lCount.data!=0&&lastCountL!=0)
{
    //update ticks for this cycle
        int leftTicks = (lCount.data - lastCountL);

//these two ifs detect and correct rollover or rollunder
    if (leftTicks > 10000)
        {
            leftTicks=0-(65535 - leftTicks);
        }
    else if (leftTicks < -10000)
    {
        leftTicks = 65535-leftTicks;
    }

//calculate distance from ticks, and store
//in global variable leftDistance
    leftDistance = leftTicks/TICKS_PER_M;
}
    lastCountL = lCount.data;
}
```

**The rest of the steps happen in** update_odom

# Calculate the total distance the robot has traveled

This is just a matter of adding the right and left wheel distances and dividing by 2 for the average.

```
double cycleDistance = (rightDistance+leftDistance)/2;
```

# Calculate the change in heading angle theta

Just a little trigonometry. The difference in wheel travel forms the side of a right triangle known in trigonometry as the *opposite,* meaning opposite of the angle we are calculating, as opposed to either the adjacent side or hypotenuse. The wheel base forms the hypotenuse, and because we are updating so quickly and the difference will be tiny in normal drive conditions, we can forget for a moment that technically the adjacent side and hypotenuse cannot be the same. The header file cmath has trig function asin (for arc sine). *Figure 11.5* illustrates this concept.

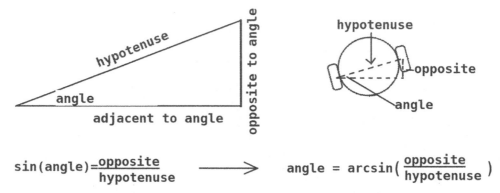

*Figure 11.5: Calculating a change in heading angle from difference in wheel travel*

```
double difference = rightDistance-leftDistance;

double cycleAngle = asin(difference/WHEEL_BASE);
```

# Add the change in heading to old heading theta

This is just the addition of the radians, but we have to handle rollover and rollunder, as the max we want to express is PI, and the min is -PI. Just add or subtract 2*PI as necessary.

```
newOdom.pose.pose.orientation.z

    = cycleAngle + oldOdom.pose.pose.orientation.z;


if (newOdom.pose.pose.orientation.z > PI)

    {

        newOdom.pose.pose.orientation.z -= 2*PI;

    }
```

```
else if (newOdom.pose.pose.orientation.z < -PI)

{

    newOdom.pose.pose.orientation.z += 2*PI;

}
```

## Calculate the distance moved in the x direction and the y directions (also known as translation)

The distance traveled in the x direction is also a trigonometry problem. Don't forget this is calculated using our heading angle theta relative to the map, not just the cycleAngle change. It doesn't make a lot of difference if you use the old theta or the new one. See *figure 11.6.*

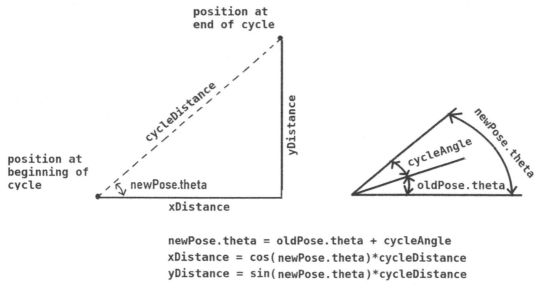

```
newPose.theta = oldPose.theta + cycleAngle
xDistance = cos(newPose.theta)*cycleDistance
yDistance = sin(newPose.theta)*cycleDistance
```

**Figure 11.6:** *Calculating the distance traveled in each direction during this cycle*

```
xDistance = cos(newPose.theta)*cycleDistance;

yDistance = sin(newPose.theta)*cycleDistance;
```

## Add the distances calculated to the previous pose estimate

Again, just addition. Whatever our position in the x direction was, we will add the distance we traveled in this cycle to that distance. The same will apply to the y direction.

```
newOdom.x = oldOdom.x + xDistance;

newOdom.y = oldOdom.y + yDistance;
```

**Publish the new odometry pose message for other nodes**

The Odometry message we publish is just a little different than the simple 2D pose data type I've been using here. We'll talk about converting and publishing at the end of the chapter.

//pseudocode.publish(newOdom);

**Save the new pose data to use in the next cycle**

```
oldOdom.x = newOdom.x;

oldOdom.y = newOdom.y;

oldOdom.theta = newOdom.theta;
```

The basic odometry we just covered can be used by itself but is typically part of a more robust system. Indeed, the standard for maintaining an accurate estimate of the position of a robot is to use multiple sensor types to fill the gaps because every sensor has its weakness. Wheel encoder-based odometry, for example, suffers from things like wheel slippage and the inability to compensate if the robot is bumped off its path or picked up and moved.

# Dead reckoning

The next evolution of the odometry is called **dead reckoning**. Dating back perhaps thousands of years, dead reckoning takes the odometry data in terms of purely measuring distance traveled and further calculated the rate of travel. Early sailors would count how many knots on a long rope rolled out for a fixed amount of time. Then, in the absence of visible landmarks or stars, they could estimate where they should be by multiplying their speed by the amount of time elapsed and then factoring in their heading angle.

In modern robotics, this becomes a useful tool for combining data from multiple sensors and deciding which to trust. More on that in *Chapter 20, Sensor Fusion.* For now, know that in addition to publishing a distance traveled based on encoder ticks, we also calculate and publish velocities in the same odometry message. We call velocity in the x, y, or z axis linear velocities and measure them in meters per second. We also measure velocities of rotation about each of the Euler angles and call them angular velocities, which we measure in radians per second.

The thing about velocity measurements that may be confusing at first is that the measurements are about the robot, not the map. Since we use polar coordinates and consider our robot to have a heading of 0 radians when facing *East* (along the x-axis), the robots x-axis is on its front-to-back center line. If the robot rotates `1.57` radians (`.5*PI`), the robots x-axis is now aiming straight up along the map's y-axis. A linear x velocity value of `.1` now means the robot is moving up along the y-axis at `.1` meters per second. When the robot is turning, it is said to have an angular z velocity. Take a look at *figure 11.7*.

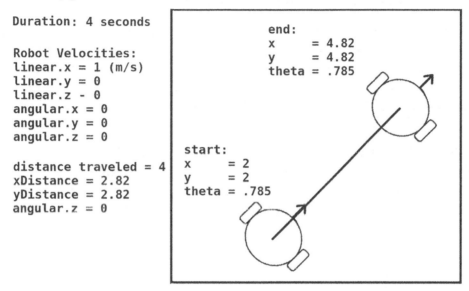

```
Duration: 4 seconds                 end:
                                    x      = 4.82
Robot Velocities:                   y      = 4.82
linear.x = 1 (m/s)                  theta  = .785
linear.y = 0
linear.z - 0
angular.x = 0
angular.y = 0
angular.z = 0
                            start:
distance traveled = 4       x      = 2
xDistance = 2.82            y      = 2
yDistance = 2.82            theta  = .785
angular.z = 0
```

**Figure 11.7:** *When publishing velocities, they are in relation to the robot and and not the map*

Notice that although the only linear velocity is along the x axis, the robot still physically moves along both the x and y axis in the map frame, following its heading `theta`.

Our simple two-wheeled, differential-drive robots would never have a linear y or z velocity unless something is wrong. Similarly, we only need to publish the angular z velocity for rotation as angular x and y do not apply.

 **Positive linear x is moving forward, and negative linear x is moving backwards. Positive angular z is rotating counter-clockwise, negative angular z is rotating clockwise.**

For our purposes, we can simply calculate the `linear.x` and `angular.z` velocities by dividing the `cycleDistance` and `cycleAngle` by the amount of time that elapses between cycles. If your update_odom() function runs `10` times per second, then you could divide distance traveled by `.1`. It would, however, be more accurate to use the system time clock and save time each cycle to compare with the current time. You can call the ROS time and cast it to seconds with the single line:

```
double secs = ros::Time::now().toSec();
```

See *wiki.ros.org/roscpp/Overview/Time* for more information on ROS time, duration, and sleep topics.

# Publishing odometry data in ROS

Among the many pre-defined ROS message types is nav_msgs/Odometry. There are a variety of existing ROS packages and tools that will be expecting an odometry position and velocity data in this format, should you decide to try them out. You're certainly under no obligation to use it, but I think down the road, you'll find it helpful to start getting used to the messages that are conventionally used even if we are omitting some of the fields.

Declaring a nav_msgs/Odometry message is creating an object that is made up of other objects – like most ROS nodes. I hope you're comfortable accessing objects in objects by now because we'll need to access data members several objects deep for this one. Look up *wiki.ros.org/nav_msgs* for more information about nav_msgs/Odometry.

We'll be focusing on getting the odometry data we've discussed so far into the nav_msgs/Odometry message, plus a couple of other minor things. In the code block below, I create the nav_msgs/Odometry message then access each of the data members we are concerned with.

```
//declare the message object named OdomMsg

nav_msgs::Odometry OdomMsg;

nav_msgs::Odometry OdomQuatMsg;


//Set the time in the header stamp

OdomMsg.header.stamp = ros::Time::now();


//set the frame id

OdomMsg.header.frame_id = "odom";


//assign the pose position and orientation data
```

```
OdomMsg.pose.pose.position.x = newOdom.x;

OdomMsg.pose.pose.position.y = newOdom.y;

OdomMsg.pose.orientation.z = newOdom.theta;


//assign the velocity data

OdomMsg.twist.twist.linear.x = linear.x

OdomMsg.twist.twist.angular.z = angular.z;


//convert orientation Euler heading angle to quaternion

tf2::Quaternion tempQuat;

tempQuat.setRPY(0, 0, newpose.theta);


//copy position and quaternion data to 2nd message

odomQuatMsg.pose.pose = odomMsg.pose.pose;
```

Converting the orientation data from Euler to quaternions might still be a little weird, but the rest should be pretty straightforward. We create a message that's easy for us to work with and one with a proper quaternion that other nodes will expect. Doing both is optional, but I like to be able to debug Euler angles at a glance.

Now all that's left is to publish our odometry messages and start all over again. The above code will be part of update_odom() below. I also included a minimal main() for reference.

```
ros::Publisher odom_pub;


void update_odom()
{
    nav_msgs::Odometry OdomMsg;
    //
    //calculate new odometry data here
```

```
    //
    pub.publish(OdomMsg);

    pub.publish(OdomQuatMsg);

}

int main(int argc, char **argv)

{
    ros::init(argc, argv, "encoder_odom_publisher");
    ros::NodeHandle node;

    ros::Subscriber subForRightCounts =
        node.subscribe("rightWheel", 0, Calc_Right);
    ros::Subscriber subForLeftCounts =
        node.subscribe("leftWheel", 0, Calc_Left);

    odom_pub = node.advertise<nav_msgs::Odometry>(odom, 0);

    odom_pub = node.advertise<nav_msgs::Odometry>(odom_quat, 0);

    ros::Rate::loop_rate(10);

    while(ros::ok)

    {
        ros::spinOnce();

        update_odom();

        loop_rate.sleep();

    }
    return 0;

}
```

# Odometry transform publisher

As we discussed in *Chapter 10, Maps for Robot Navigation,* some nodes like Gmapping require odometry data to be available as a transform. While you could certainly add the following to the odometry node above and run it alongside the odometry message publisher, but there will likely be times you'd rather let another node handle the odom->base_link transform. If you run it in its node, it is easy to comment out in your launch file. The downloads for this chapter, as well as the complete robot package for *Chapter 21, Building and Programming an Autonomous Robot,* includes a node that subscribes to the odometry message, copies the information, and publishes it as an odom->base_link transform. The odometry transform publisher tf_pub.cpp follows these steps:

1. Includes necessary header files.
2. Register node with roscore.
3. Subscribe to odometry messages and set the callback function.
   3.1  Initialize transform broadcaster
   3.2  Copy odometry message data to tf::transform
   3.3  Broadcast transform
4. Loop as long as roscore is alive.

The following code block is the entire program except for the content of the callback function.

```
//step 1

#include "ros/ros.h"

#include <nav_msgs/Odometry.h>

#include <tf/transform_broadcaster.h>

#include "std_msgs/Float32.h"


//step 3

void handle_odom(const nav_msgs::Odometry &odom)

{

//steps 3.1 - 3.3 here

}
```

```
int main(int argc, char **argv)

{

    //step 2

    ros::init(argc, argv, "tf_pub");

    ros::NodeHandle node;


    //step 3

    ros::Subscriber subOdom

    = node.subscribe("encoder/odom_quat", 10, handle_odom);


    //step 4

    ros::Rate loop_rate(30);

    while (ros::ok)

    {

    ros::spinOnce();

    loop_rate.sleep();

    }


    return 0;

}
```

The transform must make use of the full quaternion, so I make sure I subscribe to the proper message to avoid having to do the conversion from Euler angles again. The following code block is the callback function.

```
//step 3

//callback function that broadcasts odom message as transform

void handle_odom(const nav_msgs::Odometry &odom)

{

    //step 3.1
```

```
static tf::TransformBroadcaster br;

tf::Transform odom_base_tf;


//step 3.2

odom_base_tf.setOrigin(tf::Vector3(odom.pose.pose.position.x,    odom.
pose.pose.position.y, 0.0) );


tf::Quaternion    tf_q(odom.pose.pose.orientation.x,    odom.pose.pose.
orientation.y,

    odom.pose.pose.orientation.z,    odom.pose.pose.orientation.w);

odom_base_tf.setRotation(tf_q);


//step 3.3

{

br.sendTransform(tf::StampedTransform(odom_base_tf,    odom.header.
stamp, "odom", "base_link"));

}

}
```

Note that the broadcaster does need to be declared statically. The rest is just using the tf package functions to copy the data from the odometry message until we broadcast it in *step 3.3*.

Embedding the transform broadcaster in the odometry node and using a parameter to turn it *On* an *Off* may be a more elegant and common solution than a separate node. Feel free to do so if you are comfortable modifying the code. In any case, don't forget you'll need to list tf to the find_package section in your CmakeLists.txt.

# Further tracking and localization

The odometry we've been working on so far is one method of tracking the robot as it moves through space. While localization is a matter of determining where a robot is – sometimes with the help of and sometimes independently of tracking – because all forms of odometry and dead reckoning suffer from sensor noise errors and drift errors, we will eventually have an incorrect estimate of our robot's location if we don't have a way to make corrections. To do this, we can use a pose estimator to take additional information and decide whether a better guess of actual position and orientation is available.

 **Sensor noise errors can happen in large, sudden jumps while drift errors accumulate as each small error is added to the previous. And while a tiny error in distance measured may take a very long time to be meaningful, a tiny error in our heading angle theta can leave us far away from our target very quickly.**

A notable thing about localization is that the *best guess* location might make big, sudden jumps. This will play havoc on drive controllers, and so are not usually used to correct the odometry message that our drive controllers act on. Instead, the pose estimate from localization is broadcast as another message and another transform – the `map->odom` transform instead of the static `map->odom` transform I introduced earlier.

We will stick with a `static map->odom` transform for this book, and except for the manual pose updater, the rest of this chapter is to give you an idea of some localization methods available so you have a starting place for further research when you've achieved the basics we are working on here. I will say I have successfully used localization to correct the pose estimate in odometry nodes directly, but only while the robot is stationary. This can be done in our odometry node by publishing the new, corrected pose on the `initial_2d` topic we use to set the initial pose.

## Manual pose updater

This is a very useful tool that will allow the user to correct the pose manually at any time. Perhaps more importantly, it allows us to easily provide an initial pose on startup without dealing with changing code or parameters. This manual updating can be made easier by laying a grid of tape on the floor – just don't write me angry emails when your significant other doesn't appreciate the convenience.

This is, of course, the easiest pose-fixing node to implement, as it simply requires asking the user to enter x, y, and theta and then publishing the entries (don't forget to convert Euler theta to quaternion). I think this will be easy for you but is included in the chapter downloads as part of a node called `manual_pose_and_goal_pub.cpp`.

# Fiducials

Fiducials are tags placed where they will become part of a picture and used for reference. Simply, a robot wandering down a warehouse floor can read fiducial after fiducial until it reaches the right location. More modernly in robotics, each special fiducial marker results in line and vertice coordinates being produced for each fiducial in a frame. An April Tag, pictured in *figure 11.8*, is a common type of fiducial.

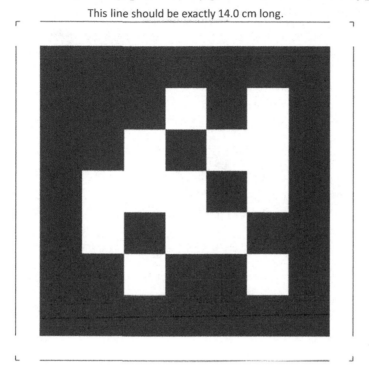

*Figure 11.8: A common fiducal called an "April Tag"*

If a robot can see these in pairs, this allows a position and orientation to be estimated fairly accurately. Alternatively, a fiducial tag can be placed on a robot allowing the robot to be tracked by a camera or system of cameras from above. The downside, of course, is that it requires a previous setup.

More information about the idea and one ROS package that is available at *wiki.ros.org/fiducials*, but I suggest you *Google* fiducial or ROS fiducial for more detailed information and more package choices.

# Laser scanner based localization

The same laser scanner (or LIDAR) that we used for generating a map can be used localization. One of the most popular methods uses a particle filter to estimate the robot's position within a known map.

Particle filtering a pose estimate starts with the robot assuming that it is equally likely to be anywhere. As information comes in, it begins to eliminate the places that it cannot be. Eventually, one location should be revealed as having the highest probability. *Figure 11.9* roughly illustrates the process.

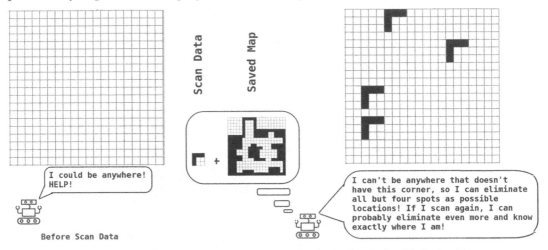

***Figure 11.9:*** *Matching scan data to a stored map to determine likely locations*

A very popular laser-based pose estimator that uses particle filtering is called **Advanced Monte Carlo Localization** (**AMCL**).

AMCL works well enough in places with a lot of features for the laser to detect and compare, but not so well in open areas. I've also had difficulties with the lower-end *XV11 Neato Botvac* scanner, I presume because of its relatively low publishing rate. With faster scanners like my Hokuyo, I've had great results. Read more about AMCL at *wiki.ros.org/amcl*.

While AMCL requires a previously stored map to localize, there is a package called `hector_slam` that provides odometry data and builds a map based on laser scan matching alone, and therefore can be used if you don't have wheel encoders. It is fairly easy to implement once you understand which messages and transforms it needs and supplies and are comfortable converting one message type to another. You can read more at *wiki.ros.org/hector_slam* and *wiki.ros.org/hector_mapping*.

# GPS and GNSS

GPS works by triangulating a position with time signals received from a constellation of satellites maintained by the U.S. Government. GNSS is the same except it uses satellite networks from several countries – including the *United States* GPS. Standard

GPS/GNSS is accurate only to within a couple of meters and is therefore only a helpful clue for determining a robot's location, but cannot be used to guide a robot precisely.

The biggest factor for this inaccuracy is that atmospheric conditions change the speed of the radio signals from the satellite to receiver, and those conditions are varying all over the planet all the time. Several methods have been developed to minimize that error — one of the most successful, called `Real Time Kinematics` (`RTK`), can provide location data accurate down to a single centimeter!

Before you get too excited for GPS, be aware that it simply doesn't work indoors with any repeatable accuracy – the interference with the satellite signals is too great and too varying. If it's an outdoor-robot, though, an RTK GPS/GNSS system may provide a location fix accurate enough that you trust it to push the data to your pose estimator. You still have to be prepared to handle errant readings – what is your robot going to do if it suddenly told that it traveled several hundred meters in 1/10 of a second?

We'll spend a whole chapter on GPS and GNSS a little later; for now, I just wanted you to know what it can and cannot do.

# Beacon-based localization systems

If you're crushed that you can't use GPS indoors, you may feel some relief to know that several systems can be used indoors in a manner somewhat similar to GPS – by triangulation and time-of-flight measurements of ultrasonic sound, radio waves, or even light projected onto the ceiling.

Most of these are aimed at industry – like the KineticIQ by *Humatics*. Other companies are starting to pander to the hobbyist-market – I found a beacon system on *Amazon* being marketed as `indoor GPS` by a company called *Marvelmind*. Not a bad price, if it works as advertised. I can't endorse either as I have not used any of these systems, but they are an option. (I have seen a presentation by *Humatics* at a conference. They do indeed have an impressive system.)

# Conclusion

From counting encoder ticks to calculate odometry data to supplementing that data with corrective *fixes* from other sensors, we've spent this chapter chipping away at the hardest of any mobile robot's basic questions:

*Where am I?*

You now have everything you need to write your odometry publisher and pose estimator nodes if you haven't already, and some ideas for how to keep bettering your location estimates. All of these improvements will help you to navigate, and accurate and steady pose estimates will also improve the maps we made in *Chapter 10, Maps for Robot Navigation.*

Now that our robot can answer the two big questions:

1. Where is this place?
2. Where am I?

We can write a program to send our robot to a location by coordinate, rather than to drive it manually like a remote-controlled car. We'll first learn how to build a basic motor controller that gives us remote control abilities, then we'll write a drive controller node so our robot can drive from a to b by itself.

# Questions

1. Your encoder counts for both wheels are steadily increasing when one suddenly decreases in value from +32765 to -32761. What does this mean, and what has to happen to prevent your robot from suddenly calculating a very large incorrect distance traveled?

2. Write a manual pose publisher that takes user input and publishes a geometry_msgs::PoseStamped message called initial_2d that our pose estimator can use to update the position.

# CHAPTER 12
# Autonomous Motion

## Introduction

Having a map of the robot's environment and knowing where we are on the map is great, but wouldn't it be even better if we could send the robot to any coordinate on the map with a couple of keystrokes or even pre-programmed routines? In this chapter, we are going to draw on some previously covered topics like control theory and motor control to write functional ROS nodes to turn velocity commands into robot motion — and to turn a location request into velocity commands.

In this chapter, we will cover the following:

- ROS robot motion overview
- The motor controller
- The drive controller

## Objective

Learning how to write ROS nodes needed to drive our ROS-powered robot.

# ROS robot motion overview

Making motion happen with ROS isn't different from anything we've already talked about. *Figure 12.1* below is just to help you picture what we are going to accomplish in this chapter.

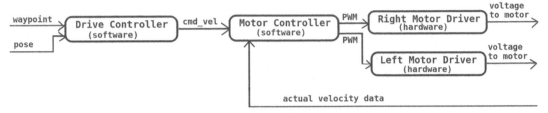

*Figure 12.1: ROS motion-related nodes and topics*

It should look similar to control loop drawings from *Chapter 8, Robot Control Strategy*. The drive controller compares the desired location (also known as a **waypoint**) with the current location and calculates appropriate linear and angular velocities to move the robot toward the desired waypoint. The motor controller receives the cmd_vel message and calculates appropriate PWM signals to output to the motor controllers, which will output varying voltage in turn.

# The motor controller - simple_diff_drive. cpp

We're going to write our differential drive motor controller first because you'll want this working before your try the drive controller – and trust me when I say that you don't want to test both the motor controller and the drive controller at the same time until they each work separately. The entire program can be found in the *Chapter 12* folder of the code repository at *github.com/lbrombach/practical_chapters*, as well as the complete robot package at *github.com/lbrombach/practical_robot*.

This particular motor controller is a partially closed-loop controller that takes cmd_vel and velocity feedback as inputs and outputs whatever signal your particular motor drivers require. In figure 12.1, I left *velocity feedback* intentionally vague because it can be acquired in a number of ways. The motor controller node could subscribe to the odometry publisher node, but I think we will subscribe directly to the wheel encoders and calculate our wheel velocities. For our L298N motor drivers, we will need to output a PWM signal for each motor as well as set forward and reverse directional pins for each motor. Refer back to *Chapter 4, Types of Robot Motors and Motor Control* if you need a refresher on controlling motors with the L298N Dual H-Bridge.

In spite of the many `if/else` blocks, `simple_diff_drive` is a very simple motor controller for a differential-drive robot with a Raspberry Pi computer and two L298N motor drivers. This motor controller does not allow for turning in an arc and instead makes an effort to make sure that the robot either drives straight or pivots. Even if it's not everything you want in a motor controller, `simple_diff_drive` is designed to help you understand what we're trying to accomplish and how to control motors with ROS and a Raspberry Pi in general.

I call this controller *partially closed* because feedback is used to correct for angular drift, but not necessarily absolute velocity. If you're new to controlling motors with your code, I highly recommend you start here and learn the basics in `simple_diff_drive`. In the long term, however, you will likely wish to graduate to a motor controller that uses a full PID instead of this simple proportional controller. You can write one or explore the `differential_drive` package, which is the simplest PID to implement that I've found (although you'll still have to write code to handle the L298Ns via Raspberry Pi GPIO). This package hasn't been maintained in a while, so you'll have to clone the repo into your own `catkin_ws/src` folder or simply use it as a guide to writing your own. Find more info at *wiki.ros/differential_drive*.

# The simple_diff_drive motor controller code steps

1. Handshake with ROS master.
2. Subscribe to wheel encoder and `cmd_vel` topics.
3. Loop through steps 4, 5, and 6 for the life of the program.
4. Check for new messages on subscribed topics, using callback functions to keep wheel velocity data current.
5. Calculate desired PWM values:
   5.1. If `cmd_vel` requests angular velocity (turning), prioritize that and turn. Otherwise, calculate PWM values to drive straight.
   5.2. If driving straight and the actual right and left wheel velocities are not the same, adjust the PWM values.
6. Set the direction pins and output the PWM signal:
   6.1. If the PWM value at this point is negative, set the GPIO direction pins for reverse. Otherwise, set the pins for forwarding.
   6.2. Increment or decrement the actual PWM output a little each loop towards the absolute (positive) value of the requested PWM value.

So six easy steps after a good bit of setup code. It seems like a lot because, at this point, we aren't just calculating a pair of PWM numbers — we have to manage six GPIO pins (four direction pins and two PWM pins). A controller with a PID could eliminate some if/else blocks for the PWM values but requires a higher level of math.

## The differential drive motor controller code outline

The following is the outline of our simple differential drive motor controller:

```
//includes

//declare constants and global variables


void Calc_Left_Vel(const std_msgs::Int16& lCount)

{

    step 4 - update left wheel velocity using encoder count data

}

void Calc_Right_Vel(const std_msgs::Int16& rCount)

{

    step 4 - update right wheel velocity using encoder count data

}


void Set_Speeds(const geometry_msgs::Twist& cmdVel)

{

    step 5 - calculate PWM values

}


void set_pin_values()

{

    step 6 - set direction pins and output signal to PWM pins

}
```

```
int PigpioSetup()

{

    //initialize pigpiod interface and GPIO pins.

    //Set initial pin states

}


int main(int argc, char **argv)

{

    //call function to initialize pipiod interface

    step 1 - Handshake with ROS master

    step 2 - Subscribe to wheel encoder and cmd_vel topics

    while(ros::ok)

    {

        //step 3 - loop through steps 4, 5, and 6

    }

    //set all motors off as node exiting

}
```

# The differential drive motor controller code

First, look over some includes and constants. We have to include both `Twist` and `Int16` message headers, as well as the Pigpio Daemon interface header. Include a few constants you'll need to adjust to your particular robot, and finally a few variables we'll just use globally for simplicity. I think most are self-explanatory, but `leftPwmReq` and `rightPwmReq` are used to calculate the PWM values – initially from a simple linear formula, then adjusted by several things before finally becoming the final target PWM values.

```
#include "ros/ros.h"

#include "geometry_msgs/Twist.h"
```

```cpp
#include "std_msgs/Int16.h"

#include <iostream>

#include <pigpiod_if2.h>


//the rate PWM out can change per cycle

const int PWM_INCREMENT = 2;


//how many encoder ticks per meter

const double TICKS_PER_M = 2250;


//Minimum and Maximum desired PWM output

const int MIN_PWM = 55;

const int MAX_PWM = 120;


//left and right motor PWM and direction GPIO pin assignments

const int PWM_L = 21;

const int MOTOR_L_FWD = 26;

const int MOTOR_L_REV = 13;

const int PWM_R = 12;

const int MOTOR_R_FWD = 20;

const int MOTOR_R_REV = 19;


double leftVelocity = 0;

double rightVelocity = 0;

double leftPwmReq = 0;

double rightPwmReq = 0;

double lastCmdMsgRcvd = 0; //time of last command received


int pi =-1;
```

The next block is our callback function that keeps calculating the left wheel velocity (global variable `leftVelocity`) every time a `leftWheel` encoder count message is received. I'm only going to show the left wheel, but you'll need to duplicate it for the right wheel.

```
void Calc_Left_Vel(const std_msgs::Int16& lCount)

{

static double lastTime = 0;

static int lastCount = 0;


//the next 2 statements handle integer rollover and rollunder

int cycleDistance = (65535 + lCount.data - lastCount) % 65535;

if (cycleDistance > 10000)

    {

        cycleDistance=0-(65535 - cycleDistance);

    }


//convert ticks per cycle to meters per second

leftVelocity = cycleDistance/TICKS_PER_M

        /(ros::Time::now().toSec()-lastTime);


//keep track of last time and last data for the next cycle

lastCount = lCount.data;

lastTime = ros::Time::now().toSec();

}
```

In the callback function `Set_Speeds()` below, we calculate PWM values for our motors. If there is a request to turn, we output the opposite values to pivot. If there is no request to turn but enough of a request to drive forward or backward, we use a linear formula to calculate the PWM value we will request ($y=230*x+39$ works for my robot based on observations of what PWM value gives what speed). Knowing that both the left and right motors will rarely actually give us the same speed given the same voltage, we attempt to correct for this speed difference (because it introduces unwanted turning) by calculating the difference in speed and averaging it over three cycles. This allows us to modify the left and right PwmReq variables with a factor that works for your robot – 125 works ok for mine. If some light calculus and an understanding of full PIDs are in your toolbox, you can avoid setting some of these variables by trial and error and be far more precise.

Lastly, we know that some low PWM values won't turn the wheels, but will make them buzz and drain the battery. I use a ternary operator in the last two lines to set the requested PWM values to 0 if that is the case. If these lines don't make sense to you, just *google ternary operator C++* to find a quick explanation. They're just a way to condense several lines of if(){...} statement into one easy line.

```cpp
void Set_Speeds(const geometry_msgs::Twist& cmdVel)

{

    lastCmdMsgRcvd = ros::Time::now().toSec();


    if(cmdVel.angular.z > .10) //cmd_vel request left turn

    {

        leftPwmReq = -55;

        rightPwmReq = 55;

    }

    else if(cmdVel.angular.z < -.10 )//cmd_vel request right turn

    {

        leftPwmReq = 55;

        rightPwmReq = -55;

    }

    else if(abs(cmdVel.linear.x) > 50 ) //else go straight.

    {

//calculate initial PWM values

        leftPwmReq =230*cmdVel.linear.x+39;

        rightPwmReq =230*cmdVel.linear.x+39;
```

```
    //average difference in actual wheel speeds for 3 cycles

    double angularVelDiff = leftVelocity - rightVelocity;

    static double prevDiff = 0;

    static double prevDiff2 = 0;

    doubleavgAngularDiff =

        (prevDiff+prevDiff2+angularVelDiff)/3;

    prevDiff2 = prevDiff;

    prevDiff = angularVelDiff;


    //apply correction to each wheel to try and go straight

    leftPwmReq -= (int)(avgAngularDiff*125);

    rightPwmReq += (int)(avgAngularDiff*125);

  }


    //don't PWM values that don't do anything

    leftPwmReq = (abs(leftPwmReq)<=MIN_PWM) ? 0 : leftPwmReq;

    rightPwmReq =(abs(rightPwmReq)<=MIN_PWM) ? 0 : rightPwmReq;

}
```

In `set_pin_values()`, below, I once again omitted any reference to the right side. Everything is the same except pin assignments and variable names.

The first thing we do is set the direction pins based on the `PwmReq` variables. While a PWM value cannot be negative, at this point a negative `PwmReq` value means we need to move the wheel in reverse. Also, recall from *Chapter 4, Types of Robot Motors and Motor Control* that we need to set the direction pin *Low* to activate it, and we don't want to set both *Low* at the same time.

After setting the direction pins, we increment or decrement the PWM output by the amount of the `PWM_INCREMENT` constant until it reaches the absolute of the requested value. This is to minimize jerkiness and wheel slippage.

Finally, we do a quick check to make sure the output stays between 0 and whatever we set for a maximum then set the PWM pin itself.

```cpp
void set_pin_values()
{
    static int leftPwmOut = 0;

    //set motor driver direction pins
    if(leftPwmReq>0) //left fwd
    {
    gpio_write(pi, MOTOR_L_REV, 1);
    gpio_write(pi, MOTOR_L_FWD, 0);
    }
    else if(leftPwmReq<0) //left rev
    {
    gpio_write(pi, MOTOR_L_FWD, 1);
    gpio_write(pi, MOTOR_L_REV, 0);
    }
    else if (leftPwmReq == 0 && leftPwmOut == 0 ) //left stop
    {
    gpio_write(pi, MOTOR_L_FWD, 1);
    gpio_write(pi, MOTOR_L_REV, 1);
    }

    //send our pwm signal

    if (abs(leftPwmReq) > leftPwmOut)
    {
    leftPwmOut += PWM_INCREMENT;
    }
    else if (abs(leftPwmReq) < leftPwmOut)
```

```
{

leftPwmOut -= PWM_INCREMENT;

}


leftPwmOut = (leftPwmOut>MAX_PWM) ? MAX_PWM : leftPwmOut;


leftPwmOut = (leftPwmOut< 0 ) ? 0 : leftPwmOut;


set_PWM_dutycycle(pi, PWM_L, leftPwmOut);

}
```

PigpioSetup() is much like other PIGPIO setup functions, but perhaps with extra pin declarations. We interface with the PIGPIO daemon that should already be running, declare and initialize our GPIO pin variables, and set the designation for pi that all of our GPIO-related function calls will need.

```
int PigpioSetup()
{
    char *addrStr = NULL;
    char *portStr = NULL;
    pi = pigpio_start(addrStr, portStr);

    //next 10 lines sets up our pins. Remember that high is "off"
    //and we must drive a direction pin low to start a motor
    set_mode(pi,PWM_L, PI_OUTPUT);
    set_mode(pi,MOTOR_L_FWD, PI_OUTPUT);
    set_mode(pi,MOTOR_L_REV, PI_OUTPUT);
    set_mode(pi,PWM_R, PI_OUTPUT);
    set_mode(pi,MOTOR_R_FWD, PI_OUTPUT);
    set_mode(pi,MOTOR_R_REV, PI_OUTPUT);
```

```
gpio_write(pi, MOTOR_L_FWD, 1); //initializes motor off

gpio_write(pi, MOTOR_L_REV, 1); //initializes motor off

gpio_write(pi, MOTOR_R_FWD, 1); //initializes motor off

gpio_write(pi, MOTOR_R_REV, 1); //initializes motor off


return pi;

}
```

Finally, our main() is typical and calls the PIGPIO Setup function, handshakes with the ROS master node, subscribes to the required topics, and calls the function that sets the PWM values (after checking that a recent cmd_vel message has been received).

```
int main(int argc, char **argv)

{

    //initialize pigpiod interface

    pi = PigpioSetup();

    if(pi()>=0)

    {

        cout<<"daemon interface started ok at "<<pi<<endl;

    }

    else

    {

        cout<<"Failed to connect to PIGPIO Daemon

        - is it running?"<<endl;

    return -1;

    }

    /////////////end pigpiod setup/start ros setup/////////


    ros::init(argc, argv, "simple_diff_drive");
```

```cpp
ros::NodeHandle node;

//Subscribe to topics
ros::Subscriber subRCounts = node.subscribe("rightWheel", 0,
    Calc_Right_Vel,ros::TransportHints().tcpNoDelay());
ros::Subscriber subLCounts = node.subscribe("leftWheel", 0,
    Calc_Left_Vel,ros::TransportHints().tcpNoDelay());
ros::Subscriber subVelocity = node.subscribe("cmd_vel", 0,
    Set_Speeds,ros::TransportHints().tcpNoDelay());

ros::Rate loop_rate(50);
while(ros::ok)
{
    ros::spinOnce();

    //If no msg recieved for more than 1 sec, stop motors
    if(ros::Time::now().toSec() - lastCmdMsgRcvd > 1)
    {
        cout<<"NOT RECIEVING CMD_VEL - STOPPING MOTORS"<<endl;
        leftPwmReq = 0;
        rightPwmReq = 0;
}

    set_pin_values();
    loop_rate.sleep();
}

//set the motors to off as node closes
```

```
gpio_write(pi, MOTOR_L_FWD, 1);

gpio_write(pi, MOTOR_L_REV, 1);

gpio_write(pi, MOTOR_R_FWD, 1);

gpio_write(pi, MOTOR_R_REV, 1);


return 0;
}
```

And that covers a primary motor controller. Since it uses the PIGPIO daemon library to interface the GPIO pins, don't forget to run `sudo pigpiod` from the command line to start the daemon before trying to run it (refer *Chapter 2, GPIO Hardware Interface Pins Overview and Use* for a refresher on GPIO pin and PIGPIOD use). Test and adjust values as needed for your robot until you can drive your robot with a `cmd_vel` publisher such as `rqt_robot_steering` that we learned to use in *Chapter 9, Coordinating the Parts*.

# The drive controller: simple_drive_controller.cpp

Once you have a working motor controller that responds appropriately to `cmd_vel` messages, you can write a simple node that calculates and publishes those `cmd_vel` values automatically, given current and desired locations. This is the drive controller node.

## Drive controller steps

1. Handshake with the ROS master node.
2. Subscribe to `odom` and `waypoint_2d` topics, and advertise as the publisher of `cmd_vel`.
3. Loop steps 4 and 5 for the life of the program.
4. Check for new messages on subscribed topics, and update current position and desired positions as new messages are received.
5. Set velocities based on the latest odometry pose and desired waypoint information:
   5.1. Check if we are close enough to the desired waypoint. If close enough, calculate velocity to make the heading equal to the final desired heading.

5.2. If not yet close enough to the desired waypoint, calculate angular velocity to turn robot toward the desired waypoint and set linear velocity to 0.

5.3. If the robot is facing the desired waypoint, set angular velocity to 0 and calculate linear velocity to move the robot toward the desired waypoint.

5.4. Publish `cmd_vel` message with values set above.

It's pretty simple and also works with the *turtlesim* node if you adjust subscribed and published topics to match what we used in the single-axis turtle controller in *Chapter 9, Coordinating the Parts.* Here is an outline of the `simple_drive_controller. cpp`:

```cpp
//include required files

//declare some constants and global variables


void update_pose(const nav_msgs::Odometry &currentOdom)

{

    step 4 – update current pose

}


void update_goal(const geometry_msgs::PoseStamped &desiredPose)

{

    step 4 – update desired pose (aka the next waypoint)

}


double getDistanceError()

{

    //helper to calculate distance error to desired location

}


double getAngularError()

{

    //helper function to calculate angular error
```

```
}

void set_velocity()

{

    Steps 5.1-5.4 – calculate and publish appropriate velocities to first
    turn towards desired waypoint, then drive to waypoint.

}

int main(int argc, char **argv)

{

    step 1 - Handshake with ROS master

    step 2 - subscribe to topics, advertise publisher

    step 3 – loop for life of program

}
```

Let's take a closer look at each section. The first block is our required includes and declaring some constants and global variables.

```
#include "ros/ros.h"

#include "geometry_msgs/Twist.h"

#include "geometry_msgs/PoseStamped.h"

#include <nav_msgs/Odometry.h>

#include <cstdlib> //for abs()

#include <math.h>

#include <iostream>

const double PI = 3.141592;

//Proportional gain for angular error

const double Ka = .35;

//Proportional gain for linear error
```

```
const double Klv = .65;

const double MAX_LINEAR_VEL = 1.0;


ros::Publisher pubVel;

geometry_msgs::Twist cmdVel;


nav_msgs::Odometry odom;

geometry_msgs::PoseStamped desired;

bool waypointActive = false;
```

The next block has our two callback functions that keep the current and desired locations up to date – as messages of the designated topics are received. The only difference is that when we receive a new goal, we set a bool flag to true in addition to updating the desired pose:

```
//updates the current location

void update_pose(const nav_msgs::Odometry &currentOdom)

{

    odom.pose.pose.position.x = currentOdom.pose.pose.position.x;

    odom.pose.pose.position.y = currentOdom.pose.pose.position.y;

    odom.pose.pose.orientation.z = currentOdom.pose.pose.orientation.z;

}


//updates the desired pose AKA waypoint

void update_goal(const geometry_msgs::PoseStamped &desiredPose)

{

    desired.pose.position.x = desiredPose.pose.position.x;

    desired.pose.position.y = desiredPose.pose.position.y;

    desired.pose.orientation.z = desiredPose.pose.orientation.z;

    waypointActive = true;

}
```

Our helper functions getDistanceError() and getAngularError() in the next block contain some familiar math.

```
double getDistanceError()

{

    double deltaX =

        desired.pose.position.x - odom.pose.pose.position.x;

    double deltaY =

        desired.pose.position.y - odom.pose.pose.position.y;


    return sqrt(pow(deltaX, 2) + pow(deltaY, 2));

}


double getAngularError()

{

    double deltaX =

        desired.pose.position.x - odom.pose.pose.position.x;

    double deltaY =

        desired.pose.position.y - odom.pose.pose.position.y;

    double thetaBearing = atan2(deltaY, deltaX);

    double angularError =

        thetaBearing - odom.pose.pose.orientation.z;

    angularError =

    (angularError > PI) ? angularError - (2*PI) : angularError;

    angularError =

    (angularError < -PI) ? angularError + (2*PI) : angularError;


    return angularError;

}
```

The next block is the `set_velocity` function, where we do all the calculations and publish the `cmd_vel` message. We start every cycle with all `0`s, then set either the angular or linear velocity with a proportional formula as needed to first turn toward the waypoint, then drive to it. The waypoints are published as a pose with a heading: once we have arrived at the location, the controller will publish angular velocity to turn to this desired heading. Once we have arrived and met the desired heading, the flag `waypointActive` is set to `false`, and velocities are all set to zero until a new waypoint message is received.

```
void set_velocity()

{

    cmdVel.linear.x = 0;

    cmdVel.angular.z = 0;


    bool angle_met = true;

    bool location_met = true;

    double final_desired_heading_error =

        desired.pose.orientation.z - odom.pose.pose.orientation.z;


    //check if we are "close enough" to desired location

    if(abs(getDistanceError()) >= .10)

    {

        location_met = false;

    }

    else if (abs(getDistanceError()) < .07)

    {

        location_met = true;

    }


        //if at waypoint, base angular error on final desired heading

        //otherwise, based it on heading required to get to waypoint
```

```cpp
    double angularError = (location_met == false) ?

       getAngularError() : final_desired_heading_error;


//check if heading is "close enough"

if (abs(angularError) > .15)

{

   angle_met = false;

}

else if (abs(angularError) < .1)

{

   angle_met = true;

}


//if not close enough to required heading, command a turn

//otherwise, command to drive forward

if (waypointActive == true && angle_met == false)

{

   cmdVel.angular.z = Ka * angularError;

   cmdVel.linear.x = 0;

}

else if (waypointActive == true

   && abs(getDistanceError()) >= .1

   && location_met == false)

{

   cmdVel.linear.x = Klv * getDistanceError();

   cmdVel.angular.z = 0;

}
```

```
    else

    {

        location_met = true;

    }


    //stop once at waypoint and final desired heading achieved

    if (location_met && abs(final_desired_heading_error) < .1)

    {

        waypointActive = false;

    }


    pubVelocity.publish(cmdVel);

}
```

Finally, we have a particularly simple main() where we have just one conditional statement, so we don't chase some default waypoint. Instead, we wait until we receive one on purpose.

```
int main(int argc, char **argv)

{

    //set desired pose.x as a flag until waypoint msg is recieved

    desired.pose.position.x = -1;


    ros::init(argc, argv, "simple_drive_controller");

    ros::NodeHandle node;


    //Subscribe to topics

    ros::Subscriber subPose = node.subscribe("encoder/odom", 0,

        update_pose, ros::TransportHints().tcpNoDelay());


    ros::Subscriber subWaypnt = node.subscribe("waypoint_2d", 0,
```

```
        update_goal, ros::TransportHints().tcpNoDelay());

    pubVel = node.advertise<geometry_msgs::Twist>("cmd_vel", 0);


    ros::Rate loop_rate(10);

    while (ros::ok)

    {

        ros::spinOnce();


    //IF a waypoint message has been received, set velocities

        if(desired.pose.position.x != -1)

        {

        set_velocity();

        }


            loop_rate.sleep();

    }


    return 0;

}
```

You can see that `simple_drive_controller` is a shorter program than the `simple_diff_drive` because it doesn't have to deal with GPIO pins. Using GPIO pins isn't tricky but does add a lot of code compared to simply calculating variables that only move images on a screen. That is the price we must pay to control machines in the physical world.

You should have no problem writing a simple waypoint publisher at this point to test this program, but you'll find `manual_pose_and_goal_pub.cpp` in your *Chapter 11, Robot Localization and Implementation* downloads that can publish both pose and goals of the same message type as the expected `waypoint_2d`, so you can just remap the topic name at the command line or launch file. Refer to *Chapter 9, Coordinating the Parts* for a refresher on topic name remapping arguments.

# Conclusion

In this chapter, you learned to create a simple motor controller that can turn ROS `cmd_vel` messages into PWM outputs to actually drive a robot in the real world, as well as a simple drive controller that can autonomously calculate and publish those `cmd_vel` messages as it receives *x, y* coordinates of both the current pose and desired pose (waypoint). This is an exciting and essential milestone toward creating fully autonomous robot, so take the time to get these nodes working well, along with the odometry node from the last chapter. Accurate odometry affects the drive controller and is critical as we start trying to follow autonomously plotted waypoints.

When you have those all working, dive into the next chapter, where we will learn a path-planning algorithm that can read a map and publish waypoints along a course that avoids obstacles. This is a crucial ability and finally opens the door to having routines that do not require human intervention – such as `Go send me a picture of what is outside the front window` or `Go explore and update your map`.

# Questions

1. What are the inputs and outputs of the motor controller node?
2. What are the inputs and outputs of the drive controller node?
3. What type of control requires more math at a higher level, but offers more precise control than the simple controllers we've written in this book?

# CHAPTER 13

# Autonomous Path Planning

## Introduction

This chapter probably needs little introduction, as one of the primary questions that keeps budding roboticists awake at night is, *How do I make my robot go places by itself?* Well, as of today, you needn't lose any more sleep over it because we're going to cover everything you need to write an autonomous path-planning program – from reading the map to publishing waypoints to putting power to the wheels.

In this chapter, we will be covering the following:

- Path planning methods and challenges
- Obstacle inflation
- The A* path planner algorithm
- Writing the path planner program

## Objectives

Learning how to write a program for a robot to autonomously plan a path and drive itself from place to place avoiding obstacles in the way.

# Path planning methods and challenges

The goal of path planning is to come up with a list of coordinates that a robot can follow, like it's playing connect-the-dots to get from one place to another without hitting an obstacle. A secondary goal is to make that path efficient, rather than letting our robots drunkenly stumble until they happen across the desired location like early robot vacuums did when looking for their home base.

## Challenges

What makes autonomous navigation difficult isn't so much the path planning itself, it's the supporting requirements – *namely an accurate map and accurate pose estimate within that map.* Our map can only be as accurate as our sensor data and pose estimates, and making accurate pose estimates is difficult without an accurate map. Add to this dynamic conditions like a lazy dog or the kid's backpack on the floor, and suddenly a path that should have been clear is no longer suitable, and an alternate must be found.

## Path planning methods

You can't research autonomous path planning without hearing about *Dijkstra's* algorithm – considered by many to be the earliest successful algorithm. *Dijkstra's* algorithm starts at the starting cell and computes the travel distance from the start cell to every neighboring cell, then from the neighboring cell to its neighboring cells and so on, keeping track of the shortest distance traveled along the way (don't worry, this concept will be clear in a few pages). Its shortcoming is that a lot of calculating is done on entirely irrelevant areas of the map since this exploration takes place in every direction — from the starting cell until the goal is found.

An algorithm that also considers the shortest straight-line distance to the goal will generally save a lot of computations, and *A\** (pronounced as **A-star**) is one such popular algorithm. In *Dijkstra*, the next cell to be checked is the one with the shortest distance back to the start cell. In *A\**, the next cell to be checked is the one with the lowest sum of travel distance from the start plus straight-line distance to the goal. The illustration below, *figure 13.1*, shows the number of cells computed to find a path in *Dijkstra's* algorithm versus the *A\** algorithm.

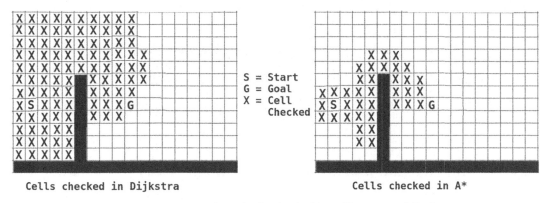

Figure 13.1: *Number of cells checked in Dijkstra vs A\* Path*

You can easily see how many cells more we must check with *Dijkstra's* algorithm, and the difference becomes even greater when there is no obstacle to go around. There are still improvements that can be made and even entirely different approaches to path-finding. Still, in my opinion, the classic $A^*$ is hard to beat for a beginning roboticist in terms of results per amount of hair-pulling frustration to learn. My more advanced readers may like to self-study $D^*$, which keeps a lot of data for re-computation purposes – like when a new obstacle pops up ($A^*$ starts all over in these cases).

# Obstacle inflation

Before we can go reading our map and plotting a path, we have to consider that our robot thinks of itself as a single point in space and doesn't know that it has larger physical dimensions. Unless we do something to prevent it, the robot will attempt to squeeze through places it cannot fit or drive too closely around corners. The answer to this problem is to trick our path-planning program into thinking that the obstacles are bigger than they are. The following *figure 13.2* compares path planning and results with and without obstacle inflation applied.

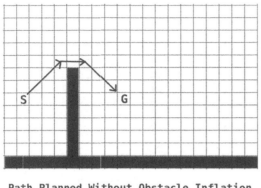
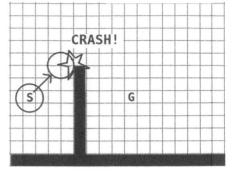

Path Planned Without Obstacle Inflation

Result Without Obstacle Inflation

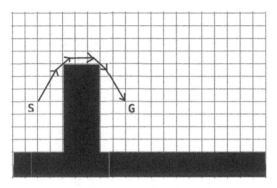
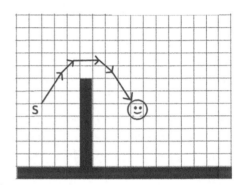

Path Planned With Obstacle Inflation

Result With Obstacle Inflation

*Figure 13.2: Path planning with and without obstacle inflation*

Do you see the extra clearance that results from path planning with artificially inflated obstacles? That's what we're trying to achieve.

# Costmaps

**Costmaps** are what the inflated maps are usually called and technically aren't just about inflating obstacles. Formally, costmaps are about reflecting the cost to traverse a cell in either time or energy, as some may be slippery or rough terrain that takes extra time and energy. There is a threshold of *cost* above which the path planner considers the cell completely impassable and avoids it as if it were occupied.

### costmap_2d

The costmap_2d package is readily available to us and only slightly different to set up than most other nodes with a lot of parameters. I'll give a summary and walk-through of getting it going, but complete documentation is available at *wiki.ros.org/ costmap_2d*.

The `costmap_2d` uses the concept of map *layers* to manage the many things going, the primary layers being:

- The static map layer – This is the map you created or are creating with all the permanent obstacles in it.

- The obstacle map layer – This is essentially another map `costmap_2d` creates on-the-fly with sensor data. It will thus include non-permanent objects like a person or object that was not present during the original map-building process.

- The inflation layer – This layer includes all of the obstacle inflation done by `costmap_2d` on both of the above layers.

Imagine that all three above layers are drawn on their transparent paper. If you stack them on top of one another, the result appears as if you only have to look at one map to see the information from all layers. This is what `costmap_2d` publishes, and what your path planning node should subscribe to.

Install `costmap_2d` with the appropriate apt-get command for your ROS version:

```
sudo apt-get install ros-kinetic-costmap-2d
```

-or-

```
sudo apt-get install ros-melodic-costmap-2d
```

So far, we've loaded parameters from the command line or a `launch` file. In the case of `costmap_2d`, we will use our launch file to load a `.yaml` parameter file. This is because we need to load the shape of our robot to `costmap_2d`, and that is not available as a normal parameter that I have been able to find. I know it's one more hoop to jump through, but I promise it's not complicated. For complete documentation and some extra tricks, check out *wiki.ros.org/costmap_2d/tutorials* – in particular, the section on configuring layered costmaps. For the very basics, follow these instructions:

1. Create a folder in the root directory of your package called `param`. For example, my navigation package is called `practical_nav`, so I used the following commands:

   ```
   roscd practical_nav
   mkdir param
   ```

2. Create a text file with a `.yaml` extension. I used `costmap_basic.yaml`

3. Specify plugins – This is how we set up which layers we want to include. For the basics, we will include a static layer and an inflation layer. `static_map` is the name of a service provided by the `map_server` node

   ```
   plugins:
     - {name: static_map,      type: "costmap_2d::StaticLayer"}
     - {name: inflation_layer,  type: "costmap_2d::InflationLayer"}
   ```

4. Specify robot footprint – this an array of points (x, y coordinates) that represent a polygon if each point is connected to the previous. My robot is round, so I just use eight points as an octagon — not a inadequate representation. The points assume (0,0) is the center of the robot. The last point will be automatically connected to the first to close the polygon.

```
footprint: [[x1, y1], [x2, y2], [x3, y3], [x4,y4],
    [x5, y5], [x6, y6], [x7, y7], [x8, y8]]
```

5. Specify other desired general parameters with the format:

```
parameterName: value_here

#for example

robot_base_frame: base_link

resolution: .1
```

6. Specify parameter specific to each layer following this example:

```
static_layer:

    map_topic: /map

    unknown_cost_value: -1

    lethal_cost_threshold: 100

    first_map_only: false

    subscribe_to_updates: false
```

A complete example (`costmap_basic.yaml`) is available in this chapter's downloads (*github.com/lbrombach/practical_chapters*) and is also part of the robot project package for *chapter 21, Building and Programming an Autonomous Robot. Figure 13.3* below is a screenshot of that file:

```
Start here ✖  costmap_basic.yaml ✖  basic_full.launch ✖

1   plugins:
2      - {name: static_map,      type: "costmap_2d::StaticLayer"}
3      - {name: inflation_layer,  type: "costmap_2d::InflationLayer"}
4
5
6   #robot with radius = .16
7   footprint: [[-0.16, 0], [-0.113137, -0.113137], [0, -0.16], [0.113137, -0.113137],
8                  [0.16, 0], [0.113137, 0.113137], [0, 0.16], [-0.113137, 0.113137]]
9
10
11  global_frame: /odom
12  robot_base_frame: base_link
13  resolution: .1
14  update_frequency: .5
15  publish_frequency: .5
16  transform_tolerance: 0.5
17  rolling_window: false
18  always_send_full_costmap: true
19
20
21  static_layer:
22      map_topic: /map
23      unknown_cost_value: -1
24      lethal_cost_threshold: 100
25      first_map_only: false
26      subscribe_to_updates: false
27
28
```

*Figure 13.3: A costmap_2d setup YAML file*

I find the YAML syntax simpler than all the tags required with the *XML* syntax we use with launch files. Load the YAML file to the ROS parameter server with the first command below; then you can start the costmap_2d node with the second command.

```
<rosparam file="$find package_name/params/file_name.yaml"

    command="load" ns="/costmap_2d" />

<node    pkg="costmap_2d"    type="costmap_2d_node"    name="costmap_2d"
output="screen" />
```

**A word of caution – about space-wasting, though. This is perhaps best illustrated first. Look at the following *figure 13.4,* displaying part of my condo before and after costmapping.**

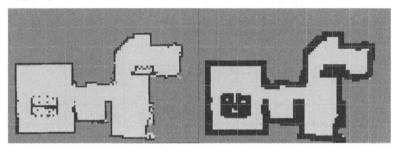

*Figure 13.4: Before and after obstacle inflation*

While inflating obstacles nicely prevents my robot from trying to go between the legs of dining room chairs (all those dots on the left of the left image), it does make worse the already wasteful nature of occupancy-grid mapping, since an entire cell is marked occupied even if an object just barely cuts through a corner of it. It can result in the robot sometimes missing a valid path. This combined wastefulness must be considered when choosing a map resolution and weighed against the amount of processing – if I use map cells that represent 5  cm instead of 10, every node has to process four times as many cells, and 1 cm resolution would require 100 times the processing. Consider this when first building your maps.

# A* path planning

Our *A** path planning node is going to subscribe to a costmap, current location from our pose estimator, and some topic that publishes a goal. With these three inputs, it is going to do some math and come up with a list of waypoints that our robot can follow to get from its current location to the goal – hopefully without hitting an obstacle along the way. We will publish these waypoints as a 2D pose that the drive controller we wrote in the previous chapter subscribes to. For the sake of making sure our terminology is understood, take a look at the following *figure 13.5.*

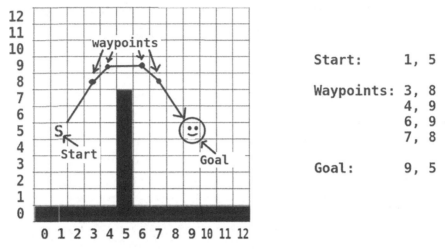

Start:        1, 5

Waypoints:  3, 8
              4, 9
              6, 9
              7, 8

Goal:        9, 5

*Figure 13.5: Defining start, goal, and waypoints*

Assuming it is already running and has a map and the robot's current location, the path planner is just waiting to receive a goal location. Upon receiving the goal location, it will come up with a list of waypoints and publish one at a time for the drive controller as the robot reaches the previous. Finally, the goal location is published as a waypoint.

# How it works

$A^*$ starts with the idea that each movement from one cell to the next will cost a certain base amount. Diagonal movements will cost `1.4` times as many sideways or vertical movements (assuming the same type of terrain), and obstacles are considered to have an infinite cost, so we won't even try to cross them. The cost of any path can be calculated simply by adding the cost of each cell traversed along the way. This cumulative cost to any cell from the starting cell is known as the **G cost**. (For some reason, it is almost universal to use the variables **G** and **H** in $A^*$, then sum them up into the variable **F** as you'll see in a moment). The following *figure 13.6* shows calculating the **G cost** for each cell along a path by adding the base cost of **10** to the previous cell's **G cost**.

| 14 | 10 | 14 |
|----|----|----|
| 10 | C | 10 |
| 14 | 10 | 14 |

Triangle: 14.14 (hypotenuse), 10 (vertical), 10 (horizontal)

G cost to traverse from current
cell (center) to each neighbor

| | | | 10+14 34 | 34+10 44 | | | |
|---|---|---|---|---|---|---|---|
| (G=0) S | 0+10 10 | 10+10 20 | inf | inf | 44+14 58 | | |
| | | | inf | inf | 58+14 G | | |
| | | | inf | inf | | | |

Calculating G cost for each cell along a path
by adding the cost to traverse this cell to the
G cost from the previous cell

*G cost to traverse occupied cells is infinite*

***Figure 13.6:*** *Calculating the G cost for each cell along a path*

*How do we come up with a base cost?* That's really up to the programmer and application. We'll be using the simplest cost measure of distance, but one could decide to consider time instead, or watts or anything else you can measure. As mentioned, obstacles will be assigned a cost of INT32_MAX to represent as close to infinity as we can. There may come a time when you assign values in between the base-cost and infinite for different types of terrain – fighting sand or mud may be possible, but why use the extra energy if a clear sidewalk is detected adjacent?

Since we are using distance and working with a 2D grid, our movement options are side-to-side, up and down, and diagonal. Using the number 1 for a cost for sideways movement results in decimals for diagonal movements, so it is an excellent trick to multiply by 10 and use a cost of 10 for sideways and vertical movements, and 14 for diagonal movements – which is roughly the hypotenuse of a right triangle with both sides of length 10.

Now is the part where $A^*$ diverges from *Dijkstra's* algorithm because in addition to the G cost, we need to calculate a **heuristic cost** we call H that is designed to help us calculate the total cost F that we use to keep moving in the right general direction.

Consider that for any given cell that is a waypoint on a path, the total cost from start to goal will be:

**total cost = cost from start to the cell + cost from cell to goal**

Because we can't know the actual cost from any cell to the goal without completing the path, the best we can do is substitute in a heuristic – or the best guess – that will increase the odds that we are heading in the right direction. Without adding this heuristic, we end up with a *Dijkstra* search pattern and a lot of wasted calculating. So because we can't see obstacles beyond the cell we're currently evaluating, the total distance formula above becomes the following:

**total cost = cost from start to the cell + heuristic**

**AKA**

**F = G + H**

The heuristic can be a lot of things, but the most common for our simple maps is to use either the straight-line distance from the cell to the goal or the **Manhattan distance**, calculated as if there were no obstacles in the way. It's not perfect, but it is a pretty good bet. I'll use Manhattan distance for all my examples just because I think it's slightly easier to read the code. Look at the following *figure 13.7* for an illustration on calculating one cell's **G**, **H**, and **F** costs before we start fitting this into an algorithm.

```
G cost - the cost to reach the cell from the start, along a certain path
H cost - The cost from the cell to the goal, ignoring obstacles
F cost - The sum of G + H costs
```

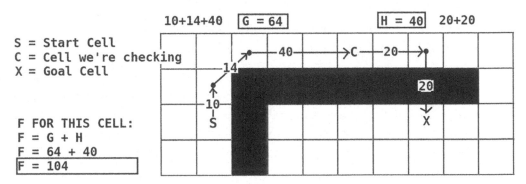

*Figure 13.7: Calculating G, H, and F, costs for one cell as part of the A\* pathfinding algorithm*

A\* works by calculating the **F** cost each of the eight cells adjacent to the starting cell (we will call these adjacent cells *neighbors* from now on). While we are visiting a cell, we also leave a note to identify which cell led to it. The neighbor with the lowest calculated **F** cost will be the next cell we move to, and calculate **F** for all of its neighbors. This chosen neighbor is called the current.

As we explore neighbors, we add them to a list called *open*. When choosing our next *current,* we iterate over this open list and select the open cell with the lowest **F** cost. Cells get removed from the open list only after they have been the *current* cell.

Once we leave a *current* cell and move to the next, we remove it from *open* and add it to a list called *closed,* so we don't re-open it and calculate all of its values again and again. When we run into an occupied cell, we immediately add that cell to the closed list as well.

The pattern repeats – moving *current* one cell at a time until the goal is found, or it is decided that there is no path from start to goal because we have run out of cells in the open list. Once the goal is found, we follow the notes about the previous cells like a trail of breadcrumbs to make a list of cells that comprise the complete path.

# The A* algorithm by the steps

I'm not going to kid you – it can take a while to get a grasp of all the nested `while()` and `for()` loops and `if()` and `else` blocks in an *A\** program, especially once you start adding actual code and it has to handle ROS messages. When we write the program later, you can refer back to this commented outline.

The first thing we need is to define what a `cell` is going to consist of. We talk about each cell being a location on our map, but we need to attach some information to it. I've tried to avoid making our own data types until now, but it's going to be difficult to do path planning without. I'll use a `struct` with all public data members for simplicity. If you aren't familiar with structs and how to access their data members, you'll want to find a tutorial now and get comfortable before proceeding.

```
struct cell

{

    int index;    //the index in nav_msgs::OccupancyGrid data[]

    int x;        //x coordinate of cell on map

    int y;        //y coordinate of cell on map

    int F;        //the total cost, calculated as G + H

    int G;        //cost from start to this cell along path

    int H;        //heuristic - manhatten distance from cell to goal

    int prevX;    //x coordinates of previous cell

    int prevY;    //y coordinate of previous cell

};
```

The first data member, index, is optional, but I find it makes for easier comparisons than checking both x and y. The `index` parameter is the index in the array that our map is stored in. Recall from the mapping chapter that every x, y coordinate has a corresponding index for a given map size. Refer back to *figure 10.8* if you need to.

Here are the basic steps of $A^*$:

1. Create two empty lists – open and closed.
2. Create a cell object called current that is equal to the start cell – which in our case will be the robot's position.
3. Add the new cell current to the open list.
4. Starting here, loop over the remaining steps until we find the goal:
   4.1. Check size of open list – if it is 0 return a failure, for there is no path.
   4.2. For every neighboring cell of current:
       4.2.1. If already in open list, calculate the new F cost and compare it to the old F cost. If new F is lower, record new F and G, and make the current cell the new parent.
       4.2.2. If not in either open or closed list, create a new cell object and add to open unless it's an obstacle, which gets added to closed instead.
   4.3. After checking all neighbors, add current to closed and remove from open.
   4.4. Find the cell in the open list with the lowest F cost and make that the new current.
   4.5. At this point, we have found the goal. Set goal's parent to the last cell found, then add the goal to the closed list so we can trace the path back to start. All cells of the path will be on the closed list.
   4.6. Starting at the goal, follow the prevX and prevY data and make a list (in order) of the path cells back to the start.

As you can see in the steps above, the algorithm isn't that difficult to comprehend, but all the nested loops and conditional statements can make it confusing to keep track of where you are and what should happen next. Let's run through a simple path-finding problem to help you visualize and embed the idea behind the algorithm before we go over all the code.

# Walking through an A* routine

As we walk through the path-finding problem in *figure 13.8*, note how I show the G cost and the H cost for that cell at the top; and the bold number in the middle is the F cost. I also note if a cell is in the open or closed list. The darkened cells are obstacles, but our program has no way of knowing that until we reach them during exploration.

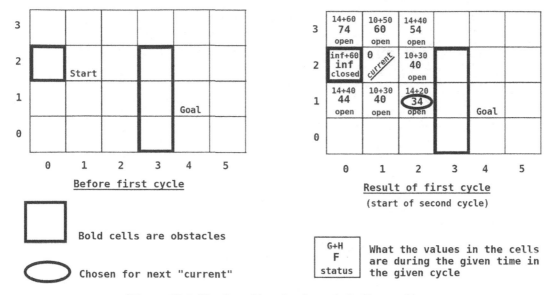

**Figure 13.8:** *The first A\* cycle of a path-finding problem*

We start on the left of *figure 13.8* with a map loaded into memory, but our path-finding node has yet to look at any information.

**Steps 1-3:** We create our empty open and closed lists, and a cell object called current using the x, y coordinates 1, 2 because that is our starting cell. We place the current cell in the open list and proceed to *Step 4*.

**Step 4:** We explore each of the start cell neighbors one at a time. None of these cells are on either list, so we have to create the cell object for each. Cell 0,2 is an obstacle, so it immediately put into "closed." For the rest, we calculate the F cost and also mark each cell prevX and prevY with our current cell 1,2 and put them in the open list.

Remember that the G cost is cumulative, but the start cell's G cost is 0, so for this first round, all neighboring cells get a G cost of just 10 or 14. The F costs are the big numbers in the middle of each cell.

Now we add the current cell to the closed list and make the cell with the lowest F the current cell. So now current is cell 2,1 and we have two closed cells and seven open cells, including current. The results of the first cycle are on the right side of *figure 13.7*, and this is the starting point for the second cycle. See *figure 13.9* below for an illustration of the second cycle.

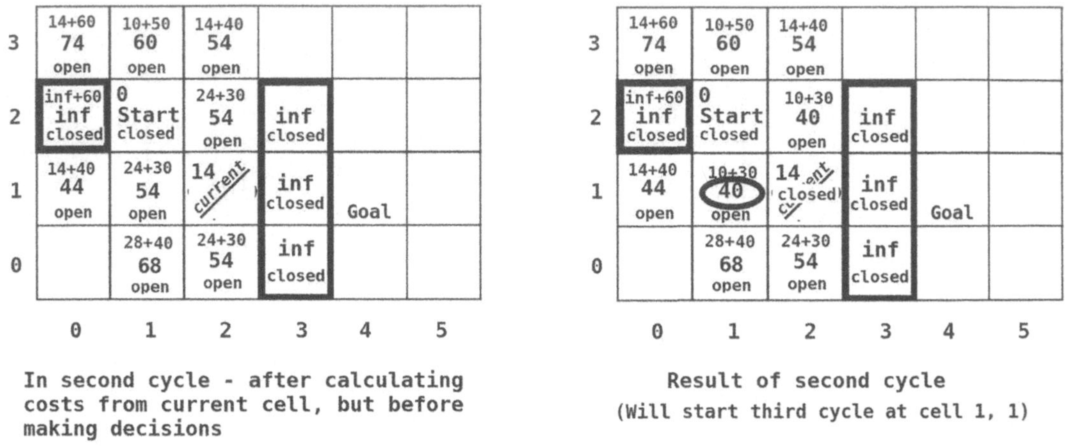

In second cycle - after calculating costs from current cell, but before making decisions

Result of second cycle
(Will start third cycle at cell 1, 1)

*Figure 13.9:* The second A* cycle

**Step 4:** (yes, step 4 again. This will repeat until we find the goal or determine there is no path. Refer to *figure 13.9*).

We look at every cell around our new current 2,1. Our previous current (also known as **start cell**) is already closed, so we skip it. 3 other cells are obstacles, so we create objects for them but place them in the closed list before we bother with any calculations.

The left picture shows the calculations we've made for the other four neighbors of the current cell, but so far, these are temporarily stored variables. Cells 1, 0, and 2, 0 have to be created and placed in open with these values. Cells 1,1 and 2,2 are already in the open list, so we compare the new values and keep whichever is lowest. In both cases, it was less costly to get to that cell from the start cell than to go through the new current, so we keep the old values.

With the calculations and comparisons done, we can close the current at 2,1 and choose a new one. Cells 1, 1, and 2, 2 have the same F cost, so we choose one arbitrarily. I happen to have chosen the one that you and I can see is leading away from the desired path, but you'll see shortly how the heuristic quickly gets us back on track. We make 1,1 the new current and, because it is already created and in the open list, we can just go back to the stop of *step 4* and proceed with our third cycle, illustrated in the following *figure 13.10*.

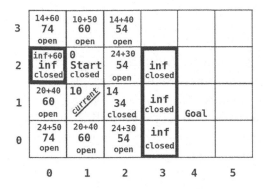

In third cycle - after calculating costs from current cell, but before making decisions

Result of third cycle
(Will start fourth cycle at cell 2,2 )

*Figure 13.10: The third A\* cycle*

**Step 4:** (The third cycle. Refer to *figure 13.10*)

With current now at cell **1,1**, we calculate G and F for all the neighboring cells that are still in the open list. Many of the old F costs are the same or lower, so we leave those cells alone. Cell **1,0** gets new, lower G and F costs, though. Its prevX and prevY are updated as well, so **1,1** is its new parent. Finally, we move **1,1** to closed and make **2,2** the new current because it has the lowest F cost of any cell in the open list. In the right image, we can see that now our cell with the lowest F cost is the other choice from the last cycle. **2,2** will be our new current for the next cycle. Look at the fourth cycle in the following *figure 13.11*.

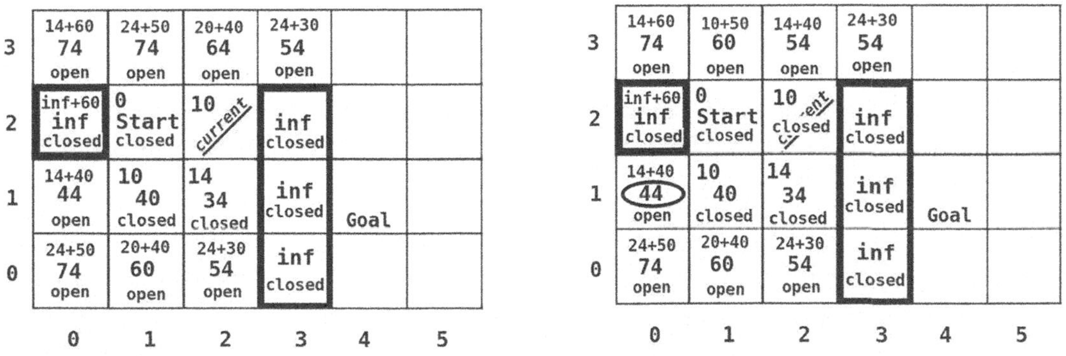

In fourth cycle - after calculating costs from current cell, but before making decisions

Result of fourth cycle
(Will start fifth cycle at cell 0,1 )

*Figure 13.11: The fourth A\* cycle*

**Step 4:** (The fourth cycle. Refer to *figure 13.11*)

Most of the current cell's neighbors are already closed, so we only have to check the three in the top row. If you look back at the result of the third cycle (in *figure 13.10*), you can see that the two cells already in the open list already have the lower F cost, so we do not update them with the new calculations or change their parent cell. The new cell 3,3 is created and added to open, and its parent cell is set to 2,2 – the current 2,2 is closed and removed from open, and a quick scan of open cells shows us that our current for cycle five will be cell 0,1. Cycle five is illustrated in the following *figure 13.12*.

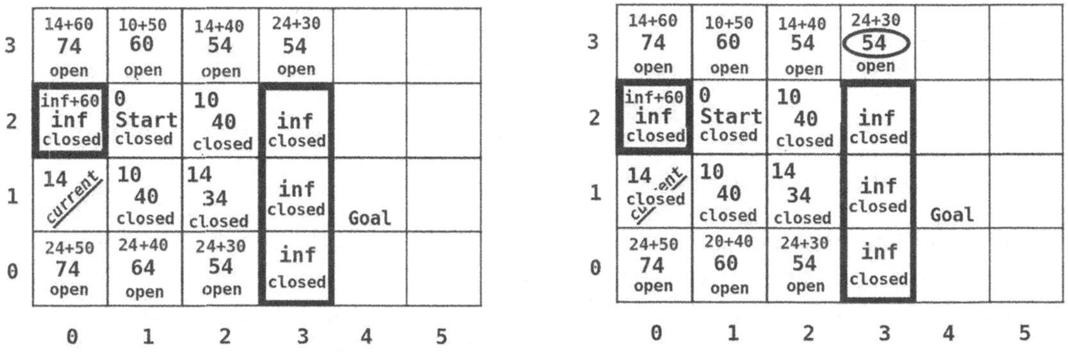

Left grid:

| | 0 | 1 | 2 | 3 | 4 | 5 |
|---|---|---|---|---|---|---|
| 3 | 14+60 / 74 / open | 10+50 / 60 / open | 14+40 / 54 / open | 24+30 / 54 / open | | |
| 2 | inf+60 / inf / closed | 0 / Start / closed | 10 / 40 / closed | inf / inf / closed | | |
| 1 | 14 / current | 10 / 40 / closed | 14 / 34 / closed | inf / inf / closed | Goal | |
| 0 | 24+50 / 74 / open | 24+40 / 64 / open | 24+30 / 54 / open | inf / inf / closed | | |

In fifth cycle - after calculating costs from current cell, but before making decisions

Right grid:

| | 0 | 1 | 2 | 3 | 4 | 5 |
|---|---|---|---|---|---|---|
| 3 | 14+60 / 74 / open | 10+50 / 60 / open | 14+40 / 54 / open | 24+30 / (54) / open | | |
| 2 | inf+60 / inf / closed | 0 / Start / closed | 10 / 40 / closed | inf / inf / closed | | |
| 1 | 14 / closed | 10 / 40 / closed | 14 / 34 / closed | inf / inf / closed | Goal | |
| 0 | 24+50 / 74 / open | 20+40 / 60 / open | 24+30 / 54 / open | inf / inf / closed | | |

Result of fifth cycle
(Will start sixth cycle at cell 3,3 )

*Figure 13.12: The fifth A\* cycle*

**Step 4:** (The fifth cycle. Refer to *figure 13.12*)

With most of the current cell (0,1) neighbors being out-of-bounds or closed, we just have to check two cells for a lower F cost. Of those, only cell 1,0 needs updating. We close the current and search for the open cell with the lowest F cost, which is clearly...oh my.

If you look over the right image in *figure 13.12*, you'll find that we have three cells in a tie for the lowest F cost. I am going to pick the one we can see is going in the right direction to save us some time, but in reality, your program might pick any of these. I think you can see that the cell I selected would become the current within a cycle or two anyway. See *figure 13.13* below to see how cycle six works out.

Left grid — *In sixth cycle - after calculating costs from current cell, but before making decisions*

| y \ x | 0 | 1 | 2 | 3 | 4 | 5 |
|---|---|---|---|---|---|---|
| 3 | 14+60 / 74 / open | 10+50 / 60 / open | 34+40 / 74 / open | 24 / current | 34+20 / 54 / open | |
| 2 | inf+60 / inf / closed | 0 / Start / closed | 10 / 40 / closed | inf / closed | 38+10 / 48 / open | |
| 1 | 14 / 44 / closed | 10 / 40 / closed | 14 / 34 / closed | inf / closed | Goal | |
| 0 | 24+50 / 74 / open | 24+40 / 64 / open | 24+30 / 54 / open | inf / closed | | |

Right grid — *Result of sixth cycle (Will start seventh cycle at cell 4,2)*

| y \ x | 0 | 1 | 2 | 3 | 4 | 5 |
|---|---|---|---|---|---|---|
| 3 | 14+60 / 74 / open | 10+50 / 60 / open | 14+40 / 54 / open | 24 / closed / current | 34+20 / 54 / open | |
| 2 | inf+60 / inf / closed | 0 / Start / closed | 10 / 40 / closed | inf / closed | 38+10 / (48) / open | |
| 1 | 14 / 44 / closed | 10 / 40 / closed | 14 / 34 / closed | inf / closed | Goal | |
| 0 | 24+50 / 74 / open | 20+40 / 60 / open | 24+30 / 54 / open | inf / closed | | |

**Figure 13.13:** *The sixth A\* cycle*

**Step 4:** (The sixth cycle refer to *figure 13.13*)

With the current cell at 3,3, we check the one *open* cell and find the new calculations too high to save. We open two new cells and look over the open list for our next cell to make current. Our program won't know it until it starts checking the neighbors, but you and I can see and be excited that the next cell to be current is going to find the goal! Let's close the last current, set 4,2 as the new current, and get started!

**Step 4:** (For the last time!)

The newest current cell *(4,2)* has one open cell and three new cells, so it may not find the goal on its first pick. No big deal; soon enough, the algorithm will detect that the cell it is exploring matches the goal, and it can finally move on from *Step 4* to *Step 5* in the A\* steps we listed before.

**Step 5:**

To get here, we must have detected the goal. We must now set the goal's parent to the current that found it. Then we add both the current and the goal to the closed list. Since we have closed every cell we have explored, we can forget about all those F, G, and H costs and focus on prevX and prevY to trace backward from the goal cell to the start. If we take one last look at the map we've been working on and I show you the prevX and prevY instead of the costs, you'll see that it worked out nicely. The following *figure 13.14* shows the previous x,y values, and the path.

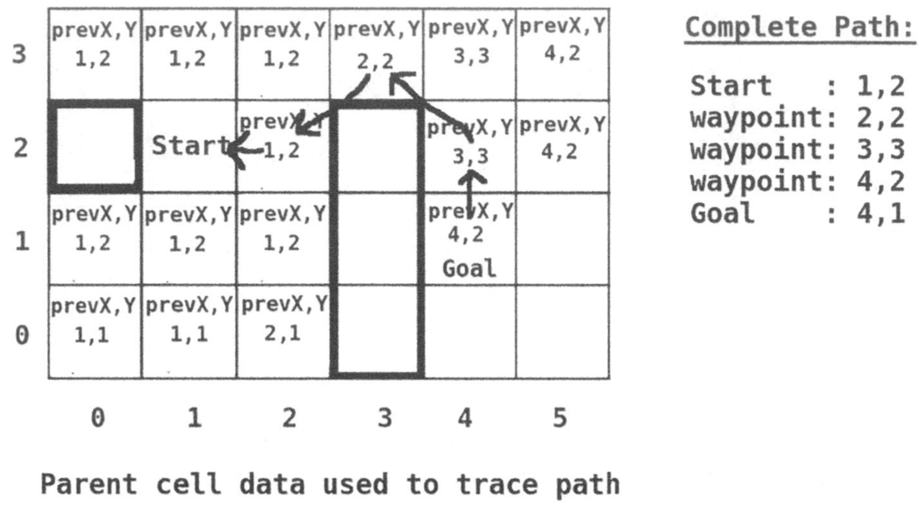

| | prevX,Y | prevX,Y | prevX,Y | prevX,Y | prevX,Y | prevX,Y |
|---|---|---|---|---|---|---|
| 3 | 1,2 | 1,2 | 1,2 | 2,2 | 3,3 | 4,2 |
| 2 | | Start | prevX,Y 1,2 | | prevX,Y 3,3 | prevX,Y 4,2 |
| 1 | prevX,Y 1,2 | prevX,Y 1,2 | prevX,Y 1,2 | | prevX,Y 4,2 Goal | |
| 0 | prevX,Y 1,1 | prevX,Y 1,1 | prevX,Y 2,1 | | | |
| | 0 | 1 | 2 | 3 | 4 | 5 |

**Complete Path:**

```
Start    : 1,2
waypoint: 2,2
waypoint: 3,3
waypoint: 4,2
Goal     : 4,1
```

**Parent cell data used to trace path**

*Figure 13.14: Tracing the path back to the starting cell after finding the goal*

**Step 6:**

*Figure 13.14* gives you an idea of how to find the waypoint back to the start by following parent cell data — then we can publish however much of the path data we need to. You might just want to publish the first waypoint for the robot to navigate to, then publish the next or rerun the algorithm if there have been map updates. If you are running some visualization, you might want to publish all of the waypoints so you can see the path in some tool like **Rviz** – that's up to your needs.

**Bonus step:** (This is optional, and I recommend not trying to add this to your code until you have a basic path planner working)

Notice that $A^*$ gives you a waypoint for every single cell the path passes through. It's not apparent how many extra waypoints this can be from our little example, but on a larger map, even a straight line can end up having dozens or hundreds of waypoints. Even here on our little map, the move from the start cell **1,2** to **3,3** requires two waypoints, and the robot would make two different movements to get there even though there is nothing in between. It's not part of the standard algorithm. Still, you can optionally add a function that looks for the farthest point on the path from the robot's current location that it can get to in one straight-line movement, then deletes waypoints that aren't necessary.

For our example, such a function might draw a line from the start to the goal, then see if any obstacle is on that line. There are, so we can't drive straight to the goal. It might then check the waypoint before the goal, and find there are still obstacles in the way. When it checks waypoint **3,3**, it will find nothing between that waypoint and the start, so waypoint 2,2 could be deleted and the robot could drive to 3,3 in one movement.

# Writing the A* program as a ROS node

Welcome to the biggest program (most lines of code) we'll write in this book – by far. Not because it's necessarily such a difficult algorithm, but instead because there are a lot of small comparisons and operations that make a relatively simple task (for a human) look very bloated in written code. This will be somewhat more the case than necessary as I am still very much writing with readability for the beginning-programmer in mind and avoiding calling libraries to do things behind the curtains so the greatest number of readers can understand as they follow the code. Unfortunately, that means more advanced programmers are going to have to read more lines of code than they might like, but the point is they should have no problem understanding and write their own *A\** program to satisfy their abilities.

That said, beginner programmers may have to take a break and study up on some less beginner-friendly **C++** concepts like *vectors* (because we'll need to be able to re-size arrays) and *structs*. I still managed to avoid classes with separate public and private data members, functions, and operator overloading and hope the trade-off means more people will be able to follow along (although I do add a copy constructor and use an item initializer list). For the first time, however, I'm going to bring up including files because there are only so many functions you can put into a program before you can't even find the main().

*A\** benefits from a lot of little helper functions. I recommend at least two include files for *A\** — one for *A\** functions and one with general helper functions (some of which are the same as helpers from other programs, so you can start to save lines of code if you can include this file in multiple programs). Not that include files are that advanced of an idea, but I can think back to a time when they weren't second nature, and I avoided them in favor of one big program. If that's you, now is the time to cross the bridge and embrace separating your programs into multiple manageable files.

## The standard stuff, helper functions, and main()

First, we need to include some things and declare some things. We have a constant, three ROS subscribers, a ROS publisher, and one global variable to hold the occupancy grid map. The only thing that might look odd is _map declaration. It is just an occupancy grid object with a special constructor to make sure we don't run out of stack memory space.

```
#include "ros/ros.h"

#include "nav_msgs/OccupancyGrid.h"

#include "nav_msgs/Path.h"

#include "geometry_msgs/PoseStamped.h"

#include      "yourPkgName/yourIncludeHeader.h"#include      <tf/transform_
listener.h>

#include <vector>

#include <math.h>

#include <iostream>


using namespace std;


//cells with map data above this are considered 100% occupied

const int OCCUPIED_THRESHOLD = 20;


//create our subscriber and publisher.

ros::Subscriber subMap, subGoal;

ros::Publisher pub;

ros::Publisher pathPub;


//this is where we'll keep the working _map data

nav_msgs::OccupancyGrid::Ptr _map(new nav_msgs::OccupancyGrid());


//global flag so we can start and stop the algorithm

bool goalActive = false;
```

After the basics, the first helper functions I want to get out of the way are to make it easy to figure out the x,y coordinate of the index of any occupancy grid data[] point, and vice versa. Recall that our mapping work is done on a 2D grid, but the map data is received and stored as a 1D array.

```
//returns the x coordinate, given an index number and a map

int getX(int index, const nav_msgs::OccupancyGridPtr &map)

{

    return index % map->info.width;

}


//returns the y coordinate, given an index number and a map

int getY(int index, const nav_msgs::OccupancyGridPtr &map)

{

    return index / map->info.width;

}


//returns the index number, given x,y coordinates and a map

int getIndex(int x, int y, const nav_msgs::OccupancyGridPtr &map)

{

    return map->info.width * y + x;

}
```

The next few functions will also be called often. We need to check that all cells are within map boundaries, or we risk throwing a segmentation fault and halting the program. We also will frequently simply need to know if a cell is considered an obstacle, and occasionally what the resolution of the map is so we can convert from grid cell coordinates to the real-world coordinates in meters.

```
//returns whether given coordinates are a valid cell n the map

bool is_in_bounds(int x, int y,

        const nav_msgs::OccupancyGridPtr &map)

{

    return (x >= 0 && x < map->info.width

        && y >= 0 && y < map->info.height);
```

```
}


//helper to check if cell is to be considered an obstacle

bool is_obstacle(int x, int y,

          const nav_msgs::OccupancyGridPtr &map)

{

    return ((int)map->data[getIndex(x, y, map)]

      > OCCUPIED_THRESHOLD);

}


//helper to return map resolution

double map_resolution(const nav_msgs::OccupancyGridPtr &map)

{

    return map->info.resolution;

}
```

The following block of helpers is just some basic math. Two important things to note: It's easy to forget when you're handling a pose coordinate or a grid coordinate (grid cell number = pose*(in meters)* / map_resolution, so grid coordinate 8,8 is pose .8,.8 in the real world ). *Do not mix grid cell coordinates with real-world map coordinates*. Also, these are basic functions that won't handle dividing by 0(as in vertical lines). Make sure the functions that call any of these checks before asking these functions to divide by 0.

```
//returns slope m from slope-intercept formula y=m*x+b

//given two coordinate pairs

double get_m(double x1, double y1, double x2, double y2)

{

    //****CAUTION< WILL THROW ERROR IF WE DIVIDE BY ZERO

    return (y1 - y2) / (x1 - x2);

}
```

```
// returns offset b from slope intercept formula y=m*x+b

//for b = y-(m*x)

double get_b(double x1, double y1, double x2, double y2)

{

    if(x1 != x2)

    {

    return y1 - (get_m(x1, y1, x2, y2) * x1);

    }

    else return x1; // if x1 == x2, line is vertical, so b = x1

}


//returns Y from slope intercept formula y=m*x+b, given x

//****DOES NOT HANDLE VERTICAL LINES****

double get_y_intercept(double x1, double y1,

            double x2, double y2, double checkX)

{

    double m = get_m(x1, y1, x2, y2);

    double b = get_b(x1, y1, x2, y2);

    return m * checkX + b;

}


//returns x from slope intercept formula y=m*x+b, given y.

//for x= (y-b)/m **DOES NOT HANDLE VERTICAL LINES**

double get_x_intercept(double x1, double y1, double x2, double y2, double
checkY)

{

    double m = get_m(x1, y1, x2, y2);

    double b = get_b(x1, y1, x2, y2);
```

```
    return (checkY - b) / m;

}
```

While the general occupancy grid contains only one bit of information about each cell, *A\** needs to track a handful of pieces of information for each cell. Following is an example of the data we need, a copy constructor, and declaring a couple of global instances of struct cell we will use throughout the program.

```
struct cell

{

    cell() : index(-1), x(-1), y(-1), theta(-1), F(INT32_MAX),

        G(INT32_MAX), H(INT32_MAX),

            prevX(-1), prevY(-1) {}


    cell(const cell &incoming);


    int index; //the index in the nav_msgs::OccupancyGrid

    int x; //x, y as grid cells coordinates

    int y;

    double theta; //not strictly for A*, but the final waypoint //is the
    goal and requires heading theta

    int F;       //this cells total cost, F = G + H

    int G;       //cost (distancetraveled) to cell from start

    int H;       //manhattan distance distance to goal

    int prevX;   //map grid coordinates of previous parent cell

    int prevY;

};

//copy constructor

cell::cell(const cell &incoming)

{

    index = incoming.index;
```

```
    x = incoming.x;

    y = incoming.y;

    theta = incoming.theta;

    F = incoming.F;

    G = incoming.G;

    H = incoming.H;

    prevX = incoming.prevX;

    prevY = incoming.prevY;

}
```

```
cell start; //creating start object

cell goal; //creating goal object
```

We generally have a callback function for every subscriber. The first callback function is to update our working map (_map) with the data from costmap published by another node. Ideally, the costmap is only published when there is new information in it.

```
//copy the supplied costmap to a new _map we created above

void map_handler(const nav_msgs::OccupancyGridPtr &costmap)

{

    static bool init_complete = false;

    //only do this stuff the first time a map is recieved.

    if (init_complete == false)

    {

        _map->header.frame_id = costmap->header.frame_id;

        _map->info.resolution = costmap->info.resolution;

        _map->info.width = costmap->info.width;

        _map->info.height = costmap->info.height;

        _map->info.origin.position.x
```

```
                = costmap->info.origin.position.x;

        _map->info.origin.position.y

                = costmap->info.origin.position.y;

        _map->info.origin.orientation.x

                = costmap->info.origin.orientation.x;

        _map->info.origin.orientation.y

                = costmap->info.origin.orientation.y;

        _map->info.origin.orientation.z

                = costmap->info.origin.orientation.z;

        _map->info.origin.orientation.w

                = costmap→info.origin.orientation.w;
    //resize data[] so it can hold the data in costmap->data

        _map→data.resize(costmap→data.size());


        cout << "Initializing map size " << _map->info.width

        << " x " << _map->info.height << endl;


        init_complete = true;

    }

    //this part we can do every time to ensure we see updates.

    for (int i = 0; i < costmap->data.size(); i++)

    {

        _map->data[i] = costmap->data[i];

    }

}
```

Our other callback is to keep our goal position updated. You can see in `set_goal()` where we set `goalActive` to `true` – this is what tells the program (that is always running in our robot) to run the path-finding function. Our start cell is always the current actual location. This could be updated with a callback upon receipt of an odometry pose message or making use of transform data like I do here. This method is more resilient to future changes as your localization methods evolve with new skills.

```cpp
//set our start cell as the current grid cell

bool update_start_cell()

{

    static tf::TransformListener listener;

    tf::StampedTransform odom_base_tf;


    listener.lookupTransform("odom", "base_link", ros::Time(0), odom_base_tf);


    //dont forget that grid cell is pose in meters / map resolution

    start.x = odom_base_tf.getOrigin().x()/ map_resolution(_map);

    start.y = odom_base_tf.getOrigin().y()/ map_resolution(_map);


    tf::Quaternion q(0, 0, odom_base_tf.getRotation().z(),
        odom_base_tf.getRotation().w());

    tf::Matrix3x3 m(q);

    double roll, pitch, yaw;

    m.getRPY(roll, pitch, yaw);

    start.theta = yaw;

    start.index = getIndex(start.x, start.y, _map);

    return true;

}


//set goal recieved and set goalActive = true

void set_goal(const geometry_msgs::PoseStamped &desiredPose)

{
```

```
//grid cell is pose in meters / map resolution

goal.x = (int)(desiredPose.pose.position.x /

    map_resolution(_map));

goal.y = (int)(desiredPose.pose.position.y /

    map_resolution(_map));

goal.theta = desiredPose.pose.orientation.z;

goal.index = getIndex(goal.x, goal.y, _map);

goal.H = 0; //must set to zero to identify when found

goalActive = true;

}
```

The next block has just two functions – one that simply iterates over a list to check if it contains a given cell by its occupancy grid index, and one that will publish the cell identified by the find_path() function as the next waypoint.

```
//check if cell with index of toCheck is in supplied list

bool contains(vector<cell> &list, int toCheck)

{

    for (int i = 0; i < list.size(); i++)

    {

        if (list[i].index == toCheck)

        {

            return true;

        }

    }

    //if not found in above loop, list does not contain

    return false;

}


//publish the next waypoint is 2d form -
```

```
//ignoring quaternion nature of PoseStamped data type

void publish_waypoint(cell nextWaypoint)

{

    geometry_msgs::PoseStamped wpt;

    wpt.header.frame_id = "map";

    wpt.header.stamp = ros::Time::now();

    //convert cell x, y coords to position in meters

    wpt.pose.position.x = (double)(nextWaypoint.x) / 10 + .05;

    wpt.pose.position.y = (double)(nextWaypoint.y) / 10 + .05;

    wpt.pose.position.z = 0;

    wpt.pose.orientation.x = 0;

    wpt.pose.orientation.y = 0;

    wpt.pose.orientation.z = nextWaypoint.theta;

    wpt.pose.orientation.w = 0;

    pub.publish(wpt);

}
```

Following are three simple math helpers for calculating the G, H, and F costs for the cell *A*\* will explore.

```
//helper to calculate G cost

double getG(int x, int y, int currentX, int currentY, double currentG)

{

    //cost is infinite if cell is obstacle

    if (is_obstacle(x, y, _map))

    {

        return INT32_MAX;

    }
```

```cpp
    //if cell is not diagonal, the cost to move is 10
    else if (x == currentX || y == currentY)
    {
        return currentG + 10;
    }
    //cost is 14.142 if cell is diagonal
    else
    {
        return currentG + 14;
    }
}


//helper to calculate H heuristic
double getH(int x, int y)
{
    return (abs(goal.x - x) + abs(goal.y - y)) * 10;
}


//helper to calculate F, but avoid integer rollover
double getF(int g, int h)
{
    if (g == INT32_MAX)
    {
        return g;
    }
    else
    {
```

```
        return g + h;

    }

}
```

Next up is the essential `trace()` function that follows the previous cell data we left along the way and sends the next waypoint to `publish_waypoint()` to publish to our drive controller.

```
int trace(vector<cell> &closed)

{

    vector<cell> path;

    //closed.back() is the goal, and will be element [0] in path

    path.push_back(cell(closed.back()));

    bool pathComplete = false;

    while (pathComplete == false)

    {

        bool found = false;

        //check the closed list for the parent cell of the last

    // cell in path[]. At first, only the goal is in path.

        for (int i = 0; found == false && i < closed.size(); i++)

        {

            //when we find the parent cell, push it to path

            if (closed[i].x == path.back().prevX

            && closed[i].y == path.back().prevY)

                {

                path.push_back(cell(closed[i]));

                found = true;

            }

        }
```

```
    //check if the path is complete
    if (path.back().index == start.index)
    {
        pathComplete = true;
    }
}

//the waypoint at path.back() is currently our start point.
//By removing it, the new back() will be our first waypoint
if (path.back().index != goal.index)
{
    path.pop_back();
}

//if goal, publish goal heading, else publish the heading we
//took to get here anyway
if (path.back().index != path.front().index)
{
    double deltaX = path.back().x - start.x;
    double deltaY = path.back().y - start.y;
    path.back().theta = atan2(deltaY, deltaX);
}

publish_waypoint(path.back());

return path.back().index;
}
```

Finally, let's get our `main()` out of the way before we get to the find-path function itself. We subscribe to topics here, advertise our publisher, and have a couple if and else blocks. Nothing new here.

```
int main(int argc, char **argv)

{

    ros::init(argc, argv, "path_planner");

    ros::NodeHandle node;


    //subscribe to map, current pose, and goal location

    subMap = node.subscribe("costmap", 0, map_handler);

    subGoal = node.subscribe("goal_2d", 0, set_goal);


    //advertise publisher

    pub = node.advertise<geometry_msgs::PoseStamped>

        ("waypoint_2d",0);


    //check callbacks every second

    ros::Rate loop_rate(1);

    while (ros::ok)

    {

        if (goalActive == true)

        {

//get current location from transform data

update_start_cell();

            //If we arrive at goal, stop until new goal received

            if (start.index == goal.index)

            {

                goalActive = false;

            }

            else

                {
```

```
        int nextWaypoint = find_path();

        if (nextWaypoint == -1)

            {

                cout << "NO PATH FOUND" << endl;

                goalActive = false;

            }

        }

    }

    ros::spinOnce();

    loop_rate.sleep();

    }


    return 0;

}
```

And that wraps up a whole lot of supporting functions. I know it's a lot of code, but none of it is very complicated if you break them down into little blocks. Keep that in mind in the next section as we look at the code for the find_path() function that is the heart of the *A\** program.

# The heart of your A\* Node: find_path()

This is where the magic happens – the *A\** algorithm that we walked through earlier. Just as this is the biggest program we'll write in this book, this happens to be the biggest function. As such, I'm going to break this function up into manageable blocks. As usual, the whole program is available for download at *github.com/lbrombach/ practical_chapters*.

Here is the outline of find_path() with all of the major brackets in place and a note about which step (from the preceding section *A\* by the steps*) is where. You can see *Step 4* takes up a lot of space by itself, so that will be further broken up as we walk through the code sections.

```
int find_path()

{
```

```
//Step 1. Create empty open and closed lists
//Step 2. Create cell object "current" that is the start cell
//Step 3. Add "current" to open list

while (Step 4 - while goal not found)
{
    for (iterate over neighbors)
    {
        for (its 2d matrix, still iterating over neighbors)
        {
            if (make sure cell is in bounds)
            {
                if (Step 4.1 check if open list is empty)
                {
                }

                if (Step 4.2.1 - cell already in open list)
                {
                else if (4.2.2 - cell not in either list)
                {
                }
            }
        }
    }

// Step 4.3 - Add "current" to closed and remove from open
{
}
```

```
        //Step 4.4 - Make "current" the cell in open with lowest F
    {

    }

    }

    //Step 5 - we have found the goal. Set goal's parents to last
        cell found and add to goal to closed list.

    {

    }


    //Step 6 - Trace the path


    return nextWaypoint;

}
```

**Step 1.** Create empty open and closed lists. I use vector for simplicity, but keep in mind that we'll do quite a bit of searching these by iteration. If more efficient data structures are in your coding toolkit, you can potentially cut run time quite a bit.

```
vector<cell> open;
```

```
vector<cell> closed;
```

**Step 2.** Create a cell object current that is the start cell. We call the copy constructor to make a copy of the start cell; then, I do all three cost calculations just because this is an easy place to see them. We just need this first cell to have a G cost of 0, and because I like to use the occupancy grid index for comparisons, I initialize that too.

cell current(start);

//special case start G must be initialized to 0

current.G = 0;

current.H = getH(start.x, start.y);

current.F = current.G + current.H;

current.index = (getIndex(current.x, current.y, _map));

**Step 3.** Add current to open list. Nothing much here. Since the open list is empty, adding the current we just made makes our start element 0 in the open[ ]. When we are done, the goal will be the last element in the open[ ], regardless of what size it reaches.

```
open.push_back(cell(current));
```

**Step 4.** This one is a doozy, so try to carefully keep track of the brackets. We iterate over the cells around current and if they are in bounds, we do steps 4.1, 4.2.1, and 4.2.2. Once we've done that for all neighbors, steps 4.3 and 4.4 find us a new current and we repeat until we are at the goal.

```
//H of 0 means we are at the goal cell

while (current.H > 0)
{
    for (int x = current.x - 1; x <= current.x + 1; x++)
    {
        for (int y = current.y - 1; y <= current.y + 1; y++)
        {
            if (is_in_bounds(x, y, _map))
            {
                Step 4.1 if open list is empty

                Step 4.2.1 - cell already in open list

                Step 4.2.2 - cell not in either list
            }
        }
    }

    Step 4.3 - Add "current" to closed and remove from open

    Step 4.4 - Make "current" the cell in open with lowest F
}
```

**Step 4.1** – If we run out of cells in the open list, then there is no path. I simply set goalActive to false and return -1.

```
if (open.size() == 0)

{

    cout << "NO PATH FOUND" << endl;

    goalActive = false;

    return -1;

}
```

**Step 4.2.1** – If the cell is already in the open list, iterate over the open list until i is equal to the index of the cell we are checking in the open list(Feel free to combine the checking and index retrieving to save code and operations). Once we have the correct index, calculate F and compare it with the existing.

```
if (contains(open, getIndex(x, y, _map)) == true)

{

    //iterate the list until we find the relevant cell

    int i = 0;

    while (open[i].index != getIndex(x, y, _map))

    {

        i++;

    }

    int tempG = getG(x, y, current.x, current.y, current.G);

    int tempH = getH(x, y);

    int tempF = getF(tempG + tempH);

    //if this calculation results in lower F cost, save the new

    //data and replace cells parents with current cell

    if (tempF < open[i].F)

    {

        open[i].F = tempG + tempH;

        open[i].G = tempG;
```

```
        open[i].prevX = current.x;

        open[i].prevY = current.y;

    }

}
```

**Step 4.2.2** – If the cell was not found in the open and is not in closed list either, we need to create the `cell` object and place it accordingly. If the calculated `F` value indicates the cell is an obstacle, it goes in the closed list. Otherwise, add it to the open list.

```
else if (contains(closed, getIndex(x, y, _map)) == false)

{

    //create the cell object with current cell data

    cell newCell;

    newCell.x = x;

    newCell.y = y;

    newCell.index = getIndex(x, y, _map);

    newCell.prevX = current.x;

    newCell.prevY = current.y;

    newCell.G = getG(x, y, current.x, current.y, current.G);

    newCell.H = getH(x, y);

    newCell.F = getF(newCell.G, newCell.H);


    //add to closed list if obstacle, else add to open list

    if (newCell.F == INT32_MAX)

    {

        closed.push_back(cell(newCell));

    }

    else

    {
```

```
        open.push_back(newCell);

    }

}
```

**Step 4.3** – Once we've checked all of the *current's* neighbors, put current in the closed list and remove from the open list.

```
closed.push_back(cell(current));

bool found = false;

for (int i = 0; found == false; i++)

{

    if (open[i].index == current.index)

    {

        open.erase(open.begin() + i);

        found = true;

    }

}
```

**Step 4.4** – Find the cell in the open list with the lowest F cost, and make that cell the new current.

```
int lowestF = 0;

for (int i = 0; i < open.size(); i++)

{

    if (open[i].F < open[lowestF].F)

    {

        lowestF = i;

    }

}


//now make the current = cell we found with lowest f cost

current.index = open[lowestF].index;
```

```
current.x = open[lowestF].x;

current.y = open[lowestF].y;

current.theta = open[lowestF].theta;

current.F = open[lowestF].F;

current.G = open[lowestF].G;

current.H = open[lowestF].H;

current.prevX = open[lowestF].prevX;

current.prevY = open[lowestF].prevY;
```

**Step 5** – At this point, we have found the goal and left the big *Step 4* `while()` loop. We set the `current` cell as the goal's parent and add the goal to the closed list.

```
goal.prevX = closed.back().x;

goal.prevY = closed.back().y;

closed.push_back(cell(goal));
```

**Step 6** – Call the `trace()` function to find and publish the next waypoint, and return its index in occupancy grid to `main()`, where find_Path() was first called.

```
int nextWaypoint = trace(closed);

return nextWaypoint;
```

And as easy as all that, you've got a ROS node that subscribes to the most recent map data, the robot's current position, and a goal and publishes waypoints for the drive controller we wrote in the last chapter.

Don't forget to uncomment `include` under include  directories and add the program as an executable in your ROS package's `cmake.txt` file (like we did in *Chapter 9, Coordinating the Parts*).

# Conclusion

I know it was a long chapter, but the ability to add autonomous path-planning to your real-world robot is one of the great, exciting milestones in robotics that starts to separate a roboticist from a remote-control toy enthusiast (which is still a fun hobby, no matter how old I get). In this chapter, you learned how to inflate the obstacles in your robot's map of the environment so it doesn't hit anything, how the $A^*$ path planning algorithm works in great detail, and wrote a working path planning ROS node for any robot.

*Congratulations!* Completing this marks a big milestone because you now have all of the fundamentals you need to build and program a basic, autonomous robot. The next four chapters are to provide a little greater detail about integrating the different sensors with the ROS ecosystem. In *Chapter 5, Communication with Sensors and Other Devices*, we learned how to communicate with sensors and get some numbers out of them. In *Chapters 14-18*, we'll learn how to interpret the data and convert it as necessary for publication in a ROS node. Let's get started with *Chapter 14, Encoders for Odometry*.

Suggested further studies:

- Pointers, `new()`, and `delete()` in C++
- The $D^*$ path planning algorithm
- RRT – The *Rapidly Exploring Random Tree path-finding* algorithm

# Questions

1. Your costmapper node receives a map with a `.1` meter-per-cell (or pixel) resolution. It has just one obstacle that is `5x1` cells. How many extra cells will be marked as obstacles in the resulting costmap if the robot is `1` meter in diameter?

2. We use distance to measure calculating the cost of movement in our $A^*$ program. What is another very common unit used to measure the cost of movement?

3. Write an `optimize()` function for your path planner that removes all waypoints between the start and the furthest cell the robot can get to in a straight line without hitting any obstacles.

CHAPTER 14

# Wheel Encoders for Odometry

## Introduction

We've talked a lot about wheel encoders and counting encoder *ticks* for odometry. We've even written an odometry publisher and a motor controller that both rely on encoder tick messages, so I suppose it's time to make sure we have a working encoder tick publisher node. As you advance your robotics' skills, tick publishers can also be an essential part of detecting when a wheel is stuck or slipping, so corrective measures can be taken and other nodes know when the encoder data is unreliable and should be ignored. For all of these reasons, the simple tick publisher has a very important role.

In this chapter, we will be covering the following:

- Optical encoders
- Hall effect encoders
- Wiring encoders
- Counting and publishing encoder ticks in ROS

# Objective

Understand and write a functional ROS node to publish wheel encoder, tick counts.

# Wheel encoders 101

Encoders are devices that help you keep track of how many turns a shaft has turned by providing a *pulse* to a GPIO pin as if someone had pressed a button. If you count the pulses, you can determine how many times the shaft has rotated and, further, how many times a wheel has rotated. Calculating how far a robot has traveled and turned with encoder pulse counts is known as **wheel odometry**.

An encoder system might be designed to pulse once per revolution or **100** times per revolution, and might be mounted on either the motor shaft or wheel shaft. Mounting on the motor often gives more pulses per revolution of the wheel, which makes for better accuracy. You have to be careful, though, because if the drive train slips, you'll be counting pulses that aren't contributing to wheel movement.

# Optical encoders

Optical encoders typically use an infrared emitter/receiver pair circuit (see *figure 5.2* from *Chapter 5, coordinating with sensors and other devices*) aimed at a disk with alternating white and black stripes. Alternatively, the emitter and receiver might be aimed directly at each other with a disk with holes or tabs that makes or breaks the infrared beam light. See *figure 14.1*.

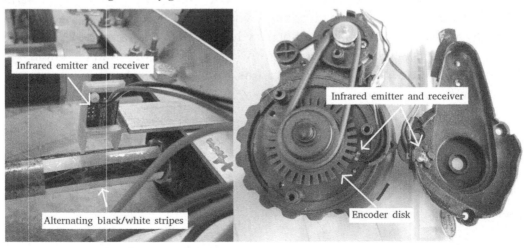

*Figure 14.1: Infrared emitter/receiver pair encoders*

The receiving infrared diode either allows current or stops current depending on whether it can *see* the beam from the emitter, and we can count every change of state by monitoring the output of the receiver with a callback function. Optical encoders are prone to interference by strong light sources or dirt obstructing the beam.

# Hall effect encoders

`Hall effect` is another common sensor type used in encoders. Instead of a receiver looking for infrared light, hall effect sensors respond to the presence or absence of a magnetic field. A disk with permanent magnets will be attached to the rotating shaft, and one or more stationary sensors are mounted close enough to detect the magnets as they pass by. See *figure 14.2* below.

*Figure 14.2: Hall effect encoders in a wheel module (left) and an industrial motor (right)*

By using two hall effect sensors instead of one, the software for the industrial motor in *figure 14.2* can determine which direction the shaft is spinning as well the number of rotations (when using a single sensor, the direction has to be determined by some other means). Wheel encoders made with hall effect sensors are more reliable than optical encoders because the former can be obstructed by dirt, or the emitter can burn out. The hall effect encoder has only small permanent magnets, and the sensor doesn't care if the dirt gets in between.

# Wiring encoders

Wiring an encoder is fairly straightforward. Optical encoders require the emitter to be wired just like an LED (because it is). This doesn't even have to be electrically connected to the same device as the receiver. The receiver gets wired like much like we are reading a switch – with one side to ground and the other side to the GPIO input pin, which needs to be pulled UP with a resistor to *3.3* volts as the typical arrangement has the phototransistor driving down.

Hall effect encoders only have one circuit, and wiring is as simple as giving the sensor the voltage it needs (and ground) and wiring the output to the GPIO input pin. The GPIO pin needs to be pulled UP, as the hall effect sensor output drives low in the presence of a magnet but floats instead of actively pulling up when the magnetic field is taken away. *Figure 14.3* below shows typical wiring schematics for both optical and hall effect encoders.

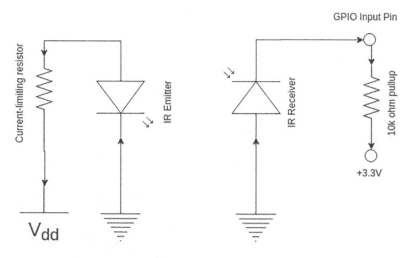

## Optical Encoder Circuit (emitter/receiver pair)

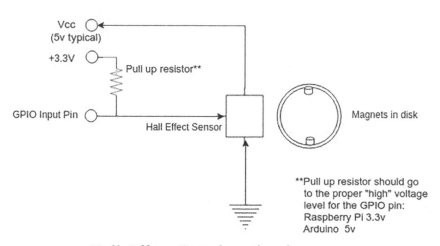

## Hall Effect Encoder Circuit

*Figure 14.3: Typical schematics for optical and hall effect encoders*

Because the basic encoders we've discussed are read as a binary digital signal, each encoder needs its own GPIO input pin and callback function. This is not difficult to manage if you have just two wheels to keep track of, but if you find yourself running short of GPIO pins, encoder modules are available that can track many encoders for you and communicate the data to your computer via serial or I2C. This is also an excellent way to handle encoders if you are using a laptop computer instead of a computer with GPIO pins like the Raspberry Pi.

# The Encoder tick publisher - tick_ publisher.cpp

This may be the easiest ROS node we write, as the data type and operations are all very simple with just a couple conditional statements to cover the direction of travel and counter *rollover/rollunder*. Most of the code is the setup of variables and GPIO pins. While the following `tick` publisher would work with a lot of details varied, it is designed for a robot with a Raspberry Pi, motor drivers with direction pins we can monitor, and encoders we can read much like a switch – such as the **hall effect** encoders found in *Roomba* wheel assemblies. This is the wheel module I use in the robot project in *Chapter 21, Building and Programming an Autonomous Robot*.

Encoder `tick` publisher by the following steps:

1. Handshake with ROS master.
2. Advertise publishers.
3. Setup PIGPIO daemon interface.
    3.1. Declare GPIO pin numbers and set pin modes.
    3.2. Initialize callbacks on GPIO pins connected to encoders.
4. Loop for the life of the program.
    4.1. Process callbacks and increment or decrement counter.
    4.2. Publish latest count data at the specified interval.

Encoder tick publisher code overview:

```
//include stuff

//declare constants and global variables


void left_event(int pi, unsigned int gpio,

        unsigned int edge, unsigned int tick)

{
```

```
      step 4.1 – process callback and increment or decrement counter

}


void right_event(int pi, unsigned int gpio,

         unsigned int edge, unsigned int tick)

{

    step 4.1 – process callback and increment or decrement counter

}


int PigpioSetup()

{

    step 3.1 - Set GPIO Pin Modes

}


int main(int argc, char **argv)

{

    step 1 – handshake with ROS master

    step 2 – Advertise publishers


    step 3.1 - call PigpioSetup()

    step 3.2 - Initialize callbacks on GPIO pins connected to encoders


    step 4 – loop through steps 4.1 and 4.2 for the life of the program

}
```

This program builds on the hello_callback.cpp program we worked through in *Chapter 2, GPIO Hardware Interface Pins Overview and Use.* Now we're just monitoring a second pin and publishing the accumulated counts as simple ROS messages.

# Encoder tick publisher code

Like other programs that are identical/redundant for both the left and right sides, I am only going to show code for the left side. You know that you need to repeat everything for the right side, using the proper GPIO pin numbers for how you wired the hardware. The entire program is available for download both in *Chapter 14*, download and *Chapter 21, Building and Programming an Autonomous Robot* complete robot package.

In this first block of code, we handle the usual includes and setting our constants. The ROS messages we publish are a simple data type called `std_msgs::Int16`, so we declare two of those globally. These are a class with one data member called `data`. For more information about the `Int16` messages, explore *wiki.ros.org/std_msgs*.

```
#include "ros/ros.h"16

#include "std_msgs/Int16.h"

#include <pigpiod_if2.h>

#include <iostream>


using namespace std;


//GPIO Pin assignments

const int leftEncoder = 22; //left encoder

const int rightEncoder = 23; //right encoder

const int leftReverse = 13; //input - goes low when left motor set to
reverse

const int rightReverse = 19; //monitor as input that goes low when right
motor set to reverse


//max and min allowable values

const int encoderMin = -32768;

const int encoderMax = 32768;


std_msgs::Int16 leftCount;
```

```
std_msgs::Int16 rightCount;
```

The next code block covers the callback function that runs every time an event (change in pin state) happens on the GPIO pin the encoder is connected to. Because this callback only knows there is a change of state and not which direction the wheel is turning, we check the direction pin attached to the motor driver for the wheel we are monitoring. The full function for an event on the left wheel's encoder is included as well as just the function declaration for the right encoder.

If you wired your encoders and motor drivers as I did in *Chapter 7, Adding the Computer to Control your Robot* (*figure 7.3*), the above pin assignments would work, and you can monitor the reverse pins for a state of low. If the reverse pin is low, we presume that the motor is turning the wheels in reverse, and we count down. Otherwise, we count up. Additionally, we check if we have reached the minimum or maximum Int16 values and handle the rollunder or rollover when necessary.

```
void left_event(int pi, unsigned int gpio,

        unsigned int edge, unsigned int tick)

{

    //If (leftReverse pin is "low")

    if(gpio_read(pi, leftReverse)==0)

    {

        //handle rollunder if already at minimum value for Int16

        if(leftCount.data==encoderMin)

        {

            leftCount.data = encoderMax;

        }

        //otherwise just count down by one

        else

        {

            leftCount.data--;

        }

    }
```

```
    else

    {

        //handle rollover if already at maximum value for Int16

        if(leftCount.data==encoderMax)

        {

            leftCount.data = encoderMin;

        }

        //otherwise just count up by one

        else

        {

            leftCount.data++;

        }

    }

}


void right_event(int pi, unsigned int gpio,

        unsigned int edge, unsigned int tick)

{

    //same as for the left_event above

}
```

The next code block is our `PigpioSetup()` function. We handshake with the PIGPIO daemon that should already be running, set the pin modes (in this case, all are set as inputs), and use the internal `pull_up` resistors as well. Finally, we return the `pi` handle for GPIO-using functions to reference.

```
int PigpioSetup()

{

char *addrStr = NULL;

char *portStr = NULL;
```

```
int pi = pigpio_start(addrStr, portStr);

//set the mode and pullup to read the encoder like a switch

set_mode(pi, leftEncoder, PI_INPUT);

set_mode(pi, rightEncoder, PI_INPUT);

set_mode(pi, leftReverse, PI_INPUT);

set_mode(pi, rightReverse, PI_INPUT);

set_pull_up_down(pi, leftEncoder, PI_PUD_UP);

set_pull_up_down(pi, rightEncoder, PI_PUD_UP);

set_pull_up_down(pi, leftReverse, PI_PUD_UP);

set_pull_up_down(pi, rightReverse, PI_PUD_UP);


return pi;

}
```

Finally, our `main()` function is as standard as it gets. Handshake with ROS and the PIGPIO daemon, advertise publishers (one for each encoder), and loop at the specified loop rate until we close the node, cleaning up as we do close.

```
int main(int argc, char **argv)

{

    ros::init(argc, argv, "encoder_ticks");

    ros::NodeHandle node;


    ros::Publisher pubLeft =

        node.advertise<std_msgs::Int16>("leftWheel", 0);


    //initialize pigpiod interface

    int pi = PigpioSetup();

    if(pi>=0)

    {
```

```
        cout<<"daemon interface started ok at "<<pi<<endl;

    }

    else

    {

        cout<<"Failed to connect to PIGPIO Daemon

            - is it running?"<<endl;

        return -1;

    }


    //initializes Pigpio callbacks

    int cbLeft=callback(pi, leftEncoder,EITHER_EDGE, left_event);


    ros::Rate loop_rate(10);

    while(ros::ok)

    {

        pubLeft.publish(leftCount);

        ros::spinOnce();

        loop_rate.sleep();

    }


    //terminate callbacks and pigpio interface as node closes

    callback_cancel(cbLeft);

    pigpio_stop(pi);

    return 0;

}
```

If you have a hard time compiling with catkin_make, make sure the package CmakeLists.txt has the following:

1. std_msgs is included in the find_package section.

2. `add_compile_options(-std=c++11)` is uncommented.

3. `libpigpiod_if2.so` is included in your target link libraries for this file.

Visit *Chapter 9, Coordinating the Parts* for a refresher on your `CmakeLists.txt`, as well as examine the `practical_sensors` package from my git repository at *github. com/lbrombach* for working examples. Don't forget that you need to start the PIGPIO daemon from the command line before running.

# Conclusion

This chapter was brief but covered some essential wheel encoder basics as well as how to track and publish encoder tick counts. These ticks are essential for odometry, velocity calculation, and even things later on like detecting wheel slip, so you know when to ignore encoder counts in pose estimation.

The next chapter is going to cover publishing ultrasonic range data in ROS. Once published, the raw data can be used by nodes looking for real-time obstacles to avoid.

# Questions

1. Why do we need an encoder tick publisher?

2. Why do we need to read the motor driver direction pins?

3. What three things must be done to the package `CmakeLists.txt` for this program/node to compile with `catkin_make`?

# CHAPTER 15

# Ultrasonic Range Detectors

## Introduction

Ultrasonic range detectors are small, inexpensive devices that measure the distance to whatever is in front of them. They work by emitting sound in the ultrasonic range and timing how long it takes to bounce back. You can either do this directly with your software or buy modules that handle this for you and report back in either serial or I2C.

This chapter is an essential guide to reading range with the very popular *HC-SR04* ultrasonic range sensor and publishing the range data as a ROS message. Other nodes (or even a modified version of this node) may use the range data for obstacle avoidance or other purposes. Ultrasonic range sensor data can be used for mapping. Still, the resolution is so weak this is not advised except as a secondary sensor – to record an obstacle where a primary scanner like a LIDAR cannot due to the very narrow laser beam or a non-reflective surface (like something black) that the LIDAR cannot see.

In this chapter, we will be covering the following:

- HC-SR04 ultrasonic range sensor basics
- Publishing ultrasonic range data in ROS
- Ultrasonic range data for object detection

# Objective

Understand how Ultrasonic range sensors work, familiarity with the `sensor_msgs::Range` data type and how to publish ultrasonic range data in ROS.

# HC-SR04 ultrasonic range sensor basics

The `HC-SR04` is as affordable as they come, but does not come with bells and whistles such as I2C or serial communication. Instead, it has two digital interface pins. One is a digital input called the *trigger* that we use to start the process, and the other is a digital output called the *echo* pin that we read, much like a switch.

Once the device is triggered, it sends a pulse of ultrasonic sound, and the echo pin (that usually sits *high*) is driven low for as long as it takes the sound to bounce off an object and return to the device (like an echo). Instead of reading a number directly, we measure the time that the echo pin sits low and calculate the distance the sound traveled based on the time elapsed. This method of detecting ranges with sound is also known as *sonar,* for Sound Detection and Ranging.

## Reading HC-SR04 by the steps

1. Output a short pulse (*10 microseconds*) of logic *high* to the trigger pin.
2. Monitor the echo pin and wait for it to switch from *Low* to *high*.
3. Save the current time in microseconds when *Step 2* takes place.
4. Monitor the echo pin and wait for it to switch back to *Low*.
5. Recheck the time. Subtract the start time from the current time to get the flight duration of the ultrasonic signal.
6. The flight duration in *Step 5* is round-trip. Divide it by *2,* then multiply by the speed of sound (34300) to get the distance in centimeters.

I think the steps are pretty self-explanatory, and the actual numbers of it will become apparent as you work through the code.

# Wiring the HC-SR04

These require 5 volts to operate and common ground with the Raspberry Pi or microcontroller, and two GPIO pins – one for the trigger and one for the echo. Look over *figure 15.1* below.

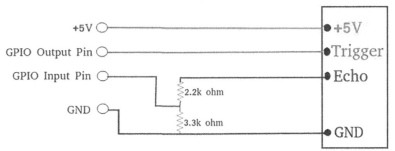

**Figure 15.1:** *Wiring an HC-SR04 ultrasonic range sensor to a Raspberry Pi*

The HC-SR04 outputs 5V on their signal (echo) line and can damage a Raspberry Pi GPIO. We need a voltage divider or logic level shifter to bring that voltage down to 3.3 volts (both discussed in detail in *Chapter 6, Additional helpful Hardware*). The trigger pin seems to have a logic-level threshold of around 2.5-2.7 volts so that we can wire it directly to a 3.3 volt GPIO pin.

# Ultrasonic range data publisher: ultrasonic_publisher.cpp

This node will read a single HC-SR04 ultrasonic range sensor and publish the data using the ROS message type `sensor_msgs::Range`, which contains more data than just the range. For example, the minimum and maximum range that our sensor is capable of, so subscribing nodes can detect and ignore readings outside of this range. Read all the details of the `sensor_msgs::Range` data type at *wiki.ros.org/sensor_msgs*.

The GPIO pin assignments assume your sensor is wired with GPIO pin *6* to the *trigger* and pin *16* for the *echo,* but modify these to suit your needs.

## Ultrasonic range publisher by the steps

1.  Handshake with ROS master
2.  Advertise publishers
3.  Setup `Pigpio` daemon interface
    3.1.  Declare GPIO pin numbers and set pin modes
4.  Initialize fixed data in range message

5. Loop for the life of the program:
   5.1. Get current range and ROS time
   5.2. Publish range message at a specified interval

Ultrasonic range publisher code overview:

```
//include stuff
```

```
//declare constants and global variables
```

```
float get_range(int pi)

{

    step 4.1 - process callback and increment or decrement counter

}
```

```
int PigpioSetup()

{

    step 3.1 - Set GPIO Pin Modes

}
```

```
int main(int argc, char **argv)

{

    step 1 - handshake with ROS master

    step 2 - Advertise publishers

    step 3 - call PigpioSetup()

    step 4 - Initialize fixed data in range message

    step 5 - loop through steps 5.1 and 5.2 for life of program

}
```

The ultrasonic_publisher node doesn't subscribe to any ROS topics, as it gets its inputs directly from the hardware. With just a couple functions, it is a simple matter of repeatedly calling the function that interfaces with the device, and publishing the data.

# Ultrasonic range publisher code

In this first block of code, we handle the usual includes and set our constants. We declare a couple of aliases for GPIO pin assignments and create an object of `sensor_msgs:Range`.

```
#include "ros/ros.h"

#include "sensor_msgs/Range.h"

#include <pigpiod_if2.h>

#include <iostream>


using namespace std;


//assign alias to the gpio pin numbers

const int trigger = 6;

const int echo = 16;


sensor_msgs::Range range;
```

The next code block covers the function `get_range()` that the loop in `main()` calls every cycle. It takes an argument of `int pi`, which is the `PIGPIO` daemon interface handle returned when we set up the interface. In other programs, you may have seen me just declare `pi` globally. I have thoroughly commented on the following block.

```
float get_range(int pi)

{

//initiate reading with 10 microsecond pulse to trigger

gpio_write(pi, trigger, 1);

time_sleep(.00001);

gpio_write(pi, trigger, 0);


//wait for echo pin to go low
```

```
while(gpio_read(pi, echo)==0){};
```

```
//get current tick (microseconds since boot) from system.
int start = get_current_tick(pi);
```

```
//wait for echo pin to return high
while(gpio_read(pi, echo)==1){};
```

```
//calculate round trip time
int echoTime = get_current_tick(pi) - start;
```

```
//speed of sound is 343 m/s, but total echo time is round trip
//half that times echo time (in seconds) is the range
return 171.5 * echoTime / 1000000;
}
```

The next code block is our `Pigpio` setup function. We handshake with the `PIGPIO` daemon that should already be running, set the pin modes, and our trigger output to `low`. Finally, we return the `pi` handle for GPIO-using functions to reference after a short delay.

```
int PigpioSetup()
{
    char *addrStr = NULL;
    char *portStr = NULL;
    int pi = pigpio_start(addrStr, portStr);

    //set the pin modes and set the trigger output to low
    set_mode(pi, echo, PI_INPUT);
    set_mode(pi, trigger, PI_OUTPUT);
    gpio_write(pi, trigger, 0);
```

```
//let pins stabilize before trying to read

time_sleep(.01);


return pi;

}
```

Finally, our main() function is pretty standard. Handshake with ROS and the Pigpio daemon, advertise publisher, enter some fixed data fields in the range message, and loop at the specified loop rate until we close the node, cleaning up as we do close.

We set the frame_id to sonar, and in the future, you may wish to publish a transform message (as briefly discussed in *Chapter 10, Maps for Robot Navigation*) between the sonar and base_link frames. The radiation_type field is so receiving nodes know what type of sensor, and 0 is accepted as a standard for ultrasonics. (1 would be for infrared sensors, which can also use the range message).

I used .35 radians (*about 20 degrees*) for the field_of_view, but these sensors seem to vary a bit, and I've seen people posting test results anywhere from *15-30 degrees*. The best thing I can suggest is to read on the *ROS wiki* for the Range message type what the field of view means, and do some testing with your particular manufacture of the sensor. Until you get around to that, I think .35 will do.

```
int main(int argc, char **argv)

{

    ros::init(argc, argv, "ultrasonic_publisher");

    ros::NodeHandle node;

    ros::Publisher pub =

        node.advertise<sensor_msgs::Range>("ultra_range", 0);


    //initialize pipiod interface

    int pi = PigpioSetup();

    if(pi>=0)

    {

        cout<<"daemon interface started ok at "<<pi<<endl;

    }
```

```
else

{

    cout<<"Failed to connect to PIGPIO Daemon - is it running?"<<endl;

return -1;

}


//set our range message fixed data

range.header.frame_id = "sonar";

range.radiation_type = 0;

range.field_of_view = .35;

range.min_range = .05;

range.max_range = 4.0;


ros::Rate loop_rate(10);

while(ros::ok)

{

    range.header.stamp = ros::Time::now();

    range.range = get_range(pi);

    pub.publish(range);

    loop_rate.sleep();

}


pigpio_stop(pi);

return 0;

}
```

If you have a hard time compiling with catkin_make, make sure the package CmakeLists.txt has the following:

1. sensor_msgs is included in the find_package section.

2. `add_compile_options(-std=c++11)` is uncommented.

3. `libpigpiod_if2.so` is included in your target link libraries for this file.

Visit *Chapter 9, Coordinating the Parts* for a refresher on your `CmakeLists.txt`, and examine the `practical_sensors` package from my git repository at *github.com/lbrombach/practical_chapters* for a working example in the *Chapter 15* folder. Don't forget that you need to start the `pigpio` daemon from the command line before running.

# Ultrasonic range data for object detection

While ultrasonic sensors have value in that they can see some things that a 2D LIDAR misses, consideration must be given to their shortcomings. Aside from the relatively poor resolution, ultrasonic sound can reflect *off* on object and away from, rather than back to the sensor if the angle is significant. This is illustrated in the following *figure 15.2*.

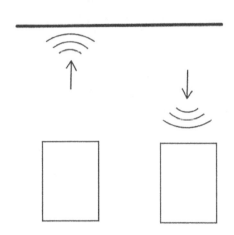

Ultrasonic range finders like roughly perpendicular surfaces and reports pretty accurately here.

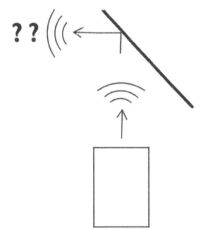

Trying to measure distance to an object at an angle causes ultrasonic devices to report the obstacle farther away than it is or not at all.

***Figure 15.2:*** *The angle of the obstacle can fool an ultrasonic sensor*

A simple version of obstacle detection is to publish a Boolean message when the detected range is less than some value you've set. This could be done in another node that subscribes to the range message, or as an added function and published message in `ultrasonic_publisher.cpp,` and it is how a lot of people start with simple bump-and-go tye robots. Additionally, sonar range data can be added to the obstacle layer of your costmap_2d costmap that we use in *Chapter 13, Autonomous Path Planning*.

# Conclusion

With other sensors with much greater precision coming down so far in price in the past decade, ultrasonic sensors are seen much less in modern robotics than in the past. They are still useful is as proximity detectors or bumpers that don't have to make physical contact to provide a warning to the robot controller (my car has several on the front and back bumpers to help me park in tight spaces). The wide, unfocused path of ultrasonic sound makes for undesirable, very low-resolution maps.

We've learned to make a simple ultrasonic range data publisher node for the HC-SR04 sensors. This is useful on its own, but we also (perhaps more importantly) became familiar with the sensor_msgs::Range data type that can also be used for infrared range, **Time of Flight** (**ToF**), or other sensors that return a single range value.

The next chapter is going to cover publishing IMU data (accelerometer, gyroscope, and magnetometer data) in ROS. These are some of the most important messages for keeping accurate pose estimates, given the shortcomings of encoder-only odometry.

# Questions

1. Why does the sensor_msgs::Range data type include minimum and maximum sensor ranges?
2. What do 0 and 1 mean when setting the value for the sensor_msgs::Range data field radiation_type?
3. What is the problem with ultrasonic range sensors and detecting objects that are not perpendicular?

CHAPTER 16

# IMUs - Accelerometers, Gyroscopes and Magnetometers

## Introduction

In addition to wheel encoder-based odometry, we can use acceleration data, angular velocity data, or measurements of the Earth's magnetic field to help track a robot's position and orientation. Frequently, several of these sensors come on one package known as an **Inertial Measurement Unit** (**IMU**). *Figure 16.1* below shows one module with an LSM303DLHC accelerometer and magnetometer, and another module with an L3GD20 gyroscope all wired up for I2C.

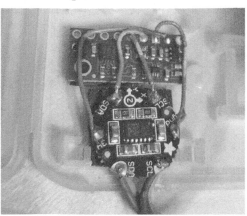

*Figure 16.1:* *An LSM303 accelerometer and magnetometer (bottom) and L3GD20 gyroscope (top)*

These are three very popular IMU components and can even be purchased all in the same module. In this chapter, we'll talk about what we can do with data from each of these sensors, how to read and interpret the data from the device, and how to format and publish it for a ROS-based robot.

In this chapter, we will be covering the following:

- Accelerometers
- Gyroscopes
- Magnetometers
- Reading and interpreting IMU data
- Formatting and publishing IMU data for ROS

# Objectives

- Understand the value and limitations of the data from each IMU sensor.
- Learn to read and interpret the sensor data.
- Gain familiarity with the `sensor_msgs::Imu` data type and how to publish it.
- Gain familiarity with the `sensor_msgs::MagneticField` data type and how to publish it.

# Accelerometers

Accelerometers measure linear acceleration in either milliG *(1/1000 of 1 G-force)* or *meters/sec^2* – usually in three axes known as the *x*, *y*, and *z* axis. It is essential to pay attention to which direction gets a positive value and which gets a negative value from your sensor so you can adjust it to the ROS standard, if necessary. *Figure 16.2* below shows the direction of acceleration along the *x* and *y* axis that are standard for ROS ground robots.

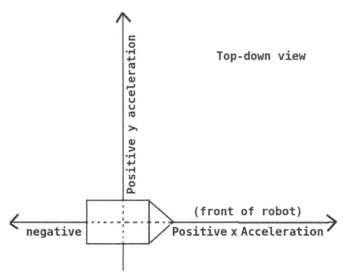

*Figure 16.2: Conventional directions of acceleration*

A steady stream of acceleration data not only allows a variety of available ROS nodes to calculate velocity (which allows us to calculate the distance traveled), but also detect collisions, wheel slippage, and how level or tipped over we are (thanks to the ever-present acceleration of gravity). We are going to use meters per second squared, as that is the standard unit used in ROS software.

Although acceleration data can still be useful as an input to various ROS packages, without a background in fundamental physics and calculus, you won't get as much out of it as you will if you understand what is going on under the hood. I recommend taking the time to find a basics physics course, as well as a calculus course that covers basic derivatives and integration if those aren't already in your toolbox.

## Accelerometer shortcomings

*Why do we need error-prone wheel odometry at all if we can just use an accelerometer?* Error.

Accelerometers are subject to different types of errors that preclude us from using them as a standalone position-tracking device. From big, sudden errors like hitting a bump, to small, steady noise errors, acceleration data errors quickly accumulate to throw position estimates far outside of reality.

## Publishing IMU Data in ROS

While a magnetometer is often included in an IMU module, only acceleration and angular velocity data (and sometimes an orientation estimate) are included in the ROS message `sensor_msgs::Imu`. ROS has a separate message for magnetic field data – `sensor_msgs::MagneticField`. As we learned in the `hello_i2c_lsm303.cpp` program back in *Chapter 5, Communicating with Sensors and Other Devices,* reading raw data from each device is usually somewhat redundant with only register addresses changing.

Once we've read the raw data, some work is done to convert it to the correct units and resolution, and again the act of publishing is redundant with just changes in variable names. Visit *wiki.ros.org/sensor_msgs* for a closer look at both message types, and *ros.org/reps/rep-0145.html* for details about the ROS IMU-related conventions.

I'm going to walk through publishing the accelerometer data in detail, but for the gyroscope and magnetometer data, I will only cover the few minor differences. These sensors I'm reading while writing this chapter are all I2C devices, which is probably the most common communication protocol for these sensors. The entire node is available for download in the `practical_robot` project on *github.com/lbrombach/practical_robot*, as well as the *Chapter 16* folder in the chapter downloads at *github.com/lbrombach/practical_chapters.*

## The ROS sensor_msgs::Imu data type

Aside from the usual Header stuff, the IMU message consists of the following IMU data components.

- `linear_acceleration`
- `linear_acceleration_covariance`
- `angular_velocity`
- `angular_velocity_covariance`
- `orientation`
- `orientation_covariance`

Sometimes, we don't use every data member in a message, and it's a good idea to follow the convention to *signal* any subscribing nodes that a field should be ignored.

For example, the *wiki.ros.org/sensor_msgs* page for the IMU message explains that if we don't have an orientation estimate, we should set the first element of orientation's covariance matrix to -1. If we are publishing one of the data members but don't know the covariance, we should set every element in the covariance matrix to 0.

IMU publisher by the steps:

1. Handshake with ROS master
2. Advertise publisher(s)
3. Setup `Pigpio` daemon interface
4. Initialize Sensor:
   4.1. Initiate I2C (or serial) connection
   4.2. Set device modes, desired units, and other required parameters
5. Initialize Fixed Data in IMU message
6. Loop for the life of the program:
   6.1. Read raw data
   6.2. Convert raw data to proper units
   6.3. Publish IMU message at a specified interval

IMU message publisher code overview:

```
//include stuff

//declare global stuff


void get_accel()

{

    step 6.1 - Read raw data

    step 6.2 - Convert raw data to proper units

}


void accelerometer_setup()

{

    step 4.1 - Initiate I2C connection

    step 4.2 - Set device modes, desired units, etc.

}
```

```
int PigpioSetup()

{

    step 3

}


int main(int argc, char **argv)

{

    step 1 - Handshake with ROS master

    step 2 – Advertise publishers

    step 3 – Initialize pigpiod interface

    step 4 – Initialize sensor

    step 5 – Initialize fixed data in IMU message

    step 6 – Loop through 6.1, 6.2, and 6.3 for life of program

    step 6.3 – Publish IMU message

}
```

The basic IMU Publisher doesn't subscribe to any nodes and publishes just one topic. This outline only shows methods for the accelerometer, but there's a good chance your IMU also has a gyroscope — either *all-in-one* or on another module. Even if the gyroscope is not on the same little module, you should use this node to read and publish its data on the same message – just add functions for gyro_setup() and get_gyro().

## The IMU message publisher code

In the first block of code, we include the required header files and declare some global variables:

```
#include "ros/ros.h"

#include "sensor_msgs/Imu.h"

#include <pigpiod_if2.h>

#include <iostream>
```

```
//RPi typical I2C bus is 1. Find yours with "ls /dev/*i2c* "

const int I2Cbus=1;


const int LSM303_accel=0x19; //accelerometer I2C address

const int L3GD20_gyro = 0x6b; //gyroscope I2C address

const int LSM303_mag =0x1e;

const float RAD_PER_DEG = 0.0174533;

const float TESLA_PER_GAUSS = .0001;


int pi = -1;

int ACCEL_HANDLE=-1;

int GYRO_HANDLE=-1;


sensor_msgs::Imu myImu;
```

Even if they are all on one chip or module, the gyro, accelerometer, and magnetometer each have their I2C address, so we have to initiate an interface with each individually. Hence, the accelerometer and gyro have different handles. Getting all three devices in one module may save a little wiring, but doesn't affect your code at all. We declare them globally here, but they receive a proper value during the setup() function. We also declare the IMU message.

```
void accel_setup()

{

ACCEL_HANDLE=i2c_open(pi,I2Cbus, LSM303_accel,0);

if (ACCEL_HANDLE>=0)

    {

    cout<<"Accelerometer found. Handle = "<<ACCEL_HANDLE<<endl;

    }

else

    {
```

```
        cout<<"Unable to open I2C comms with Accelerometer"<<endl;

    }


//set frequency

i2c_write_byte_data(pi, ACCEL_HANDLE, 0x20, 0x47);

time_sleep(.02);


//set config register to update continuously,

//LSB at lower addr, resolution at +- 2g, Hi-Res disable

i2c_write_byte_data(pi, ACCEL_HANDLE, 0x23, 0x09);

time_sleep(.02);

}
```

In accel_setup( ), we get an I2C handle and write to two configuration registers. See your device's datasheet to figure out which registers to write to and what values. If the datasheet doesn't make sense to you, head over to the *Practical Robotics YouTube* channel at *www.youtube.com/practicalrobotics* for a video tutorial.

```
void get_accel()

{

    //read the data for x from the registers and combine.

    int xLSB = (int)i2c_read_byte_data(pi, ACCEL_HANDLE, 0x28);

    int xMSB = (int)i2c_read_byte_data(pi, ACCEL_HANDLE, 0x29);


    //combine bytes and shift to remove trailing zeros

    myImu.linear_acceleration.x

        =(float)((int16_t)(xLSB | xMSB<<8)>>4)/1000*9.81;


    //*if 16 bit value instead of 12, omit the >>4 shift. Ex:

    // myImu.linear_acceleration.x

    // =(float)((int16_t)(xLSB | xMSB<<8))/1000*9.81;
```

```
//repeat for y data and z data, changing only the address for

//the data registers


myImu.header.stamp = ros::Time::now();

}
```

In get_accel(), the goal is to read three values: x, y, and z acceleration. Each of these is coded in two bytes that we have to combine like we briefly discussed in *Chapter 5, Communication with Sensors and Other Devices.* Remember that my particular model of the *LSM303*(I have the *LSM303DLHC*) uses only 12 of 16 bits from the two bytes and is somewhat oddly left-justified. After combining the two bytes into a single value, we have to shift back 4 bits to the right to get a decent number. This may not be the case with your accelerometer – if you're a bit lost, I have a much more detailed video tutorial about combining bytes at *www.youtube.com/practicalrobotics.*

Once we've correctly combined the bytes and shifted bits as necessary, we divide the output first from *milliGs* to *G* by dividing by 1000; then, we multiply the number of *Gs* by 9.81 to convert *Gs* to *meters/second^2.*

```
int PigpioSetup()

{

    char *addrStr = NULL;

    char *portStr = NULL;

    pi = pigpio_start(addrStr, portStr);

    return pi;

}
```

PigpioSetup() is easier than usual because we aren't using any GPIO pins except for the I2C bus. Since we don't have to set modes or pullups, we just handshake with the Pigpio daemon and return the handle.

```
int main(int argc, char **argv)

{

    ros::init(argc, argv, "imu_publisher");
```

```
ros::NodeHandle node;

ros::Publisher pub
    = node.advertise<sensor_msgs::Imu>("imu/data_raw", 0);


//initialize pipiod interface

int pi = PigpioSetup();


accel_setup();


//set our range message fixed data

myImu.header.frame_id = "imu";


//set covariance of unused data members to "not used"

myImu.orientation_covariance[0] = -1;


//set accel covariance to unknown

for(int i = 0; i<9; i++)

{

    myImu.linear_acceleration_covariance[i]=0;

}


ros::Rate loop_rate(10);

while(ros::ok)

{

    get_accel();

    pub.publish(myImu);

    loop_rate.sleep();

}
```

```
//puts accelerometer into sleep mode

i2c_write_byte_data(pi, ACCEL_HANDLE, 0x20, 0x00);


//close I2C connection and disconnect from the daemon

i2c_close(pi, ACCEL_HANDLE);


pigpio_stop(pi);

return 0;

}
```

Nothing in main() should look new except that we take care to fill out the orientation_covariance to signal that orientation data is to be ignored, and set the acceleration_covariance to all zeros to signal the covariance is unknown. If you are not going to publish gyroscope data, you should also set angular_velocity_covariance[0] to -1.

If you have a hard time compiling with catkin_make, make sure the package CmakeLists.txt has the following:

1. sensor_msgs is included in the find_package section.
2. add_compile_options(-std=c++11) is uncommented.
3. libpigpiod_if2.so is included in your target link libraries for this file.

Visit *Chapter 9, Coordinating the Parts* for a refresher on your CmakeLists.txt, and examine the practical_sensors package from my git repository at *github.com/lbrombach* for working examples you'll find in either the practical_chapters or the practical_robot section. Don't forget that you need to start the PIGPIO daemon from the command line before running.

# Gyroscopes

As opposed to measuring linear acceleration, a gyroscope's job is to measure angular velocity – the rate at which the device is turning — in either degrees per second or radians per second. The apparent use for gyroscope data is to keep track of our orientation, which is excellent because wheel-encoder-only odometry heading calculations are pretty bad. *Figure 16.3* below shows the ROS convention for angular velocity values.

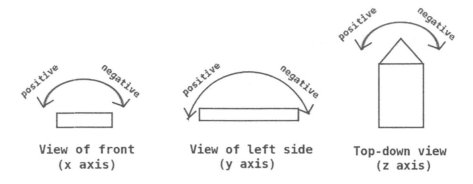

The gyroscope measures angular velocity about each axis.
ROS convention is that counter-clockwise motion is positive
(when looking at the front of that axis)

*Figure 16.3: The direction of angular velocity about the x, y, and z axis*

Make sure your sensor outputs the correctly signed (positive or negative) values in radians per second or you adjust them to match the ROS convention.

## Gyroscope shortcomings

Gyroscopes are pretty great at measuring quick changes, but the readings drift unacceptably over time. For this reason, gyroscopes are almost never used alone to track heading.

## Adding gyroscope data to the IMU node

Whether the gyroscope is on the same physical module or not makes no difference, and the data should still be published on the same message as the accelerometer data. Adding it (or using it without an accelerometer) is as easy as a few simple changes to the accelerometer publisher. The steps are identical, but the I2C address, register addresses, and conversion values will be different. Presuming we are adding gyro publishing to the accelerometer node, we just add a setup() and get() functions for the gyroscope.

```
void gyro_setup()

{

    GYRO_HANDLE=i2c_open(pi,I2Cbus, L3GD20_gyro,0);

    time_sleep(.02);
```

```
    //set frequency, power on and enable all 3 axes

    i2c_write_byte_data(pi, GYRO_HANDLE, 0x20, 95);

    time_sleep(.05);

}
```

Aside from different addresses, the only other difference is the configuration value sent to the register known as *CTRL1* at address 0x20. The L3GD20H datasheet says that the default value at this register has the unit powered down. The value 95 (0b01011111) puts the unit in normal power mode and changes the update frequency from the default of 12.5 to 25 Hz. Plenty of other configuration options and features are available, but this will do for us.

```
void get_gyro()

{

    //readings in default scale of 245 degrees per sec

    //sensitivity at 245 deg/sec is .00875 degrees per digit

    int xLSB = (int)i2c_read_byte_data(pi, GYRO_HANDLE, 0x28);

    int xMSB = (int)i2c_read_byte_data(pi, GYRO_HANDLE, 0x29);

    myImu.angular_velocity.x

        =(float)((int16_t)(xLSB | xMSB<<8))*.00875*RAD_PER_DEG;


    //repeat for y and z, changing register addresses

}
```

The L3GD20H uses all 16 bits from the two bytes, so we can just shift the high byte to the left 8 places for a raw value. Multiplying by the raw value by .00875 gets us degrees per second, then we can convert that to radians per second to adhere to the ROS convention. RAD_PER_DEG is a const float I declared and is equal to 0.0174533.

And that's all there is to it. You'll obviously need to call these functions in main() alongside the accel_setup() and get_accel() function calls, and set each angular_velocity_covariance[0-8] to 0 in the same for loop as the acceleration_covariance[].

# Magnetometers

Magnetometers are used to measure magnetic field strength in units called either **Gauss** or **Tesla**. Because a magnetic field is a vector (with strength and direction), a magnetometer can measure the *x*, *y*, and *z* components of the said vector. If the sensor is located in an area with a stable magnetic field, this can be useful for determining orientation.

The accepted convention for units of magnetism in ROS is Tesla. Your sensor may be configurable to output the unit of your choosing, or you may need to convert in your software before you publish it. This one is easy because `1 Tesla = 1000 gauss`.

Magnetometers are sometimes erroneously called electronic compasses, and I'm afraid if you were hoping for a simple solution to tracking magnetic heading with a magnetometer, you're about to be disappointed.

What one has to understand is that calculating a compass heading requires proper calibration and an understanding that the vector of the Earth's magnetic field is not going straight North and South, but instead are offset by an angle that varies at different locations all over the world. The field vector also has a vertical component that must be compensated for if the device tilts more than `10` degrees or so from the level, else it wreaks havoc on your calculations. The amount of tilt that can be tolerated depends not only on the direction of tilt but the location on Earth because the closer you are to the poles, the greater the vertical component.

## Magnetometer shortcomings

The problem with relying on a magnetometer is that a lot of things can distort the magnetic field vector being measured. Metal on the robot, electromagnetic noise coming from motors, and nearby metal objects can all distort the field. Distortion from the robot itself can (and must) be measured and removed through calibration offsets, but metal things in the environment are trickier because they are not consistent.

The problem is significant enough that I've given up using the magnetometer at all for heading calculations indoors. Even after careful calibration and placement far away from motors, as the robot drives past desks or metal cabinets, the readings go haywire. Even avoiding metal furniture, I've discovered that areas in the basement must have large pipes or construction rebar hidden in the concrete because of suddenly unreliable readings in those places. I still include the magnetometer in robots that operate outdoors in open areas. Still, I'd need to do much testing and tweaking before I relied on magnetometer data for a robot operating near cars and such.

# Adding magnetometer data

Although **magnetometer** (**mag**) data is published in a separate message, it is not unusual to include reading and publishing mag data in the same node as the IMU message. Because mag data is a separate message, we have a few more lines of code to add than when we added the gyroscope data. The chapter downloads and the robot project files at *github.com/lbrombach* include versions of the IMU publisher with and without the magnetometer.

```
#include "sensor_msgs/MagneticField.h"

int MAG_HANDLE=-1;

sensor_msgs::MagneticField mag;
```

First, we have to include the `sensor_msgs::MagneticField.h` file. Then we declare another handle to address the magnetometer, as well as create the message object of type `sensor_msgs::MagneticField`.

```
void mag_setup()

{

    MAG_HANDLE=i2c_open(pi,I2Cbus, LSM303_mag ,0);

    time_sleep(.05);


    //set sample frequency to 15hz

    i2c_write_byte_data(pi, MAG_HANDLE, 0x00, 16);

    time_sleep(.05);


    //set scale to +- 1.3 gauss

    i2c_write_byte_data(pi, MAG_HANDLE, 0x01, 32);

    time_sleep(.05);


    //set mode - 0 for continuous, 1 for single read , 3 for off

    i2c_write_byte_data(pi, MAG_HANDLE, 0x02, 0);

    time_sleep(.05);

}
```

In mag_setup(), we have three registers to configure. Here, I set the register at address 0x00 to 16, so the magnetometer samples just faster than the frequency I intend to run the node (10 Hz). We also set the scale and, finally, the mode to start the device sampling.

```
void get_mag()

{

    //readings in default scale of +/- 1.3Gauss

    // x,y gain at that scale ==1100, z gain = 980

    int xLSB = (int)i2c_read_byte_data(pi, MAG_HANDLE, 0x04);

    int xMSB = (int)i2c_read_byte_data(pi, MAG_HANDLE, 0x03);

    mag.magnetic_field.x

        =(float)((int16_t)(xLSB | xMSB<<8))/1100*TESLA_PER_GAUSS;


    int yLSB = (int)i2c_read_byte_data(pi, MAG_HANDLE, 0x08);

    int yMSB = (int)i2c_read_byte_data(pi, MAG_HANDLE, 0x07);

    mag.magnetic_field.y

        =(float)((int16_t)(yLSB | yMSB<<8))/1100*TESLA_PER_GAUSS;


    int zLSB = (int)i2c_read_byte_data(pi, MAG_HANDLE, 0x06);

    int zMSB = (int)i2c_read_byte_data(pi, MAG_HANDLE, 0x05);

    mag.magnetic_field.z

        =(float)((int16_t)(zLSB | zMSB<<8))/980*TESLA_PER_GAUSS;

}
```

I included all of the get_mag() instead of just the data for x because a couple points of important detail require your attention. The first thing you might notice is that the conversion factor from digits in the reading to *gauss* also known as gain, for z is different than x and y. This is no mistake and can be found in the datasheet under the register description for register CRB_REG_M, which is the one at address 0x01 that we set to scale to 1.3 Gauss. Once we convert raw values to Gauss, we convert to Tesla to meet the ROS convention.

The second important thing to notice is that the register addresses for y and z data are out of order compared to every other x, y, z readings we've taken. By this, I mean that y has always been the two registers after x, and z the two registers after y. In this case, the order of register addresses is x, z, y. Even I thought this was a typo at first, but some testing shows it to be accurate. My LSM303 is a DLHC variant that is one of a few LSM303 variants that put z before y. It is essential to always check the register descriptions in the datasheet for your specific device as presuming data sheet with the same prefix will do can get you in trouble.

# Mounting the IMU

When mounting any of the IMU sensors on your robot, it should be oriented so the z *axis* reads roughly *1000milliG* or *+9.81 m/s^2* (when stationary and level), because this will be how the device represents the acceleration of gravity (or, more correctly, this is the net effect of gravity on a stationary object – kind of like a stationary boat facing into a flowing river would register forward speed) and the x and y axis should read very close to 0. If you then lift the front of the robot straight up, the x *axis* should be the one that reads *+9.81 m/s^2*. Mounted with this orientation, the robot will read positive acceleration as it speeds up in the forward direction. See *figure 16.4* below.

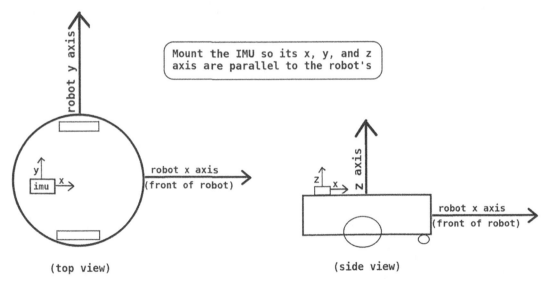

*Figure 16.4: Correct orientation for mounting IMU*

While it is possible to re-map the data and compensate for mounting in other orientations in your programs, it is usually easier to simply mount it this way to begin with.

# Conclusion

In this chapter, we've learned how to read sensor data from three very common IMU components. Hopefully, the examples are thorough enough that if you find yourself with different sensors, you will be able to make the necessary changes to register addresses and values with these examples and the datasheet for your component.

With the ability to read IMU data from any sensor and publish the data, you've taken a big step toward hugely improved autonomy. As you gain experience and explore available ROS packages, you'll find a number of them work with data. For the most accuracy (especially important with the magnetometer), you can study on your own how to calculate and apply the calibration offset data. Start with the datasheet or resources page on the manufacturer's website.

Expanding on our ability to solve the robot's *Where am I?* problem the next chapter dives into GPS/GNSS satellite location devices. These are quite a game-changer in the right circumstances and are the only sensor that allows our robot to locate itself from a cold start all over the world.

# Questions

1. Where can you find detailed information about ROS IMU-related conventions?
2. True or false: Getting all sensors in one module makes the code cleaner because you'll only have to deal with one I2C address.
3. True or false: Magnetometers are especially useful for indoor robots.

# CHAPTER 17

# GPS and External Beacon Systems

## Introduction

By now, you've realized just how big a challenge robot localization is. Wheel odometry with an IMU can help quite a bit, but over time the error will grow unacceptably, and another means of verifying location is needed. Fortunately, systems that use land-based beacons or even satellites have become more accurate and more affordable. We'll spend this chapter discussing some of these options and learning how to use a GPS and publish its data for your ROS-based robot.

In this chapter, we will be covering the following:

- How beacon systems work
- GPS and GNSS basics
- GPS/GNSS-RTK for 2 cm accuracy
- GPS/GNSS limitations
- GPS/GNSS data
- Publishing GPS data to ROS

# Objectives

Understand how beacon systems work, their value, and their limitations. Learn how to get, understand, and publish GPS/GNSS data in ROS.

# How beacon systems work

Beacon systems work either by triangulation or trilateration. Triangulation works by knowing the angle from the device being located to the beacons. With two or more beacons spotted, the lines drawn from the robot to beacons can be drawn and the where they intersect is the location of the device. This is much less common in robotics than trilateration so that we will focus on the latter for this chapter.

Trilateration uses measurements of the distance from the beacon to the receiver on the robot, usually acquired by very precise synchronizing of clocks that transmit the time. The time that signal is received minus the time stamp on the signal is the time of flight of the transmission. The receiver multiplies the time of flight by the speed of light or sound (depending on the system being used) to calculate the distance from the beacon. Radio signals used by systems like GPS and GNSS travel at the speed of light, while the signal from ultrasonic beacons travels at the speed of sound.

Imagine you know the exact location of some landmarks but don't know where you are. *Figure 17.1* below shows how you can narrow down your location with accurate distance measurements to these landmarks or beacons on a 2D plane.

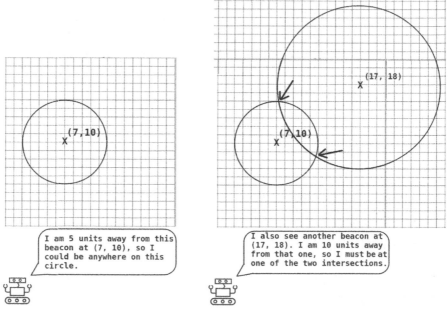

*Figure 17.1: Using trilateration (using distances to known reference points) for localization*

Drawing a circle with range data to the third reference shows only one location intersected by all three circles revealing your location on a 2D plane (or on the surface of the Earth (left image in the *figure 17.2* below). If the beacons are space-based, we can use a fourth to determine altitude data as well. See the right image in *figure 17.2* below.

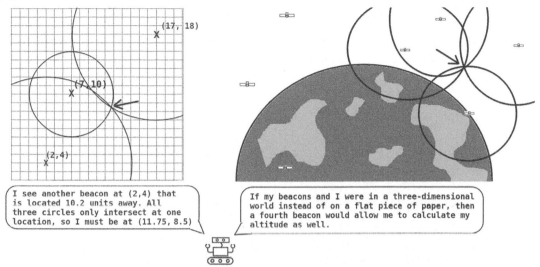

**Figure 17.2:** *Trilateration on a two-dimensional plane (left) and in three dimensions (right) - with satellites*

Keep in mind that three or four is the minimum number of beacons we require signals from. Operating at this minimum is error-prone, as a single hiccup can result in a location estimate kilometers off. The better systems are capable of listening to a dozen or more beacons at once and filtering out the signals that just don't make sense.

# GPS and GNSS basics

**Global Positioning System (GPS)** and **Global Navigation Satellite System (GNSS)** are satellite-based beacon systems that can be used around the globe. GPS is the oldest and technically refers only to the system operated by the *Unites States*, while GNSS includes systems operated by several different agencies. These include GPS by the *U.S. Glonass* by *Russia, Galileo* by the *European Union, BieDou* by *China,* and a few others.

If you are shopping for a receiver and a GPS unit doesn't specifically mention GNSS, you'll likely be limited to the *U.S. satellites*. In this game, the more satellites your receiver can see, the faster you can get a lock and the more accurate it will be. Further, GPS/GNSS is a line-of-sight system, which means the receiver needs to be able to *see* the satellites directly. Using indoors, in valleys, or under heavy tree canopies will result in horrifically inaccurate location data or none at all. An external antenna mounted as high on the robot as possible and away from anything else can go a long way in improving your location accuracy.

# GPS/GNSS accuracy

The least expensive units I've tried (GPS-only and tempting for under *$10*) have been pretty awful – slow and always losing signals. Save your money and spend an extra *$20* for a decent GPS/GNSS unit like the *GPSV5* with the antenna in *figure 17.3* below to save yourself a lot of frustration. You can find GPS modules that output I2C, serial data for the GPIO UART, or USB serial.

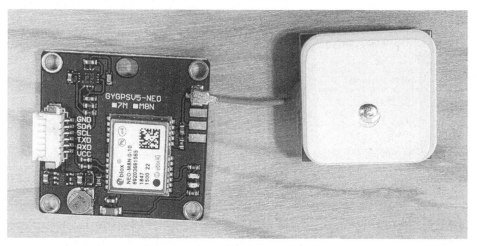

*Figure 17.3:* The GPSV5 GPS/GNSS receiver with I2C and serial connections

Standard GPS/GNSS is accurate only within a couple of meters and is, therefore, only a helpful clue for determining a robot's location and cannot be used to guide a robot precisely.

The most significant factor for this inaccuracy is that atmospheric conditions change the speed of the radio signals from the satellite to the receiver, and those conditions are varying all over the planet all the time. Several methods have been developed to minimize that error — one of the most successful, called **Real Time Kinematics** (**RTK**), can provide location data accurate down to a couple of centimeters!

 **In casual conversation, people tend to use *GPS* to refer to both systems. I may be guilty of this myself. It's not a big deal if you're talking with friends, but be careful when you're shopping for components.**

# GPS/GNSS-RTK for 2cm accuracy

RTK is a method of correcting the error from atmospheric interference by using a second receiver as a base station that can broadcast correction data to the mobile receiver in your robot. The `base station` can calculate the error data because it is placed in a known location and knows what values it should be receiving from the satellites. Because the atmosphere varies so much from location to location, the correction data is less and less useful to the mobile receiver the farther it gets from the base station. Generally, you want to be within `20 miles` (`32 KM`) or so, although data from networks of RTK receivers can be used to calculate virtual base station data in places in between.

In the past, RTK stations were privately owned, and you had to pay hefty fees for access to the correction data. Fortunately, more and more government programs are making RTK available for a nominal fee or even free. In the `United States`, check with your state's `Department of Transportation`. Alternatively, the private companies `Leica` and `Trimble` (that provide service to most of the states that have a program) cover a great deal of the countries. Finally, a community-based network called RTK 2 go may be have a station near you – check out *rtk2go.com* to use or contribute if you have your own base station.

If no RTK stations are available near you or cost too much, you are not out of luck – some RTK GPS modules can be configured to act as your private base station. I think the most affordable I've found the `Sparkfun GPS-RTK2 Board` – just don't forget you'll need two of them unless you have public RTK data available. The *www. sparkfun.com* website has some tutorials if you want to learn more about how RTK works or how to set up an RTK GPS.

# GPS/GNSS limitations

Besides the fact that standard GPS is nowhere near accurate enough to rely on as an absolute localization solution, the line-of-sight limitation of the signals means that using it indoors is a no-go. Also, be prepared for trouble acquiring enough satellite signals if you are in between buildings, in a valley or depression, or even under dense tree cover. GPS works best out in the open because more satellites allows for greater accuracy. An external antenna like the one pictured next to the `Sparkfun RTK-GPS` in *figure 17.4* below can help reception and let you mount the receiver somewhere protected from the elements. Still, it can't make up for major line-of-sight violations.

***Figure 17.4:*** *A Sparkfun RTK-GPS with an external, waterproof antenna*

Installing your own network of beacons can solve this problem but comes at a hefty price. If you have a large operating area, the price of beacons can far exceed the cost of the rest of a robot, but applications with multiple robots can find it a fantastic solution. There is at least one relatively affordable indoor beacon system made by a company called **Marvelmind**, but I have yet to get my hands on one to test it.

# GPS/GNSS data

Hopefully, you are familiar with the **latitude/longitude** (**lat/long**) coordinate system that uses degrees, minutes, and seconds to express location on the globe. While there are other (arguably friendlier for most robotics projects) coordinate systems, we will use lat/long because:

1.  Most GPS/GNSS receivers are set to use lat/long by default, and many have no other options.
2.  The standard ROS message for a satellite location fix is degrees of latitude and longitude.

If you are not familiar with using degrees, minutes, and seconds of latitude and longitude, there are plenty of tutorials to be found with a quick check of *Google* or *YouTube*. Take a break from this book and check some out if you need to – I'm afraid the rest of this section will be hard to follow otherwise. *Ready to continue?* Good!

## NMEA data strings

One of the wonderful things about most GPS/GNSS receivers is that you don't have to do anything to get data out of them if you've wired them up for serial (and sometimes this is easy as plugging in a USB cable). So far, every one I've used has been this way – once hooked up and powered up, it automatically looks for satellites and starts streaming serial data. Different modes and options are often available, but for basic use, there is no need to bother. Also, be advised that if you want to use I2C instead of serial, you'll need to actively poll the registers and sometimes change modes before you get data. For this reason, I much prefer using serial mode unless there is some compelling need to do otherwise.

**A quick check that the receiver is working and that you have the correct permissions and port can be done with the** `cat` **command from the terminal command prompt.**

`cat /dev/ttyACM0`

**(or whichever port it is connected to, if different from** `ttyACM0`**) should start displaying all the streaming data if everything is in order.**

The data the device streams are a repeated bunch of something called **NMEA strings**. **The National Maritime Electronics Association** (**NMEA**) is the organization that created the standard format for transmitting GPS/GNSS data. While the NMEA sentences have standard structure, there are several different ones, and decoding them can be tedious. *Figure 17.5* below shows a screenshot of some NMEA sentences streamed to my GPIO UART from a GPSV5 receiver, and a breakdown of a GGA-type sentence – one of the more common ones.

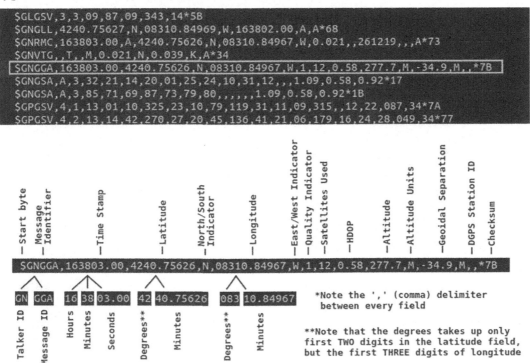

*Figure 17.5: Breaking down a common NMEA Sentence*

Fortunately, the first few characters include a message identifier so the software knows how to proceed with decoding. Having a standard sentence format for each type means we don't have to write custom software for each different manufacturer or model of receiver – the same software will work for most cases. For more information about this and other (and there are many others) NMEA sentences, *Google* NMEA 0183 – this is the official NMEA specification.

## Some key lat/long data representations

By now, you are hopefully familiar with the lat/long convention of dividing the globe into degrees, minutes, and seconds and representing that data in a format with a little different symbol for each. If you have a handheld GPS/GNSS, that is likely how the data is displayed on the screen. NMEA sentences and the ROS message we'll be using, however, use what appears as a single value with a decimal. Be further aware that the format from an NMEA sentence is different than the ROS NavSatFix message. Check out *figure 17.6* below for three different representations of the same data grabbed from the NMEA sentence at the top of the image.

```
$GNGGA,163805.00,4240.75630,N,08310.84960,W,1,12,0.60,278.3,M,-34.9,M,,*7D
                        (Original NMEA Sentence)


Traditional         :  DD⁰ MM' SS.SSSS"    example: 42⁰ 40' 45.3792" N    83⁰ 10'50.9772" W


NMEA GGA Sentence:  DDMM.MMMMM             example: 4240.75630, N        08310.84960, W


ROS NavSatFix       :  DD.DDDDDD           example: 42.679272            -83.180827
```

*Figure 17.6: Three ways to represent the same latitude and longitude data*

Observe in the second row that the NMEA GGA-type sentence doesn't directly list seconds like the traditional format but instead includes seconds as the decimal part of minutes. Since there are 60 seconds in one minute:

```
60 sec/min x .7563 minutes = 45.37 seconds
```

Also important to note about the NMEA sentence is that leading zeros are included in the number of transmitted so the number of received bytes before the decimal remains constant. Latitude is always four digits before the decimal, and longitude is always five (Because latitude only goes ranges from 90W to 90E, but longitude ranges from 180S to 180N).

Moving down one row is the values from the same NMEA sentence converted for a ROS sensor_msgs::NavSatFix message. Here, not even minutes are directly represented as the entire value is degrees. (The portion after the decimal is minutes represented as a partial degree). Therefore:

```
60 min/deg x .679272 = 40.7563 minutes
```

And just like we did for the NMEA sentence, seconds are now the decimal part of the minute.

Finally, You may have noticed that we don't mention *North, South, East,* or *West* in the ROS format. That would take up another data field that the developers decided could be easily represented instead by using a single signed value. Positive values are *North* of the equator or *East* of the prime meridian, and negative values are *South* or *West*.

# Publishing GPS/GNSS data in ROS

In past chapters on different sensors, I have walked you through writing entire ROS nodes (also known as **Programs**). This was to make sure you understood both the principles behind the devices, the tasks we were trying to accomplish, and the nuts and bolts of getting data to a ROS project in the proper formats. Equally important, however, is knowing how to find and implement ROS nodes written by others that can speed your project along or perhaps add the functionality you couldn't have written yourself.

Because GPS/GNSS modules (that I'm aware of) all transmit the same NMEA sentences, this is the perfect application for finding a generic ROS package to receive, convert, and publish the data for us. In this section, we're going to get some practice downloading and installing a ROS package from the Internet as well as learning how to pass parameter arguments when necessary to customize how a node runs.

The end goal is the publication of the ROS sensor_msgs::NavSatFix message. This message contains latitude, longitude, and altitude information, if available. For complete details, visit *wiki.ros.org/sensor_msgs* and click the link for NavSatFix. There are NMEA sentences for heading and velocity data too, and the ROS node we are about to explore publishes that (on its topic) as well when the receiver provides it.

## The ROS package: nmea_navsat_driver

When you download a ROS node, it will frequently come in a package with other related nodes. While we only plan to use one of the included nodes in the nmea_navsat_driver package, it is worth looking over all three included nodes:

- nmea_topic_serial_reader – This node could be used if you have some use for the NMEA sentences other than what the nmea_topic_driver does.

This node simply reads the sentences from the designated serial port and publishes them as a ROS message of type `sensor_msgs::Sentence`.

- `nmea_topic_driver` – This node could be used if you got data from a source other than the USB or GPIO serial ports. You could publish the NMEA sentence as a topic in some other node, and this node would complete conversion and publish the `NavSatFix` message.

- `nmea_serial_driver` – This node combines the above nodes to do it all — except for publishing the raw NMEA sentences.

The node we are going to use is the `nmea_serial_driver`, but first, we have to download and install it.

## Installing the nmea_navsat_driver package

There are two basic ways to install ROS packages from the internet. The first works if the package is in the repository for your ROS distro. Installing then is as easy as using apt-get:

```
sudo apt-get install ros-kinetic-nmea-navsat-driver
```

or

```
sudo apt-get install ros-melodic-nmea-navsat-driver
```

Alternatively, use the second method if the package you want is not available in the repository, or if for some reason you need to modify the code for your application (although it is preferable to *fork* the repository, then clone *your* fork to your local machine to make the changes).

The code for the `nmea_navsat_driver` package is located at *github.com/ros-drivers/ nmea_navsat_driver*. Installing it takes three easy steps:

1. Navigate to your root `catkin_ws/src` folder.
2. Clone the repository into your source folder.
3. Compile the new package with `catkin_make`.

Refer to *Chapter 9, Coordinating the Parts* for a review of the ROS/Catkin workspace file structure if needed. Then issue the following commands:

```
cd /home/lloyd/catkin_ws/src
```

```
Git clone https://github.com/ros-drivers/nmea_navsat_driver.git
```

```
cd ..
```

```
catkin_make
```

Don't forget the `cd..` because you need to be in `/src` to close, but have to back up one folder level to run `catkin_make`. Once it compiles (hopefully without error), install the GPS for serial communications and make sure the antenna is in a clear, open area on a good ground plane (a ground plane is a metal base like the roof of a car or even just a metal sheet). If you're lucky, you just need to plug a USB cable in, otherwise refer back to *Chapter 5, Communication with Sensors and Other Devices* for more information on connecting serial devices and making sure you have the proper permissions to access the port.

# Reading ROS package documentation

This section is going to include a few extra lessons on launching nodes from the command line. Mostly, you need to get used to reading the package docs and sifting through the parameters so you can pass the correct ones when the default ones don't work for you. For example, this node defaults to trying to open and read from the USB serial port at `/dev/ttyUSB0`, but the GPS on the robot I'm using is wired to the GPIO serial UART pins and is addressed at `/dev/ttyAMA0`. Please navigate to the official documentation at *wiki.ros.org/nmea_navsat_driver* before we continue.

This is a pretty typical page for a ROS package you might find for any ROS application. Near the top, you'll find a name and e-mail address for the maintainer, as well as a link to the code's *GitHub* page. The overview section has valuable information about what the node or nodes can and cannot do, version limitations, and often known bugs or compatibility issues. A little farther down are listed nodes.

For each node, there is a list of topics that the node subscribes to. Sometimes not every subscribed topic is required. There is also a list of the topics the node publishes. All of these are usually links to the *Wiki* page for that message type so you can get clarification on what the node does. Finally, for each node, there will be a list of parameters.

Parameters are values in the node's code you should customize for your specific application and hardware. Think of them as `const` values in a program, but you get to initialize them. They'll have some default value if you pass nothing, but you have to be careful and know that these default values are acceptable or results can be unpredictable.

Look with care at the section for the `nmea_serial_driver` we are going to run momentarily. You can see the topics it is capable of publishing at the top under **Published Topics** – we are most interested in the `NavSatFix`. You don't see any **Subscribed Topics** because it doesn't subscribe to anything – instead, it takes input from the hardware. To make sure the node can find and interpret the data sent by the hardware, we need to check and set some parameters. Let's look at each parameter listed:

- port – This is the /dev location you have the GPS/GNSS receiver connected to, and the node assumes you're using USB. If not connected via USB, you might need to specify /dev/ttyAMA0, /dev/ttyACM0, or a handful of others. If you have more than one USB serial device connected, you may need to try /dev/ttyUSB1 or /dev/ttyUSB2. Refer back to *Chapter 5, Communicating with Sensors and other Devices* for more on finding your port.

- baud – This is the data transfer speed and defaults to a slightly older standard of 4800. Both GPS units pictured in this chapter communicate at 9600 – check the spec sheet for yours and make a note of it.

- frame_id – this is especially important if you are using some corrected GPS/GNSS data like RTK. The default of GPS is fine, just know that when you eventually set up transforms that the GPS frame is at the receiver's antenna – not the receiver itself.

- time_ref_source – I would leave this at the default as well.

- useRMC – RMC is a different NMEA sentence than the one we used in our example and contains velocity data as well. You'll have to decide if you need velocity data or covariance data – for now, we'll be leaving this at the default of false.

And that's all there is to it. This node is pretty tame with this small handful of parameters, while others have a long, long list of them. I understand that it can be intimidating or inconvenient to sift through a long list of parameters when you just want to type rosrun.. and move on – be warned that impatience usually comes back to haunt me in the form of extra troubleshooting because I didn't take the time to read the docs.

# Running the nmea_serial_driver node with parameters

You're an expert at starting non-parameterized nodes by now with

```
rosrun package_name node_name
```

But that is likely going to return you an error with the nmea_serial_driver. In my case, the receiver is connected to /dev/ttyAMA0 and runs at 9600 baud, so we have to change those two parameters. Passing parameters via command line is similar to command line topic name remapping that I suggested you explore in *Chapter 9, Coordinating the Parts*. One key difference is that you have to add an underscore to a parameter, or the argument is interpreted as a remap. For example:

```
rosrun nmea_navsat_driver nmea_serial_driver

    _port:="/dev/ttyACM0" _baud:=9600
```

This means that run the node using /dev/ttyACM0 at 9600 baud, but

```
rosrun nmea_navsat_driver nmea_serial_driver

    port:="/dev/ttyACM0" baud:=9600
```

Means change every topic named port to /dev/ttyACM0 and every topic named baud to 9600. This is not what we want, so remember to add the underscore for setting parameters via the command line.

**Note:** The commands in the above two blocks are each a single command – they just don't fit on the page on one line.

 While the command line is convenient for setting a couple of parameters, the dozen or more parameters some nodes require are far too many to type every time you launch a node. For these, you'll want to use a launch file. See *wiki.ros.org/roslaunch* for more – especially the video embedded at the bottom.

# Conclusion

We've covered a good amount of information about beacons and how they can help solve the localization problem – focusing on the satellite-based systems known as GPS and GNSS. We talked about their uses and limitations, such as inaccuracy unless we use a method like RTK to correct for atmospheric distortions to the GPS signals, and we even touched on systems that can be used indoors if you can afford to buy and set up your beacons.

In the next chapter, we are going to dive into the details of LIDAR – we'll learn some theory and operating principles, look at the differences between some different units, and learn how to read data from them and publish them adequately formatted data to ROS.

# Questions

1. What is the minimum number of beacons necessary to trilaterate a Position (without altitude data).

2. What is the necessary accuracy of satellite navigation systems without correction data like RTK?

3. What must be added to a parameter name to pass a parameter while starting a ROS node from the command prompt with rosrun?

CHAPTER 18

# LIDAR Devices and Data

## Introduction

Despite advances in millimetre-wave radar and computer vision techniques, light detection and ranging, also known as LIDAR, devices are still more or less the robotics industry standard for mapping environments.

In this chapter, we will learn all of the basics you need to choose, install, and run LIDAR devices. We'll talk about different types, what they can and cannot do, and we'll make sure you understand how to read the data. Finally, we'll walk through setting up a popular model and getting the data published in ROS.

In this chapter, we will cover the following topics:

- LIDAR basics
- LIDAR limitations
- LIDAR types
- LIDAR selection considerations
- LIDAR data — the sensor_msgs::LaserScan message
- LIDAR mounting considerations
- Setting up, running, and testing a common LIDAR unit
- Visualizing LIDAR data with RViz

# Objective

Understand how LIDAR works along with its uses and limitations. Learn how to interpret LIDAR data and the sensor_msgs::LaserScan message type. Learn how to set up a popular LIDAR model and start publishing LIDAR data in ROS.

# LIDAR basics

LIDAR devices measure how long it takes a pulse of laser light to travel to an object and back. Because it uses a tight laser beam, the resolution is second-to-none, and the data makes for incredibly detailed maps of the environment.

LIDAR rangefinders measure only a single point, and motors are used to spin mirrors or the whole apparatus to take multiple measurements in a circle for two dimensional (2D) data. *Figure 18.1* below shows the 2D LIDAR data for a robot in a simulated environment. The simulator is called **Gazebo,** and the LIDAR scan visualization is in a tool called **Rviz**.

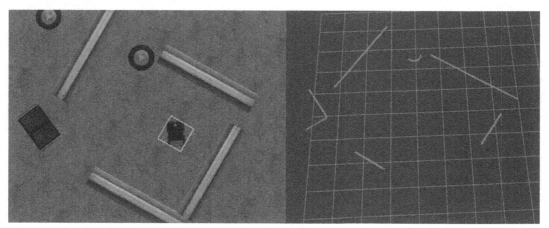

*Figure 18.1: A robot in a simulated environment (left) and a visualization of its LIDAR scan data (right)*

Notice that LIDAR cannot show us the entire shape of an obstacle, but can only measure to the leading edge of the closest object. To draw the whole dumpster on the left or barrel at the top, we would save this data and drive around to scan from a different location.

Also note that while the data appears in the visualization as red lines, the data provided by the laser scan comes as a single point – the points are just so close together that they tend to appear as lines or curves when plotted in a visualization tool like Rviz.

Some people will argue technical differences, but the fact is that the terms *LIDAR*, *Laser scanner*, and sometimes just *Laser* are generally used interchangeably to refer to any device that uses laser light to provide a bunch of precision range values covering an arc or complete circle. I use them interchangeably in this book.

# LIDAR limitations

LIDAR's pinpoint-accurate beams are both a blessing and a curse. This same precision that gives us such wonderfully detailed maps means that the LIDAR can't detect anything even one centimeter above, below, or to the side of the beam – illustrated in *figure 18.2* below. 2D, or scanning, units have a rotating component to eliminate the problem in the side-to-side direction, but robots relying on them still require secondary sensors.

*Figure 18.2: LIDAR will not detect anything above or below the very thin beam*

Another shortcoming of LIDAR that some dark colors and materials simply absorb the laser light, and the unit won't detect it at all. My team experienced this issue when a brave teammate sat in a chair, trusting our collision avoidance routine. All was well until the 50 KG robot approached from behind and slammed into the back of the chair with significant force. The problem? We failed to stop and think – the chair was black and invisible to our LIDAR.

# LIDAR types

LIDAR range devices vary wildly in features and price — from about $100 to well over $10,000 in U.S. dollars. Let's discuss some of the options so you can make a better choice when you're ready to shop for one.

# Unidirectional (single point) LIDAR

These are small, relatively inexpensive devices that return only a single measurement rather than many points from a scan or sweep. These aren't too often seen on the type of ground robot we've been focusing on in this book, but you may see them on drones or some other specialty application. *Figure 18.3* below is an example of such a device.

*Figure 18.3:* *A VL53xx series time of flight distance sensor alongside a micro SD card and Hokuyo scanning laser range finder for scale*

Because of their low cost, attempts are sometimes made to add a servo or stepper motor and make a do-it-yourself scanning LIDAR. This absolutely can be done but requires a significant amount of development time and results in relatively weak resolution and scan rate. For a fraction of the work and the same amount of money, there is a much better option I'll tell you about at the end of this section.

# 2D LIDAR

2D scanning LIDAR provides multiple ranges that cover an arc or a complete *360* degree circle by rotating mirrors or a whole sensor assembly with a motor. This array of accurate ranges with pinpoint precision is what makes LIDAR data useful compared to a handful of ultrasonic sensors that might detect an object several inches away from the center of aim. These cost a bit more than non-scanning laser range devices but are much more useful unless your application requires the smallest possible package. Below, *figure 18.4* consists of laser scanners from two popular manufacturers.

*Figure 18.4: The popular Hokuyo (left) and RPLIDAR brands each offer several models of laser scanner*

2D laser scan data like we saw in *figure 18.1* is useful for creating fantastic maps and can be provided by a laser scanner like the *Hokuyo* in *figure 18.4*. The RPLIDAR is a remarkable sensor for a fraction of the price but runs at about one-quarter of the speed and resolution. It does, however, scan a full *360* degrees where the *Hokuyo* pictured only has a *270* degree **field-of-view (FOV)**.

2D LIDAR is the most common in use today and is the type that I am talking about anytime I refer to LIDAR data in this book. We'll even walk through setting up and starting the popular RPLIDAR later in this chapter.

# 3D LIDAR

While 2D LIDAR is still king, 3D LIDAR has made some significant advances. It adds some exciting capabilities – namely, the ability to detect objects and draw a map for the ground level and the level the device is mounted. And another level above that. And another above that. And so on and so one until we have a collection of maps that we can stack together into one 3D map of the world that our robot can understand. No longer do we have the problem of our path appearing to be clear at the robot's `eye level,` but a curb or dog being invisible just below the sensor. It's much more coding and processor intensive, but a fantastic breakthrough in robot navigation!

3D LIDAR units have a narrower horizontal field of view than 2D LIDARS (sometimes *30* degrees compared to *270* or *360* degrees). Still, they can provide several scans at different vertical angles and can, therefore, see things a 2D laser would miss. This data may very useful for even a ground robot dealing with uneven terrain, but it will come at a significant cost both in terms of processing and cost. 3D LIDAR is rapidly gaining popularity among self-driving car developers in particular, although other robot companies (and the occasional hobbyist) with deep pockets are also coming on board.

# Salvaged robot vacuum LIDAR

There's no denying that a LIDAR unit can be just too expensive for a lot of individuals. With even the most affordable costing over *$100* (which is fantastic, given that a few years ago, the least expensive options were *$800-1500*), it's quite an investment for a learning project. Fortunately, the rise of robot vacuums that use LIDAR and intelligent navigation has resulted in surplus and salvaged LIDAR units available to individuals willing to do a little extra work to hack and re-purpose them. *Figure 18.5* belowshows a salvaged LIDAR from a *Neato Botvac*.

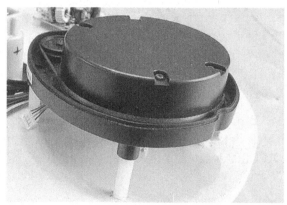

*Figure 18.5: A laser scanner removed from a dead Neato robot vacuum*

People are getting rid of their older robot vacuums all the time, and you may be lucky enough to land one for free. If that is not the case, I have purchased these salvaged Lidar units for as little as *$35* on *eBay*. Still, I have to recommend acquiring even the least expensive purpose-made 2D scanning LIDAR if at all possible (as far as I know, that is the RPLIDAR A1) because of several downsides of free or very cheap LIDAR salvaged from robot vacuums:

- You'll have to make connectors rather than plug-and-play.
- You'll have to control motor-speed – that means a little extra circuitry and software to write.
- These do provide *360* ranges in a full-circle field-of-view but are significantly slower (per scan) than even the RPLIDAR. This can be a problem when mapping or otherwise relying on data on-the-move.

- The software to run them will have to be written by you or can be downloaded from at least two sources I know of, but these are unofficial, and you'll have to do everything without manufacturer support.

- If you want to interface via USB, you'll still have to purchase a USB serial-to-TTL serial converter like an FTDI.

Hacking devices is a little outside the scope of this book, but it is something I personally get a kick out of. If this is something you'd like to do, I have a video tutorial for hacking the *Neato Lidar* on *The Practical Robotics Youtube channel* at *www.youtube.com/practicalrobotics*.

# LIDAR selection considerations

Some characteristics to consider when selecting a LIDAR are:

- **Field of view** – Some can give you a *360* degree view, others only *270* degrees or less. 3D units will specify both horizontal and vertical fields of view.

- **Resolution** – How many increments the device reports over its field of view. Less expensive units that I love for indoor projects where the ranges are shorter give one measurement per degree. Higher-resolution units are more suitable for commercial use, outdoors, or anywhere with longer distances to measure and benefit from four measurements per degree (or one measurement every ¼ degree).

- **Range** – Four meters of the range is *OK* for most homes and smaller offices, but get outside or in a big, open office or shop and you'll appreciate being able to detect things *12* or more meters away.

- **Indoor/Outdoor rating** – LIDAR units rated for only indoor use tend to be more sensitive to interference from sunlight and may not be weather-resistant at all.

- **Scan rate** – How long it takes to complete a scan. A bit less critical for slower robots. Becomes very important as the speed of the robot or objects around the robot increase.

- **Ethernet versus USB connection** – The only reason I bring this up is that units connecting via Ethernet have some IP addresses and networking hoops you have to jump through. Not a big deal, but it can be frustrating if you're not familiar with networking stuff while devices that attach with USB are more or less plug-and-play.

# LIDAR data: The sensor_msgs::LaserScan message

Fortunately, LIDAR units you buy new should have ROS drivers written by the manufacturer, so you shouldn't have to write the laser data publisher node. I do want to discuss the LaserScan message in detail so you can troubleshoot when necessary, decode the message for some specialty node you write yourself, or even create the message to fake a laser scan message with range data from other sensors. Below is a screenshot (*figure 18.6*) of the ROS docs for the LaserScan message – you can see the whole page and click to some extra information by heading to *wiki.ros. org/sensor_msgs* and clicking on LaserScan.

**File:** sensor_msgs/LaserScan.msg

## Raw Message Definition

```
# Single scan from a planar laser range-finder
#
# If you have another ranging device with different behavior (e.g. a sonar
# array), please find or create a different message, since applications
# will make fairly laser-specific assumptions about this data

Header header          # timestamp in the header is the acquisition time of
                       # the first ray in the scan.
                       #
                       # in frame frame_id, angles are measured around
                       # the positive Z axis (counterclockwise, if Z is up)
                       # with zero angle being forward along the x axis

float32 angle_min      # start angle of the scan [rad]
float32 angle_max      # end angle of the scan [rad]
float32 angle_increment # angular distance between measurements [rad]

float32 time_increment # time between measurements [seconds] - if your scanner
                       # is moving, this will be used in interpolating position
                       # of 3d points
float32 scan_time      # time between scans [seconds]

float32 range_min      # minimum range value [m]
float32 range_max      # maximum range value [m]

float32[] ranges       # range data [m] (Note: values < range_min or > range_max should be discarded)
float32[] intensities  # intensity data [device-specific units].  If your
                       # device does not provide intensities, please leave
                       # the array empty.
```

*Figure 18.6: A screenshot of the the official ROS docs for the LaserScan message (linked at wiki. ros.org/sensor_msgs)*

The LaserScan message is intended for a single 2D laser scan, although it is possible to combine multiple LaserScan messages into one if you have more than one scanner. Unidirectional laser rangers, including ultrasonic range finders, would generally use the Range message – though multiple readings from multiple fixed sensors and rotating the whole robot have been combined into a LaserScan message with varying results. 3D scanners have used different message formats but seem to be settling on the `PointCloud` or `PointCloud2` message. You can find links to data about the `Range` message and both `PointCloud` messages at the ROS wiki for sensor messages.

The header is standard for all ROS messages – There, you'll find a data members for the time stamp and the frame ID. The frame ID is usually just `laser` unless you have multiple scanners. The time stamp should be set by the node using the `ros` clock. For example:

```
scanMessageName.header.stamp = ros.Time.now();
```

The next three lines are critical – because they define what heading angle each data element refers to.

- `angle_min` – The minimum angle in radians that will be measured. The range measured at this angle is written to the first element of the `laserMsg.ranges`, which is an element `[0]`. This should be a negative number.

- `angle_max` - The maximum angle in radians that will be measured. The range measured at this angle is written to the last element of the `laserMsg.ranges[]`. The size of `ranges[]` varies with the field of view and the `angle_increment`.

- `angle_increment` – The angle between each reading or `ranges[]` element. The angle for any `ranges[i]` element can be found with `angle = i * angle_increment + angle_min`.

For some reason, it is typical for specs and sales brochures to list field of view in degrees, but `angle_min`, `angle_max`, and `angle_increment` are listed in radians. It is much to your benefit to get used to at least estimating conversions back and forth in your head. *Figure 18.7* below shows the angle min, max, and increment for 360 and 270 degree field-of-view LIDARs with different resolutions.

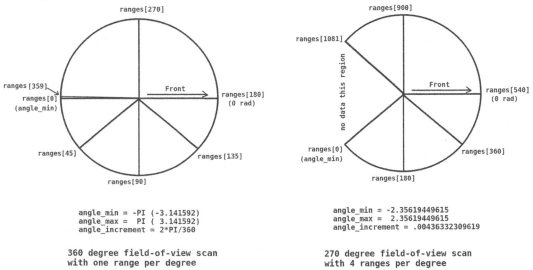

*Figure 18.7: visualizing angle_min, angle_max, and angle_increment with ranges[] element numbers*

The RPLIDAR A1 we are going to set up in a few moments has a `ranges[]` element arrangement like the example on the left, while the image on the right has values from the *Hokuyo UST-10Lx*. Notice that the highest index number is smaller for the *360* degree LIDAR because of the lower `angle_increment` (also known as *resolution*).

After the `angle_min`, `angle_max`, and `angle_increment` data members, we have two data members regarding timing and two regarding `range_min` and `range_max`. The ROS doc is pretty clear on the time members, so I'll leave them alone. The `range_min` and `range_max` values indicate the capabilities of the laser scanner – you must check values in the `ranges[]` field against these and discard any reading with a value outside of this range.

Finally, the `sensor_msgs::LaserScan` message contains two arrays: `ranges[]` and `intensities[]`. The intensity is an indicator of the strength of the reading (signal returned), and too weak a signal may be discarded or otherwise considered with caution in programs reading the message. The `ranges[i]` and `intensities[i]` index refer to the same reading/angle for a given index. Please note that I am using the term `array` for `ranges[]` and `intensities[]` for simplicity and because the ROS docs present them this way, but know that these are implemented as vectors and can be resized with `.resize()` as necessary. This should be irrelevant if you are reading the message but must be done if you are creating your message.

# LIDAR mounting considerations

The LIDAR should be oriented like we orient an IMU. That is, the front faces along the *x axis* of the robot. This will result in the central element of the scan measuring distance directly in front of the robot. *Figure 18.8* illustrates how the `ranges[]` elements line up on a *360* degree `Field of View` (`FOV`) LIDAR ideally oriented with `ranges[min]` and `ranges[max]` at the back of the robot and the middle of the `ranges[]` array directly in front of the robot.

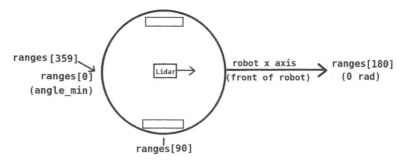

**Top View of properly oriented RPLIDAR**

*Figure 18.8: How ranges[] elements line up when a 360 degree Field of View (FOV) LIDAR with one range per degree is ideally oriented*

*Figure 18.8* shows a LIDAR centered on the rotational center of the robot (also known as base_link) and ideally oriented. Still, they can be mounted anywhere – or even turned or tilted, so the natural scan is misaligned. These offsets can be compensated for by broadcasting a transform message or hard-coding a transform in nodes that use the laser data. We touched on this concept in *Chapter 10, Maps for Robot Navigation*, if you need a refresher. The RPLIDAR in the image below is mounted *10 cm* forward of center on the robot, so my transformX value would be .1 because values are to be in meters.

**Figure 18.9:** *An RPLIDAR mounted just forward of center*

Finally, LIDARs usually get mounted on the highest point of the robot except for perhaps an antenna or boom for some instrument. You may be able to filter this obstruction out by placing the LIDAR closer than the range_min. Keep in mind that the closer the object is, the greater the resulting blind spot will be. Another option is to place the LIDAR so the obstruction is already in a blind spot if the scanner has one. If those aren't options, you can modify the scanner driver to set the ranges in that area to some out-of-bounds range. Any nodes that receive the scan message should be set to ignore out-of-bounds ranges.

# Setting up, running, and testing a common LIDAR unit

For this section, we are going to set up an RPLIDAR A1, run the node, and check that it is publishing a proper LaserScan message. There isn't a lot to it and is mostly an exercise in USB serial communication that we covered in *Chapter 5, Communication with Sensors and Other Devices*. The procedure should be similar for any USB-connected laser scanner. We are going to install the ROS package provided by the

*Slamtec/Robopeak* team that developed the RPLIDAR – you should look over the package docs at *wiki.ros.org/rplidar*.

My instructions vary a little from the official wiki tutorial docs from the *Slamtec/ Robopeak* team because I want to teach you some extra details that you'll find useful in your robotics journey. You can find the official tutorial at *www.github.robopeak/ rplidar_ros/wiki/How-to-use-rplidar*.

# Setting up an RPLIDAR by following these steps:

1. Navigate to your `catkin_ws/src` folder and clone the RPLIDAR software repository:

   `git clone https://github.com/robopeak/rplidar_ros.git`

2. Use `cd ..` to move back up one folder level and compile the new package with:

   `catkin_make`

3. Connect the RPLIDAR via USB and find the port and set permission according to what we learned in *Chapter 5, Communication with Sensors and Other Devices.*

4. Start `roscore` and the RPLIDAR node by running the following commands in two separate terminal windows:

   `roscore`

   `rosrun rplidar_ros rplidarNode`

   `--OR-- (if the port is different than /dev/ttyUSB0, you have to pass a port parameter when you launch the node)`

   `rosrun rplidar_ros rplidarNode _port:="dev/YOUR_PORT"`

5. The turret should be spinning, and the RPLIDAR should be streaming data. The `rplidarNode` should be converting the data to a `LaserScan` message and publishing it with the topic name `scan`. Open a new terminal window and confirm with the command:

   `rostopic list`

   You should see all of the published topics listed. `/scan` should be among them (or something similar if you have a different model scanner).

6. View the `LaserScan` message in the terminal with one of the following commands. The first command will begin a continuous stream of scan messages that will be difficult to read. The second command adds a `-n` tag that will display however

many messages you request with the following integer. I request one message in the example:

```
rostopic echo scan
```

--or--

```
rostopic echo -n1 scan
```

The message will be long, but if you scroll back up to the top, you'll see an output of every field that the message contains. *Figure 18.10* shows a `LaserScan` message echoed to the terminal.

```
lloyd@lloyd-GE63-Raider-RGB-8RE:~$ rostopic echo -n1 scan
header:
  seq: 271980
  stamp:
    secs: 1571275172
    nsecs: 245216727
  frame_id: "laser"
angle_min: -2.35619449615
angle_max: 2.35619449615
angle_increment: 0.00436332309619
time_increment: 1.73611151695e-05
scan_time: 0.0250000003725
range_min: 0.019999999553
range_max: 30.0
ranges: [2.131999969482422, 2.130000114440918, 2.13100004196167, 2.121999979019165, 2.1129999160766
6, 2.0929999351501465, 2.0869998931884766, 2.072999954223633, 2.072999954223633, 2.062000036239624,
 2.0490000247955322, 2.0409998893737793, 2.0369999408721924, 2.0309998989105225, 2.0199999809265137
, 2.0139999389648438, 2.006999969482422, 2.003000020980835, 1.996000051498413, 1.9919999837875366,
1.980999946594283, 1.9750000238841858, 1.9709999561309814, 1.9689999818800188, 1.9579999446868896, 1
.9520000219345093, 1.937000036239624, 1.9299999475479126, 1.9259999990463257, 1.916000085830688, 1
.909000039100647, 1.909000039100647, 1.902999971138977, 1.8990000486373901, 1.8980000019073486, 1.8
919999599456787, 1.8839999437332153, 1.88100004196167, 1.8589999675750732, 1.8550000190734863, 1.85
50000190734863, 1.8530000448226929, 1.8530000448226929, 1.8530000448226929, 1.8350000381469727, 1.8
309999704360962, 1.8220000267028809, 1.8109999895095825, 1.8009999990463257, 1.7990000247955322, 1.
7970000505447388, 1.7979999780654907, 1.7949999570846558, 1.7949999570846558, 1.7869999408721924, 1
.7790000438690186, 1.7710000276565552, 1.7660000324249268, 1.7589999437332153, 1.753999948501587, 1
.7510000467300415, 1.7519999742507935, 1.7489999532699585, 1.7339999675750732, 1.7380000352859497,
```

*Figure 18.10: The LaserScan message echoed to the terminal with rostopic echo*

You can see the time stamp, the `frame_id`, and all of the *angle, time,* and *range min/max* data (this scan was with a *Hokuyo* – the RPLIDAR will have different values). Finally, you can see the ranges[] data – starting at element 0 and continuing sequentially to the last element. After ranges[], intensities[] are printed to the screen in the same manner. Make a note of the frame ID before – we'll need it in a moment.

And that wraps up basic setup and testing. One important thing to remember from *Chapter 5, Communication with Sensors and Other Devices* is that if you have more than one USB device, you can't guarantee which one will be `ttyUSB0` and which will be `ttyUSB1`, etc. unless you set *udev rules* for them. The RPLIDAR package comes with a nifty script to make this easy. Check out the RPLIDAR tutorial page for more info on this.

# Visualizing the LaserScan message

This last thing this chapter introduces you to is a visualization tool called Rviz. **Rostopic echo** is very useful too, but checking all that data purely by looking at hundreds of numbers is pretty tedious. This is by no means a complete Rviz how-to, as we can't possibly fit it all in this book, but it should get you started. I'm always adding content to my *YouTube* channel at *youtube.com/practicalrobotics* – keep an eye there for some extra tutorials to build on this basic knowledge. With roscore and the rplidarNode still running, start Rviz in another terminal:

```
rosrun rviz rviz
```

It may take a minute, but up should pop the Rviz main window like the one in the screenshot (*figure 18.11*) below.

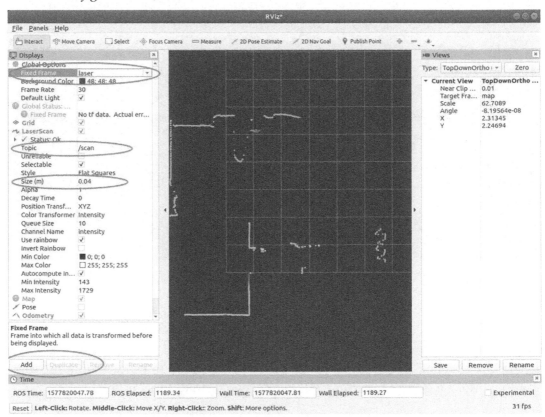

***Figure 18.11:*** *The RViz vizualization tool main window*

Your main viewing window is probably blank, but that's ok. I brought you to this section instead of using the RPLIDAR launch file so you could get a little experience setting these views up for yourself. Rviz has many more useful visualizations and tools than plotting laser data – some tutorials setting up visualizations for maps, pose, odometry, paths, and more can be found on the *Practical Robotics YouTube* channel.

Listed in the left panel underneath the **Global Options** and **Global Status** are the visualizations that are set up. If you don't see some of them, they are turned off, not being published, or there is some configuration error. The topics you can see that I have set up are **Grid**, **LaserScan**, **Map**, **Pose**, and **Odometry**.

**Map**, **Pose**, and **Odometry** are collapsed, but I have **LaserScan** expanded so you can see two columns of parameters and values. The column on the left is the parameter name, and the column to the right is the value for that parameter. I have circled four parameters we are particularly concerned with for this tutorial.

If your list of visualizations does not include **LaserScan**, we need to add it. If it does have a LaserScan, skip the first step and start at *Step 2*.

**The steps to set up a visualization in Rviz are:**

1. Click the **Add** button, and a window like the image below will pop up:
   1.1. Make sure **By display type** is up front and look over the list of available visualizations.
   1.2. Click on **LaserScan** and type in a display name if you want something other than the default LaserScan. You may wish to use custom names if you have more than one laser scanner.
   1.3. Click **OK**.

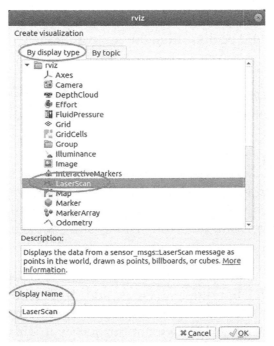

*Figure 18.12:* The window to add a vizualization to RViz

Set up the visualization parameters. Back in the left panel of main Rviz window:

1.1. Use the arrow next to **LaserScan** to expand the full menu.

1.2. Next to the **Topic** parameter, click the value field drop-down. You should see all of the topic names of all of the LaserScans being published. Select **scan**. If **scan** is not an option, find your topic with **rostopic list** and type it.

1.3. Under the **size** parameter, it may be set too small to see the points. I find **.01** too tiny – start with **.04** and play around a little with this value until you find where you like it.

2.  Under **Global Options**, click the value field next to **Fixed Frame**. Remember the **frame_id** from when you did the **rostopic echo** of a **scan** message (refer *figure 18.10*)? Enter that value here. It should be **laser** right now but could be something else.

And now, you should see your scan plotted in the main viewing window. If it isn't working after *Step 3*, check that your laser scanner and node are both running, and try zooming out or in if necessary. Further troubleshooting clues can be found in the **LaserScan** section in the left pane – if it says status:warn or status:error click on the arrow to expand the warning, and it may say something like **no message received** (check your scanner and node) or **transform for frame ___ to ___ does not exist** check that you have the exact frame_id in the **Global Fixed Frame** field. If the **Global Fixed Frame** field is different (say, you want to see the laser scan on top of a map being published, so the **Fixed Frame** is set to **Map**), you have to publish a transforming message between the map frame and the frame_id of your scan message. That could be done from the command line with:

```
rosrun tf static_transform_publisher 0 0 0 0 0 0 map laser 10
```

Visit *Chapter 10, Maps for Robot Navigation* for a refresher on transforms if needed, or dig even more in-depth at *wiki.ros.org/tf wiki.ros.org/tf/Tutorials.*

# Conclusion

Affordable LIDAR had really advanced the robotics industry miles beyond the early days when robots needed to follow a painted line to avoid disaster. What once cost thousands for the lowest-end units can be had for a couple of hundred dollars (*US*) new or salvaged from robot vacuums for under *$50*.

We spent this chapter learning some LIDAR basic operating fundamentals and limitations, a bit about the different types, and a great deal about the sensor_ msgs::LaserScan message before installing, setting up, and testing a common, affordable LIDAR device. Finally, we got our feet wet with Rviz – a very useful software tool for visualizing all sorts of ROS messages.

From the beginning of the book to this point, you have covered enough information to make a basic, autonomous robot from nothing – but we aren't done teaching it new tricks just yet! In the next chapter, we are going to dip our robot's toes into the ever-advancing world of computer vision so our robot cannot only plot an obstacle on its map and avoid it, but identify certain objects or features for new skills or enhanced navigation abilities.

# Questions

1. What are the two major limitations of LIDAR?
2. Why does the `sensor_msgs::Range` data type include a minimum and maximum sensor ranges?
3. What are the commands to list all topics being published in ROS and to echo a ROS message to the screen?

# CHAPTER 19
# Real Vision with Cameras

## Introduction

Computer vision is the vast, rapidly expanding science of extracting useful information from images – usually taken with a camera mounted on our robot. There is no sensor that can provide such a vast amount of information about a robot's environment for such a small cost as a modest camera, and out of that data has arisen a number of different methods for filtering and interpreting the data.

As surely as each image carries thousands of times more data than a typical laser scan message, making use of that data in a form a computer can use is full of many challenges. Some of these challenges we are able to tackle in an evening as individuals (and, fortunately, software libraries are available to make quick work of some of the most common methods), while others may take a team of developers months of work. Still other challenges are so complex that it is thought no human team of developers could ever complete the necessary code, and in those cases we must turn to experts in yet another special field – machine learning.

I am by no means an expert in computer vision field, but will use this chapter to introduce you to some of the ways computer vision is used in robotics, introduce you to one of the most popular computer vision libraries, and walk you through some of the basics that you'll undoubtedly find useful as you continue your studies in the field.

In this chapter, we will be covering the following:

- Reading photos or individual frames from video.
- Filtering out visual clutter to make what we are looking for easier to spot.
- Detecting objects of interest.
- Transforming pixel data into something more useful for our robot.

# Objectives

Install and start using computer vision software. Learn some fundamentals of image data types, how to detect lines, basic shapes, and colors within a ROS node.

# What is an image?

The short story is that an **image** is a 2D array (also known as matrix) of pixels. Pixels are the little dots that that can be individually changed in color and sometimes other qualities in order to change what we see when we look at them. If you recall back in *Chapter 10, Maps for Robot Navigation,* when we created a *map,* we created it by setting elements of a matrix to either 0 or 100 to represent whether a particular grid square was occupied or not. When we saved a map to a file, the map_saver node took those values and saved them as pixel data that most any image program could open so you could see the map data as an image.

Pixels store the information in data members called **channels**. A grayscale pixel could have as little as one channel (and this is a common type), but a color pixel definitely uses three channels. There are a number of different formats for storing color information in these three channels, but one of the most common (and I think, easiest to understand) types is called the **Red, Green,** and **Blue (RGB)** where each element is assigned a value of 0-255 for the amount of that color to be added to the total color.

We use something called a **Scalar** to reference pixel values, and a RGB scalar that sets a pixel or pixels to all *red* would be (255, 0, 0) since only the red channel should be *On* and the green and blue channels should be completely *Off*. Different colors are achieved by mixing different values for each color, much like mixing paints in art class. Black is represented by setting each channel to 0, while white is achieved by setting all three channels to 255. We'll get plenty of practice with Scalars shortly.

Scalars in the OpenCV **library we are going to use is a four-element vector, but we simply use three channels for color images pixels, and for most grayscale image pixels we can simply set the first element. We might write** cv::Scalar(255) **to set a grayscale pixel to white.**

Other pixel/image types we will use are *BGR*, *grayscale*, and *HSV*.

- **BGR** – Same as RGB but the order rearranged. Setting a BGR to *red* would use cv::Scalar(0,0,255).

- **Grayscale** – We already spoke about. We will mostly just need to set one channel in our cv::Scalar, but three channel grayscale does exist.

- **HSV** – This is a bit of a different animal than BRG and RGB. It still has three channels, but the channels are *Hue*, *Saturation*, and *Value*. Hue is a 0-179 value that represents all colors, Saturation is a 0-255 value that indicates how much of the hue shines through in the pixel. Like...*How intense a hue is*. Value is how brightly a pixel radiates its colors.

# Image attributes

Some image attributes you'll frequently need to be aware of are:

- **Size** – The total number of pixels also known as *width\*height*
- **Width** – The number of columns of pixels
- **Height** – The number of rows of pixels
- **Channels** – How many channels of information each pixel stores
- **Pixel depth** – How many bits each channel stores. There are variations, but we'll be working with 8-bit depth pixels. This explains why we assign color scalars values from 0-255.

# Pixel coordinates

The concept of individually addressable pixels is how we can make images, or read their data and perform mathematical checks on images to find edges or shapes. This is not unlike marking or checking a specific grid square when working with an occupancy grid map. There is one significant difference, however, to addressing an image pixel or addressing a grid square or cell of an occupancy grid – it is illustrated in the image (*figure 19.1*) below:

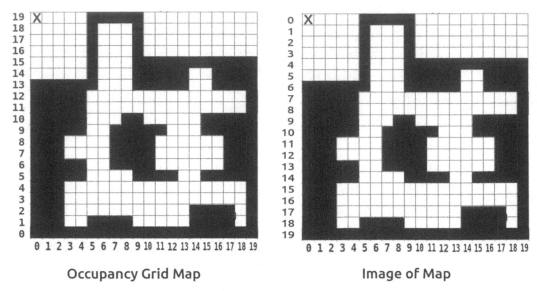

Occupancy Grid Map                              Image of Map

*Figure 19.1: Addressing cells and pixels in maps vs images. Do you see the difference?*

While the information from each grid cell can be copied directly to a single image pixel (that is how it is done, by the way), care must be taken to note the difference in addressing of rows between the two types. While the pixel marked with an **X** in the upper left-hand corner would be addressed as (**0,19**) in your map program, images are rendered from the top down, and the upper-left pixel is addressed as cv::Point(0,0) if you were working on an image.

**But what about video?**

**Video feeds – whether a live feed or a saved video file – are just a series of images played one after the other. When we process live video, we just grab one of the images (or all, one after the other). These individual images are also called frames.**

A Note about ordering coordinates: We'll only be using the (x,y), also known as (column, row) convention, as is the order for cv::Point and .size(), but due to the cv::Mat being a matrix with a mathematical connection, some functions – notably the .at<type> function – use (row, column). This can be quite a source of confusion and errors until you get the hang of it. Be sure to pay attention to the coordinate order in definitions when you look them up on your own.

# Checking or installing the required software

We're going to spend a lot of time in this chapter working with the OpenCV image processing libraries. Before we go on, let's make sure you have the software you'll need to continue. If you set up a Raspberry Pi with the *Ubiquity Robotics* image, you should be all set with OpenCV already installed and ready to work in ROS. If that's the case, skip ahead to the testing section. Otherwise, follow the steps below to install OpenCV and the ROS packages required to support OpenCV operations.

## ROS Kinetic

You're still in luck if you're not running the Ubiquity Raspberry Pi image but are still running ROS Kinetic because the ROS Repository has OpenCV pre-packaged for you. Just update your repository, then install opencv with:

```
sudo apt-get update
```

```
sudo apt-get install ros-kinetic-opencv3
```

It doesn't get any easier than that. There are a few ROS tools for bridging OpenCV and handling images in ROS we need, but they should have been installed automatically if you did the full desktop ROS install. If the tests below give you errors during the catkin_make or running, run the following to install important packages:

```
sudo apt-get install ros-kinetic-perception
```

```
sudo apt-get install ros-kinetic-vision-opencv
```

## ROS Melodic

I really, really wish the maintainers kept an easy-to-install OpenCV apt package for Melodic, but I'm afraid this is going to require some extra steps. For the most complete info, head to *opencv.org* and click on **Tutorials**. The first tutorial has a link to the installation instructions – follow them carefully. Here are a couple notes from my experience:

- In the **Required Packages** section: I recommend you run all three listed commands – even the optional one. You may not like to use python, but there is every chance you'll find a package you want to use that requires these files. I have circled the 3 commands in *figure 19.2* below.

**Required Packages**

- GCC 4.4.x or later
- CMake 2.8.7 or higher
- Git
- GTK+2.x or higher, including headers (libgtk2.0-dev)
- pkg-config
- Python 2.6 or later and Numpy 1.5 or later with developer packages (python-dev, python-numpy)
- ffmpeg or libav development packages: libavcodec-dev, libavformat-dev, libswscale-dev
- [optional] libtbb2 libtbb-dev
- [optional] libdc1394 2.x
- [optional] libjpeg-dev, libpng-dev, libtiff-dev, libjasper-dev, libdc1394-22-dev
- [optional] CUDA Toolkit 6.5 or higher

The packages can be installed using a terminal and the following commands or by using Synaptic Manager:

```
[compiler] sudo apt-get install build-essential
[required] sudo apt-get install cmake git libgtk2.0-dev pkg-config libavcodec-dev libavformat-dev libswscale-dev
[optional] sudo apt-get install python-dev python-numpy libtbb2 libtbb-dev libjpeg-dev libpng-dev libtiff-dev libjasper-dev
          libdc1394-22-dev
```

*Figure 19.2: Recommended installation commands from opencv.org*

- In the **Building OpenCV From Source Using CMake** section: When you configure CMake, you want to add the optional parameter to include the `contrib` modules that you cloned. You would add the following to your cmake command, taking care to use your own directory paths and not mine:

  `-D OPENCV_EXTRA_MODULES_PATH=/home/lloyd/opencv/opencv_contrib/`

That covers the OpenCV installation, but there are a few ROS tools for bridging OpenCV and handling images in ROS we need. They should have been installed automatically if you did the full desktop ROS install, but run the following to install important packages if the tests below give you errors during the `catkin_make` or running:

`sudo apt-get install ros-melodic-perception`

`sudo apt-get install ros-melodic-vision-opencv`

# Testing OpenCV in ROS

I've put together a simple ROS package for testing OpenCV in ROS. It contains three short nodes that make good learning templates, so I'll go over them in detail later. For now, you can just clone and build my test package from the command line:

`cd ~/catkin_ws/src`

`git clone https://github.com/lbrombach/opencv_tests.git`

`cd ..`

`catkin_make`

Presuming we have no errors to figure out, run the first test node. You'll need to have roscore running, then in a new window:

```
rosrun opencv_tests cv_test_node
```

If all goes according to plan, the current version of OpenCV should print in the terminal, and a new window will open up with an image that it blank other than a blue square in the middle. The window will wait for you to press a key, then it will close the window and the node will exit automatically.

So far, this tests the OpenCV installation but not yet the ROS tools for handling images in ROS. Please place a bookmark here and read the next section's introduction and complete *Step 1: Publishing Images in ROS*. Then come back and run the second test node called `cv_bridge_test`. To test the rest of your ROS tools for image and OpenCV, open four terminal windows and run these commands in this order – one in each window:

```
roscore
```

```
rosrun usb_cam usb_cam_node
```

```
rosrun opencv_tests cv_bridge_test
```

```
rosrun rqt_image_view rqt_image_view
```

The `cv_test_bridge` node subscribes to the camera images published by the `usb_cam_node`, draws a blue square on it, then publishes the modified image under the topic name `image_output`. Use the `rqt_image_viewer` to verify that you can see both the `/usb_cam/image_raw` and the `image_output` images. These steps confirm that `cv_bridge`, `image_transport`, and so on are all playing together nicely.

# Image processing software (OpenCV) and ROS:

OpenCV is possibly the most widely used computer vision library in the robotics world, and perhaps beyond. Open source and free, there is no shortage of books, tutorials, and documentation for using the many algorithms that have been developed and improved over the years. This is fortunate because even if I were a computer vision expert (which I definitely am not), it would take volumes and volumes to provide a full course.

A notable difference you need to be aware of when reading most OpenCV materials is that instead of running OpenCV programs standalone, we run them in ROS nodes. This means that instead of our OpenCV program accessing a camera feed directly, a ROS node accesses the camera feed and publishes a ROS message of type `sensor_msgs::Image` that our image processing node subscribes to. The image then has to be converted before we work on it. The general steps to do a computer vision operation with OpenCV in ROS workflow are as follows:

1. Publish images from a camera as type `sensor_msgs::Image`.
2. Subscribe to and receive image messages in a different node.
3. Use `cv_bridge` to convert the RGB image that ROS uses to a BGR image that OpenCV can work with.
4. Perform desired operations/detections on the image.
5. Publish any non-image data (like location or size of detected objects or lines) as their own ROS message.
6. Convert modified image back to RGB.
7. Publish result image under its own topic.

If you've done any standalone OpenCV work, this may seem like we're adding unnecessary steps. Why not grab the image directly in our node, publish just the non-image data, and skip all the converting nonsense? Although that can work, you're losing a lot of functionality that the handling of images through ROS brings. Besides that ROS image messages can be viewed in several utility nodes like `rqt_image_view`, publishing images as messages means that any number of nodes can receive the same image frame and do completely different tasks at the same time – even across several computers.

What's more is that the images can be recorded and replayed later in perfect sync with any or all other messages (like laser scan data). This is tremendously helpful for figuring out why something didn't work as expected. Trust me – it's well worth getting used to a couple extra steps to get so much more power down the road.

# Step 1: Publishing images in ROS

The ROS node I recommend for connecting to a camera and publishing images is called `usb_cam_node` from the `usb_cam` package. There is some misinformation out there claiming that this node only works with USB cameras and not with the raspicam that connects to a Raspberry Pi with its special ribbon cable, but that simply isn't true. The `raspicam_node` by our friends at *Ubiquity Robotics* is a fine node for the raspicams, but it has been my experience that the `usb_cam` node can run either camera type. I have not had the same luck reliably running a USB camera with the `raspicam_node`, so why keep track of two nodes when one will do the job for me?

# Installing the usb_cam_node

Documentation for the usb_cam_node can be found at *wiki.ros.org/usb_cam*, and since it is available in the official ROS repositories for both ROS Kinetic and ROS Melodic, it should install as easily as typing at the command line:

```
sudo apt-get update

sudo apt-get install ros-kinetic-usb-cam


- or -


sudo apt-get update

sudo apt-get install ros-melodic-usb-cam
```

If for some reason your apt cannot find it, you can follow the link in the *Wiki* doc to the *git* repository to make sure the address below is still current, and navigate to your catkin_ws/src directory. From there, clone the repository and then run catkin_make:

```
git clone https://github.com/ros-drivers/usb_cam.git

cd ..

catkin_make
```

# Running the usb_cam_node

Before we launch the node, pull up the usb_cam *Wiki* page on a web browser and look over some parameters with me. Many of them can be left at their default values until you have a specific need, but a couple we need to get right or nothing works:

- video_device – This is the /dev/location of your camera. Find a list of all available video devices by typing ls /dev/video* in a terminal window. If you have any cameras connected, you should see them listed starting at /dev/video0. If you have a built-in camera or more than one you've installed yourself, the one you want to read may be at /dev/video1 or /dev/video2. If you have only one camera it usually will be /dev/video0 and you don't have to specify this manually.

- pixel_format – This is the other critical parameter and the reason many don't know that you can use this node with a raspicam. Notice that the default value is mjpeg, which stands for **motion jpeg**. If you're using one of the *Logitech* webcams, you can leave this alone as `mjpeg` is the native image type to those cameras. If you are trying to run a raspicam, those have a `yuyv` pixel format, so you need to pass that parameter when launching the node.

- `framerate` – This is how many images the node will try to publish per second. You can probably leave this at default but can save a little bandwidth by publishing less frequently if you don't need that many frames.

If your only camera is a USB camera, you may not need to pass any parameters as the defaults should work. You can start the node with:

```
rosrun usb_cam usb_cam_node
```

If there are errors, look for clues in the output message. If the node doesn't shut down, it may still be publishing and just issuing warnings – these may not be enough to interfere with operations. One of my cameras causes the node to whine about a deprecated pixel format, but everything still works so I haven't been inclined to dig into the program.

 **Don't forget that in order to pass parameters via the command line, you have to precede the parameter name with an underscore _ or ROS interprets your command as a name remap.**

If you have a raspicam and a USB cam and want to start publishing from the raspicam, don't forget to pass the correct `pixel_format` parameter:

```
rosrun usb_cam usb_cam_node _pixel_format:="yuyv"
```

If you have a raspicam or built-in camera and a USB cam and want to start publishing from the USB cam, don't forget to pass the correct video_device parameter:

```
rosrun usb_cam usb_cam_node _video_device:="/dev/video1"
```

- or -

```
rosrun usb_cam usb_cam_node _video_device:="/dev/video2"
```

## Test the camera output

A quick check of `rostopic list` at the command line can tell you the topic names the node is publishing to. By default, this should be /usb_cam/image_raw and /usb_cam/image_raw/compressed. You can see the raw pixel data with `rostopic echo`:

```
rostopic echo -n1 /usb_cam/image_raw
```

If the output is all zeros, either the image is all black or something is wrong. A bunch of numbers other than zero is a good sign, but let's actually see the image using a tool called `rqt_image_view`:

```
rosrun rqt_image_view rqt_image_view
```

This may take a minute to pop up if you're running a slower machine like a Raspberry Pi, but a window like the one in the image (*figure 19.3*) below should pop up. It may be blank at first – don't worry just yet.

*Figure 19.3: Viewing ROS sensor_msgs::Image messages with rqt_image_viewer*

There is a drop-down field at the upper-left that I have circled. Click the drop-down to see a list of messages the node is capable of displaying. Click the one you want to see. If you started the image viewer before you started the node that published the images, the new topics may not be visible. In that case, just close and restart the image viewer.

 **You can run more than one instance of the image viewer so you can visualize both input and output images at the same time (or outputs different nodes have done on the same image).**

# Step 2: Subscribe to image in a different node

Subscribing to and publishing image messages is a little more involved than our usual message-types because we should use the `image_transport` package. Much more detail is available at *wiki.ros.org/image_transport*, but in short it allows for much more efficient transport of image data. We're going to walk through creating a vision package using my `opencv_tests` package as an example. Although you have the code in front of you, I suggest you go through the steps for yourself.

# Create your ROS vision package

Go ahead and create your own ROS package for your vision projects. Refer back to *Chapter 9, Coordinating the Parts* if you need a refresher on what we're doing here, and use my package as an example. Navigate to your catkin_ws/src folder in a terminal, and run the command (all one command):

catkin_create_pkg cv_learning roscpp sensor_msgs image_transport cv_bridge

Then open the CMakeLists.txt in the cv_learning folder that was just created and add find_package(OpenCV REQUIRED) at the bottom of the section titled Find catkin macros and libraries. Use line 17 in the image (*figure 19.4*) below as an example.

```
opencv_tests > M CMakeLists.txt
   1    cmake_minimum_required(VERSION 2.8.3)
   2    project(opencv_tests)
   3
   4    ## Compile as C++11, supported in ROS Kinetic and newer
   5    # add_compile_options(-std=c++11)
   6
   7    ## Find catkin macros and libraries
   8    ## if COMPONENTS list like find_package(catkin REQUIRED COMPONENTS xyz)
   9    ## is used, also find other catkin packages
  10    find_package(catkin REQUIRED COMPONENTS
  11      roscpp
  12      cv_bridge
  13      image_transport
  14      roscpp
  15      sensor_msgs
  16    )
  17    find_package(OpenCV REQUIRED)
  18
```

*Figure 19.4:* *Getting the package CMakeLists.txt ready for OpenCV nodes*

Then add your first node (executable) at the bottom of the file – whatever you want to call it. In addition to the usual target link library stuff, we have to make sure to link the OpenCV libraries with ${OpenCV_LIBS}. *Figure 19.5* below shows how I did it for the opencv_tests package.

```
213    add_executable(cv_test_node src/cv_test_node.cpp)
214    target_link_libraries(cv_test_node ${OpenCV_LIBS} ${catkin_LIBRARIES})
215
216    add_executable(cv_bridge_test src/cv_bridge_test.cpp)
217    target_link_libraries(cv_bridge_test ${OpenCV_LIBS} ${catkin_LIBRARIES})
218
219    add_executable(image_transport_test src/image_transport_test.cpp)
220    target_link_libraries(image_transport_test ${OpenCV_LIBS} ${catkin_LIBRARIES})
```

*Figure 19.5:* *Adding executables and target link libraries to the CmakeLists.txt must include* *${OpenCV_LIBS}*

Save the CMakeLists.txt and create your cpp file using the same name in the package cv_learning/src folder. Now we're ready to start coding it.

# Coding the image message subscriber

A basic subscriber to an image message requires the following includes:

```
#include <ros/ros.h>
```

```
#include <image_transport/image_transport.h>
```

```
#include <cv_bridge/cv_bridge.h>
```

```
#include <sensor_msgs/image_encodings.h>
```

We will also need a subscriber. Instead of a ros::Subscriber, we are going to use a Subscriber from the image_transport namespace.

```
image_transport::Subscriber image_sub;
```

In our main function, we initialize our node with the ROS master and create ourselves a node handle, as usual. Additionally, we use that node handle to create an ImageTransport object. The first three lines of my main() function are as follows:

```
ros::init(argc, argv, "cv_bridge_test");
```

```
ros::NodeHandle nh;
```

```
image_transport::ImageTransport it_(nh);
```

Now we can subscribe to an image message. Below, the image_sub we created uses our ImageTransport (named it_) to subscribe to images published on the /usb_cam/image_raw topic with a buffer size of 1. When an image is received, it is passed to the handle_image() callback function.

```
image_sub = it_.subscribe("/usb_cam/image_raw", 1, handle_image);
```

And finally, we need our usual loop to check the subscribers. I set this one for 30 times per second, but don't be surprised if your node can't process that many frames per second as you add complexity.

```
ros::Rate loop_rate(30);
while(ros::ok)
{
    ros::spinOnce();
    loop_rate.sleep();
}
```

With main() complete, we just need to write a callback function. This function receives the ROS image message that we will convert and process. For now, we just need to receive it.

```
void image_handler(const sensor_msgs::ImageConstPtr &img)

{

    //process image here

}
```

In image_transport_test.cpp, I also declared a sensor_msgs::Image and simply copy every data field from the received message, then publish the new message. You can see the received image and output images in rqt_image_view but they will look exactly the same – we have not implemented any OpenCV functions yet. You can read more about the sensor_msgs::Image at *wiki.ros.org/sensor_msgs*.

## Step 3: Use cv-bridge to convert the RGB image ROS uses to a BGR image OpenCV can work with

The image data type OpenCV works with is called cv::Mat (which is just Mat from the cv namespace). We might as well include all three OpenCV libraries we will use. Look over cv_bridge_test.cpp from my opencv_tests package for an example.

```
#include <opencv2/core/core.hpp>

#include <opencv2/highgui.hpp>

#include <opencv2/imgproc.hpp>
```

Then back in the handle_image() function, we can create a Mat image and use cv_bridge to convert our ROS message to the Mat.

```
cv::Mat image;

image = cv_bridge::toCvShare(img,

        sensor_msgs::image_encodings::BGR8)→image;
```

Now image of type Mat is a converted version of the ROS image message OpenCV can work with.

# Step 4: Perform desired operations on the image

There are far too many possible OpenCV operations to include them all here. As in cv_bridge_test.cpp, we'll simply modify the image by drawing a square on it. We'll cover some basic OpenCV operations later in this chapter.

```
//declare Rect named rectangle that originates at (150,150)

//size is 100 x 100

cv::Rect rectangle(150, 150, 100, 100);


//set a Scalar for use later - initialized as blue

cv::Scalar color(255,0,0);


//draw rectangle on image, using the Rect and Scalar we declared

//the last argument is for line size. 1 means 1 pixel wide,

// while -1 means fill the rectangle

cv::rectangle(image,rectangle, color, -1);
```

In cv_bridge_test, all this is done on one line so you can see how you can save space in your code. Declaring these custom OpenCV variables (rectangle and color) separately allows for some changes based on your programming earlier in the program – just like any other variable.

# Step 5: Publish any non-image data as their own ROS message.

This is something our test examples don't include, but rather than just changing the image, you can publish data you've extracted from the image as well — just like you would any message we've worked with so far. This might be something from the std_msgs like std_msgs::Int8 with a count of how many red balls the program found, a string with an object classification, or some custom message with location of an object so your robot can steer toward or away from it. I am currently experimenting with publishing a LaserScan message with ranges derived from image data instead of a laser for a special application. Just know that you are not limited to drawing on the image.

## Step 6: Convert modified image back to RGB

When we've done everything we want to with OpenCV, we need to convert the image back to something ROS works with.

```
sensor_msgs::Image::Ptr output_img;
```

```
output_img = cv_bridge::CVImage(img→header,
        "bgr8", image).toImageMsg();
```

The first line creates a message. The second line uses `cv_bridge` to copy the header from the original image message, then converts the BGR CV image we've been working on to a RGB ROS format and places that in the `output_img` as well.

## Step 7: Publish result image under its own topic

Aside from converting our image, we need three things to publish the message:

*   To declare `image_transport::Publisher`
*   To register our publisher with the ROS master
*   Call the `publish()` function

Much the same as we use the `image_transport::Subscriber` instead of a `ros::Subscriber`, we use a publisher from `image_transport` as well.

```
image_transport::Publisher image_pub;
```

You can see in the `cv_bridge_test.cpp` that I declare this globally but initialize it in `main()`, where we normally register our publishers with the ROS master. The following line is in `main()`:

```
image_pub = it_.advertise("image_output", 1);
```

As usual, the part in quotes is the topic name that the node will publish. Change this as necessary – sometimes you may publish more than one image for various reasons and they each need their own topic name.

The final thing we need to do is call the `publish()` function.

```
image_pub.publish(output_image);
```

This should be fairly straightforward – just pass the image you want to publish as an argument.

That completes a basic outline you can use over and over. At various times, you may not need to republish an image and others you may create an image without needing to subscribe to any. There is further reading available at *wiki.ros.org/vision_ opencv/Tutorials.*

# More image processing basics

Before I throw more functions at you, let's discuss a few important matter that are going to come up.

# Kernels, apertures and blocks

A lot of operations that happen on an image require iterating over the image matrix pixel-by-pixel. When calculating what to do to any one pixel, the values of the neighboring pixels are considered. The number of neighboring pixels included is defined as its own little matrix called the **aperture**, **kernel**, or **block**. This is most commonly a square but can sometimes be a non-square rectangle. *Figure 19.6* below illustrates kernels on a very small example image.

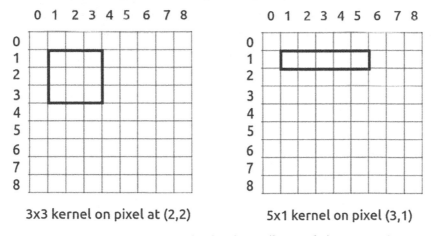

3x3 kernel on pixel at (2,2)          5x1 kernel on pixel (3,1)

*Figure 19.6:* kernels on a ridiculously small example image matrix

If the above example on the left were doing a blur operation, the pixel at *(2,2)* would be set to the average value of all pixels in the kernel mini-matrix. The kernel would then be iterated over every pixel in the image and the averaging repeated. Some functions allow you to define a shape as well – when you are calling a function that takes an argument of `Size Ksize`, you get to choose two different dimensions for that argument as follows.

```
cv::Size(width, height);
```

Other operations will ask for `int block_size`. In this case, simply pass an integer and a square mini-matrix is passed over the image. For example, instead of using `cv::Size(3,3)` you would just pass the value 3. There is technically a difference between a block and a kernel, but they both deal with which neighbors influence the outcome of an operation. Further reading on the *Sobel operator* can help clear this up for you.

# The importance of working on copies instead of original images

A lot of OpenCV function calls take both an input image and an output image as arguments (you'll see these as `InputArray src` and `OutputArray Dst` in the function definitions). While nothing is stopping you from passing your original image as both the source and destination, in many cases this will change the output from what the function's algorithm is designed to do. For example, the `blur()` function that assigns an average of all pixels in the kernel to one pixel, then moves on to the next pixel. If the output of the operation is on the same image as the input, when the kernel moves to the next pixel, some of that pixel's neighbors have already been changed, so the calculated average will be different than if we were reading from an unaltered original image. *Figure 19.7* below illustrates this problem.

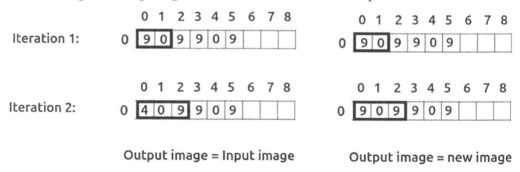

*Figure 19.7:* *What happens when the output image of a blur() operation is the same as the input image*

Just two iterations over a single row is enough to show the problem. The 3x1 kernels are set over the input values – The first iteration ignores the out-of-bounds pixels, and the output of the averaging operation sets pixel 0 to 4. For iteration two, the thread using the image for input and output will now average the values of 4, 0, and 9 instead of 9, 0, and 9.

Another reason to work on copies instead of originals is that it is sometimes desirable to overlay some new information on an original image, like drawing detected lines or circling a detected object. Some of the operations we do won't just blur the image a little – they will completely change it.

Over time, you will learn which operations can be done safely using the same image for input and output, but until then, get in the habit of making and using copies. You'll see this in action as we continue the chapter.

# A word about lighting

One of the biggest challenges in computer vision comes from changes in lighting. Reflections from lighting can completely wash out sections of an image that should be detected as a color. Sometimes we can compensate for this – until the angle changes or the source of light moves. This is one of the reasons so much work is going into developing machine learning for computer vision. For us, it's something to be aware of and it will help you along if can work in fairly consistent lighting conditions while you're learning.

# Step 4 revisited - more possible OpenCV operations

This is by no means a comprehensive or advanced course on the many algorithms OpenCV has waiting for us. This is a handful of very common, tried-and-true operations you'll no doubt find useful well into any further studies.

# Converting color format: cvtColor()

There are many reasons you'll need to convert an image from one color format to another. Working on a grayscale image, for example, can make detecting some things easier and definitely reduces the amount of work subsequent algorithms have to do because it's a simpler image type. HSV image types are much friendlier for isolating specific colors. Presuming we have an original image Mat image, we could convert to grayscale and HSV with the following code:

```
cv::Mat gray, hsv;

cv::cvtColor(image, gray, CV_BGR2GRAY);

cv::cvtColor(image, hsv, CV_BGR2HSV);
```

The first line creates two empty Mat objects named gray and hsv. The cv::cvtColor(InputArray src, OutputArray dst, int code) function leaves the source image alone, and puts the results in the destination image – resizing and configuring it as necessary. The code argument is from an enumeration list. There is another version of that enum list, so in some tutorials, the same conversions might use the enum COLOR_BGR2GRAY and COLOR_BGR2HSV.

# Blurring images: blur(), medianBlur(), GaussianBlur()

We humans are very good at ignoring imperfections in images, so until we start working with images in a computer, it may not occur to us that things we presume to be a solid color are actually riddled with tiny specks of several colors that we intuitively interpret as sort of an average color. Sometimes this is how a material is made; sometimes an object's texture gives it tiny shadows and reflections that alter what gets recorded in the pixel data.

These and other imperfections that our brains naturally filter out and ignore can be enough to make our programs incorrectly determine object boundaries or not detect the thing it is looking for at all. A couple common blurring functions are available to smooth out these imperfections so the programs detection algorithm has less noise across its kernel.

*Figure 19.7* illustrated a simple averaging blur, although we usually have a square kernel of *3x3* or *5x5* or even bigger. A median blur that uses the median value of all pixels in the kernel (instead of the average) is also available, as well as special type of blur called a `Gaussian blur`. In a Gaussian blur, the weight of each pixel depends on how close it is to the central pixel with the central getting the most weight and the `furthest pixel` the least. The following is an example of calling each blurring function assuming an original image called `image`.

```
cv::Mat blur, med_blur, gaus_blur;

cv::blur(image, blur, Size(5,5));

cv::medianBlur(image, med_blur, Size(5,5));

cv::GaussianBlur(image, gaus_blur, Size(3,3), 0);
```

One note about the `GaussianBlur()` call, notice it has one extra argument at the end — this is a double value called `sigmaX`, used to change the standard deviation of weights for the Gaussian kernel. Setting it to `0` simply lets the algorithm calculate the value based on the kernel size. The definitions of each of these functions:

```
void blur(InputArray src, OutputArray dst, Size ksize)

void medianBlur(InputArray src, OutputArray dst, Size ksize)

void GaussianBlur(InputArray src, OutputArray dst, Size ksize,
    double sigmaX, double sigmaY=0,

        int borderType = BORDER_DEFAULT)
```

# Edge detection: Canny()

Detecting edges is an important step in detecting all sorts of things – from painted lines to the contours of an object – and is helpful in determining what the object is. Edge detection is a matter of finding gradients across an image kernel — Areas where the pixel values change rapidly (above a certain threshold we set) are considered to be edges. As such, edge detection is very sensitive to noise in the image, and blurring is required for reasonable results in most cases. Edge detection is also usually best done on grayscale images. Look over the following code that starts with an original image called image.

```
cv::Mat gray, blur, canny;

cv::cvtColor(image, gray, CV_BGR2GRAY);

cv::GaussianBlur(gray, blur, Size(3,3), 0);

cv::Canny(blur, canny, 100, 200, 3);
```

The above code first creates three image objects, passes the original image to cvtColor(), passes the resulting gray image to the GaussianBlur() function, and, finally, passes the resulting blur image to the Canny() function. The Canny function sets every pixel that is not part of an edge to zero and every pixel that is part of an edge to white. The result is a black and white image you can see in the image (*figure 19.8*) sequence below.

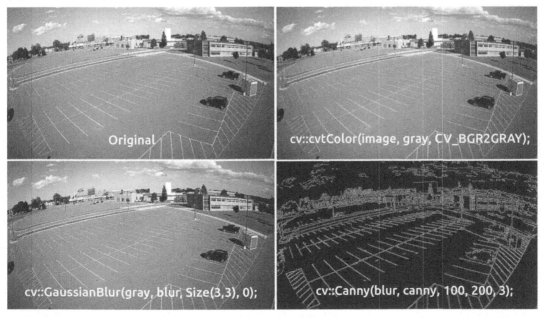

***Figure 19.8:*** *An image going through several CV operations*

The definition for the cv::Canny() function is:

```
void Canny(InputArray src, OutputArray dst, double threshold1,
    double threshold2, int aperatureSize=3,
    bool L2gradient = false)
```

Canny uses a two-threshold method of determining edges:

- Any gradient found above the higher threshold2 value is definitely considered to be an edge.

- Any gradient found between the two threshold values might be an edge, so it is only included if it is touching another edge.

- Any gradient found below the lower threshold1 is definitely not an edge.

The int aperatureSize is akin to a kernel or block and can be left blank for the default of 3, or adjusted if desired. **L2gradient** is a different equation for determining edges and sometimes yields a better result. It is something for you to experiment with, but until you get the hang of the other variables, I'd ignore these two and leave them to their defaults. Definitely experiment with the threshold values, however, and notice how much they affect the output image.

# Edges on image to numerical lines: HoughLinesP()

At some point, we need to move from images that make sense to human eyes to some collection of numbers our robot can understand — and perhaps add to a map or path-planning algorithm. We will do that with HoughLinesP, an algorithm that takes a binary (black and white) image like the one Canny() provides and detects straight lines. Not only can the HoughLinesP() function find straight lines – it can be set to connect broken lines into one solid line. Let's see how it works on the image I took on a roadtrip. Below is the original freeway image (*figure 19.9*) and the result of the Canny() steps we took above.

*Figure 19.9: Original image of freeway (left) and the Canny() result (right) we will provide to HoughLinesP() line detection function*

The following code takes the Canny() result as an argument but doesn't directly output an image. Instead, it takes a vector we will have to create and fills that vector with line data in the form of begin and end points.

```
//create container for line data

cv::vector<Vec4i> lines;


//find lines in canny image and output them to lines vector

cv::HoughLinesP(canny, lines, 2, CV_PI/180, 50, 50, 100);
```

Vec4i is a container that holds four integers addressable with the [] operator as any array. The lines are stored in them as x1, y1, x2, y2. HoughlinesP() adds an element of type Vec4i to your vector called lines for every line it finds.

The definition of HoughLinesP() is as follows:

```
void HoughLinesP(InputArray src, OutputArray lines, double rho,

        double theta, int threshold,

        double minLineLength=0, double maxLineGap=0)
```

Without diving too far into the **Hough space** and the inner working of Hough Lines detection (although I highly recommend further research so you can make the most of the function) the HoughLinesP function first finds all possible lines, then has to determine whether each possible line is a brand new line or part of an existing line. The argument rho is a distance resolution parameter that affects whether a possible line is considered a new line or part of an existing line. Since Hough finds all the possible lines and then accumulates *votes* (only possible lines that accumulate enough *votes* are finally accepted as lines), a smaller rho results in a greater number of `possible lines` for consideration. Each of these possible lines will receive fewer votes than if they had been considered one big line, so the final result of a smaller rho is fewer lines output.

In summary: `Smaller rho = fewer lines found.`

Much simpler than rho are the theta and threshold parameters. Theta is the angle (in radians) within which a line is considered to be one straight line and not two lines of different angles. `CV_PI` is just a constant for `pi`, so I have passed the equivalent of one degree of resolution for theta. The threshold parameter is how many *votes* a possible line must reach in order to be finally considered a line and added to the output vector.

The final two parameters are filters applied to lines that have passed the above tests. Any line shorter than `minLineLength` will be discarded, while `maxLineGap` defines how much space is allowable between two lines to consider them the same line instead of two separate lines (this applies only to the same line that may be broken up – like a dashed line on a road). I set a moderate `minLineLength` and a somewhat generous `maxLineGap` because of the angle the image was taken from.

Now that we have a vector of lines, we can access them to publish them as numerical data or draw them on an image. Calling `.size()` returns how many lines are stored in the output vector, and for each of those, a pair of points (x1, y1) and (x2,y2) are stored for a single line.

```
//copy original image for drawing on

cv::Mat imcopy = image.clone();


//make blank image of the same size for drawing on

cv::Mat drawing = Mat::zeros(canny.size(), CV_8UC3);


//iterate over output vector lines, drawing the lines

for(int i=0; i<lines.size(); i++)

{

    cv::Vec4i line = lines[i];

    int x1 = line[0];
```

```
int y1 = line[1];

int x2 = line[2];

int y2 = line[3];

cv::line(drawing, cv::Point(x1, y1), cv::Point(x2, y2),

    cv::Scalar(255,0,0), 2);

}
```

The above code creates a copy of the original image (called `imcopy`) and a blank image (called `drawing`) of the same size. We can draw the lines detected by `HoughLinesP()` on either or both of these images. I do this by iterating over the output vector called lines, and read each element into it's own `Vec4i` variable i called line. This is optional, as is reading each element of line into an integer, but I did so to make it clear how to access which values.

The function I use to draw is called `line()` and takes as arguments:

- A Mat image to draw on
- A point (an x, y pair of pixel coordinates)
- Another point
- A Scalar (for color of the line)
- A width of the line.

Following is the output of the above code using the lines we detected on the original image in *figure 19.10*.

***Figure 19.10:*** *Lines detected with HoughLinesP() drawn on a blank image and overlayed on top of the original image*

If you look back at the original image, you can see how carefully setting `minLineLength` and `maxLineGap` were able to detect the apparently short dashed road marking and connect them. Unfortunately, HoughLines will often find lines where we aren't looking – like all the horizontal lines.

The first way to deal with unwanted horizontal lines is to add a simple `if()` statement in the above code snippet to filter lines that we feel are too far horizontal. We can find the angle of the lines easily with the `atan2()` and `abs()` functions we've used in previous chapters (`#include <cmath>`).

```
double lineTheta = abs(atan2(y1,y1, x1, x2));

double maxtheta = 2.65;

double minTheta = .5;

if(lineTheta < maxTheta && lineTheta > minTheta)

{

    //draw or add line to output here

}
```

Because of the camera perspective, the road lines I want to detect appear at around *35-40* degrees, so I set the `if()` filter to reject anything shallower or much steeper with `minTheta` and `maxTheta` (`atan2` returns theta in radians, so my `min` and `max` are in radians as well). I also applied the `abs()` function so I don't have to deal with negative angles. The filtered output is pictured below in *figure 19.11*.

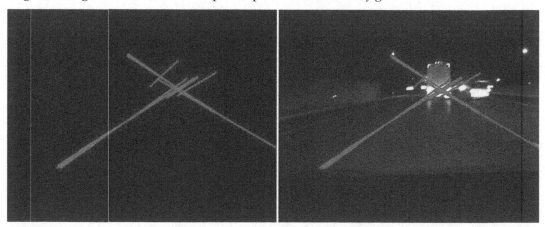

*Figure 19.11: Hough lines drawn after filtering out horizontal lines*

Much improved, but there are still some errant lines we'd like to get rid of. In fact, some of the lines that should be included extend farther than we'd like them to, creating false data beyond the point where they cross. We can use image masking to make sure we only find lines in the parts of the image that we want to include.

# Image masking: bitwise_and()

A mask will be a black and white image the same size as your image of interest, with the areas you are interested in set to white and the areas you want to ignore set to black. The `cv::bitwise_and()` function compares pixel data from one or two images and your mask. If the mask's pixel is black, the AND comparison returns *false* and the output pixel is set to 0 *(black)*. If the mask's pixel is *white*, the other values are assigned to the output pixel.

To create a mask, we start with a blank image like we've created before. It must be the same size as the input and output image, and it must be a single-channel (the last argument CV_8U). We then draw any shape we want on that blank image and fill it with white. The code snippet below creates two masks – one simply masks the upper 2/5 of the image, and the other is a bit more elegant polygon.

```
cv::Mat mask1 = Mat::zeros(canny.size(), CV_8U);

cv::rectangle(mask1, cv::Rect(0, image.size().height*2/5,

            image.size().width, image.size().height*3/5),

        cv::Scalar(255,255,255), -1);


//create polygon-shaped mask

//create blank drawing

cv::Mat mask2 = Mat::zeros(canny.size(), CV_8U);


//create vector of points to hold polygon vertices

vector<cv::Point> poly(4);


//create trapezoid-shaped polygon in poly

poly[0]=cv::Point(0, image.size().height);

poly[1]=cv::Point(image.size().width/3, image.size().height*2/5);

poly[2]=cv::Point(image.size().width*2/3,

        image.size().height*3/5);
```

```
poly[3]=cv::Point(image.size().width, image.size().height);


//fill the area in mask2 defined by poly with white

cv::fillConvexPoly(mask2, poly, Scalar(255));
```

You can see that a rectangle-shaped mask is much easier to create (just two lines of code), while a polygon mask allows you to crop much closer to your region of interest. You can make any polygon you wish – just make the vector bigger and keep adding points.

The `cv::rectangle()` function draws directly on an image like the `lines()` function. The required arguments are:

- `cv::Mat` image to draw on
- `cv::Rect` (origin x, origin y, width, height)
- `cv::Scalar` (for color)
- `int` for line thickness (setting thickness to `-1` fills the rectangle with the scalar color)

The `cv::fillPolyConvex()` function seems simple because you have to define all the coordinates earlier in a vector of points. `FollyPolyConvex()` requires only the following arguments:

- `cv::Mat` image to draw on
- the vector of `cv::Points`
- A Scalar for color (single channel only require one argument – we use 255 for white here)

The two masks created are show in the following *figure 19.12*:

*Figure 19.12: Rectangle and polygon-shaped masks*

To apply the mask to an image, we use the `cv::bitwise_and()` function described above.

```
cv::bitwise_and(canny, canny, masked, mask1);
```

The `bitwise_and()` function requires the following arguments:

- Input `cv::Mat` image 1
- Input `cv::Mat` image 2 (use image 1 if there is only 1)
- Output `cv::Mat` image (same size as the inputs)
- (Optional) A mask image (of type `cv::Mat` – same size as inputs)

One word of caution when using a polygon-shaped mask: Sometimes, `HoughLinesP` will detect the mask's edge as a line. It can be useful to make the upper lines of the polygon shallower than the minTheta value we used when filtering out the horizontal lines. In this case (presumably because the background is dark) it was not a problem and the output after applying either mask is the same. The result is shown in the following *figure 19.13*.

*Figure 19.13: HoughLinesP() result after first masking the Canny() result*

After masking undesired areas and filtering lines of the wrong orientation, we are able to arrive at just the lines that matter. But sometimes we don't want to filter by shape or edge – *what if we want to find an objects of a certain color?* For that, we'll need to use convert our image and apply another kind of filtering function.

# Filtering by Color: cvtColor() and inRange()

Imagine programming a robot to detect stop signs – even with its distinct octagonal shape, it is likely to be lost in a field of detected lines in a busy urban environment. A similar scenario can be imagined if we wanted a robot to find ripe fruit to pick from a tree, or a ball in a field. The uncluttering of contours from the image can be helped by eliminating everything from the image that isn't the correct color. Then, the only contours left are those surrounding objects that are the correct color.

 **Contours are what we call continuous edges. While lines have to be straight to be defined, a contour can be any curve – even an outline of an entire object.**

The general steps to filter images by color are:

1. Blur a copy of the image.
2. Convert blurred copy from *BGR* to *HSV*.
3. Apply `inRange()` to find pixels in within a certain color-range.
4. Apply output of `inRange` as a mask over original image.

**Step 1:** Blur a copy of the image.

The first step in removing everything from an image that isn't the correct color is to blur the image. You'd be surprised how many pixels in a certain area that appear to be uniform are actually white, black, or some other color. What type of blur and how big a kernel to use will vary widely based on everything from lighting conditions to image resolution to type of background and texture of the object you want to find. A fair bit of experimenting to gain experience in selecting these values is in order.

**Step 2:** Convert the blurred copy from BGR to HSV.

Three color-channel images like *BGR* and *RGB* are very difficult to filter by because every color is a mixture of three separate values. As mentioned early in the chapter, HSV images are still three channels of information, but only the first channel contains the color value -- called **hue**. (The remaining two channels are for how saturated the pixel is with the color and how intense, or bright, the pixel is). This means all colors fall within the range of a single integer value from 0-179 in OpenCV – as pictured in the following *figure 19.14*. (Traditional HSV is a *360* degree circle, so traditional HSV color values are exactly 2x the OpenCV value). This is because we store data for each channel in 8 bits, and the maximum value for an 8-bit integer is 255 – the entire range doesn't fit unless we scale it down).

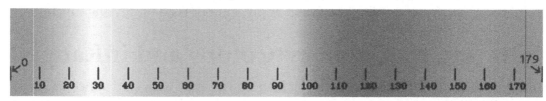

*Figure 19.14: The HSV color spectrum in OpenCV*

This image will be best viewed on your own computer screen, so I added a ROS node in the `opencv_tests` package you downloaded from github.com/lbrombach. With `roscore` running in another terminal, run the `hsv_colors` node with:

```
rosrun opencv_tests hsv_colors
```

The node starts with an all-red image that pops up on your screen and then fills from left to right with the full spectrum of OpenCV HSV hues (`0-179`). Finally, a numerical scale is added to the image so you can see which colors fall near which hue values. (*Saturation* and *Value* channels are set to the maximum of 255). The window should close and the node will shut down when you press a key.

**Step 3**: Apply the `inRange()` filter to find pixels of a certain color.

Notice that red exists on both ends of the HSV hue spectrum. While colors like blue fall completely within a single range of perhaps `100-130`, with red we may have to check for colors from `0-10`, and again for colors from `170-179`. Depending on what we're specifically looking for and the environment, we likely have to further reduce one or both of those filters to eliminate more unnecessary clutter.

The `inRange()` function looks for all the pixels in a range you specify and returns a black and white image (a mask, essentially) with pixels that were in range marked white and the rest black. Since colors are rarely exactly one color, we define a range to look for. For other colors, you would only have to call `inRange()` once, but I chose to look for a red stop sign to show you how to combine two masks into one. The following code combines *Steps 1 - 3* to blur our original image, convert it to *HSV*, and create two masks.

```
using namespace cv;

Mat blurred, hsv, mask1, mask2;

blur(image, blurred, Size(3,3), Point(0,0));

cvtColor(blurred, hsv, CV_BGR2HSV);

inRange(hsv,Scalar(0, 40, 100), Scalar(2, 255, 255), mask1);

inRange(hsv, Scalar(176, 40, 100), Scalar(179, 40, 255), mask2);
```

We, of course, have to create our empty `Mat` objects to hold the outputs of our functions. We then call `blur()` with our original image and `cvtColor()` functions to get the blurred *HSV* we will send to the `inRange()` color filter. The following *figure 19.15* shows the original image and the blurred *HSV* image.

**Figure 19.15:** *Image of a stop sign in a busy city. Original image (left) and converted to HSV (right)*

The visual representation of the HSV image is a bit misleading because the image display expects a BGR image and interprets the HSV's three channels as such. Still, we can see it has been converted.

The next two lines in the above code create our two masks. The `inRange()` function requires the following arguments:

- An input `Mat` image
- A lower-boundary `cv::Scalar`
- An upper-boundary `cv::Scalar`
- An output `Mat` image

The input and output images we are used to by now. The boundary scalars we have to remember are *HSV* scalars – not *BGR* scalars. These are three-element scalars (`hue`, `saturation`, `value`) and `inRange()` compare each element, so if any of them are out of the specified range, the pixel is rejected. You can see that I have a fairly narrow range for `hue`, but `saturation` and `value` are both pretty broad – although sometimes it helps to tighten those up as well. The two masks created by the preceding code are in the following *figure 19.16.*

**Figure 19.16:** *Two inRange() results looking for the same red stop sign*

While one result is much better than the other, it is still going to be pretty difficult to identify. How can we combine these two masks into one, better mask? Do you remember the `bitwise_and()` function that rejects any pixel that is not part of both images? There is also a `bitwise_or()` function that will include any pixel that is part of either image.

```
Mat mask3;

bitwise_or(mask1, mask2, mask3);

imshow("combined_mask", mask3);
```

The `bitwise_or()` functions requires the same arguments as the `bitwise_and()` function:

- Input `cv::Mat` image 1
- Input `cv::Mat` image 2 (use image 1 if there is only 1)
- Output `cv::Mat` image (same size as the inputs)
- (Optional) A mask image (of type `cv::Mat` – same size as inputs)

This time we didn't include a mask argument, although we could have if we had accepted the biggest contour as the region of interest and created a mask around that big contour. This would further reduce clutter that is still present. The following *figure 19.17* is the result of combining the two masks.

***Figure 19.17:*** *The result of combining the two inRange() results from figure 19.16*

The edges of the lettering and even the sign are much more clear and more likely to be recognized if fed to a shape or text-recognition algorithm. I'm afraid such things are beyond our scope, though not difficult for you to research yourself.

# Miscellaneous helpful ROS tool

While you won't have to look far for examples on how to read an image or video from file for your OpenCV experimentation, you'll find it much more helpful in your robotics career to use something called **rosbag**.

Rosbag is a ROS package with tools to record and play back all of your ROS message traffic. It's great to be able to read a video from an .mp4 file, but wouldn't it be more useful to be able to play back ROS image messages along with *laser*, *imu*, and any other ROS message traffic just as if you were operating the robot in real-time? It's super easy to record every single message or just a few specific topics. To record all message traffic from the command line:

```
rosbag record -a
```

This will record to the current directory with a default file name ending in .bag. When you want to play back the bag file:

```
rosbag play nameOfFile.bag
```

There are many more tools and options available. Check them out at *wiki.ros.org/rosbag/Commandline*.

# Advanced OpenCV and beyond

We've gotten our feet wet with a few common, simple, and useful tools, but computer vision is a wide and ever-expanding world. OpenCV is a great platform, and a number of very advanced object detection and recognition programs are built to work with it. To name just a couple:

- OpenCV **Optical Character Recognition** (**OCR**) uses a very robust deep learning engine to read text from images.

- Darknet is an impressively advanced neural network framework that allows computer-vision laypersons like myself to use some of the most advanced, open-sourced object-recognition models using the now-famous *YOLO3* method.

**Some extra advice about Darknet:** Visit *pjreddie.com/darknet* for a whole lot of learning on *Joseph Redmon's* amazing work and tutorials, but visit *github.com/leggedrobotics/darknet* for a ROS package version. FYI, I've not been able to get it to run on a Pi3 – only a Pi4 (this is the only reason I can think of to put a Pi4 on a robot and waste that much battery, although an *Nvidia Jetson Nano* is a much better choice still). The Darknet ROS package outputs image messages like the one shown below in *figure 19.18*.

*Figure 19.18: The bounding boxes published by darknet object classification*

The output image is neat for humans to view, but less useful for robots. Fortunately, Darknet ROS also publishes bounding box messages – coordinates of the boxes in the frame and what they are.

# Cloud-based image recognition

As the use cases for reliable image recognition have grown, tech corporations like *Google, Amazon,* and *Microsoft* have begun looking to profit from it. This is a good thing, because the amount of resources they can put into training models and the size of their databases far exceed what us individuals can dream of. The downside, of course, is that these are not free. They're pretty affordable to play with but could get expensive if you tried streaming *24/7*. These also require a reliable, fast internet connection. All of the above have friendly getting-started pages easily found with a quick *Google* search.

# Conclusion

We've covered quite a lot of an entirely new subject in this chapter – learning what makes up a computer image, how to pass them around in ROS, and how to manipulate them to find lines and specific colors. There is still much to learn, so keep at it when you're done with the final project in this book – and we're almost to the final project!

Before we build and program an entire robot from the ground up, we should learn how to bring together some of the material we've learned to use individually. We've explored several tools for keeping track of our robot, why an accurate pose estimate is critically important, and some of the shortcomings of each tracking method. In the next chapter, we are going to learn how to bring several methods together to provide a much-improved pose estimate: `We are going to learn Sensor Fusion`.

# Questions

1. What is different about pixel coordinates than the coordinates of an occupancy grid map?

2. When starting the `usb_cam` `usb_cam_node` to publish camera image in ROS, what parameter must you pass if you are using a Raspberry Pi Raspicam?

3. Why is it usually important to blur an image before calling detection functions like `Canny()` or `inRange()`?

4. What do the two threshold values mean to the `Canny()` function?

5. What must we create to store the output of the `HoughLinesP()` function?

6. Before applying the `inRange()` filter function, what must we convert a BGR image to?

# CHAPTER 20
# Sensor Fusion

## Introduction

By this part in our robotics journey, we know all too well that no single sensor can provide all the data a robot needs to perceive and navigate its environment accurately. Sometimes the sensor doesn't have high enough resolution, and sometimes the resolution is so high that sometimes it introduces noise in the readings. Sometimes the math we use to extrapolate data introduces an error that only gets compounded over time.

All of these things cause sensor readings to come with some amount of uncertainty, or doubt, as to how much we can trust a reading or perception. For these and other reasons, we use sensor fusion algorithms to consider the data from multiple sources and derive an estimate of reality with less uncertainty than any single sensor can provide.

The pose estimate is usually the first place sensor fusion is applied in a mobile robot and will be the focus of this chapter. An accurate pose estimate is critical for intelligently navigating a mapped space, as well as making an accurate map to begin with.

In this chapter, we will cover the following:

- Sensor fusion made easy: Improving odometry with an absolute orientation sensor
- A more comprehensive approach with Kalman filters
- Using the robot_pose_ekf ROS node

# Objective

A more accurate robot pose estimate. Familiarity with the Kalman Filter and the robot_pose_ekf package.

# Sensor fusion made easy

One factor that I think has tremendously advanced the robotics field (among others) is manufacturers realizing the massive demand for pre-assembled modules rather than just individual components. Even the simple things (such as relay modules that used to require an afternoon of etching, wiring, and soldering a number of components to a circuit board can now be ordered for a few bucks) are huge time-savers and allow you to spend those hours learning something new instead of wasting hours doing the routine, mundane task of assembly. Beyond the simple things? Manufacturers have advanced from pre-manufacturing simple modules (for single devices like relays or a single sensor) to manufacturing modules with several sensors. Some of these modules will just be several sensors on a single board, while others will have their microcontroller running advanced sensor fusion algorithms so you don't have to — the fused data is there for you to read.

# The Bosch BN0055 absolute orientation sensor

It's not my intention to steer you towards specific products (I have no sponsors or affiliations with any manufacturer or seller of any product mention in this book). Still, I'd be doing you a disservice if I didn't introduce you to this particular gem.

So far the IMUs we've talked about provide raw data about acceleration, velocity, and magnetic field strength data that we must continuously read and perform various maths on to come up with an estimate of which way our robot is facing. Even then, our estimate is likely to have a high degree of uncertainty unless we use even more complicated filtering techniques that we'll discuss shortly. If your IMU is a Bosch BN0055 like the one pictured below (*figure 20.1*), all of these things are already done for you!

**Figure 20.1:** *BOSCH BN0055 Absolute Orientation IMU - my new favorite!*

When I first started writing this book, I thought this section was going to suggest that if you wanted an accurate, fused orientation estimate from an IMU module that you would have to spend hundreds of dollars. What makes the Bosch BN0055 stand out is (besides its stellar performance that I'll get to in a moment) is its size and price. While it isn't the first module to output an accurate, fused heading estimate, it is the first I've seen that isn't in a box the size of a Raspberry Pi or bigger. It's also the first I've seen to cost less than Raspberry Pi. The one pictured is by *Adafruit*, and there is another version called the **BN0055-USB-Stick** that plugs right into the USB-port without using I2C or an FTDI.

*Edit to add: Since first writing this chapter, I've discovered and tested another BN0055 based module by Devantech that works as well as the Adafruit module with the same software.*

# Provided data

The BN0055 contains an accelerometer, gyroscope, and magnetometer, and you can read all of the raw data just as with any other IMU. It also provides acceleration vectors with the gravity component removed for you, if you wish. The real draw for me, however, is the absolute orientation data. Provided in both quaternions and Euler angles, knowing which way your robot is facing is as easy as querying the module and reading the numbers it provides.

# Improved odometry

Inside the wheel odometry publisher is not the usual place to fuse sensors, I did so as an experiment and have been amazed. What I did was use the same odometry node we wrote in *Chapter 11, Robot Localization and Implementation* but added a subscriber to the BN0055 publishing on the IMU topic. If an IMU message is received with valid orientation data, it is converted from quaternions to Euler angles, and the Odom heading estimate is simply updated with the *z (yaw)* angle from the IMU. (The danger here, of course, is that a sizeable sudden jump in the heading can cause havoc on the drive controller. This hasn't been a problem since I am reading the IMU 10 times per second, but I know that it could be if somehow IMU messages are lost). *Figure 20.2* below shows the before and after of one short experiment.

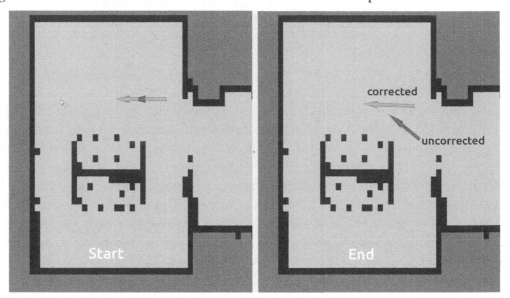

*Figure 20.2:* *Odometry estimates with and without heading correction*

Since the vast majority of wheel odometry uncertainty is introduced when turning, I expected significant improvement in the little indoor robot I built to go along with this book (The same one you can build in *Chapter 21, Building and PROGRAMMING AN AUTONOMOUS ROBOT*). The results show that `significant improvement` is an understatement and my odometry-based pose estimate rivals the accuracy of the much more complex `robot_pose_ekf` node (*extended Kalman filter*) that I'll introduce you to later in the chapter.

What you're looking at in *figure 20.2* is my dining room (that's a table and chairs in the middle) and two arrows that represent the odometry node's location estimate on the same robot at the same time. It's hard to see both arrows in the left pane because the estimates are the same before the robot moves. The pane on the right shows both estimates more clearly after they have diverged. After just a few laps around my dining room, then being ordered to return to the start, the uncorrected estimate is so far off that it is unusable for autonomous navigation on its own. The corrected estimate (that I was using for input to the path planner and drive controller) brought the robot back almost precisely to the start position (it's within the 10 cm tolerance I have set in the drive controller). *Now this is usable odometry!*

# Integrating the BN0055 – The hardware and ROS publisher

The sensor itself can use serial or I2C to communicate, and the Adafruit module I have is configurable to do either. One big warning is that the BN0055 uses a technique called `clock-stretching` with I2C communication. This is something a Raspberry Pi cannot do with its I2C interface so you'll have to use serial mode to use the BN0055 with a Raspberry pi. This can be either the GPIO UART or with an FTDI and USB port. From what I'm told I2C mode works just fine on Arduinos and Nvidia Jetson Nanos. The USB-Stick version obviously uses serial via USB.

Publishing the information is done on the same topics as any other IMU – it just also populates the orientation field instead of marking it *do not use*. Getting the information from the BN0055 is a bit more involved than from other IMUs because the fusion algorithm requires calibration data — either you have to calibrate it every time you power it on, or you can store the calibration data in a file and re-load it as necessary. Fortunately, software is available to handle this for you.

The two versions (*Adafruit* and *USB-Stick*) versions don't speak the same language, so each has its own ROS package. I was surprised that I could not find a ROS package for the Adafruit version that would work in serial mode, so I released one that includes a simple setup utility that lets you run calibration, save configuration and calibration data to file, and reload it later as well a few other features. The other node is the publisher node that reads the calibration file if necessary (it will be every power-cycle), sets the device into fusion mode, and starts publishing the IMU message with the fused orientation data. Clone and compile it from the command line (make sure you're in your `catkin_ws/src`):

```
git clone https://github.com/lbrombach/bn0055_fusion_imu.git

cd ..

catkin_make
```

From there it will be ready for you to run the setup node. If you don't run the setup node it will load the config and calibration data from MY device – that won't be the same for yours.

I can't give any details on the software for the USB-Stick software as I have not used it. BOSCH provides some windows software for configuration and calibration, and the ROS package I have been told works well can be cloned from *https://github.com/mdrwiega/bosch_imu_driver.git*

# Integrating the BN0055 – The odometry node

Whichever version you get (or any other IMU that outputs accurate heading data), once it is publishing in ROS, the short road to using that data is to correct the heading in the odometry node as I have. The steps to correct the heading in your odometry node are pretty simple:

1.  Subscribe to the IMU message.
2.  Verify that the orientation field is not marked as *do not use*.
3.  Convert the quaternion information in the orientation field to Euler angles.
4.  If this is the first heading update received from the IMU, store the offset between the current heading and the IMU heading instead of updating the heading.
5.  For all subsequent IMU messages received - update the heading with the IMU data plus the recorded offset.
    5.1.  Update the variable that stores the IMU heading and mark the flag telling the odometry calculation node to use the IMU heading.
    5.2.  Apply the IMU heading in the odometry calculation function.

## Step 1: Subscribe to the IMU message

You should be a pro at subscribing to messages by now.

```
#include <sensor_msgs/Imu.h>


int main(…)

{

    ...

    ros::Subscriber subImu;
```

```
subImu = node.subscribe("imu", 100, update_heading);

    ...

}
```

I leave room for a 100 message queue, although I doubt we'd ever approach that unless we have other significant problems. update_heading is what I named the callback function.

# Step 2: Verify orientation is not marked Do Not Use

*Steps 2, 3, 4*, and part of *step 5* all happen in the callback function. *Step 2* is handled with a simple if() check. According to the sensor_msgs::Imu wiki, IMU messages published with a -1 in the first element of the associated field's covariance matrix means *do not use*. *Step 2*, as well as the layout of the whole function, are below:

```
void update_heading(const sensor_msgs::Imu &imuMsg)

{

    //step 2

    if(imuMsg.orientation_covariance[0] != -1)

    {

    step 3 - Convert quaternion to Euler

        if(this is first message received from IMU)

        {

        step 4 - calculate and save offset

        }

        else

        {

        step 5.1 - Apply the saved offset and save the heading

        }

    }

}
```

## Step 3: Convert quaternions to Euler angles

This conversion will use the `tf/transform_broadcaster.h` file, so we need to include that at the top of our file. The rest takes place inside our callback function:

```cpp
#include <tf/transform_broadcaster.h>


void update_heading(const sensor_msgs::Imu &imuMsg)

{

    ...

    tf::Quaternion q(imuMsg.orientation.x, imuMsg.orientation.y,

        imuMsg.orientation.z, imuMsg.orientation.w);

    tf::Matrix3x3 m(q);

    double roll, pitch, yaw;

    m.getRPY(roll, pitch, yaw);

}
```

## Step 4: Save Offset information IF this is first IMU message

If the IMU has no way of knowing what the robot's initial heading is, it always starts reporting a heading of 0. To prevent the BN0055 from overriding any current estimate with 0, we will use the first message to compare the current heading estimate with the IMU's heading estimate and record the difference. To keep track if this is the first IMU message received or not, I have simply declared global variables near the top of the file and to store this flag as well as the calculated offset. As always, apply your best programming technique.

```cpp
bool imuHeadingInitialized = false;

double headingOffset = 0;


void update_heading(const sensor_msgs::Imu &imuMsg)

{

    ...
```

```
if( imuHeadingInitialized == false)

{

    headingOffset = oldOdom.pose.pose.orientation.z - yaw;

imuHeadingInitialized = true;

}

else

{...}

}
```

# Step 5.1: If NOT the first IMU message – Save the IMU heading

A global variable is used so the odometry calculation function can access the heading later, as well as a global Boolean flag, so it knows that the imuHeading is new. The heading is calculated by adding back in the offset we recorded earlier.

```
bool haveNewImuHeading = false;

double imuHeading = 0;


void update_heading(const sensor_msgs::Imu &imuMsg)

{

    ...

    else

    {

        imuHeading = yaw + headingOffset;

haveNewImuHeading = true;

    }

}
```

# Step 5.2: Apply the new heading in the odometry calculation function

My odometry calculation node is called `void update_odom()`. I apply the IMU heading at the end of the function – right before copying the new odometry message to `oldOdom` and publishing the new message. We also have to set our flag to `false,` so we don't use the same IMU heading over and over if we don't get a new message before the next cycle.

```
void update_odom()

{

    ...

    if(haveNewHeading == true)

    {

        newOdom.pose.pose.orientation.z = imuHeading;

        haveNewImueHeading = false;

    }


    oldOdom... = newOdom...;

    odom_pub.publish(newOdom);

}
```

And that's it. I'm sure plenty of *by the book or not at all* roboticists would not approve. Still, I'm also sure that plenty of practical roboticists will see the value of getting such a significant improvement for such a relatively simple implementation. In my experience, it has quite literally been the difference between a machine more or less limited to remote control and a robot capable of truly navigating a space on its own for a good while – perhaps indefinitely if a few fiducial markers or other beacons are scattered about that the robot can routinely visit and confirm its location and orientation as part of its routine.

# Sensor fusion 2 – A more comprehensive approach

While I'm confident that the more straightforward approach above can significantly improve the reliability of the odometry system, it is not a comprehensive solution and still prone to errors in distance measurement and an inability to tell if the robot is stuck with wheels spinning but not going anywhere. We're still going to have a much more robust system if we can use all the data from the IMU and not just it's heading. Further, if we can bring other sources of data into the equation like GPS data, laser-based odometry, or a commercial solution like the output from a visual odometry unit, we are approaching a system that can be reliable through a variety of condition changes. The problem, of course, is if each of these sensors is at times completely unreliable – how do we know which to believe at any given time? Let me introduce you to the `Kalman` filter.

## The Kalman filter

The backbone of many sensor fusion algorithms, the Kalman filter, can consider several measurements, predictions, and uncertainty matrices to make a more accurate estimate of the actual state of the thing we are trying to measure. We won't get into the specific math of implementation, but a basic understanding of how it works is essential to using already-available ROS nodes successfully. Let's consider for now the single variable of velocity.

We have several sources of velocity information. We have our encoders to compute how far we travel each second. We have an accelerometer – which can give us velocity by integrating the acceleration data over time. We may have a GPS that allows us to compute velocity as we do with our encoder odometry or perhaps we have a GPS model that computes velocity for us. In addition to these instantaneous values computed for the present, we also can predict the future based on information from all of the above.

We know that each of these comes with some amount of presumed uncertainty – the reality that the reading or prediction may be off by some amount – and we have to accept the value as *hopefully somewhere close to reality*. Presume that we've been calculating velocity with accelerometer data: We've started from a known velocity and accelerated at a measured rate for a measured amount of time, and the integration over time indicates a final velocity for a certain moment in time. Instead of accepting the final result as precisely accurate, we have to realize that reality is most likely within a range — this range is related to the variance. *Figure 20.3* illustrates what I mean.

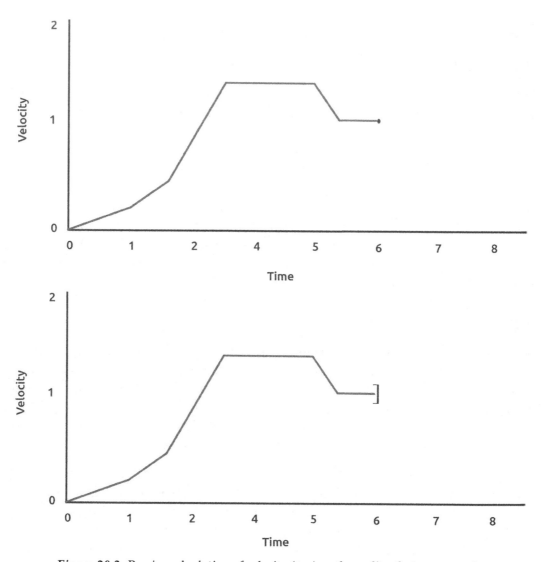

**Figure 20.3:** *Precise calculation of velocity (top) vs the reality that we can only be accurate within a range (bottom)*

After a series of accelerations over **6** seconds, our function reflected by the top graph calculates that our velocity at `time = 6 seconds` is precisely `1 meter per second`. The bottom graph represents the reality that due to a variety of errors in measurement, we can probably accept that the actual velocity at `t=6` is within this range that is `+/- .05 m/s` or so from the calculated value and it would be a mistake to accept the precise measurement. If we have data from several sensors, we can compare their ranges and eliminate some of the possible values. *Figure 20.4* shows a zoomed-in view and the addition of another range of possible velocities calculated from encoder odometry.

The drawing on the left shows a range calculated by an odometry function that is of similar size (`this won't always be so`) but slightly lower than the range calculation with accelerometer data. We don't know where the real value is within either of these ranges, only that it is most likely within each range. This means that any part of the range from one that does not overlap the other can be eliminated, leaving us with a smaller range as pictured on the right in *figure 20.4*.

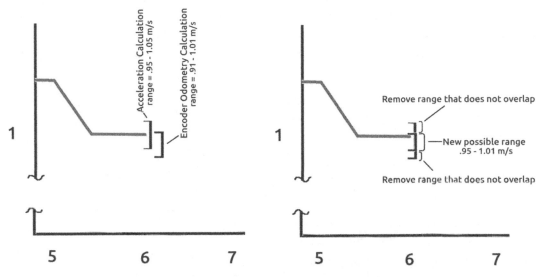

**Figure 20.4:** *Narrowing down range of possible values*

By applying this narrowing down with more and more ranges from other sensors and even predictions, we can arrive at a better estimate of velocity than any of these providers on their own. And more than merely chopping off sections that don't overlap, we can consider the certainty or uncertainty of each range and weight the ones we trust the more heavily than ones with significant uncertainty. This brings us back to the question – *How do we know which values to trust the most?*

# The covariance matrix

My illustrations are a fair bit over-simplified for ease of understanding, but the Kalman filter does not weight each position in each range equally. Instead, it takes from each input the precise value (that I said we aren't going to trust) it reports as well as some variance values to calculate the range and assumes a Gaussian distribution of the possible values over the range. Getting the variance values to publish is a hassle if not provided by the sensor, but essential for good results. Every robot is different, so copying the variance values from another robot is definitely not ideal – particularly in the case of odometry from encoders.

We've talked about the covariance field in our various ROS message-types before without discussing what it means, but it cannot be ignored in this chapter. Hopefully, you've had a statistics class in the past as I can only provide a quick run-down of the covariance matrix and how the robot_pose_ekf node uses it.

If we have a set of velocity estimates of a single axis (the $x$ *axis*), the average of those estimates is called the **Mean**. Now, if we individually compare each estimate to the mean, the difference of the data and the mean is that individual estimate's deviation. Finally, the variance of that particular set of data is found by squaring each deviation, then averaging the results. *Figure 20.5* below shows calculating the variance of a small data set.

Data:
2.0
2.2
2.2
2.1
2.1

Calculate Mean (average) :

$$\frac{2.0 + 2.2 + 2.2 + 2.1 + 2.1}{5} = 2.12$$

Calculate Deviations:
(data - mean = deviation)

2.0 - 2.12 =  -.12
2.2 - 2.12 =   .08
2.2 - 2.12 =   .08
2.1 - 2.12 =  -.02
2.1 - 2.12 =  -.02

Calculate Variance:
(square all means, then average)

-.12 x -.12  = .0144
 .08 x  .08  = .0064
 .08 x  .08  = .0064
-.02 x -.02  = .0044
-.02 x -.02  = .0044

$$\frac{.0144 + .0064 + .0064 + .0044 + .0044}{5} = .0072$$

Variance = .0072

*Figure 20.5: Calculating Variance*

This variance is one value in our covariance matrix. Before we get confused, I should clarify the difference between variance and covariance, and show you why we are entering variances into the covariance matrix. Start by looking over *figure 20.6*.

|   | x | y | z |
|---|---|---|---|
| x | Vx | Cxy | Cxz |
| y | Cxy | Vy | Cyz |
| z | Cxz | Cyz | Vz |

Standard 3x3
Covariance Matrix
C = covariance value
V = Variance value

|   | x | y | z |
|---|---|---|---|
| x | .0072 | 0 | 0 |
| y | 0 | Vy | 0 |
| z | 0 | 0 | Vz |

Starting to populate the covariance matrix with the data set from fig 20.5

*Figure 20.6: A 3x3 covariance matrix*

**Variance** is a measure of how far a single variable might deviate from the mean. In the left image in *figure 20.6*, we can see the cells marked with a **V** are where we are comparing an element with itself – **the variance**. The variances fall along what is routinely called **the diagonal**. Looking to the image on the right, I entered the variance we calculated above in the field for **Vx. Vy** and **Vz** have not been calculated yet, but as the robots we've talked about can only move along their *x axis*, we don't have to. According to the robot_pose_ekf package document (at *wiki.ros.org/robot_pose_ekf*), the direction is given to enter a significant value on elements that are not relevant so they can be ignored. Whenthetime comes, you can use **999999**. Other packages have different directions, so be sure to read up when you try new things.

**Covariance** is a measure of how two variables vary in relation to each other. The *off-diagonal* cells are where we enter covariance values. Since our robot's velocity in the y direction does not change in any particular relationship with the velocity in the x direction, we can say that there is no correlation and simply enter **0**. This is true for all of the off-diagonal cells in all the covariance matrices we need for the robot_pose_ekf node.

# Covariance matrices in ROS messages

There are two types of covariance matrix in ROS that I know of – *3x3* and *6x6*. These are pre-defined fields in some types of the pose, IMU, and twist messages, to name a few. When you look at the message documents, however, they reference a float64[] array. *Figure 20.7* has screenshots from two message documents – the sensor_msgs::Imu message and geometry_msgs::PoseWithCovariance message.

```
Header header

geometry_msgs/Quaternion orientation
float64[9] orientation_covariance # Row major about x, y, z axes

geometry_msgs/Vector3 angular_velocity
float64[9] angular_velocity_covariance # Row major about x, y, z axes

geometry_msgs/Vector3 linear_acceleration
float64[9] linear_acceleration_covariance # Row major x, y z
```

```
# This represents a pose in free space with uncertainty.

Pose pose

# Row-major representation of the 6x6 covariance matrix
# The orientation parameters use a fixed-axis representation.
# In order, the parameters are:
# (x, y, z, rotation about X axis, rotation about Y axis, rotation about Z axis)
float64[36] covariance
```

***Figure 20.7:*** *Screenshot of how covariance is listed in ROS message documents*

I've circled the covariance data member listings – notice that covariance fields for a *3x3* matrix have an array of size 9, and a *6x6* matrix has an array of size 36? It's likely apparent to you by now, but we use a 1D array to hold the data from our matrix the same way we do for an occupancy grid map. Fortunately, the docs have comments to specify the order. The *3x3* matrix we made in *figure 20.8* would be represented as in the image below:

$$[Vx, \quad Cxy, Cxz, Cxy, \qquad Vy, Cyz, Cxz, Cyz, \qquad Vz]$$
$$[.0072, \quad 0, \quad 0, \quad 0, 999999, \quad 0, \quad 0, \quad 0, 999999]$$
$$index = \quad [0] \; [1] \; [2] \; [3] \qquad [4] \; [5] \; [6] \; [7] \qquad [8]$$

**Figure 20.8:** *The 3x3 covariance matrix in array form*

One last note on matrices in ROS before we get to the `robot_pose_ekf` node – because it was a linear velocity covariance matrix we made in *figure 20.8*, it belongs as part of the *6x6* twist covariance matrix – which will be part of your odometry message. The other elements for that are for rotational velocity in the *x, y,* and *z* axis. We don't need to measure **Vx** and **Vy** for rotational velocity for our ground robot – just the *z axis*. Use a significant value for rotational **Vx** and rotational **Vy**, and you just need to calculate for rotational **Vz**.

# The robot_pose_ekf node

The `robot_pose_ekf` uses an extended Kalman filter to estimate your robot's pose and can subscribe to three ROS topics for input information – two odometry topics and one IMU topic. There are a lot of details in the Wiki page about how it uses the various topics – what information it takes and what is ignored, how to configure, and how to use one of the odometry topics for GPS data (if you're clever you can use this other topic for some other form of odometry like laser-based odometry). Take the time to read up at *wiki.ros.org/robot_pose_ekf*.

## Installing robot_pose_ekf

The package is in the ROS repository for both *Kinetic* and *Melodic,* so installing is as easy as using `apt-get`:

```
sudo apt-get install ros-kinetic-robot-pose-ekf

cd ~/catkin_ws

catkin_make
```

- OR -

```
sudo apt-get install ros-melodic-robot-pose-ekf

cd ~/catkin_ws

catkin_make
```

Alternatively, you can clone the repository (link in the Wiki page) into your `catkin_ws/src` directory and then `catkin_make`, but unless I plan to tinker with the code, I find this just clutters my workspace.

# Running the robot_pose_ekf

To successfully run `robot_pose_ekf`, you need a few things:

- `roscore` running
- At least one of the odometry topics publishing (with covariance) on the topic `odom`
- IMU data (with covariance) being published on the topic `imu_data`, or a second odometry message with covariance.
- A static transform publisher is running from your `base_link` to `imu` frame.

The node also takes several parameters so it knows which sensors to use and some other things. The `robot_pose_ekf` node publishes a `geometry_msgs::PoseWithCovarianceStamped` message on the topic `robot_pose_ekf/odom_combined`.

Instead of trying to pass many topic names remaps and parameters via command line, this is a great node to launch with a launch file. The `robot_pose_ekf` package comes with a couple examples of launch files, and the first thing you'll want to do is at least make one for the package you've been working on. In the base directory of the ROS package you've been building nodes in:

1. Create a folder called `launch`.
2. Create a file called something like `ekf_launch.launch`.
3. Copy the contents of the example launch file in the `robot_pose_ekf` Wiki page. (screenshot below – *figure 20.9*).
4. Edit the parameter marked in the screenshot below, so the node doesn't look for that topic.
5. Save the file.

```
<launch>
  <node pkg="robot_pose_ekf" type="robot_pose_ekf" name="robot_pose_ekf">
    <param name="output_frame" value="odom"/>
    <param name="freq" value="30.0"/>
    <param name="sensor_timeout" value="1.0"/>
    <param name="odom_used" value="true"/>
    <param name="imu_used" value="true"/>
    <param name="vo_used" value="true"/>* make this false *
    <param name="debug" value="false"/>
    <param name="self_diagnose" value="false"/>
  </node>
</launch>
```

**Figure 20.9:** *The robot_pose_ekf example launch file*

To run the node, make sure your pre-requisites are running (or add them to the launch file). You can also add the tf publisher or run it from the command line with:

rosrun tf static_transform_publisher 0 0 0 0 0 0 base_link imu 20

Then you can run the launch file with:

roslaunch name_of_your_package ekf_launch.launch

To see if it's running, you can use

rostopic echo robot_pose_ekf/odom_combined

To see the topic messages, and

rosrun robot_pose_ekf wtf.py

To see a quick self-diagnosis/status report.

# A final note on transforms and roslaunch

We haven't spent much time as I would have liked on these topics due to time and space constraints, but you're getting to the point where you're really going to need to understand these to keep advancing – especially the transforms.

We've done our best so far to dial in odometry and drive nodes so we can operate in a single frame and not be distracted by transforms from world to odom and odom to base_link at every step. Eventually, however, performance is capped without transforms and experimentation with different ROS packages isn't possible.

On my second point – If you're still manually opening a dozen windows and starting a dozen nodes, it just won't do to keep wasting that much time. `roslaunch` is your friend – it's time to play.

# Conclusion

We've spent this chapter refining our robot's ability to keep track of its location. This refinement is critical if we are ever to be able to leave our machines unattended to work truly autonomously. We've learned how to quickly get a significant improvement over plain, wheel encoder-only odometry by using a sensor with a built-in sensor fusion algorithm, and we learned how to fuse that improvement with other pose estimates using a Kalman filter node for a more robust result.

The final chapter brings together the previous 20 chapters and walks through combining everything we've learned to build a complete, autonomous robot that is ready for you to continue learning and experimenting with. From loading software on bare machines to choosing and wiring electronic components to building a map of the environment and navigating from place to place, we're going to do it all.

# Questions

1. When using an orientation sensor like the BN0055 to update the heading in the odometry publisher node, what is essential to do when the first message is received?

2. What is the variance?

3. Where do we put the variance in a covariance matrix?

CHAPTER 21

# Building and
# Programming an
# Autonomous Robot

## Introduction

In the past twenty chapters, we learned the basics of many individual subjects necessary to make an autonomous robot. From blinking an LED for the first time to reading and interpreting data from all sorts of sensors to sending signals out to a motor driver to control wheel speed, and to writing a program that can plot a series of waypoints for our robot to navigate itself from place to place — take a moment to look back and congratulate yourself on how much you've learned on this journey so far and get ready to finally put all the parts together to get started on your masterpiece. Don't fret if not everything is crystal clear yet – I have become a believer that there will always be questions and always parts of the vast field of robotics where you feel a need to improve. *I know I do.*

In our final chapter, we are going to put together everything we've learned to build a robot that can navigate and drive itself from place to place. I'm going to write this chapter to the best of my ability that you can follow along carefully and build the exact robot I used for all my examples and code testing, or use this chapter as a template — following along generally but doing each step your way to end up with a very different robot. That's the beauty of having learned how these things work instead of me telling you to copy and paste — you are much better enabled to experiment with your techniques and build a robot to suit your own requirements and desires.

On that note, this chapter is meant to be more than just a checklist but less than a detailed step-by-step instruction set. Instead, this is more of a guided checklist to help you coordinate everything you've already learned in the preceding chapters. Building an autonomous robot is a big project and sometimes we just need a nudge for which step to take next. I'll try to provide that direction, extra pointers along the way, and plenty of reminders of which chapters to refer back to.

This chapter is divided into two general parts:

1.   Building the robot platform.
2.   Programming your robot.

In part one, we'll put together the physical robot. The body, motors, sensors, and computer – then we'll wire it all up. Part one isn't about the software, but we'll test each component along the way. If you have purchased a robot platform, you still may want to read along to make sure the minimum components (sensors) are all interfaced and ready to go for the programming section.

In part two, we'll put together our software packages and launch files so we can start all of the programs and behaviors you want to run with one convenient command. Then we'll build a map of the robot's environment, save a list of locations we can serve just by entering a number, and finally discuss how you can expand on these basic behaviors by writing your routines. It would be entirely reasonable to read the whole book, then build the robot in part one of this chapter, then spend the second part of this chapter going back and more thoroughly tackling each chapter relevant to the step you're on.

In this chapter, we will cover the following:

•   The robot platform – General overview and parts list
•   Assembling the robot platform
•   Programming – general overview
•   Programming your robot – Detailed steps
•   Run your autonomous robot!
•   What next?

# Objective

The grand finale: A working, autonomous robot!

# Part 1 - Building the physical robot platform

I thought long and hard about what kind of robot to build to go along with our lessons and, I have to admit, it was difficult to resist the temptation to build a big, 4 wheel drive machine like the 50Kg beasts my team has built for autonomous robot competitions. What I ultimately decided was that a robot platform that was available to the most significant number of people was far more critical than a flashy one.

Among the requirements, I determined it was important to use no specialty tools. Although a power drill was handy, everything can be done with hand tools and a soldering iron. I resisted the temptation to make brackets and mounting parts with my 3D printer. Instead, I designed the entire robot to be made with parts I bought at my hardware store except for electronic components that came from *Amazon* or *eBay*.

Aside from being far more affordable than a large robot, building one roughly the size and shape of a robot vacuum was a thousand times handier than a large robot – allowing me to pack it on the road and keep working in hotels or my camper. I thought I would get around to 3D print some optional body parts just for looks but honestly, I've grown pretty fond of its raw beauty and simplicity. Not to mention having everything exposed makes it so simple to check wires or swap sensors. Quite frankly, it's a fantastic robot that can keep growing along with your skills as a robot developer for years and years.

# The robot platform – General overview and parts list

Generally speaking, we are going to build a robot with two drive wheels and a castering nose or tail-wheel. You are, of course, welcome to make this any size you'd like, but you'll have to adapt and improvise more — a fun challenge if you're up for it! The essential components you'll need for the basic platform are:

- Wheel/Motors modules – consist of the 3 items below. They can be bought all together or piece-by-piece.
    o Wheels
    o Motors
    o Gearboxes

- Motor driver(s)
- Caster wheel
- Battery and charger
- Base/chassis

And to turn your platform into a robot, you'll need some electronics:

- Computer
- LIDAR (or some ranging device)
- Wheel encoders
- IMU
- Voltage converter for computer
- GPIO header breakout board
- Camera
- Voltage meter/display (optional)
- Analog to digital converter (optional)

See *figure 21.1* below:

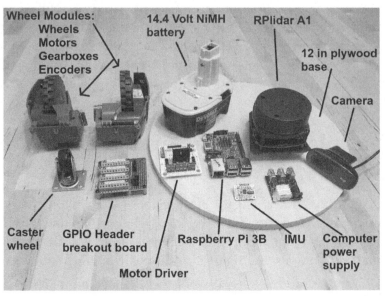

**Figure 21.1:** *The major components that I have chosen for this project*

And a few tools:

- Drill – hand or powered
- Soldering Iron

- Screwdrivers (regular and small sizes)
- Needle nose pliers (small)
- Wire connector crimpers

The above two lists are your primary requirements. It's not a lot that you need, and you can always add extras you want like servo motors to move the camera without moving the robot or ultrasonic sensors to add collision avoidance along the edges below the LIDAR beam. Let's briefly look at each item:

# Wheel/motor modules

I put these together because it's so common to acquire them pre-assembled. You won't be attaching a wheel directly to a motor, or you'll end up with an uncontrollable mess, so you want a motor with a gearbox. A little arithmetic can help you choose the wheel/motor/gearbox combination. The maximum theoretical speed will be close to `motor_rpm/gear_ratio*wheel_circumference` but, in reality, you may see speeds a bit less as the weight of the robot (and other forms of resistance) slows down the motor (a small motor meant for a toy car obviously won't be able to maintain it's rated speed if you ask it to tow your real car). Online stores that sell gear motors for robots often have tutorials or tools to help you choose an appropriate combination. *Figure 21.2* below shows the wheel modules I am using for this build.

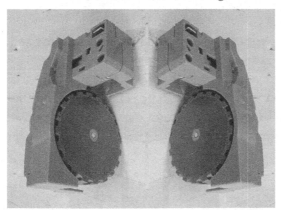

*Figure 21.2:* The iRobot Roomba wheel modules

**My choice:** iRobot Roomba wheel modules

We'll be using my favorite wheel/motor module for this project because not only is it probably the best deal, but it's also very well-made, resilient, and simplifies the build by coming all together with motor, gearbox, wheel, encoders, and even spring loaded drop switch. We know it's designed for long-term use and speeds that are appropriate for our project, and works fantastically at *12* or *14.4* volts. Any Roomba model from *500, 600, 700, 800,* or *900* series uses the same wheel, so they are very easy to find new or used online. You can salvage them for free, if you're lucky, or I've bought them for as little as *USD 40* per pair on *eBay*. I have a tutorial with detailed instructions for removing from a Roomba, connection diagrams, and schematics of the internals at the *YouTube* channel I put together to accompany this book at *www. youtube.com/practicalrobotics.*

# Motor driver(s)

You are certainly not limited to using the motor drivers we discussed in *Chapter 4, Types of Robot Motors and Motor Control.* Still, it may be a good idea to review that chapter before making a selection. Be reminded that some motor drivers can handle only one motor, while others can handle two. You need two rated for the voltage and current requirements of your motors.

**My choice:** L298N dual H-Bridge motor driver

The motor driver I'm using is the *Velleman* VMA409 version from *Chapter 4, Types of Robot Motors and Motor Control.* Other, less expensive L298N modules are available and wiring will be similar — Just make sure you buy a module and not a bare L298N chip unless you like making your circuits.

# Caster wheel

This just a wheel that swivels freely whichever way it is dragged and can be purchased at most hardware or home improvement stores. I mistakenly bought one that is too small and had to make a spacer to keep the robot level. It worked out because it gave me a handy place to mount an ultrasonic sensor (pictured below – *figure 21.3*), but it would have saved time if I had bought one **7.51cm** (*3 inches*) tall to begin with.

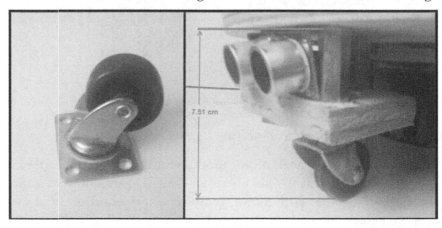

*Figure 21.3: The nose caster, make-shift spacer and ultrasonic sensor mount*

# Battery and charger

We don't want our robot stuck to a wall receptacle, so we need a battery. The choices are numerous, but you want something rechargeable as little battery packs with *AA* or even *D* batteries are going to die quickly and become far costlier than a rechargeable battery in just a handful of uses. Whatever battery type you choose, get a proper charger for that specific type as lithium ion, lithium polymer, `nickel-metal hydride` (`NiMH`), sealed lead acid, and absorbed glass mat batteries all have different charging properties.

Batteries are rated in volts and amp-hours (*AH*). If we have *2.5* AH (also known as *2500* milliamp hour) battery, it's going to last twice as long as a *1250* milliamp hour battery. Recall from *Chapter 2, GPIO Hardware Interface Pins Overview and Use* that power comes from volts times amps, so a *2.5* AH, *12* volt battery has twice as much available power as a *2.5* AH, *6* volt battery and will last much longer. There's nothing worse than having to stop working after *20* minutes to charge your robot for a couple of hours so this is an excellent place to spend a few extra bucks if you have it. I recommend at least *2.5* AH at *12* or *14.4* volts, which is coincidentally about what my power tool batteries have to offer. Electric scooter batteries are a bit big for this project but great for larger robots. Computer power-banks like the one pictured in *figure 21.4* store a lot of power for their size and weight but are expensive, and you have to consider that they have their electronics that could decide to shut down on you at an inconvenient time.

*Figure 21.4: A 2.4 AH,14.4 volt power tool battery (left),*
*and a multi-voltage laptop power bank (right)*

**My choice:** A *14.4* volt, NiMH power-tool battery (pictured in *figure 21.4*, on the left). Simple, durable, cheap if you find a generic replacement, and I already have chargers for them everywhere.

## Chassis/base

We, of course, need something to hold everything together and mount all the parts to. You can get as fancy as you want, but I have to advise that your first robot (probably all of your robots, but especially your first one) will go through a lot of tweaks, adjustments, and changes so spending a lot of time and money on the first attempts might not be the best idea. Instead, I suggest you stick with something basic and easy to work with and spend the extra time and money learning and experimenting with different sensors and components rather than a fancier body. You can always build the masterpiece when you have a better idea of what your robot is going to be doing.

**My choice:** A simple, `30 x 1.2` cm (`12 x 1/2` inch) circle of birch plywood that I found pre-cut at my home improvement store for just a few *US* dollars. Yes, there was a time I would have wrinkled my nose at the suggestion of building a wooden robot but, robot but, after making a number of them out of metal and realizing how much bigger of a pain it is to mount something or move something over a centimeter, I have been sold on a wooden chassis as the most practical prototyping material. You can just get it done so much quicker, and my wife is a good bit less cranky when she finds a bit of sawdust than when she found a metal sliver with her bare feet.

## Computers

We talked a good bit about this in *Chapter 1, Choosing and Setting up a Robot Computer*. Since the motors won't be spinning a lot of the time, this will probably be the number one power-consumer on board. Avoid the temptation to get the biggest and fastest if you don't need it.

**My choice:** Raspberry Pi model 3B

I'll repeat what I said in *Chapter 1* – The `Pi 3B+` is not worth the extra power consumption for such little improvement, and at this time, skip the `Pi 4` unless you're very comfortable with fussing with Linux and installing software and dependencies manually. I'm using the regular model `3B` for the project and it's plenty fast for the job. since I wrote this chapter, I've learned that `Ubiquity Robotics`, whose Linux + ROS image I introduced in *Chapter 9, Coordinating the Parts* has a new image that works with the Raspberry Pi 4. I've not tested it and, like anything new, it can to be expected to have some bugs. If you like extra computer-tinkering, try if you're willing to drain your battery much faster for the speed. If you're still learning about computer and Linux machines, I suggest sticking with the `Pi 3B`**

# LIDAR or another ranging sensor

We're going to want to see obstacles and build our map with range data. This can be the most expensive device on your robot, and I understand any reluctance to spend that kind of money, but we addressed earlier the shortcomings of trying to build a map with sonar data. If you're building an outdoor robot, keep in mind that there are special outdoor-rated LIDAR units that have more powerful lasers and are better-suited to see through interference from the sun (not to mention weather-proofing).

If you're brave and have the money, you can get a 3D laser, a stereoscopic camera system with ranging data, or a mm-wave radar device. We haven't talked about handling that data, so I recommend you start with the basics and get a 2D laser scanner if you're not comfortable digging through the ROS message docs and searching for packages to do what you need.

**My choice:** The Slamtec RPLidar A1

At about *$100 U.S.*, it's a great little unit we installed in *Chapter 18, LIDAR Devices and Data*. If that is out of reach or you are a bit like me and enjoy salvaging and hacking things, the laser scanner from *Neato Robot* vacuums can be found on *eBay* for under *$40 U.S.* (or salvaged for free if you're very lucky). The resolution is the same as the RPLidar A1, but the range and scan-speed suffer. This can reduce map quality but is a workable option. Hacking these is outside the scope of this book, but I have a complete tutorial on the *Practical Robotics YouTube* channel at *www.youtube. com/practicalrobotics*.

# Wheel encoders

We talked about some different options in *Chapter 14, Wheels Encoders for Odometry*. I much prefer a basic hall-effect type for our purposes.

**My choice:** Included in the Roomba wheel modules

These are hall-effect type encoders.

# IMU

You can use any IMU you can find or write a ROS publisher node for (refer back to *Chapter 16, IMUs: Accelerometers, Gyroscopes, and Magnetometers* and *Chapter 20, Sensor Fusion*).

**My choice:** BN0055 absolute orientation sensor

As we talked about in *Chapter 20*. The one I have is by Adafruit, but I recently found and tried one by Devantech that's a good bit cheaper and works with the same ROS node we installed in *Chapter 20*.

# Voltage converter for computer

This needs to convert the voltage from your main battery down to something your computer can use – usually 5 volts. Don't forget it has to supply at least enough current for the computer and a few accessories/sensors. Refer back to *Chapter 6, Additional Helpful Hardware.*

My choice: USB buck converter by DROK

For no special reason other than a four-pack was cheap on *Amazon,* and they are rated at 24 watts so they should be good for over 4 amps at 5 volts. Pictured below in *figure 21.5*, I mounted an extra one for future use, though just one has handled the Raspberry Pi 3B, LIDAR, and all other sensors just fine.

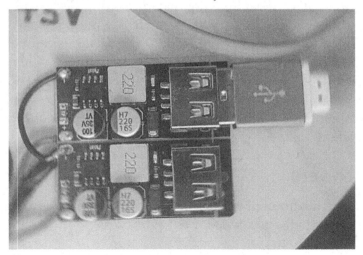

*Figure 21.5: A pair of DROK USB Buck Converters power everything except the motors*

# GPIO header breakout board

Discussed back in *Chapter 2, GPIO Hardware Interface Pins Overview and Use*, these are technically optional but it's very easy to stick wires in the wrong place without a nicely labeled breakout board. I prefer the ones with screw-terminals.

**My choice:** Pictured below

I don't think they usually have unique names so you just have to browse the picture to find the features you like. I went with one that fits right on top of the Pi to save space and has well-labeled terminals and just a little extra room to solder some connectors to – made by *CZH-Labs*. See *figure 21.6*

*Figure 21.6: GPIO header breakout board by CZH-Labs*

# Camera

This is another matter of preference. Some people are much more sticklers for crisp, hi-res pictures than I am. I just want to be able to tell if I'm looking at my dog or a raccoon. This is technically optional and can be added at any time. Still, I think you'll appreciate being able to see what your robot sees and get into some of the computer vision stuff we did in *Chapter 19, Real Vision with Cameras*.

**My choice:** Logitech C270 USB webcam

It simply works for all of my purposes and is inexpensive.

# Voltmeter

Low voltage is not good for your computer so it's good to be able to keep an eye on it without using your multimeter. The little voltmeters in *figure 21.7* cost just a couple of dollars each on *Amazon*. They don't take a lot of power, but I added the little button switch to turn it off when I'm not looking at it because I'd rather have a precious few minutes more of operating time.

*Figure 21.7: An LED voltmeter/display*

Another good option is to use an analog-to-digital converter to read the voltage into the computer. Published as a ROS message (`sensor_messages::BatteryState`), you could write a node to monitor the battery level and signal you or send the robot to its charging station when the battery is low.

## Miscellaneous materials

The above covers the major components, but we'll still need a few things to stick it all together.

- **Wires** – I mostly used jumper wires and stripped and soldered them as needed for all the sensor connections that aren't USB. For power from the battery to the motors and *5* volt buck converter, I used stranded *18* gauge wire since the jumper wires are just too small and could melt or even catch on fire.

- **Terminal strips** – Something to make a *5* volt, *12* volt, and ground rails to attach things to easily. Get something with covered terminals to help prevent accidental short circuits.

- **Nylon screws and standoffs** – An assortment of *2.5* and *3* mm. I drill a small pilot hole in the wood, run in a metal *2.5* or *3* mm screw, then remove it and screw a nylon screw or standoff right into the wooden chassis. Very handy.

- **A switch or two** – Optional but handier than unplugging the computer, etc.

# Assembling the robot platform

Once you've acquired all the parts and materials, you can assemble the robot platform. This section may take a little adaptation and ingenuity of your own, since you may have chosen different components than I have. You may also simply prefer to make changes – such as hiding components on the bottom or under a cover. It's all up to you. The general steps for assembly are:

- Prepare the computer
- Prepare the wheel modules
- Plan the layout
- Prepare the chassis
- Mount the wheel modules and caster
- Mount the motor driver, terminal strips, and computer power supply
- Prepare the GPIO Breakout Board
- Mount the computer, GPIO breakout board, and IMU
- Complete wiring and mount battery
- Mount LIDAR and camera

## 1. Prepare the computer

You likely took care of this back in *Chapter 1, Choosing and Setting up a Robot Computer.* Make sure your computer has an appropriate Linux version, and ROS Installed. Optionally, an IDE like *Codeblocks* as well as *OpenCV* if you plan to do any computer vision work. If you are using the recommended Raspberry Pi, the Ubiquity Robotics from *Chapter 9, Coordinating the Parts* is an excellent time-saver as ROS and OpenCV are already installed.

## 2. Prepare the wheel modules

In this step, assemble the motors, gearboxes, and wheels if they aren't already together. Same with your wheel encoders. Then make some sort of connector with two leads for the motor and however many you need for the encoder – probably *3* or *4*. I used a small piece of a prototyping PCB board and some screw terminals I had. My wheel modules need *5* connections, total. Check out the diagram and picture in *figure 21.8* below.

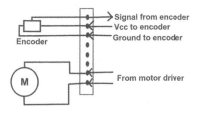

*Figure 21.8: Wheel module connector*

## 3. Plan the layout

Before you start mounting anything, take the time to place everything where you think you want it to go. Consider the fact that you'll need access to things for connectors and electrical test-points as you'll inevitably have troubleshooting to do from time to time. You might not have a monitor on the robot (although that can be a fun and convenient touch), but there will likely be occasions it's just easier to plug a monitor in rather than work over SSH or VNC. Leave room for the video, power, and USB plugs on the computer. Mark any holes or notches you want to cut to route wires. Also, any holes for mounting things – which I often trace with a pencil while the component is lying on the surface. See *figure 21.9* below.

*Figure 21.9: Marking the base for drilling*

**What you read in the rest of this section may influence where you decide to mount things, so read the rest of these steps before you start drilling in *step 4*.**

## 4. Prepare the chassis

Now actually cut or drill the holes you need – especially any large ones like the one I have in the center. Smaller holes later for screws are less of a big deal, but you don't want to put the stress of drilling a big hole or sawing on the chassis once the wheel modules are mounted.

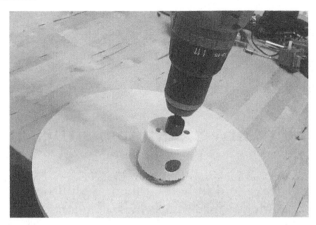

*Figure 21.10: Drilling and cutting before mounting the wheel modules*

# Mount the wheel modules and caster

The closer your main wheels are to the center-line, the less you have to worry about hitting things and getting stuck when you turn. The cost of this, however, is you'll have to be more careful about placing things because the robot will easily pop a wheelie. Add some heavier things forward of the wheel-axis to prevent this – the battery, for example.

How to mount will depend on what you've selected. The company that sold you your wheel module may have a mount or bracket available. You have something you have to make your bracket or clamps. Whatever the case, do your best to make sure the wheels are as parallel and aiming straight ahead as possible.

The Roomba wheel modules have enough flat area that I can screw them right to the chassis, but there is a curved spot, so I use nylon standoffs for spacers. Just make sure you don't drill through too far through the plastic and hit something important. Because the wheels are sure to take a bit of abuse, use screws that go all the way through the wood with washers and nuts like I did in *figure 21.11* below.

*Figure 21.11: A few standoffs make for a level mount for the Roomba wheel modules*

# Mount the motor driver, terminal strips, and computer power supply

Be careful if you still have to drill holes – there is stuff on the bottom-side now. Mount the items on standoffs – for 3 mm screws/standoffs, I use a 2.5 mm or 7/64" drill, the run a metal screw or 3 mm tap in the make the threads. Then even a plastic screw or standoff screws right into the wood and holds well (for parts that don't take a beating, anyway). For 2.5 mm screws and standoffs, I use a 2 mm or 3/32 drill. See *figure 21.12*

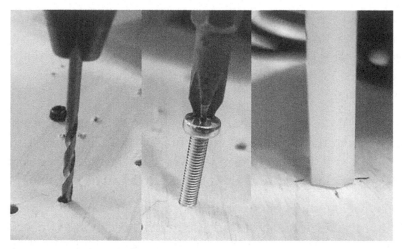

*Figure 21.12: Drilling, tapping threads, and screwing standoffs directly into plywood works well*

# Prepare the GPIO breakout board

This is optional, but I've regretted it every time I didn't. If your breakout board has a little blank prototyping area for soldering components, you can use it to make a little quick—connect section for serial and I2C devices. The I2C is especially useful because I always seem to have a reason to add or remove one, or even just test a device that has nothing to do with my robots — it's always useful to be able to plug something in without disturbing other wiring. It can also reduce the number of wires coming from the breakout board — and that's always a good thing. The image below (*figure 21.13*) shows my minimal serial (with IMU plugged in) and I2C buses and how I wired them.

*Figure 21.13: An I2C Bus to make for easy adding and removing of I2C devices*

# Mount the computer, GPIO breakout board, and IMU

In the past, I've made a mistake during the layout of leaving room for a device and its plug, but not considering that I need a little extra room actually to plug and unplug them. Don't do that.

Also remember that the computer needs to be either kind of open for airflow or you have to provide some airflow with a fan. Finally, put the IMU as far as possible from the motors, battery, and wiring - especially if you plan to use the magnetometer.

# Complete wiring and mount battery

Refer back to *Chapter 7, Adding the Computer to Control your Robot* for a complete diagram of how I wired my version of the robot. The pin numbers from *Chapter 7* match every example in this book, starting with that chapter, as well as the complete example robot code package I'm using for this chapter. Avoid using the same-colored wire for everything or troubleshooting will be a confusing nightmare.

A few extra tips are illustrated in *figure 21.14* below:

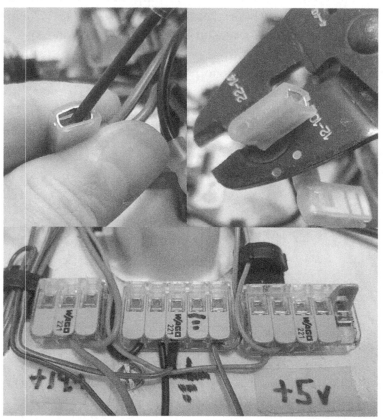

**Figure 21.14:** *Loosening and crimping a spade connector to make the battery connection (top left and top right). Lever nuts used as a terminal strip.*

In the top photos, I connect to the battery with regular spade connectors I pry open just a little bit – they fit snugly and make a good connection for such a small robot. Don't use pliers to crimp them – use proper wire crimpers. In the bottom photo, I've found the lever nuts by wago work well in place of terminal strips with screws. Just lift the lever, insert the wire, and flip the lever back down.

## Mount LIDAR and camera

I'm going to refer to you back to *Chapter 18, LIDAR Devices and Data* for some LIDAR general mounting considerations. I used nylon standoffs and a sturdy scrap of plastic cut from an old project lid to make an elevated platform to ensure the LIDAR turret was the tallest thing on the robot. This same piece of plastic served as an easy place for me to mount my camera (after some disassembly of the supplied mounting-clip). See *figure 21.15* below.

**Figure 21.15:** *The LIDAR and camera mount*

# Part 1 - Conclusion

If we've done everything correctly, we now have a completed machine waiting for some code to give it something to do and I'm sure you're eager to get it moving. I encourage you to slow down for a moment and double and triple-check your wiring. Get some rest if you aren't fresh – I can't tell you how many poor components have gone to heaven because I kept working while tired and made a silly mistake.

If the wiring is looking messy and hard to follow, try to neaten it up and keep wires short. Strap them together in neat little bundles that make sense (all the wires to one wheel module together, same with the other, etc.). Secure the bundles to the base to keep them out of the way. *Figure 21.16* below omits just the wires going to my I2C and Serial connectors on the breakout board.

*Figure 21.16:* *My nearly-complete robot I used to test all of the code in our lessons*

If at any time something doesn't work in the next section, go back through that circuit. If the circuits are looking complex and you're feeling overwhelmed, try to look at one thing at a time and ignore the rest like I sometimes have had to ignore my kids to get this book written.

- *What is suppose to make the thing go?*
- *Is that thing connected to the right place?*
- *Is the right signal coming from that place?*
- *Is that device getting the right signal and power?*
- *Is the GPIO pin doing the right thing?*
- *Is the pin number correct in the code?* You get the idea.

You just built a marvelous machine and learning tool with dozens of wires, components, and connections, and there will be thousands of lines of code – it would be almost bizarre if there were no errors or setbacks. *It's ok — you can fix it.*

*Does nothing work?* Don't worry about the IMU if you're working on the right wheel. Just fix one thing. Then you can fix another. Then another if need be. *That's how you'll get it all done.*

With that, it's time to bring this creature to life. Take a break, charge the battery, and come on back for `Part 2 - Programming Your Robot`.

# Part 2 - Programming your robot

You've come so far, and now it's time to start breathing life into your robot. Honestly, you've probably done much of this or at least studied most of it in previous chapters, so this is a guide on coordinating all the many programs. First, we'll get all the software you wrote or downloaded in order and make sure each step is working, and then we'll streamline launching the many parts together. Then we'll make and save a map, and make sure you can fire up your trusty robotic companion with a single command – with the new map loaded and ready to go. Finally, we'll talk about what comes next.

## Programming – General overview

Much like you can customize your build, you can customize your software in many ways. Fortunately, ROS makes it easy to write or download a new node and try it without having to delete the existing ones. We're going to get you running a basic setup — How far you go from there is up to you. I assume that you have set your computer up with Linux and ROS at a minimum, and are comfortable with SSH. When using a Raspberry Pi, I personally still write my code for ROS packages in the Codeblocks IDE but I just work with plain files instead of Codeblocks projects. They get compiled with catkin, so Codeblocks is just for editing and saving - I just like the tabs and autocomplete.

To start, you might want to clone the code repository that I use with the exact robot built in Part 1 of this chapter. It may be a helpful reference if you get stuck either with a single program or with the whole project not working well together. If you just want it to refer to (recommended), just clone it wherever it will be handy:

```
git clone https://github.com/lbrombach/practical_robot.git
```

If you want to try to run your robot with this package, clone it into your `catkin src` folder and compile it with `catkin_make`:

```
cd ~/catkin_ws/src
```

```
git clone https://github.com/lbrombach/practical_robot.git
```

```
cd ..
```

```
catkin_make
```

If you get errors about duplicate names, it's because you cannot have two packages or nodes with the same names. I'm afraid you'll have to rename or temporarily move your packages out of the catkin workspace.

Running my code repository will still require you to run through many of the programs as if you'd written them yourself because of specific things like wheel base and how many ticks per meter the encoders report and setting the `min` and `max` PWM values for your motors and batteries, etc. It's really meant to help you get unstuck as you follow the lessons in the book but it is nice that you can experiment and try things, and if it gets hopelessly messed up, you can delete the whole folder a clone it again.

# Programming your robot – Detailed steps

I'm going to proceed as if you're building from scratch rather than just cloning the `practical_robot` repository. I will reference packages and nodes by the names in the repository, but I suggest that you change them just a little so you have the option of cloning the repository into your catkin workspace later. If you already cloned it into your `catkin_ws`, you won't have a choice. Choose names very similar, so you don't have a hard time keeping associating yours with mine.

The general steps to program your robot:

1. Create a project folder
2. Get sensors publishing data
    2.1. Create a package for sensor data publishers
    2.2. Add wheel encoder publisher
    2.3. Add IMU data publisher
    2.4. Install LIDAR driver
    2.5. Install camera image publisher
3. Get platform driving under remote control
    3.1. Create a package for navigation and motion nodes
    3.2. Add the motor driver controller
    3.3. Check RQT graph
    3.4. Manual drive launch file
4. Get robot tracking and publishing position
    4.1. Create a package for localization
    4.2. Add odometry publisher
    4.3. Manual pose and goal publisher

5. Get robot driving to waypoints (without obstacle avoidance)
   - 5.1. Add drive controller
   - 5.2. Manual waypoint launch file
6. Map the robot's environment
   - 6.1. Update manual drive launch file
   - 6.2. Generate and save your map
7. Get saved map loading in launch files
8. Get robot autonomously navigating the mapped environment
   - 8.1. Add path planner
   - 8.2. Full launch file

## 1. Create a project folder

This is a folder in the `catkin_ws/src` directory to organize the three ROS packages we are going to make. Refer back to *Chapter 9, Coordinating the Parts* for a refresher on how the file structure works. This is just a folder, not a package yet, so we don't need a catkin command yet.

```
cd ~/catkin_ws/src
```

```
mkdir practical_robot
```

## 2. Get sensors publishing data

The robot needs information about itself and the rest of the world before it can do anything. Let's set up our sensors first. *It's ok* if you don't have them all yet. The minimum we need is the encoders data publisher – you can come back to finish the others later.

### 2.1 Create a package for sensor data publishers

This package is to organize the nodes (programs) you wrote for any sensor data. This is not for nodes you download, as those you will download to the root `catkin_ws/src` folder. Create the package from the new `practical_robot` folder you just created.

```
cd ~/catkin_ws/src/practical_robot
```

```
catkin_create_pkg practical_sensors roscpp std_msgs sensor_msgs
```

This will create the new folder `practical_sensors`, as well as everything else that gets created with a ROS package. At this time, I will refer you back to *Chapter 9* for details on setting up the `CMakeLists.txt` – you will need to enable *C++* 11 compile options and include the directory where your

PIGPIOD library file (`libpigpiod_if2.so`) is located. Don't forget, and you have an example that should closely match what you need.

## 2.2 Wheel encoder publisher

In your `practical_sensors` (or whatever you named it) package `src` folder, create the `.cpp` file and write your wheel encoder publisher node (as in *Chapter 14, Wheel Encoders for Odometry*). For example, the full file path of mine is:

`~/catkin_ws/src/practical_robot/practical_sensors/src/tick_publisher.cpp`

Save it and update the `CMakeLists.txt` file for the `practical_sensors` package so the catkin can find and compile your node. Again, refer to *Chapter 9, Coordinating the Parts* and the download for more direction.

When done, navigate to your root `catkin_ws` folder and compile to make sure everything is okay.

`cd ~/catkin_ws`

`catkin_make`

Hopefully, everything compiles just fine. If not, do your programmer thing and look at the errors and try to figure it out. Googling errors can be helpful, and probably most often traceable back to something missing or incorrect in the `CmakeLists.txt`.

Once you get a successful compilation, test your wheel encoder node. You'll need four terminal windows. Issue one of these commands in each window (don't forget to substitute the names you used):

`roscore`

`rosrun practical_sensors tick_publisher`

`rostopic echo leftWheel`

`rostopic echo rightWheel`

If you recall from *Chapter 9, Coordinating the Parts,* roscore starts the ROS master, and the second line starts the `tick_publisher` node that should be publishing a count of how many ticks each wheel accumulates. It won't go both up and down yet, though, because it monitors the motor driver direction pins for that and those are not powered yet. Spin the wheels a little by hand to see the numbers climb. If you see no changes or you got a message that the topic is not yet published, use *Ctrl + C* or *Ctrl + Z* to stop and use `rostopic list` to see a list of available topics. Spelling mistakes are my biggest nemesis. Make sure everything is working on each step before moving on.

### 2.3 IMU data publisher

For this step, make sure you have the appropriate driver for your IMU. If you have the BN0055 or any other IMU you are going to download the driver package for, go to the `catkin_ws/src` folder to clone it. If you wrote or will write your own as we did in *Chapter 16, IMUs: Accelerometers, Gyroscopes, and Magnetometers* the `.cpp` file goes in the same `practical_sensors/src` folder that `tick_publisher.cpp` does. Update the `CmakeLists` and compile with `catkin_make` again. When everything compiles ok, test your IMU node by running it with `rosrun`, and use `rostopic echo imu` to view the data.

### 2.4 Install LIDAR driver

Install the appropriate drivers for your laser scanner if you haven't already. With `roscore` running, run your laser scanner and view the scan to make sure all is good to go. Refer to *Chapter 18, LIDAR Devices and Data* for more information.

### 2.5 Install camera image publisher

Refer to *Chapter 19, Real Vision with Cameras* for instructions on installing and testing the `usb_cam` node.

## 3. Get the platform driving under remote control

With at least wheel encoder data, we can now add a motor control node that accepts velocity commands and turns them into PWM signals for the motor drivers and drive the robot remotely.

### 3.1 Create a package for navigation and motion nodes

This package is to organize the nodes (programs) you write for moving the robot, so I include the path planner, the drive controller, and the motor controller in it. Create this package in the `practical_robot` folder:

```
cd ~/catkin_ws/src/practical_robot


#below is a single command
catkin_create_pkg   practical_nav   roscpp   std_msgs   sensor_msgs
geometry_msgs tf
```

Get your `CMakeLists.txt` ready – Like the `practical_sensors` `CmakeLists.txt`, you still need to enable `c++11` compile options and include the directory where your PIGPIOD library file (`libpigpiod_if2.so`) is located.

## 3.2 Motor driver controller

Your motor driver `.cpp` file goes in the newly created `pratical_nav/src` folder. Refer back to *Chapter 12, Autonomous Motion,* and perhaps back as far as *Chapter 4, Types of Robot Motors and Motor Control* them for more motor control info. The motor drive controller in the example download (called `practical_nav/src/simple_diff_drive.cpp`) has a couple of additions I left out to keep the *Chapter 12* tutorial simple. Still, you might like to explore them to enhance performance a bit without making the leap to a full PID controller just yet. Add your node to the `practical_nav` `Cmakelists.txt` and run `catkin_make` to compile your node. Test it with three windows, one command per window:

`roscore`

`rosrun practical_sensors tick_publisher`

`rosrun practical_nav simple_diff_drive`

`rosrun rqt_robot_steering rqt_robot_steering`

Assuming your `tick_publisher` is working correctly, you should be able to command your robot back and forth, as well as to turn. (You may have to type the topic your `simple_diff_drive` node is listening to – probably `cmd_vel` – in the topic window).

If the robot responds but not as expected, you may need to reverse the motor wires at the motor driver to reverse one or both wheels or otherwise confirm the hardware is working. Maybe there is an error in your code's logic. You'll have to find it.

If nothing happens at all, it still might be one of the above problems, but the first thing to check is topic names. Actually – you can skip to *step 3.2* for a great way to check topic names.

## 3.2 Check rqt graph

Whether you have trouble above or not, now is a perfect time to get to know `rqt_graph` – which is a node in the package `rqt_graph`. What rqt graph does is shows you all of the running nodes and the topics they publish and subscribe to, as well as the connections, in a visual graph. Launch rqt graph with the following command:

`rosrun rqt_graph rqt_graph`

A window should pop up after a moment that looks something like *figure 21.17 below*:

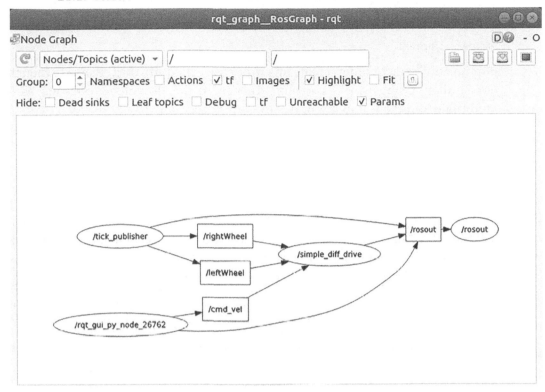

**Figure 21.17:** *The rqt_graph node output*

The ovals have the names of nodes that are running, and the rectangles are message topics. You can see that `tick_publisher` publishes `rightWheel` and `leftWheel`, which `simple_diff_drive` subscribes to. If one node misspelled one of those topics, you would see the misspelled topic as well but it wouldn't be connected to anything. `rqt_gui_py_node` is just how `rqt_robot_steering` and all of the `rqt_*` tools show up.

The view may change dramatically with some of the checkbox options – I encourage you to mess around with them and see the differences. Being able to de-clutter as necessary is handy when this graph inevitably gets very busy.

## 3.3 Manual drive launch file

The next thing I want to do is make your life easier – because opening so many windows and starting all those nodes by hand is a time-consuming drag, and it's only going to get worse. Much worse.

Navigate to your practical_nav package root folder and create a new folder called launch (*don't change this one –name it* launch).

```
cd ~/catkin_ws/src/practical_robot/practical_nav
mkdir launch
```

In the new launch folder, create an empty file called minimal_manual.launch or similar. Using minimal_manual.launch in the download package as a template add the following nodes to your launch file:

- Your encoder tick publisher

- Your motor driver controller

- RQT robot steering

When looking at the example, don't forget that lines with !-- are comments, so the whole launch file is just three lines plus the <launch> and </launch> that denote the beginning and end of the file. Refer back to *Chapter 10, Maps for Robot Navigation* for more launch file information.

When it's done, you can launch all three nodes (plus roscore if it's not already running) at once with:

```
roslaunch practical_nav minimal_manual.launch
```

*Pretty handy, right?* You may also wish to start your usb_cam and rqt_image_view nodes with the launch file – now you can chase your dog from the other room!

4. **Get robot tracking and publishing position**

I admit that it's plenty of fun to drive my robots remotely, but what we are really after is getting it to drive to places by itself, right? Before that can happen, our robot has to be able to keep track of where it is. Let's add some basics to do just that.

### 4.1 Create a package for localization

This package is to organize the nodes (programs) you write for keeping track of localizing the robot. It depends on a few more packages, so the create_ command is longer, but it's the same idea as creating the previous two packages:

```
cd ~/catkin_ws/src/practical_robot
```

```
#below is a single command
```

```
catkin_create_pkg practical_localization roscpp std_msgs tf tf2_
ros geometry_msgs sensor_msgs nav_msgs
```

Get your `CMakeLists.txt` ready as before – I don't think this package requires the PIGPIOD library, but it can't hurt to have the path there in case you add a node later that does.

### 4.2 Add odometry publisher

Add the `.cpp` file of your odometry publisher of choice to the `src` folder in the newly created package. The example you downloaded has two – a simpler odometry only node, and a node that accepts IMU messages with heading data to help with the orientation as we discussed in *Chapter 20, Sensor Fusion*. Update the localization package's `CmakeLists.txt` and compile.

### 4.3 Manual pose and goal publisher

As we discussed in *Chapter 11, Robot Tracking and Localization*, we usually want some means of setting the initial pose of our robot without changing code or correcting its pose during operation. Referring to *Chapter 11*, add a `.cpp` file to the new package that can issue manual pose estimates – I use the same node to issue goal messages. I publish both messages in the easy to read method we've been using in this book (Euler angles instead of quaternions) and as full-quaternion messages to match standard practice (and Rviz clicks that serve the same purpose). Use the example called `manual_pose_and_goal_pub.cpp` as a guide or simply copy the code if you wish. Update the localization package's `CmakeLists.txt` and compile.

Test both nodes before continuing by using `rostopic echo` and monitoring the outputs. Depending on how you wrote your odometry publisher, it may not start publishing until it receives an initial pose message.

## 5. Get robot driving to waypoints (without obstacle avoidance)

Once you have the kinks worked out with your motor driver controller and odometry nodes (your robot should behave acceptably when given `cmd_vel` messages and reports acceptable odometry data), you can give it the ability to drive straight from where it is to a point specified in a waypoint message. There will be no obstacle avoidance but, later on, our path planner will publish these waypoints automatically. For now, they will be published by the manual publisher we just added or the `rviz_click_to_2d.cpp` node I snuck into the example download.

## 5.1 Add drive controller

Add your drive controller .cpp file to the practical_nav/src folder, add it to your CmakeLists.xtx file and compile it with catkin_make. This is the second program we wrote in *Chapter 12, Autonomous Motion* that I called simple_drive_controller (not to be confused with simple_diff_drive). Remember: simple_diff_drive.cpp is a motor controller that accepts cmd_vel messages and outputs PWM signals for the motors. The simple_drive_controller accepts desired locations (waypoints) and outputs the cmd_vel message.

When it compiles and is working correctly, make a new launch file in the next step to test everything.

## 5.2 Manual waypoint launch file

**If you look at the launch file in the downloads for reference, you'll see a lot of extra lines in my basic_manual_waypoint.launch file – ignore them for now and just worry about the entries I talk about here. The rest is optional stuff you may or may not want to add later, but no need to clutter your file or desktop just yet**

In your practical_nav/src folder, create another launch file named something like basic_manual_waypoint.launch. Start by copying and pasting everything that's in the minimal_manual.launch, then adding lines to launch the following nodes:

- Your IMU publisher node
- Your odometry publisher
- manual_pose_and_goal_pub
- simple_drive_controller

Before you try your new launch file, we have to adjust the simple_drive_controller line – we have to remap the topic name. The node we wrote in *Chapter 12, Autonomous Motion* listens to the topic waypoint_2d, but this is the topic published by the path_planner. For this purpose, we want to listen directly to the topic that path_planner usually listens to – which is goal_2d.

While the rest of the node-launch entries look like this:

```
<node pkg="pkg_name" type="node_name" name="node name" />
```

The entire entry to launch your drive controller should look like this:

```
<node pkg="pkg_name" type="node_name" name="node name">
```

```
    <remap from="waypoint_2d" to="goal_2d" />
```

```
</node>
```

You may also want to comment out or delete the entry for `rqt_robot_ steering`, since two nodes that publish the `cmd_vel` message may interfere with each other and confuse the motor controller. When you're done, run the launch file with:

```
roslaunch practical_nav basic_manual_waypoint.launch
```

If all goes according to plan, you should be able to publish a goal with `manual_ pose_and_goal_pub` node. When the drive controller receives it, the robot should turn towards it and drive it. Refer back to *Chapter 10, Maps for Robot Navigation* and *Chapter 11, Robot Tracking and Localization* for information about the coordinates, and *Chapter 12, Autonomous Motion* for a refresher on how both the motor controller and the drive controller work.

Getting the drive controller and motor controller to work nicely together with your specific robot platform can take some fiddling, so have some patience and try to make just one change at a time. Also, make a backup copy before you change anything so you can also go back a step without starting all over, though sometimes starting all over is just what you have to do. Take the time to get it right, though – everything depends on it.

## 6. Map the robot's environment

Once you've got the above complete, we're close to autonomy! Now let's map the area the robot will be working so the path planner has something to work with.

### 6.1 Update manual drive launch file

We want to manually drive while generating a map so we can accelerate and turn very slowly to minimize both wheel slip – the more accurate our odometry, the more accurate our map. Additionally, laser scans taken while moving can be blurred (for lack of a better word). The `gmapping` package can try to compensate, but nothing is better than minimizing that blur to begin with. Being very patient and mapping very slowly can pay off big, so we won't use our drive controller and instead will control the robot with `rqt_robot_steering`.

Either edit the `minimal_manual.launch` file or create a new file and copy the `minimal_manual.launch` contents to it to start. Reference the file `basic_ manual_steer.launch` in the downloads for this section. Ignore the sections labeled `arguments` and `map_server` - you don't need them for this. Then let's add the following to your launch file:

- `base_link` to laser static transform publisher
- The odometry transform publisher from *Chapter 11, Robot Tracking and Localization* – mine is called `tf_pub.cpp`
- Your IMU publisher
- Your LIDAR driver node. If your device defaults to a `frame_id` other than `laser`, set the parameter here. Also, remap the topic if your device driver defaults to anything other than `scan`.
- Your odometry publisher node
- Your manual pose and goal publisher

The RPLidar A1 has a different coordinate system than our robot, with it mounted as in all the photos from our build section. I had to transform it by `.1` meters in the x direction, flip it over `180` degrees (PI rads) around the y axis, and rotate it `180` around the z (yaw) axis. Since static transforms can be published with arguments x y z *roll pitch yaw* my final `base_link` to laser transform is `.1 0 0 0 3.1415 3.1415`.

The `gmapping` package will provide the map to odom transform so if you see my `map -> odom` publisher in the downloads, just ignore it or comment it out if you copied it for later use. You will need it if you run this launch file later but are not running `gmapping`.

That's it for this launch file. We are going to run `gmapping` in a separate launch file since that is so far all on its own. Add this launch file now (we covered making this in *Chapter 10, Maps for Robot Navigation*).

## 6.2 Generate and save your map

Use the launch file you just created to start the system and set the initial pose with your manual pose publisher. Make sure your odometry publisher and odometry to `base_link` transform are reporting correctly (should be the same) before launching `gmapping`. Maybe check that your laser scan (and transform) looks correct in Rviz.

Launch your `gmapping` launch file (mine is called `gmapping_only.launch`, for reference). Follow the steps we went through in *Chapter 10* to create and view the map – let me repeat the part about driving slowing. When you have mapped the area, create a folder in your `practical_nav` package called `maps` and with a command prompt IN that folder, save it with `map_server` (also covered in *Chapter 10*).

```
cd ~/catkin_ws/src/practical_robot/practical_nav

mkdir maps

cd ~/catkin_ws/src/practical_robot/practical_nav/maps

rosrun map_server map_saver -f myFirstMap
```

## 7. Get saved map loading in launch files

To start any launch file session off with a map automatically served for both the path planner and your viewing pleasure, add the argument section that I told you to ignore earlier to the launch file. These go at the top, so they are easily kept track of as launch files get cluttered. Normally when you run `map_server` from the command line, you would pass it an argument with the path to your map YAML file. In the launch file, you do that by adding:

```
<arg name="name_of_arg" default="value" />
```

This gives you the option of passing an argument via command line or letting the file run with the default. ROS also provides a handy $(find) tool so you don't have to type an absolute path – although you could. My argument entry looks like:

```
<arg name="map_file"
    default="$(find practical_nav)/maps/myFirstMap.yaml"/>
```

Now everywhere `map_file` appears in this launch file, the full path to `myFirstMap.yaml` will be entered. That allows me to run launch server with the following entry:

```
<node name="map_server" pkg="map_server"
    type="map_server" args="$(arg map_file)" />
```

## 8. Get robot autonomously navigating the mapped environment

You're almost there! Let's cross our fingers for no hiccups and get to it!

### 8.1 Add path planner

Add your path planners `.cpp` file from *Chapter 13, Autonomous Path Planning* to the `practical_nav/src` folder, then update the `CmakeLists.txt` and compile it with `catkin_make`.

### 8.2 Full launch file

Make another launch file – you can reference `basic_full.launch` in the download. It starts everything in `basic_manual_steer.launch` and adds:

- Serving the saved map

- The map to odom static transform publishers
- Costmap_2d
- Path_planner

Before anything else, let's remember to comment out the topic remap from waypoint_2d to goal_2d in the simple_drive_controller entry — It's time to let our little birds fly! Also, remove the manual_pose_and_goal_pub entry – either use the rviz_click_to_2d node or run the manual one in a different terminal window because there is going to be too much output for one window.

Gmapping won't be here to publish the map to odom transform, so add that static transform publisher now. Use 0 0 0 0 0 0 for arguments to lock the map frame and odom frames together.

We have to get costmap_2d to use the parameter file we made in *Chapter 10, Maps for Robot Navigation*. Create a folder in your practical_nav package called param and make sure your parameter.yaml file is in it (mine is called costmap_basic.yaml). Then, in the line above the costmap_2d entry, use the following rosparam entry so it looks like this:

```
<rosparam    file="$(find    practical_nav)/params/costmap_basic.yaml"
command="load" ns="/costmap_2d/costmap" />

<node pkg="costmap_2d" type="costmap_2d_node" name="costmap_2d"/>
```

Finally, add the path planner entry. Remember that path_planner looks for the topic costmap but costmap2d will publish under costmap_2d/costmap/costmap so we need to remap that topic name:

```
<node pkg="practical_nav" type="path_planner"

      name="path_planner" output="screen" >
<remap from="costmap" to="costmap_2d/costmap/costmap" />
</node>
```

# Run your autonomous robot!

Holy smokes – it's time for your first autonomous run! Follow these steps:

- Open at least two terminal windows.
- Roslaunch your basic_full launch file in one.
- Run your manual_pose_and_goal_pub node in the other.
- Set your initial pose.

- Set a goal destination.
- Smile and pat yourself on the back :)

# Some troubleshooting tips

Once again, run `rqt_graph` to look for disconnected topics – *which node has a topic misspelled or maybe failed to start for whatever reason?*

Run `roswtf` all by itself at the command line. It will run a couple of checks and tell you if more than one node is publishing a transform (you should never have more than one publisher for each transform) or if any topics aren't connected to anything. It's quick and helpful.

Slow down and look at individual nodes. Use `rosnode kill simple_diff_drive`, so the robot stays put and you can walk through every other node. *Is the odometry message correct? Does the drive controller publish an appropriate* `cmd_vel` *message for given current odometry and waypoint? Does the costmap make sense given the map topic? What is* `path_planner` *doing?* These are a lot of programs and each has to do their part – I often find it helpful to add `cout <<` statements to debug variables, then running several nodes in their windows instead of from the launch file.

Use Rviz to keep an eye on several things at once – you can see the map, laser scan, pose, and path from the planner, all in one place and at the same time. There's a lot to Rviz we didn't have room for in this book, but I have a video tutorial for you at the *youtube.com/practicalrobotics* channel.

Transforms are a big source of errors – either because they are published with the wrong values or wrong names or not at all. Use `rosrun tf view_frames` to see your transform tree, or `rosrun tf tf_echo parent_frame_name child_frame_name` to see the data for any given transform. For example, if `path_planner` is starting you at the wrong place – it gets start location data form the odom to `base_link` transform. I would run:

```
rosrun tf tf_echo odom base_link
```

Walk someone else through how everything is supposed to be working. It helps if you have someone there for real, but pretend if you have to. Try to make them understand what is supposed to be happening – every detail. I have to thank *Dr Abhilash Pandya* of *Wayne State University* for this one – he taught me that the first time I met him and I have used it a hundred times since.

Finally, take a break and come back later or even tomorrow. I don't know how often I've woken up and somehow knew exactly what the problem was.

Keep at it – This can be a game won by persistence. Like a journey of thousands of miles – Robotics is a journey of thousands of lines of code. If you fix even one at a time, you will get there.

# What next?

The great thing about our little robot is what a great platform it is to continue learning the next thing. You could choose to go over the basic programs we wrote and enhance them one at a time, or you might choose to write some new behaviors to give your robot some new usefulness. Thankfully, ROS makes it possible to do either without the risks that come with modifying *one big program*. You may even wish to embark on a whole new robot build – more confident now that you have a full-set of foundational tools at your disposal.

The direction you take is up to what you find the most exciting or relevant to you. The only thing for sure is that if you enjoy the satisfaction of learning and implementing new robotics tricks – you will never run out of new challenges. Here are just a few suggestions:

## Dynamic obstacle avoidance

Left out of our mapping chapter intentionally, this should be a nice warm-up to breaking out on your own. The way we set up `costmap_2d`, it provides only obstacle values for static objects, so your path planner will avoid walls and furniture, but not your dog or mother-in-law if they happen to be in the path. Read up in the `Costmap_2d` *Wiki* page and see if you can add the obstacle layer.

## PID controllers

You've certainly noticed how challenging (even frustrating, sometimes) it can be to get the robot to go straight with an open-loop or proportional controller motor controller. Writing a PID controller can be a satisfying challenge and is the first step towards getting your robot to drive from place to place in a continuous arc.

## A master controller that manages various routines or tasks

Using what we learned in *Chapter 8, Robot Control Strategy* (or another method, if you already have one you like), add a collection of tasks for your robot to complete.

Each task can be an object with a destination pose and an action – like drive to the dog's bowl and check if it's full or empty. Tasks can also be a collection of tasks, so the robot goes and checks a series of things.

## Implementing the map to odom transform (full localization)

For learning reasons, we kept things simple and locked our map and odom frames together and did our best with odometry – even enhancing it in *Chapter 20, Sensor Fusion*. In reality, pose estimates in odometry are going to drift away from the reality in the map frame. This means that the robots may be doing everything right but still, be closer to a wall than it thinks it is.

You can explore localization methods and packages like advanced *Monte Carlo Localization* (*wiki.ros.org/amcl*) or work on other localization methods to correctly publish the map to odom transform for a tremendous accuracy improvement. It will take a little work on your path planner and drive controller nodes to integrate this correction, but it's worth it!

## Keep an eye on facebook.com/practicalrobotics and youtube.com/practicalrobotics

With writing wrapping up, I'm excited to have time to create some video content that provides the next step in a lot of the subjects we tackled here. Whether it's a new trick, an enhancement on our basics, or answering reader's questions – You will find that content in the links above.

And please, be sure to send me questions, photos of your projects, and modifications – I can't wait to see and share them! You can message me on the *Facebook* page, and I'm also working on a forum so we can all support each other and continue to learn together. Details will be announced on the platforms above and I hope to see you there. Let's make robots happen.

# Conclusion

In this chapter, we've implemented all of the learning and experience we acquired from this book first to build, then program an autonomous robot. We used our electronics knowledge, Robot operating system, and programming skills to bring sensors and controllers together to achieve a machine that can map its environment and intelligently navigate to anywhere on that map. Now that we have a platform to continue learning, we talked about some things we can do next to keep learning and improving our robots.

# Index

## Symbols

2D LIDAR  360, 361
3D LIDAR  361
.launch files  172

## A

accelerometer
    about  326, 327
    IMU data, publishing in ROS  328
    IMU message publisher
        code  330-333, 335
    ROS sensor_msgs::IMU data
        type  328-330
    shortcomings  328
Ackerman steering
    about  53
    versus differential drive  52
actuator  130
advanced OpenCV  408, 409
alternating current (AC) motors
    versus direct current (DC) motors  73
Ampere (Amps)  21
Analog to Digital Converter (ADC)  26, 97
analog voltages
    creating, with PWM  81, 82
angle conventions  178-180
A* node
    find_path() function  294, 296-301

A* path planning
    about  267, 268
    steps  271, 272
    walk through  272-278
    working  268-270
aperture  391
A* program
    helper function  279-282, 284-289, 291,
        292, 294
    writing, as ROS node  279
Arduinos  118

## B

bang bang controller  137
base_link frame  194
beacon-based localization systems  235
beacon systems
    working  344, 345
BGR image OpenCV
    RGB image ROS, converting
        with cv-bridge  388
binary signals
    about  94
    communication summary  97
    from analog sensors  96, 97
    serial communication primer  97
    switches, debouncing  95, 96
    UART serial  98
    wheel encoders  96

Bits Per Second (BPS)  98
bitwise_and() function
    about  401-403
    arguments  403
block  391
blur() function  394
Bosch BN0055
    data, providing  413
    hardware, integrating  415
    odometry node, integrating  416
    orientation sensor  412, 413
    ROS publisher, integrating  415
Bosch BN0055, odometry node
    IMU heading, saving  419
    IMU message, subscribing to  416
    odometry calculation
        function, heading applying  420
    offset information, saving  418
    orientation, verifying  417
    quaternions, converting
        to Euler angles  418
brushed DC motors  73
brushless DC motors (BLDC)  76
brush-type DC motors  73, 74

**C**

Canny() function
    about  395
    threshold method  396
channels  376
closed-loop controller  133, 134
code blocks
    installing, for Raspberry Pi  15, 16
color
    filtering by  403-407
commercial robotics industry  147, 148
commutator  74
computer
    basic requirements  122
    GPIO pins, wiring to robot  124, 125
    mounting  123
    power running  123
control loop  130

control loop, fundamental
    about  130, 132, 133
    affect  131, 132
    observe and compare  130, 132
    react  130, 132
costmap_2d package
    about  264, 266, 267
    map layer, using  265
costmaps  264
cloud-based image recognition  409
covariance  425
covariance matrix
    about  423-425
    in ROS message  425, 426
C++ programs
    used, for accessing
        Raspberry Pi GPIO  35
cv-bridge
    used, for converting RGB image ROS
        to BGR image OpenCV  388
cvtColor() function  393, 403-407

**D**

dead reckoning  216, 224, 225
differential drive
    about  52
    versus Ackerman steering  52
Digispark  119
direct current (DC) motors
    versus alternating
        current (AC) motors  73
distance conventions  178-180
double pole, double throw (DPDT)  78
drive controller
    about  250
    simple_drive_controller code  250-255,
        257, 258

**E**

encoder tick publisher
    about  307, 308
    code  309-314
Euler angles convention  179

## F

fiducials 232, 233
full desktop Ubuntu
    installing, on laptop/desktop 10
Future Technology Devices International
        (FTDI) 117, 118

## G

Gauss 338
GaussianBlur() function 394
Gazebo 358
General Purpose
        Input/Output (GPIO) 2, 19
Global Navigation Satellite System (GNSS)
    about 234, 235
    accuracy 346
    basics 345
    data 348
    data, publishing in ROS 351
    limitations 347, 348
    Real Time Kinematics (RTK) 347
Global Positioning System (GPS)
    about 234, 235
    accuracy 346
    basics 345
    data 348
    data, publishing in ROS 351
    limitations 347, 348
    Real Time Kinematics (RTK) 347
Gmapping
    about 201
    map, creating 205
    obtaining 202
    parameters, in launch files 202-204
    running 202-204
Gmapping 101 201, 202
GPIO event callback functions 43-46
GPIO pins
    about 18, 19
    as inputs 33, 34
Graphics Processing Unit (GPU) 2

gyroscope
    about 335
    data, adding to IMU node 336, 337
    shortcomings 336

## H

hall effect encoders 305
HC-SR04
    about 316
    overview 316
    wiring 316, 317
HC-SR04 ultrasonic range sensor
    basics 316
heading angle
    angle_increment 365
    angle_max 365
    angle_min 365
heading conventions 178-180
hello_blink, GPIO project 38-41
hello_button
    digital input, to control
        digital output 42, 43
HoughLinesP() function 396-400
hue 404

## I

I2C communication primer 104, 105
I2C devices
    setting up, with Raspberry Pi 105, 106
    usage 104
    using, with Raspberry Pi 105, 106
I2C program
    example 106-110
    testing 106-110
image
    about 376
    attributes 377
    edges, to numerical lines 396-400
    OpenCV, testing in ROS 380, 381
    operations, performing on 389
    pixel coordinates 377, 378

publishing, in ROS  382
ROS Kinetic  379
ROS Melodic  379, 380
software, installing/checking  379
subscribing, in node  385
types  377
image copies
    color format, converting  393
    edge detection  395
    image, blurring  394
    lighting  393
    OpenCV operations  393
    working on  392
image, in node
    image message
        subscriber, coding  387, 388
    ROS vision package, creating  386
image, in ROS
    camera output, testing  384, 385
    usb_cam_node, installing  383
    usb_cam_node, running  383, 384
image masking  401-403
image processing software
    aperture  391
    basics  391
    block  391
    kernel  391
    OpenCV  381, 382
    ROS  381, 382
Inertial Measurement Unit (IMU)
    about  122, 325
    mounting  341
input data, types
    about  26
    Analog input  26
    breadboards  27, 28
    Digital input  26
    electronics hardware  27
    GPIO pins, as outputs  31, 32
    I2C inputs  26
    Serial  26

switches  29, 30
two pin numbering systems  32
inRange() function  403-407
Integrated Development
        Environment (IDE)
    about  5
    installing  14
    setting up  14

**J**

Jetson Nano  3

**K**

Kalman filter  421-423
kernel  391

**L**

large pre-built robots  53, 54
laser frame  194
laser range finding (LIDAR)
    basics  358
    data  364-366
    limitations  359
    mounting considerations  366, 367
    selection, considering  363
    types  359
    unit, running  367
    unit, setting up  367
    unit, testing  367
LaserScan message
    about  364
    visualizing  370-372
laser scanner based localization  233, 234
latitude/longitude (lat/long)
    about  348
    data representation  350, 351
LIDAR selection
    characteristics  363
linear function  139
live map
    visualizing  205, 206

logic level converters 116, 117
logic shifters 117
Long Term Support (LTS) 10
Lubuntu
   about 9
   installing, on Raspberry Pi 11-13

## M

magnetometer (mag)
   about 338, 339
   data, adding 339-341
   shortcomings 338
map
   saving 206, 207
   using 206
map frame 194
map layer, costmap_2d package
   inflation layer 265
   obstacle map layer 265
   static map layer 265
mapping
   with Gmapping 201
master controller
   about 128
   designing 135-137
medianBlur() function 394
messages 153-157, 159
modified image back
   converting, to RGB 390
motor controllers
   about 84, 90, 91, 238, 239
   differential drive motor controller
      code 241, 243-245, 247, 248, 250
   differential drive motor controller
      code outline 240
   simple_diff_drive motor controller
      code 239
   with L298N dual H-Bridge
      motor driver 86-89
motor drivers
   about 77, 84, 85
   on/off control 77, 78

motor types
   about 72, 73
   alternating current (AC) motors, versus
      direct current (DC) motors 73
   brushless DC motors (BLDC) 76
   brush-type DC motors 73, 74
   servos 74, 75
   stepper motors 75, 76
multimeter 23

## N

National Maritime Electronics
      Association (NMEA) 349
NMEA data strings 348, 349
nmea_navsat_driver package
   about 351
   installing 352, 353
nmea_serial_driver node
   running, with parameters 354, 355
node
   image, subscribing in 385
nodes 146, 153-157, 159
nodes, nmea_navsat_driver
   nmea_serial_driver 352
   nmea_topic_driver 352
   nmea_topic_serial_reader 351
non-image data
   publishing 389

## O

obstacle inflation
   about 263, 264
   costmaps 264
occupancy grid maps (OGMs)
   about 182-184
   building, with sensor data 184, 185, 187
occupancy grid maps (OGMs), with
      sensor data
   free cells, marking 190
   map, publishing
      as ROS message 191-193

map, updating  190, 191
occupied cells, marking  187-190
odometry
about  216
distance calculated, adding
    to position estimate  223, 224
distance traveled, calculating  223
distance traveled, calculating
    for robot  221
distance traveled, calculating
    for wheel  220
heading angle theta, change adding  222
heading angle theta, change
    calculating  222
improving  414
odometry data
publishing, in ROS  226, 227
odometry transform publisher  229-231
Ohms  21
on/off controller  137
OpenCV
testing, in ROS  380, 381
open-loop controller  133, 134
operating system
installing  9, 10
Raspbian  8
selecting  7
setting up  9, 10
Ubuntu  8, 9
Optical Character Recognition (OCR)  408
optical encoders  304
output data, types
about  24
Analog output  25
Asynchronous Serial Communication  25
Digital output  25
I2C inputs  25

path planning
challenges  262
methods  262, 263
PIGPIO
Code::Blocks, linking to  37
installing  35, 36
PIGPIO library
installing  36, 37
setting up  36, 37
PIGPIO programs
running  38
power supplies
5 volt supplies  114, 115
about  114
adjusting  115
pre-built robots
cons  55
pros  55
priority array  136
process controller
bang bang controller  137
designing  137
designing, to accept error  142
minimum output, setting  143
proportional controller
    (P controller)  138-141
programmers 101
electronics  19
programs  351
proportional controller
    (P controller)  138-141, 143
proportional integral derivative (PID)  143
publishers  153-157, 159
Pulse Width Modulation (PWM)
about  25, 75, 81
as control signal  83
using, to create analog voltages  81, 82

## P

packages  153-157, 159
Parallel  22

## R

Raspberry Pi
about  1

code blocks, installing for 15, 16
difference 2
for robot controller 2, 3
Lubuntu, installing on 11-13
setting up 99
Raspberry Pi 2B 5, 6
Raspberry Pi 3B 6
Raspberry Pi 3B+ 6, 7
Raspberry Pi 4 7
Raspberry Pi GPIO
accessing, with C++ programs 35
Raspberry Pi models
purpose 3, 4
Raspberry Pi 2B 5, 6
Raspberry Pi 3B 6
Raspberry Pi 3B+ 6, 7
Raspberry Pi 4 7
Raspberry Pi Zero 5
Raspberry Pi Zero W 5
Raspberry Pi Zero 5
Raspberry Pi Zero W 5
Raspbian 8
real robotics
learning 3
Real Time Kinematics (RTK) 235, 346
Red, Green, and Blue (RGB) 376
relay modules 115, 116
remote-controlled cars
re-purposing 59
remote-controlled cars/trucks
cons 68
hacking 67, 68
pros 68
result image
publishing 390
RGB image ROS
converting, to BGR image OpenCV
with cv-bridge 388
robot
tracking and localization 231, 232
robot, building tips
about 56
batteries 57

building materials 56, 57
drive trains 57
parts sources 58, 59
robot control
implementing 128, 129
robot control software
versus robot operating system (ROS) 147
robot operating system (ROS)
about 146
image, publishing in 382
kinetic installation, on
Raspberry Pi 3B 149-152
melodic installation, on
laptop/desktop 149
odometry data, publishing in 226, 227
OpenCV, testing in 380, 381
overview 152, 153
setup 148, 149
tips 160
transforms, using in 193-196
versus robot control software 147
robot platforms
about 53
assembling 443, 444
battery and charger 437
building 433
camera 441
caster wheel 436
chassis/base 438
computer, mounting 447
computer power supply, mounting 446
computers 438
computer voltage converter 440
conclusion 449, 450
GPIO breakout board, mounting 447
GPIO breakout board, preparing 447
GPIO header breakout board 440
IMU 439
IMU, mounting 447
large pre-built robots 53, 54
LIDAR and camera, mounting 448
LIDAR sensor 439
miscellaneous materials 442

motor driver 436
motor driver, mounting 446
overview 433, 434
small pre-built robots 54, 55
terminal strips, mounting 446
voltmeter 441, 442
wheel encoders 439
wheel modules and caster, mounting 445
wheel/motor modules 435
wiring and mount battery 447, 448
robot_pose_ekf node
about 426
installing 426
running 427, 428
robot position
creating 212, 213, 214
Euler angles, converting
to quaternions 214, 215
quaternions, converting
to Euler angles 215, 216
updating 232
robot programming
about 451
autonomous robot, running 464
dynamic obstacle, avoiding 466
enhancing 466
map, implementing
to odometry transform 467
master controllers 466
overview 451
PID controllers 466
practicalrobotics 467
steps, implementing 452-464
troubleshooting tips 465
robots
size and operating environment 50-52
robot vacuums
interfacing, with Roomba 61, 62
re-purposing 59
Roomba, un-freezing 65
with interface 59, 60
without interface 66
rosbag 408

ROS file system 161
ROS Kinetic 379
roslaunch 172, 173, 428
ros.launch files 172, 173
ROS Melodic 379, 380
ROS nodes
creating 160
writing 160, 163-167, 169-171
ROS package
about 351
creating 160-162
documentation, reading 353, 354
writing 160
ROS programs
downloading 171, 172
executing 171
reviewing 171, 172
running 172
ROS robot motion
overview 238
ROS tool 408
Rostopic echo tool 370
RPiREF 32
RPLIDAR
setting up 368, 369
Rviz tool 358, 370

# S

salvaged robot vacuum LIDAR 362
saved map
loading 207, 208
Scalar 376
scratch-built robot
cons 57
pros 57
sensor data
receiving 180, 181
used, for building occupancy
grid maps (OGMs) 184, 185, 187
sensor fusion 412
sensor fusion 2 421
sensor_msgs 364
Series 22

servo motors 74
servos 74, 75
single-board computer (SBC) 1, 18
small pre-built robots 54, 55
stepper motors 75, 76
subscribers 153-157, 159
switch bounce 46

# T

Tesla 338
theta 178
topics 153-157, 159
transform data
    obtaining, in nodes 199, 200
    viewing, from command line 201
transforms
    about 193, 194, 428
    overview 193
    publishing, from nodes with
        transform broadcaster 197, 198
    publishing, with static transform
        publisher 196
    using, in robot operating
        system (ROS) 195, 196
    using, in ROS 193, 194
transistor 77-81
types, LIDAR
    2D LIDAR 360, 361
    3D LIDAR 361
    salvaged robot vacuum LIDAR 362
    unidirectional LIDAR 360

# U

UART serial
    about 98, 99
    communication, testing 99-103
    serial port, error fixing 103, 104
Ubuntu 8, 9
ultrasonic range data
    for object detection 323
ultrasonic range data publisher
    about 317, 318
    code 319-322
unidirectional LIDAR 360

# V

variance 425
Virtual Network Computing (VNC) 5
visual studio code (VS Code)
    installing, for laptop/desktop 14, 15
voltage divider 116
Volts 20

# W

Watts 22
wheel encoders 101 304
wheel odometry 96, 216-218, 220, 304
winding 75
wiring encoders 305-307